PENGUIN BOOKS
BURNING DOWN THE HOUSE

Julian E. Zelizer is the Malcolm Stevenson Forbes, Class of 1941 Professor of History and Public Affairs at Princeton University, a CNN political analyst, and a contributor to NPR's *Here & Now*. His most recent books are *Fault Lines: A History of the United States Since 1974* (coauthored with Kevin Kruse) and *The Fierce Urgency of Now: Lyndon Johnson, Congress, and the Battle for the Great Society*, winner of the D. B. Hardeman Prize for best book on Congress. Zelizer has been awarded fellowships from the New-York Historical Society, the Russell Sage Foundation, the Guggenheim Foundation, the Brookings Institute, and New America.

Praise for *Burning Down the House*

A *New York Times* Notable Book

"Briskly entertaining . . . Zelizer writes about all of this with aplomb, teasing out the ironies and the themes, showing that what made Gingrich exceptional wasn't so much his talent as his timing." —*The New York Times*

"Zelizer holds an endowed chair in history at Princeton but writes like a journalist. (A whisper to the faculty lounge: That is a compliment, not a disparagement.) His book has color and forward momentum. His story has drama and life lessons. His subject is, depending on your point of view, either heroic or odious. One way or another, no one can argue with Zelizer's thesis that Gingrich changed American politics. . . . A remarkable, riveting story." —*The Boston Globe*

"We live today in the world Gingrich wrought, and the story of how he wrought it is the focus of *Burning Down the House* by Julian E. Zelizer. . . . His book provides an engaging, unsettling and, alas, timely look at the torch that Gingrich took to our system of self-government." —*The Washington Post*

"A lively and exceptional read." —*Los Angeles Review of Books*

"Today's hyperpartisan politics can be traced to Republican congressman Newt Gingrich's 1989 ouster of Democratic House Speaker Jim Wright, according to this meticulously researched account. . . . Zelizer's witty, well-informed narrative . . . successfully presents this episode as a foretaste of congressional warfare to come. Political junkies will be thrilled." —*Publishers Weekly*

"[A] compelling work of political history . . . Zelizer's accessible study of political behavior and leadership directly relates to today's tumultuous political scene. Anyone interested in American politics will devour this book." —*Library Journal*

"[A] thoughtful study of [Gingrich's] politics in action . . . Sharp, lucid . . . A masterfully written political road map for anyone wondering how we got to where we are, a bad place indeed." —*Kirkus Reviews* (starred review)

"Newt Gingrich tied American politics to a rock and threw it down a well. That rock is still falling. Julian Zelizer's new book takes readers to the edge of that well, not to listen for the splash but to grab the rope and pull."
   —Jill Lepore, author of *These Truths: A History of the United States*

"With intensity and detail, Julian Zelizer recreates a drama that resounds in modern history. Most are well-acquainted with Newt Gingrich and his combative style, but here is the moment when he transformed Congress and all of American politics."
   —Steve Kornacki, author of *The Red and the Blue*

"In this essential history of Newt Gingrich, Zelizer shows that Donald Trump isn't so much an innovator as an imitator. Zelizer argues that Gingrich wrote the modern Republican Party's destructive playbook, and the Democrats and the media have yet to figure out an effective response."
   —Jane Mayer, author of *Dark Money* and chief Washington correspondent at *The New Yorker*

"In this perfectly timed book, one of America's premier historians tells the story of how our present madness began—with a cunning, lying, hypocritical character assassin named Newt Gingrich. Zelizer offers a hugely important narrative of the 'evil wind' that Gingrich brought to American politics by deposing the Speaker of the House and casting the country into decades of bad feeling."
   —Jonathan Alter, author of *The Center Holds*

"How did we arrive at today's hyperpartisan, polarized, gridlocked, and dysfunctional politics? In this rich and riveting tale of Newt Gingrich's rise to power, ace historian Julian Zelizer makes a compelling argument that the former Speaker of the House is to blame." —John A. Farrell, author of *Richard Nixon: The Life*

"A gripping read about the rise of a ruthless, no-holds-barred Republican mode of politics and its main architect—Newt Gingrich. Anyone struggling to contend with our current political crisis—meaning, everyone—will be well served by reading this timely book by one of our leading lights on the history of the U. S. Congress."
    —Joanne B. Freeman, author of *The Field of Blood*

"Newt Gingrich was one of the most consequential figures in American politics in the twentieth century, with major responsibility for our current political turmoil. A lot has been written about the rise and fall of Newt. It takes a good historian to provide insight, new material, and context to what we already know. Julian Zelizer is a first-rate historian. Even for those of us present at Gingrich's emergence into national life, especially through his assault on Democratic Speaker Jim Wright and throughout his career, *Burning Down the House* enlightens and enriches our understanding of a pivotal time in American life."
    —Norman J. Ornstein, coauthor of *It's Even Worse Than It Looks: How the American Constitutional System Collided With the New Politics of Extremism*

ALSO BY JULIAN E. ZELIZER

BURNING DOWN THE HOUSE

Newt Gingrich,
and the Rise of the
New Republican Party

JULIAN E. ZELIZER

PENGUIN BOOKS

PENGUIN BOOKS
An imprint of Penguin Random House LLC
penguinrandomhouse.com

First published in the United States of America by Penguin Press,
an imprint of Penguin Random House LLC, 2020
Published in Penguin Books 2021

ISBN 9780143110705 (paperback)

THE LIBRARY OF CONGRESS HAS CATALOGED THE HARDCOVER EDITION AS FOLLOWS

Names: Zelizer, Julian E., author.
Title: Burning down the house : Newt Gingrich, the fall of a speaker, and
the rise of the new Republican Party / Julian E. Zelizer.
Other titles: Newt Gingrich, the fall of a speaker, and
the rise of the new Republican Party
Description: New York : Penguin Press, 2020. |
Includes bibliographical references and index.
Identifiers: LCCN 2019044440 (print) | LCCN 2019044441 (ebook) |
ISBN 9781594206658 (hardcover) | ISBN 9780698402751 (ebook)
Subjects: LCSH: Gingrich, Newt. | Rhetoric—Political aspects—
United States. | Communication in politics—United States. |
United States. Congress. House—Speakers. |
Republican Party (U.S. : 1854–) | Political culture—United States. |
United States—Politics and government—1989–
Classification: LCC E840.8.G5 Z45 2020 (print) | LCC E840.8.G5 (ebook) |
DDC 328.73/092—dc23
LC record available at https://lccn.loc.gov/2019044440
LC ebook record available at https://lccn.loc.gov/2019044441

Printed in the United States of America
1st Printing

Designed by Amanda Dewey

For Abigail, Sophia, Nathan, and Claire

CONTENTS

SPEAK LIKE NEWT

On the evening of July 13, 2016, the former Speaker of the House Newt Gingrich marched through the hallways of an Indianapolis television studio as he prepared to appear live on Fox News. The past twenty-four hours had been a whirlwind. The Republican presidential nominee, Donald Trump, was seriously considering naming Gingrich his vice presidential running mate. Gingrich loved being back in the spotlight; to him, the thrill of politics was like a narcotic.

Suddenly Gingrich had a chance to return to the heights of power he had missed since his Republican colleagues had pressured him to step down as Speaker of the House, one of the most influential positions in Washington, back in November 1998. His downfall had been sudden, amid the climactic days of President Bill Clinton's impeachment, only four years after Gingrich had led the Republicans to take control of the House of Representatives for the first time since 1954. Following his dramatic departure from Congress, Gingrich experienced many professional ups and downs. The best of times came when he offered commentary on Fox News or filled the role of resident policy wonk at the conservative Heritage Foundation. He also enjoyed earning money as a consultant.[1] But his disappointment was palpable when his 2012 bid for the Republican presidential nomination fell flat, bested by the former Massachusetts governor Mitt Romney, the smooth patrician to Gingrich's feisty populist.

But now Donald Trump might be offering Gingrich, who turned seventy-three that June, one last chance to step back into the center of power. Many experts argued that Gingrich had a pretty good shot at winning the vice presidential sweepstakes. His sexual past paled in comparison to the exploits of "The Donald" during his adventurous years in New York City. Gingrich was also one of the few senior figures in the Republican Party whom Trump had not knocked to his knees. The former Speaker exuded the kind of gravitas that the reality TV star lacked, displaying an easy fluency in public policy and foreign affairs. He also had an instinct for partisan warfare unequaled by almost any Republican besides Trump.

Moreover, Gingrich's competitors were flawed. The New Jersey governor, Chris Christie, had been damaged by a scandal about a manufactured traffic jam back in the Garden State. The Alabama senator Jeff Sessions seemed so much like a hard-line southern reactionary that he would instantly kill any hope that Trump could win over northern and midwestern independents. And the Indiana governor, Mike Pence, with his choirboy demeanor, felt much too boring a pick for the former star of *The Apprentice*, with his appetite for sensation and sizzle.

Gingrich was to be interviewed that night by Sean Hannity, the pugnacious Fox host whose tough-guy persona attracted a passionate right-wing audience. The day of the Fox interview, Trump had met with Gingrich in a two-thousand-square-foot penthouse suite at the Conrad hotel, a posh five-star high-rise in downtown Indianapolis. Trump had intended to fly back to New York the previous evening after attending a rally with Governor Pence, but a flat tire on the airplane had grounded him overnight. Hannity, a close friend and ally of both Trump and Gingrich, had secretly allowed the former Speaker to fly on his private jet to Indianapolis to make sure that their scheduled meeting took place.

For about two and a half hours, Trump's campaign chairman, Paul Manafort, son-in-law, Jared Kushner, and children Eric, Donald Jr., and Ivanka sat in as the presumptive Republican nominee and the former

Speaker held a free-flowing conversation about the role of the vice president, relations with Capitol Hill, and the many issues facing America after Barack Obama's presidency. Gingrich found Trump exhilarating, a fresh voice who would not be muted by the ostensible experts. The last great Republican firebrand saw the new one as a kindred spirit, one who shared Gingrich's ruthless and defiant attitude toward political convention and his mastery of the media.

That night Gingrich strode through the usually sleepy local studio; all the campaign activity had amped up the station's energy level, but having Gingrich on-site created a pronounced buzz. He was one of the rare former members of Congress who was recognized on the streets. Walking through the studios, Gingrich looked to some on the newsroom staff more like the overweight college professor he had been in his early years, lost in his own thoughts, than someone who might soon be next in line for the presidency. Although he was wearing the classic outfit of the Washington male politician—a dark suit with a royal blue shirt and a red power tie—Gingrich didn't have the normal polish. His suit was a little too boxy; its occupant was slightly rumpled.

Gingrich didn't care: this was the look that he had nurtured since entering politics thirty-seven years earlier as a young congressman from Georgia. He liked that his colleagues thought of him as the man with the big ideas, the intellectual turned politician. He had used that image to intimidate his opponents into submission, whatever the issue being debated. It was rare that Gingrich, with his trademark smirk, didn't seem to think that he was 100 percent correct about the topic being discussed. While he looked as if he might fit naturally in a seminar room, deep down Gingrich had the take-no-prisoners mentality of the toughest partisan figures who had ever served on Capitol Hill. He had practically written the handbook on cutthroat congressional tactics and spinning the media for partisan advantage; indeed, during his speakership, conservatives had literally circulated a memo on how to "speak like Newt."

As the makeup artist finished powdering his face and the production crew attached a small microphone to his lapel, Gingrich had good reason to feel that Trump would never have become the nominee without him. It wasn't just that Gingrich had been a loyal supporter throughout the primaries but also that the unlikely, unorthodox, nativist populist campaign Trump had mounted, which aimed to tear down the political leaders of *both* parties and to destabilize the entire U.S. political system, was Gingrich's creation. Trump's media-centered strategy and his determination to capitalize on public distrust of Washington were the same weapons that Gingrich had deployed upon his arrival on Capitol Hill, when he went after the Democratic majority in the 1980s.

Like Trump, Gingrich believed that anything was possible in politics. He hated it when colleagues told him that things were always going to be the way they were—especially when they said that Republicans would always be the country's minority party. When Ronald Reagan was president from 1981 to 1989, Gingrich had worked diligently as a backbencher to remake the Republican Party's then-staid, country-club, business-oriented brand into something far more hard hitting and confrontational. He committed himself to being a foot soldier in the Reagan Revolution. His goal: shove the national policy agenda to the right and wrest power away from the Democrats who had controlled the House for three decades. To almost everyone, it was a pipe dream.

But Gingrich came to the House in 1979 from a Georgia district that had been reliably Democratic for generations. He had won, and so could others in his party if they played by new rules, which he himself would invent. Gingrich promoted a style of smashmouth combat aimed at delegitimizing his opponents by whatever means possible. Politics, as he saw it, was like warfare. The only way to win a battle, he decided, was to unleash the full fury of one's firepower on the foe. Now Trump was using the same approach on his way to the presidency.

The camera light flashed on in the Indianapolis newsroom, and the interview began. Listening to Hannity's voice through his earpiece, Gingrich jumped into the discussion with verve. As the Fox anchor offered the Georgian friendly questions about his meeting with Trump and his vice presidential prospects, Gingrich turned up the wattage. Speaking in his familiar professorial style, Gingrich launched a fusillade of persuasion, listing the obvious similarities between himself and Trump that would make them ideal partners: "I'm an outsider, I'm oriented toward moving the great base of the party, communicating big ideas, being on television." Gingrich paused to mutter that he probably shouldn't say what he was thinking aloud, then connected the dots between his own congressional career and Trump's presidential campaign: "Look, in many ways, Donald Trump is like a pirate. He's outside the normal system, he gets things done, he's bold, he's actually like a figure out of a movie. In a lot of ways, my entire career has been a little bit like a pirate. I've taken on the establishment of both parties, [I'm] very prepared to fight in the media."

Then Gingrich took the conversation with Hannity in an unexpected direction. As much as he wanted the job, Gingrich said, he could not resist pointing out why he might not be the best selection. Displaying his trademark audacity, on the eve of this historic decision, he pointed Trump toward Gingrich's second choice: Mike Pence. Trump would have to decide whether he wanted a "two-pirate ticket," Gingrich said. If Trump didn't want to run with such a like-minded person, Pence might be better as a stabilizing force. This admission appeared to take Hannity by surprise, but it was classic Gingrich: he had always tended to say exactly what was on his mind, for better or worse.

After the interview ended and the crew removed his mic, Gingrich walked out of the studio. Whatever the next few days brought, he could feel as though he had won. Trump was thriving in the political world that Gingrich had created. Gingrich would always be Michelangelo to Trump's *David*.

In Gingrich's world, Republicans practiced a ruthless style of partisanship that ignored the conventional norms of Washington and continually tested how far politicians could go in bending government institutions to suit their partisan purposes. Republicans went for the head wound, as Trump's adviser Steve Bannon said, when Democrats were having pillow fights.[2] The new GOP goal was not to negotiate or legislate but to do everything necessary to maintain partisan power. If it was politically useful to engage in behavior that could destroy the possibility of governance, which rendered bipartisanship impossible and would unfairly decimate their opponents' reputations, then so be it. Gingrich-era Republicans were willing to enter into alliances of convenience with extremists who trafficked in reactionary populism, nativism, and racial backlash. The party kept counting on Gingrich's media-centered strategy, tailoring its actions and statements to push the national conversation in its favor, even if that depended on mixing fact and fiction and practicing a new, brass-knuckles politics of smear.[3]

The style of partisanship that Gingrich popularized supplanted the bipartisan norms of the committee era of Congress (1930s–1960s) as well as the responsible partisanship that had been promoted as an alternative by Watergate-era reformers (1970s), when leaders and the rank and file were loyal to their party agenda while still adhering to formal and informal rules of governance. Gingrich's approach to partisanship was an entirely different beast. Nothing and nobody was sacrosanct.

To be sure, this was not the first time in American history that conditions on Capitol Hill bottomed out. Congress had been through numerous periods of vicious partisanship, such as the decades leading up to the Civil War, when relations disintegrated so badly that bloody altercations on the floors of the House and the Senate were regular occurrences until the government broke down into total dysfunction.[4] While Gingrich's era of partisanship did not witness outright physical violence between members, what did take root was the normalization of a no-holds-barred style of partisan warfare where the career of every politician was seen as expendable and where it was fair game to shatter routine legislative processes in pursuit of power, even when there was not an issue as monumental as slavery on the table. In Gingrich's era, a crippling form of partisanship came to permanently define how elected officials dealt with almost every issue, ranging from who should lead the parties to mundane budgeting matters to decisions over war and peace.

Before Gingrich could help midwife the new American politics, he had to sweep the old order aside. His rise to power dates back to a tumultuous twenty-nine-month period from January 1987 to May 1989, when, as a relatively junior congressman within the minority party, he brought down one of the most powerful people in Washington—the Democratic Speaker of the House, Jim Wright. The brutal battle shocked Washington and forever transformed American politics. In two hundred years of House history, Wright was the first Speaker to be forced to resign. Gingrich's campaign against Wright for allegedly violating ethics rules that Congress had imposed in the aftermath of Watergate turned the forty-five-year-old Georgian from a reckless bomb-thrower whom most Republican leaders kept at arm's length to one of the party's top national leaders. He secured a leadership position as a result of his efforts. Nobody took Gingrich lightly after he brought down the Speaker.

As the brash young 1980s maverick with the chubby baby face and the helmet of prematurely graying hair, Gingrich had a central insight: the transformational changes of the Watergate era—with stricter rules to constrain the power of elected officials and congressional reforms that opened up Congress to public scrutiny—could be used to fundamentally destabilize the entire political establishment and benefit insurgents, including Republicans. President Richard Nixon had resigned in August 1974, but Democrats were not immune to new forces that exposed politics to the harsh light of the media. Inspired by *The Washington Post*'s Bob Woodward, Carl Bernstein, and Ben Bradlee, a new generation of journalists arrived in Washington determined to uncover official wrongdoing. None of them wanted to miss the next big scandal. And many of the new reforms prohibited activities once considered normal.

Even before Gingrich won his first election, he realized that the well-intentioned post-Watergate reforms, written with the help of idealistic newcomers to Congress known as the Watergate Babies, could be deployed against the entrenched Democratic majority. Ethics codes, televised floor proceedings, rules empowering rank-and-file members of Congress—all could be used by an increasingly assertive Republican caucus to take control of the House. The arena now became establishment versus outsider, not just liberal versus conservative. It would become a winning formula.

Gingrich also saw that the congressional Democrats were vulnerable even as they seemed to be at the peak of their power. Since 1932, the

Democrats had dominated the Hill with few exceptions (including interludes in 1947–1949 and 1953–1955), and Watergate had led to an even bigger surge in their numbers. But power had its pitfalls. A corrosive network of private money, lobbyists, and interest groups surrounded legislators, creating a web of nebulous relationships that looked bad to a distrustful public. When Speaker Tip O'Neill retired in 1986 and was replaced by Wright, Gingrich pegged the new Speaker as a sitting duck.

Wright, the son of a populist Democrat, viewed politics through the lens of 1955, the year that he arrived in Washington. Filled with grandiose ambitions, the Texan joined a Democratic establishment that had been shaped by President Franklin Roosevelt and his New Deal. For Wright, politics was about legislating effectively and about members keeping their districts happy, whether by helping constituents with federal agencies or by directing federal largesse toward local businesses to create jobs for the electorate. That had been a winning formula for decades, one that propelled Wright to reelection again and again. Even after Reagan's landslide victory in 1980, Wright and the House Democrats were still in the saddle.

But when he was elected Speaker, Wright didn't comprehend how profoundly Vietnam and Watergate had shattered trust in government and destabilized the leaders of both parties. The war and the scandal produced sweeping reforms that changed the way Congress worked: leaders were more vulnerable, the process was more open, and every member had to abide by stricter rules of behavior. The old rules of governing no longer applied. Wright didn't see that the people in Washington had changed too. The investigative journalists, the good-government reformers, the special prosecutors, the renegade legislators—they were as much a part of the establishment as the party leaders and the cigar-chomping lobbyists. And these ragtag upstarts could make or break a career and, as it turned out, damage an entire political party in the process.

By the time he launched his crusade against the Speaker in 1987, Gingrich had come to understand that in the modern media era politics was as much about perception as substance. The way journalists framed a story and the narratives they crafted about an issue could be as powerful as the facts. From the first day he set foot on the floor of the House in

1979, Gingrich had been peddling a tale about the illegitimacy of the Democratic majority, and he found that he was not alone within his party; after Wright's first day as Speaker in January 1987, Gingrich made the villain of that tale the corrupt Texan now leading the House Democrats.

Gingrich's House colleagues—an earlier, less brazen brand of Republicans—might not have understood that the way a politician spun a story often determined the outcome of a struggle. But Gingrich did. As an erstwhile historian at a west Georgia college, with a Ph.D. from Tulane University, he knew that good storytelling mattered. Gingrich would throw out an argument or an accusation, let an idea circulate in the media ecosystem, and when his critics pounced, he would turn their words against them. For Gingrich, the central battle was shaping the way voters conceived of the basic problem at hand. First Gingrich made Wright the embodiment of the House's ills; then Gingrich drove him to resign; then Gingrich took his majority and his gavel.

When the Republicans gained control of Congress in 1994, Gingrich would emerge as their leader, the avatar of a new generation of Republicans who were more aggressive, more partisan, and less restrained by traditional norms. Before Wright stepped down, the Speaker warned his colleagues to avoid the "mindless cannibalism" that the intensification of partisan warfare would bring. He was too late. Drawn to power, emboldened by success, the Republican Party embraced Gingrich's politics. Most of the GOP acted as though the destruction of Speaker Wright proved that shattering the rules of an institution could be an effective way to seize political power. Gingrich's generation, in turn, would spawn their own successors with the Tea Party in 2010.

These Young Turks, who won their seats in a backlash against President Barack Obama, were willing to do whatever was necessary to win. When Republicans threatened to trigger a global economic meltdown by sending the U.S. government into default over a spending dispute with President Obama, the Utah representative Jason Chaffetz told reporters that he realized that his leadership's willingness "to let a default happen" was "a negotiating chip, and said he didn't mind at all."[5] Tea Party Republicans thrived in a partisan universe that revolved around Roger Ailes's media empire; Fox News played to a zealous crowd of voters who rarely bucked the party line.

In the end, Trump decided that two pirates were indeed too much for one ticket. He considered having Gingrich as his running mate but concluded that Governor Pence brought more to the ticket. Pence had been Manafort's strong preference, as he feared that Gingrich would be too much of a distraction.[6] Unlike Gingrich, Pence would serve as a bridge between his campaign and evangelical voters who were distrustful of the thrice-married, testosterone-filled reality television star. Pence was a good-looking, media-savvy, disciplined politician, one who would not steal the spotlight away from his attention-seeking boss.

Gingrich could live with Trump's decision. He had come to believe that Trump was a transformative figure, and he didn't want to do anything to get in his way. He could take pride in watching the 2016 presidential election, which confirmed that his political style and Republican politics had become one.

On Inauguration Day, January 20, 2017, Gingrich was downright giddy, exuding the same sense of excitement as a young boy entering a stadium to see his favorite sports team. At 10:18 A.M., Gingrich strode into the capital with his fellow former Speaker John Boehner, who was boasting to colleagues that he was "texting buddies" with the president-elect. With his wife, Callista, by his side, Gingrich walked through the crowd, stopping to schmooze with some of the Republican Party's stars, including Senator Ted Cruz of Texas, who was photographed attentively listening to the Georgian. Wearing a dark overcoat, Gingrich appeared to thoroughly enjoy playing the role of senior statesman. The atmosphere reminded him of the day when Ronald Reagan took the oath of office thirty-six years earlier. Trump, now America's forty-fifth president, delivered a bleak inaugural address on the west front of the Capitol, sketching a portrait of a nation in crisis and vowing, "This American carnage stops right here and stops right now." Gingrich loved it. He called the speech "decisive and impressive—delivered slowly, firmly and with conviction. . . . It was exactly the message Americans needed to hear."[7]

Although Gingrich did not become part of Trump's cabinet, the former Speaker emerged as one of the president's chief supporters in the media—in some ways, the forum Gingrich had long felt was most meaningful. Gingrich had been playing to the television cameras for his entire career, and he would now devote his energy to "developing the agenda, pushing the agenda, explaining the agenda."[8] As Trump took the helm, Gingrich appeared frequently on conservative television and radio programs to pontificate about why the liberal establishment had it all wrong about this maverick president. He even published *Understanding Trump*, a vigorous treatise explaining why Trump was a historic figure. "It is astonishing to me, as a historian," Gingrich wrote, "how the elite media and much of the political establishment refuse to try to understand Donald Trump. They have been so rabidly opposed to him, so ideologically committed to left-wing values, and so terrified of the future that they haven't stopped and considered how extraordinary his success has been. President Trump is one of the most remarkable individuals to ever occupy the White House."[9]

Gingrich had planted; Trump had reaped. The rise of Gingrich's merciless version of the Republican Party was inextricably linked to the fall of Speaker Wright. Gingrich perfected his new style of partisan politics through the successful crusade against the powerful Texan. In the process, he elevated himself from the backbench to the party leadership. He persuaded a growing number of Republicans to embrace his raucous ways, by weaponizing ethics rules and manipulating well-meaning journalists. Slowly but surely, starting right after Ronald Reagan left office, the Grand Old Party started to look more and more like Newt.

The cataclysmic political battle between Wright and Gingrich had been an epic struggle between the old Washington and the new, and the new Washington would prevail. The new Washington was rougher, less stable, and far more ruthless. In the new Washington, almost anything was permissible. In partisan politics, it was almost impossible to go too far. We can date precisely the moment when our toxic political environment was born: Speaker Wright's downfall in 1989.[10]

One

THE MAKING OF A RENEGADE REPUBLICAN

When Newt Gingrich arrived on Capitol Hill in January 1979 to begin his first term as a U.S. representative from Georgia, he still saw himself as an outsider. The supremely confident Gingrich, who liked to describe himself as a "Pennsylvania-born army brat," had a love-hate relationship with authority figures. Whether it was dating an older woman—his high school teacher—despite his stepfather's admonition against doing so or applying to be the president of a college just a few months after joining as a junior faculty member, Gingrich had never been deferential to any of the bosses in his life. His favorite film in the late 1970s was *Animal House*, a raucous comedy about a fraternity of misfits who made life impossible for the dean.[1]

Although he didn't like the people in charge, he thirsted for the power that they unjustly held. As a teenager, Gingrich explained to a teacher that he planned to move to Georgia when he was older to create a Republican Party. It didn't concern him that some Republicans already lived in the Peach State; he would do it better. On this and most issues, Gingrich tended to believe in the essential rightness of his views and was often unable to even hear what his opponents were saying. Extraordinarily arrogant, totally self-absorbed, and brutally ruthless, he rarely allowed anything or anyone to stand in his way. He arrived in Washington at the end of his fellow Georgian Jimmy Carter's troubled presidency determined to tear everything down.

A tough upbringing shaped Gingrich's demeanor. He grew up in a home that lacked much compassion. His parents, Kathleen "Kit" Daugherty and "Big" Newton McPherson Jr., separated just months after he was born on June 17, 1943, in Harrisburg, the capital of Pennsylvania. The couple had met at a roller-skating rink, a working-class hangout where teenagers congregated to flirt and mingle. Kit instantly found herself attracted to the charismatic Newton. But the initial excitement wore off as she discovered that the hulking, six-foot-three Newton was an alcoholic with a penchant for loitering at bars, playing pool, and gambling. In short order, his drinking habits deteriorated. Bar fights were a regular occurrence. He became physically intimidating and even abusive to her during his binges.

Still, Kit said yes when he proposed, hoping that marriage would mature him and make him take more responsibility for his behavior. It proved difficult for her to live with that rationalization for long. Before the wedding, Kit (only sixteen years old) got cold feet as his long nights at the bars increased. Kit told her mother that she didn't want to marry Newton. But her mother, a widow who had enjoyed a wonderful marriage, pressured her into going through with the wedding, reminding her daughter that the announcement was all set to run in the local newspaper, so it would be embarrassing to the family if she pulled out at the last minute.

The union only lasted three days. Kit walked out on her husband after he assaulted her for waking him up from a drunken stupor. Rather than reform his ways, Newton decided to join the navy during World War II. Within a few weeks, Kit learned that she was pregnant. Their son, whom she named Newton Leroy (Newt for short), was born in June. Her husband returned from the war on a temporary leave in August only to formally begin the divorce process. Kit moved back in with her mother to save money.

With no father at home and with his mother working at a local factory on wartime production, Newt depended on his extended family for nurturing during the war years. His grandmother, aunts, and uncles—all of whom lived in the working-class, Republican town of Hummelstown, just east of Harrisburg and on the way to Hershey—tried to offer Newt the parental support that he otherwise lacked. The small, picturesque community, founded before the American Revolution, was largely populated by government workers who commuted to Harrisburg and employees of the Hershey chocolate plant. From a young age, Newt was encouraged by his family to find solace in reading and study; his grandmother, a teacher, instilled a strong commitment to education in her children and grandchildren, even though many of their family members were blue-collar workers who had not attended college.

Three years after her divorce, Kit Daugherty married an army lieutenant colonel named Robert "Gus" Gingrich, who was studying biology at Gettysburg College. He was on temporary leave from the military while recovering from a hernia. Robert was willing to raise Newt as his own but offered his young stepson scant warmth.

Robert, who liked to wear his lieutenant colonel uniform to his high school reunions in Hummelstown, also had a hardscrabble beginning. He was abandoned by his unwed teenage mother and grew up as a foster child until a family adopted him at age sixteen. Robert concluded that children needed to become self-sufficient and steely. He thought that Newt's grandmother had been too doting and that the boy needed to toughen up. Newt and his sisters—Susan, born in 1948, and Roberta, born in 1951—feared their father's temper and intolerance of anyone who broke the rules. Newt grew up thinking that Robert was his biological father, but hugs, fishing, playing catch, and other gestures of paternal affection were few. "He can go a whole day and say only fifty words," Gingrich's mother said.[2] Newt usually felt alone in his home, finding comfort in his extensive collection of snakes and books about zoology.

The end of World War II didn't make things much easier for the

Gingrich family. They were not among the millions of veteran families that found prosperous lives in the growing suburbs of 1950s America. Between the ages of three and eleven, Gingrich lived in a modest apartment in Hummelstown, on top of a fumy gas station. He shared a room with his grandmother, who kept one eye open for much of the night because she was terrified of his many jars of snakes. (He named one of the reptiles "Oscar Aloysius Stinky III.")

The dinner table was always lively at the Gingrich home, albeit with clear rules. Newt's father would go around the table to grill each child about what they had learned in school that day. None of the kids dared challenge their father. "Dad was the ruler of the house," Gingrich's sister Susan recalled.[3]

Once the Korean War started, Robert was again called on to serve. Kit found herself working hard to raise the kids even as she continued to struggle with depression. The kids spent as much time taking care of her as she did them.

Newt and his sisters learned to fend for themselves.[4] "I was a 50-year-old at 9," Gingrich recalled.[5] At age eleven, telling his mom that he was going to the library, Newt bought a bus ticket to Harrisburg to see two documentaries about African wildlife. He was enchanted by the films and left the theater wondering why Harrisburg didn't have its own zoo. As he walked onto the street, Newt noticed a sign pointing to city hall. Instead of heading back toward the bus, an inspired Gingrich walked directly over to the government building. The receptionist, amused to hear a young boy so earnestly asking her about why the city didn't have a zoo, sent him upstairs to meet with the assistant director of parks and recreation. The two had a serious conversation, reviewing old files, budgets, and well-worn maps. The civil servant explained to Gingrich that if he wanted to pursue the idea further, he needed to return the following week to make his case directly to the city council. He ordered a cab to drive Gingrich home, handing him a thick book of laws and regulations as a souvenir for his efforts. Gingrich returned dutifully the next Tuesday and waited his turn to address the council. The zoo did not get built, but Paul Walker, the editor of a city newspaper, the *Harrisburg Home Star*, was so captivated by watching this neatly dressed, polite young boy make his case to a roomful of government officials (which was much more interesting to him than the other matters on the agenda, namely garbage collection) that he published a story about the curious incident.[6] "An 11-year-old is fighting in City Hall here in an attempt to establish a zoo in the city's Wildwood Park," Walker wrote, in an article titled AMBITIOUS ZOO KEEPER which was picked up by the Associated Press. "Young Newton Gingrich told Mayor Claude Robins and four city Councilmen that he and a number of youthful buddies could round up enough animals to get the project started if granted use of the park."[7] Walker also allowed Gingrich to write an article that appeared on the front page of the local giveaway paper, about why Harrisburg needed a zoo.[8]

Not everything about Gingrich was serious. He loved to memorize comedy routines from television stars such as Red Skelton and Dick Van Dyke. He also had a mischievous side. His favorite prank was to pretend that his friend Dennis Yantz had beaten him up on the sidewalk. When someone pulled over to see if he was okay, Gingrich would push Yantz aside, jump up, and yell, "Surprise!" He would laugh in delight as he watched the startled stranger jump back.[9] One of Newt's go-to places in Harrisburg was the movie theater, where he especially enjoyed classic Westerns and war films on the big screen. Newt loved to watch his movie heroes, including John Wayne, track down and kill the bad guys, no matter how powerful they were.

Newt had an insatiable appetite for learning and new ideas. Following his father's service in the Korean War, the family moved to Fort Riley in Kansas. Newt instantly stood out in the classroom. He expanded his early interest in zoology, obsessively studying different species and endlessly talking about them with his teachers and classmates. "Newtie," as his mother called him, fed his snakes hard-boiled eggs as she looked on apprehensively. At Fort Riley, he had the opportunity to spend time with Lucius Clay, the famed U.S. colonel who had administered occupied Germany after World War II, who now schooled the precocious boy in international relations and the art of war. According to one biographer, Newt could stand in a roomful of parents and feel totally at ease, without the nerdy awkwardness he displayed around other kids.

In 1956, when Newt was thirteen, the family moved again, when the military stationed Robert Gingrich in France. The entire family packed up and moved with him. His father purchased an expensive set of the *Encyclopedia Britannica*, which Newt treasured, devouring every entry. But his relationship with his father remained icy. When the fifteen-year-old Newt and a friend stayed out late one night, breaking his father's 11:00 P.M. curfew rule, Robert snatched his son up by the shirt and pinned him to the wall. After a few seconds, the father let go, dropping the teen to the ground; without looking back, he walked away, confident that his son would never repeat the mistake again.[10]

Such tense moments were not all that young Newt experienced with his dad. On a weekend trip, he was deeply moved by the World War I battlefield at Verdun, where the barbed wire and trenches were still visible; the young American picked up helmets buried in the dirt and saw the bones of 100,000 deceased servicemen stacked behind a glass window. The visit brought home to Gingrich the grim reality of the devastation inflicted by war, as well as the ongoing threats that democracy still faced.[11] This was the height of the cold war, and Newt interpreted issues through a moralist lens, viewing politics as an epic struggle between good and evil. Over the course of an entire school year, he wrote a two-hundred-page, single-spaced paper about the balance of global naval power.[12] During the family's more than three years overseas—they spent the last leg of the tour in Stuttgart, Germany—he devoured various armed forces publications and listened to armed forces radio shows. While he admired his stepfather's continued service, Newt concluded that being a politician "was the most effective thing I could do to ensure that the US would remain free."[13]

The Gingrich family returned to the United States in 1960. Robert was stationed at Fort Benning in Columbus, Georgia, where Newt entered the racially segregated Baker High School as a junior. Gingrich thrived in the classroom and excelled at debating. His high school classmates voted him

"Most Intellectual." The only student carrying around an overflowing briefcase and wearing a pocket protector, Newt was hard to miss. While other teens were eagerly learning to drive, his mother recalled, he preferred to sit in the passenger seat and read.

At seventeen, Newt returned to Hummelstown, where he spent the summer of 1960 with his extended family. He sought out Paul Walker, the journalist who had written about his impromptu effort at lobbying as a child. Walker agreed to mentor him, even helping him to find work on some radio and television shows that a friend hosted. Gingrich spent most of his time calling to ask local businesses to purchase ads, the paper's main source of revenue. Walker, a loyal Democrat, introduced Newt to local politicians and lobbyists during their lunches at Davenport's Restaurant, where Gingrich was invited to listen in on the city's power brokers.[14] Although his father and Walker were both Democrats, Newt was drawn to the small-government philosophy of the GOP.

Gingrich started to gain a feel for political organization as well as communication. Harrisburg was filled with churches and military installations, a city inhabited by working- and middle-class Republicans who were a central target of national party leaders seeking to broaden their electoral reach. When Gingrich learned that the city planned to temporarily shut down the State Museum for major renovations, he was upset; it was one of his favorite places to spend time. He exhibited his instinctive political skills by sharing the information with Walker, who in turn leaked the news to local reporters. Thanks to the ensuing backlash, the state kept the museum open during the work.[15]

Back in Georgia that fall, inspired by his work in Harrisburg, Gingrich volunteered for Richard Nixon's 1960 presidential campaign, sending out mailers, making phone calls, knocking on doors, and organizing school debates to build interest in Nixon's candidacy. He and his coterie of high school friends—and there were not many southern Republicans in those days—were profoundly disappointed when Nixon lost narrowly to Senator John F. Kennedy. They spent all night drowning their sorrows in intense political conversation. One book that made a big impression during these years was Theodore White's *Making of the President, 1960.*

Gingrich was fascinated with this gripping account of the 1960 presidential election, particularly White's discussion of an idea-oriented wing of the Republican Party that dated back to the nineteenth century. White argued that the GOP had become alienated from the "intellectual mainstream" since the end of Theodore Roosevelt's presidency when the "regulars" took control of the party machinery. The GOP paid a long-term price for the decision, White argued in a point that captured Gingrich's attention, including in 1960 with Richard Nixon, who had not offered voters any vision.[16]

In high school, Newt also loved to play football. With a 190-pound frame, he persevered, earning a spot on the starting lineup as a defensive tackle, a position usually filled by more massive figures. He thoroughly enjoyed being on the playing field, tackling or being tackled.[17] Although he was not a gifted athlete, Gingrich exhibited an intense level of psychological grit. His coach Foster Watkins, who admired Gingrich's tenacity, taught him that when he got hit hard, he should get up immediately and play on.[18] Newt loved the aggression of the game. The lessons he learned from his coaches, just like the experiences in the war-torn environment of Europe, stuck with him as he developed a combative outlook on politics.[19]

In his senior year, at age eighteen, Gingrich fell in love with his high school geometry teacher, Jacqueline Battley, who was twenty-five. They entered into an illicit relationship, which became known to his parents only when Gingrich accidently drove her car into a ditch near the military base. Newt had to call his father to get him out of the jam, and he revealed that he and the teacher were a couple. Robert strongly disapproved and made Newt promise that the romance would end, a promise he soon broke.

Concerned about their son's relationship, Kit and Robert persuaded Newt to attend Emory University, which had become coed in 1953, with the hope that Jacqueline and Newt would go their separate ways. Newt thrilled to university life, even on a campus that revered jocks and fraternities. Although his grades were merely above average, his passion for learning and politics intensified. In 1962, Newt founded a local chapter of the Young Republicans on a campus steeped in the traditions of the South, including loyalty to the Democratic Party.

His parents' plan to separate their son from Jacqueline did not work. She secured a teaching job near Atlanta, and the couple was married in a Baptist church in 1962. Newt, who had grown up Lutheran, embraced life as a Baptist out of respect for his wife's family traditions. Robert, still unwilling to accept the relationship, boycotted the wedding. Kit didn't feel comfortable attending without Robert, so she also stayed away. "It was so hard. I was torn between my husband and my son," she later recounted.[20] Newt was still a college student when Jacqueline gave birth to a daughter, whom they named Kathy.

After graduating from Emory in 1965, Newt began a doctoral program in history at Tulane University in New Orleans. He had decided in college that he would like to pursue an advanced degree in history to perhaps secure a teaching job. He arrived at the height of the turmoil across college campuses stirred by the civil rights movement and the Vietnam War. In a community torn between liberal groups like Students for a Democratic Society and the conservative Young Americans for Freedom, Gingrich led a successful protest against censorship when the administration tried to block the publication of graphic nude photographs in a student publication. Generally, though, Gingrich left the protesting to others, feeling pressure to graduate and start earning a living. Jacqueline, who was supporting the family financially through her teaching, gave birth to a second child, Jackie Sue, in 1966. Newt remained singularly focused. He concentrated on writing his dissertation on Belgian colonial policy in the Congo from 1945 to 1960, taking breaks to attend the St. Charles Avenue Baptist Church with his wife.[21] He seemed like a stranger to the heady, rebellious atmosphere of campus life in the late 1960s. His friend David Kramer, dismayed that Newt really didn't understand what the Beatles' *White Album* was all about, brought him to see the psychedelic rock band Jefferson Airplane. Newt was unimpressed. Afterward he asked, "Is there any political value in this?"[22]

Politics provided him with much more of a rush than rock 'n' roll. If anything distracted him from his studies, it was campaigns and elections.

Gingrich took some time out of his graduate studies to campaign for the New York governor, Nelson Rockefeller, in the 1968 Republican primaries. Gingrich had a "political philosophy that was unformed" because he was a "Republican out of general feeling, not out of firm ideology," one friend noted.[23] He agreed with the Republican skepticism about too much government, but he was not a right-wing ideologue. He also believed that the GOP could appeal to African Americans given the support that historically existed in portions of the party for racial equality. In 1968, the pragmatic appeal of a moderate Republican like Rockefeller was even stronger for Gingrich and others in the GOP because of the way that Lyndon Johnson had successfully branded Senator Barry Goldwater as a radical right-wing extremist.

Rockefeller lost, but Gingrich found himself inspired by Nixon's 1968 victory and the restoration of Republican power in the White House. He enjoyed Nixon's pugnacious attitude toward his opponents and his appeals to the kinds of blue-collar conservatives Gingrich had known in Hummelstown. Whereas the moderate Rockefeller had promised to unite liberal northeastern and midwestern Republicans, Nixon was making a bold play for blue-collar Democrats in the North, as well as reaching into Dixie. Nixon seemed to appeal to a wide range of voters, standing as a politician who knew how to reach into the conservative parts of the Republican and southern Democratic electorate while claiming enough of a civil rights record from his time as vice president to retain the center. Nixon wasn't wedded to any particular issues as much as he was concerned with winning elections. Like Newt's other hero, Teddy Roosevelt, Nixon struck him as a role model for his own generation of Republicans, a shrewd, pragmatic strategist who was attempting to build a durable governing Republican majority with sizable blue-collar support.[24]

His enchantment with populism did not yet extend to the intellectual realm, where he completed a dissertation that offered a sympathetic look at Belgian colonialism. Based on one year that he and Jacqueline spent in Brussels (1969–1970), archival documents, and interviews with Belgian officials (he never traveled to the Congo or interviewed relevant local figures), Gingrich concluded that the colonial government had failed to modernize the local education system or to nurture an elite capable of sustaining economic growth. "The Belgians get very low marks for their efforts to develop a political elite and much of the country's post-independence chaos is due to this Belgian failure," Gingrich noted. Though the dissertation was critical of Belgium, his main beef was with the design of its policies rather than the inherent merits of colonialism.[25]

Newt did not serve in Vietnam, a war that he publicly supported, as a result of student and marriage deferments. The military wouldn't take him anyway, because he was nearsighted and flat-footed, which caused him deep embarrassment around his stepfather. With his doctoral degree in hand, Newt obtained a professorship in September 1970 at a small liberal arts institution, West Georgia College, located in the sleepy rural town of Carrollton.

The quiet campus in the western part of the state, known for its agricultural and textile companies, was dominated by the Baptist church rather than by student rabble-rousers. Newt soon developed a friendship with Steve Hanser, a professor of German history who introduced him to critical concepts from the history of warfare. Gingrich became fascinated with the teachings of the military theorist Carl von Clausewitz, who argued that "war is the continuation of politics by other means." He earned points with Jackie's family by volunteering to teach Sunday school at the local Baptist church.

But academia never satisfied Gingrich. By the time he reached Georgia, Gingrich was already ruminating over the possibility of running for office.[26] He didn't find the time or interest to publish his dissertation, and he lacked the patience for the slow crawl of university life. He couldn't understand why the administration rejected his application to serve as university president after one year on the job or why the dean didn't select him as chair of the department a year later.

To satisfy his ambitions, Gingrich turned to politics. For decades, Democrats had dominated the South without serious Republican opposition. But starting in the 1960s, a younger generation of Republicans felt the moment was ripe to break the Democratic monopoly in Dixie. The South was growing and prospering, resulting in new districts with better-educated suburban voters who wanted to move beyond the racism of the Dixiecrats who had fought tooth and nail against President Lyndon Johnson's civil rights legislation. Republicans also argued these voters would support an antitax, pro-business agenda that could draw further commerce and growth to the South.

Gingrich sought to capitalize on these changes. West Georgia College was located in Georgia's Sixth District, represented since 1954 by the veteran conservative John Flynt, a quintessential Dixiecrat who had strongly opposed civil rights and a silver-haired patrician who had received a Bronze Star Medal for his service in World War II. The district was so rural that it lacked hotels or large public spaces where Flynt could meet with sizable groups of constituents. Republicans suspected that the state's Democratic assembly had designed the district in this way so that Flynt had a permanent excuse to avoid lengthy encounters with his voters in order to limit the opportunities they had to directly raise complaints with him about any problems with his service.

Flynt was struggling to keep up with his changing constituency by the 1970s. The district was reapportioned in 1971 to include a few more urban and suburban areas, a result of the Supreme Court's one-man, one-vote ruling in 1964 expanding voting rights. For decades, thinly populated rural areas, which tended to be overwhelmingly white and conservative, had been given as many if not more representatives as densely populated, racially mixed urban areas. The new Sixth District stretched from Fulton to the outer parts of Muscogee, including the farmland of the west Georgia countryside as well as the booming suburbs of Atlanta, home to one of the busiest international airports in the nation, sleek shopping centers, and fancy new restaurants. Voters in the reconfigured Sixth District were united by an overall hostility to high taxation, by a business-friendly posture, and by an eagerness to reject the stereotypes of old-line southern racism even while racial inequality remained deeply embedded in the residential and educational character of its neighborhoods.[27]

In 1974, Gingrich ran against Flynt. The challenger's operation had the feel of the 1960s counterculture, not buttoned-down, country-club conservatism. Even at the dawn of his political career, Gingrich was all about taking on the establishment, not only pursuing right-wing ideas. This attitude proved helpful for a Republican in a deeply Democratic territory, helping attract a wide variety of Vietnam-era political activists. Gingrich's ragtag campaign team was composed primarily of disaffected Democrats and devout Republicans who shared a desire to topple the local leadership.

Without much money to spend, Gingrich's first campaign was a no-frills operation. Volunteers built their own signs using donated wood and cheap silk screens. After spending hours canvassing voters, they worked late into the evening to make their own campaign materials in an empty warehouse that relied on gas lanterns.[28]

Gingrich promised to bring honesty and transparency into office. "The Politicians Had Their Chance. Now You Can Have Yours," read Gingrich's brochures.[29] He tirelessly worked civic events and went door to door, assuring every voter he met that he would not hole up in Washington like his opponent. He promised to appear in the district at least once a month and to open an office near the Atlanta airport to satisfy Georgians living in Fulton County, the densely populated and well-educated area that bordered the city, whose residents often complained about never seeing Flynt. Tapping into the national rage over Watergate, Gingrich charged that Flynt reflected the brokenness of Washington. "I can no longer sit idly by while my future—and the future of this country—is endangered by political hacks who do not understand what is happening to the people they supposedly represent," Gingrich said.[30]

If anything, Gingrich was the liberal in this particular race. He supported environmentalist policies, earning the endorsement of the League of Conservation Voters. Gingrich also promised to take a more progressive stance on civil rights, hoping to appeal to black residents of west and southwest Atlanta who had been reapportioned into the Sixth District, voters previously represented by the civil rights activist Andrew Young.[31] The Democratic campaign consultant Bob Beckel, who was working for the reformist National Committee for an Effective Congress, became one of Gingrich's first admirers. Beckel, who would chair Walter Mondale's presidential campaign a decade later, saw Gingrich as a new class of

Republican—more cosmopolitan, more educated, and more suburban than rural—who would offer a better option than the conservative Flynt. Respected journalists like *The Washington Post*'s David Broder paid attention too, identifying Gingrich as the fresh voice southerners needed in the post-civil-rights era. The *Atlanta Daily World*, the oldest black newspaper in Georgia, whose publisher was a friend of Gingrich's, offered its endorsement. "Gingrich is only 31 years old," the editors argued, "but he is a college teacher and is progressive in his views. And he is also fair-minded on racial issues."[32]

From his very first campaign, Gingrich understood that corruption was a powerful theme to deploy against a senior congressional incumbent, a way to turn an opponent's strength into a weakness. Members of Congress naturally developed close connections with powerful interests in their districts, and they often did things that, at a minimum, looked as though they were taking advantage of their power for their own economic benefit.

One of the stories that Gingrich liked to talk up involved Flynt and an unpaved road. Flynt had wound up in a controversy over a dirt road that bordered his home in the city of Griffin. One of the congressman's neighbors, Skeeter Norsworthy, owned a home that was also adjacent to the road. In 1973, Norsworthy ran for Griffin committeeman promising to pave every city road. After he won the election, the city had the road paved at a cost of $12,000. The city paid for one-third of the bill. Flynt received a $4,000 assessment while Norsworthy shared his $4,000 assessment with four neighbors living on the other side of the road to cover the remainder of the cost. But Flynt had transferred the title to his property to a former aide, who never paid the assessment. When a local newspaper wrote about the story, someone anonymously sent the city a check to pay the bill, after which Flynt retook the land title.[33]

Gingrich also went after Flynt for having rented space on his farm to a Ford Motor Company plant to use as a parking lot and shortly thereafter offering an amendment to the Clean Air Act that the manufacturer endorsed.[34] The only television spot that Gingrich ran showed him standing in a pile of five-pound bags of sugar, to highlight the contributions Flynt received from the industry.

Gingrich's first campaign was exciting, but it wasn't yet enough to knock off Flynt. The senior Democrat, as an incumbent, would continue to ladle congressional pork into the district. And 1974 was a hard year for Republicans all over the country; after Watergate, the party suffered from its connections to a discredited president who was forced to resign. Voters elected large Democratic majorities to the House and the Senate.

Gingrich's first showing was still impressive. The *Christian Science Monitor* reporter John Dillin singled out Gingrich to his readers as evidence that Republicans "can recruit young, attractive candidates" and "challenge even Democratic incumbents head-on." While most "Gingrich-style" candidates were attracted to the Democratic Party because of Watergate, Dillin wrote, Gingrich's campaign was significant to the GOP because he offered an exception to the rule.[35] In a Democratic year, Gingrich won 48.5 percent of the vote in a district where registered Republicans composed less than 10 percent of the electorate. He attracted strong broad-based support in the suburbs, the target electorate for the new Republican Party.[36] He even did relatively well with black voters in Andrew Young's former district, who felt little loyalty to a racist southern Democrat like Congressman Flynt.

Even as he earned support from the center, Gingrich kept his eye on the growing conservative movement eager to rebuild the GOP after Watergate. By the mid-1970s, several factions of conservatives were starting to coalesce into a full-blown movement that sought to push American politics to the right. Religious conservatives were inspired to enter into politics in response to the Supreme Court's legalizing abortion in 1973, the campaign for an Equal Rights Amendment (ERA), and IRS regulations cracking down on all-white private school academies; business and Wall Street conservatives sought to cut taxes, curtail unions, and deregulate the economy; while neoconservative Democrats were abandoning their party to join hawkish Republicans in championing a more militaristic foreign policy. Though the New Right, as it was called, was still coming together when Gerald Ford was in the Oval Office, conservatism was seen as a legitimate and powerful force. The movement's leaders employed novel tactics to attract members and money, such as Richard Viguerie's use of direct mail to raise large numbers of small donations. Think tanks like the American Enterprise Institute served as incubators for rightward policy ideas that were capturing the imagination of young conservatives who began to dream about the end of the New Deal era.

In 1975, Gingrich attended an election-campaign "school" in Wisconsin run by one of the movement's emerging stars, the fiery conservative activist Paul Weyrich, an evangelical Republican building bridges between religious activists and the Republican Party leadership. Weyrich had come to prominence three years earlier by co-founding the Heritage Foundation, a conservative think tank in Washington, and saw himself as a movement builder. As one of the founders of the New Right, a network of political action committees, think tanks, and activists determined to make the Republican Party more conservative, Weyrich enjoyed nurturing lesser-known Republican candidates who could knock off Democratic incumbents or win open seats.

Weyrich conducted small workshops in his native Wisconsin, funded by his Committee for the Survival of a Free Congress, which were becoming legendary for giving inexperienced candidates insights about the nuts and bolts of running effective campaigns. Gingrich attended one of these classes in a conference room in the Marc Plaza Hotel in Milwaukee on a bitterly cold December afternoon. Sitting in the first row among a group of talented classmates, Gingrich was eager to learn how to take out Flynt when he ran against him, as he intended, for a second time in 1976. Gingrich being Gingrich, he couldn't sit still for very long. Just a few minutes into the class, the student sounded like the teacher. In his high-pitched, squeaky voice, arms waving like an orchestra conductor's, Gingrich dominated the discussion, and everyone turned to hear what he had to say. Weyrich sat back in stunned silence. Gingrich argued that all the candidates in the room could be more effective if they ran on a shared message. Weyrich, Gingrich informed his teacher, should be responsible for ensuring that this coordination happened.

Weyrich was deeply impressed and sensed that Gingrich was someone special.[37] Although Gingrich was still much more of a middle-of-the-road Rockefeller Republican than Weyrich, he liked the Georgian's intensity and passion, as well as his vision for the Republican Party. The two men hit it off right away. "I made a conscious effort to make Newt a star of the conservative movement," Weyrich recalled. "We had magazines, bulletins, and I got him featured on the cover of every one. No one had heard of him. I made an effort to be Newt's promoter."[38]

Two years after his first campaign, Gingrich, still teaching at West Georgia, challenged Flynt for a second round. This time around, Gingrich made congressional corruption his central theme, hoping that the GOP baggage from the Nixon years would now prove less heavy, and he portrayed Flynt as being part of the corrupt establishment even as he chaired the House Ethics Committee. Gingrich formally announced his second run by blasting a pay raise that Congress was considering for itself. Given that the salary of legislators was "4½ times the income of the average Georgia family," Gingrich called the proposal "immoral."[39]

After decades in power, southern Democratic politicians in the 1970s enjoyed such built-in advantages as troughs of campaign funds and gerrymandered districts. The corruption of politics, Gingrich declared, offered his party its best argument for taking on a powerful Democratic incumbent in the one-party South—perhaps the only rationale compelling enough to undercut the benefits of incumbency. When Flynt's 1973 land dealings became public, the congressman admitted that it was the "worst mistake I ever made." Gingrich agreed, calling the scandal "petty, arrogant behavior that does not befit a member of Congress, and certainly not the chairman of the ethics committee."[40] When Flynt rejected an invitation to debate Gingrich on the grounds that he had too much work to do in Washington, Gingrich pounced. "There is a chair in the House of Representatives in Washington," Gingrich exclaimed at his kickoff rally, "a chair that belongs to the people of this district."

The facts on the ground had changed too. By Gingrich's second run, senior congressional Democrats had come under fire for scandals of their own. Wilbur Mills, the powerful chairman of the House Ways and Means

Committee, had to step down in December 1974 after being caught jumping into Washington's Tidal Basin with a stripper named Fanne Foxe. The Ohio Democrat Wayne Hays, the head of the Committee on House Administration and the Democratic Congressional Campaign Committee (DCCC), resigned after being caught using public funds to pay his girlfriend, Elizabeth Ray, to work as his secretary, even though she admitted to a reporter that she didn't know how to type.

The class of '74, popularly known as the Watergate Babies (in part because eighty-seven of them were under forty years of age), deposed three senior committee chairmen—Edward Hébert of the Armed Services Committee, William R. Poage of the Committee on Agriculture, and Wright Patman of the Committee on Banking and Currency—for being unresponsive to the demands of younger Democrats.[41] Such actions by freshmen had been unheard of in previous decades, when the norm was for younger members to defer to senior leaders.

During a speech to the Young Republicans of Fulton County in 1976, Gingrich warned, "The news media continues to uncover more and more Congressional corruption every day. We have seen padded payrolls and falsified travel vouchers, bribery and forgery, all by the men we elect to pass our laws and lead this country, and all by powerful members of the Democratic Party."[42]

Turning from the national to the local, Gingrich sharpened his corruption case against Flynt. The House Ethics Committee that he chaired was notorious for sitting on its hands when fellow members, especially Democrats, were accused of ethics violations. The joke on Capitol Hill was that the best way to bury an ethics complaint was to send it to Flynt's committee. To drive the point home to voters in Georgia's Sixth, one Gingrich campaign ad depicted him knocking on the door of the Ethics Committee, with the caption explaining that he was there to ask "Flynt to open it up to public scrutiny."[43]

In the 1976 campaign, Gingrich showed voters his full potential by devoting more attention to issues besides political corruption. He endorsed a tougher stance toward the Soviet Union and opposed proposals for national health insurance. The Republican promised to vote against the Humphrey-Hawkins bill being debated in Congress, which would fund federal public works programs as a way to lower unemployment, and he threw his support behind antiunion right-to-work laws. Abortion legislation, Gingrich told voters, should be left to the states. He reached out to moderates by championing most of the government's efforts to protect the environment.

Gingrich continued to receive attention from national conservatives. The 1964 Republican nominee, Barry Goldwater, stopped by a fundraising luncheon for Gingrich at the Airport-Sheraton Hotel as part of a tour of the region aiming to mobilize Republican voters.[44] Gingrich, who still identified and was seen as a moderate Republican, began to show indications that he was sympathetic to the conservative movement, including its figurehead, Ronald Reagan, who challenged President Gerald Ford in the 1976 Republican primaries. The Fords and Rockefellers of the party, Gingrich warned in an op-ed for *The Baltimore Sun*, were in "grave danger of overestimating conservative . . . goodwill."[45] The *Atlanta Daily World* endorsed Gingrich again, saying that the race "pits youth, intelligence, compassion and ability in the person of Newt Gingrich against an aging incumbent whose 22 years in office represents some of the worse [*sic*] you can find in Washington's so-called 'Establishment.'"[46]

Gingrich had refined his case, but he came up short again—this time by less than a percentage point. Republicans were still paying for Watergate, and the Democrats had nominated a popular Georgia Democrat, the former governor Jimmy Carter, for president. Running as a sincere, trustworthy outsider to Washington, Carter won the White House, and Democrats increased their margins in both the House and the Senate.

After his defeat, Gingrich kept poking at Flynt and the Democratic Congress. During a speech in Atlanta, he rejected the notion that his fellow Georgian Jimmy Carter's election as president had somehow cleansed Washington of its problems. "Our legislative system," Gingrich insisted with his attention turned to Capitol Hill, "has become morally, intellectually, and spiritually corrupt. Indeed, the patterns of corruption have become so firmly established that they overwhelm reform-minded freshmen when they arrive, and convince them by the time they become sophomores to accept what is, rather than struggle for change. In Sam Rayburn's memorable phrase, they learn quickly to get along by going along." What this meant in practice, according to Gingrich, was "closing one's eyes to a thousand bad things," all for the promise of making a difference.[47] The break Gingrich needed came in February 1978, when the sixty-three-year-old Flynt made the surprise announcement that he would not run again. Flynt didn't like the way the class of '74 had changed life on the Hill, and his own district was steadily moving away from the racial conservatism that had sustained him.

Gingrich had already been campaigning; now he was all in. He and his wife no longer had his professorial income to draw from; Gingrich had never published his research, and without the prospect of tenure he had resigned from West Georgia College. His marriage to Jackie had become rocky; they had been in and out of counseling while repeatedly considering divorce. They lived in a modest house with cheap furniture. Money was going to be a big issue this time around. Gingrich's mother worried that her son wouldn't be able to provide for his family.[48]

To finance his campaign, Gingrich turned to a group of wealthy Georgia donors, headed by a local developer named Chester Roush, who offered him a whopping $13,000 to write a novel (Gingrich didn't write the book). The donors structured the donation, which well exceeded Gingrich's salary as assistant professor, as a tax shelter to minimize their losses. Gingrich, according to this plan, would use the private advance as income to sustain his run.[49] He also relied on the national party for assistance. He brazenly arranged a meeting in Washington with the deputy chairman of the Republican National Committee (RNC), Eddie Mahe, who was scouring the country for new faces who could help the party take advantage of President Carter's falling approval ratings. When Mahe, unaware that his executive assistant had set up this meeting, entered his office, he found Gingrich seated in front of his desk. Mahe peered through his Coke-bottle glasses at the mysterious gentleman in the madras jacket and polyester pants and thought, "How did this dork get in here?" Even though

Mahe had a busy day ahead of him, he sat down and asked Gingrich what he wanted. Without missing a beat, Gingrich delivered a three-and-a-half-minute monologue about how Republicans could win in southern districts that had been solidly Democratic via the story of his own campaign. Mahe was hooked.[50]

The RNC decided to invest in this fresh face. The National Republican Congressional Committee (NRCC) contributed $50,000 to Gingrich's campaign, and the party provided him with a seasoned manager named Carlyle Gregory from Virginia and a talented consultant named Bob Weed. Gingrich cleaned up his looks: he lost weight, trimmed his long sideburns, and purchased a Washington-worthy wardrobe. According to a Gingrich biographer, "The used car salesman ties, shirts, and suits had been banished (hopefully burned), and the long sideburns had been eighty-sixed, along with the steel-rim glasses. He was now photographed in attire befitting a young politician on the go: red ties and solid blue, gray, or black suits."[51]

Gingrich's third campaign took on a more conservative tone than his previous runs. With the economy tanking, American power in decline, and conservative activism on the rise, politics was shifting rightward at the national level and within his own district. Gingrich had been enthralled upon hearing the New York congressman Jack Kemp, a former professional football player, deliver a passionate one-hour speech at the Georgia Republican state convention about supply-side economics. Kemp touted deficit-inducing tax cuts for wealthier Americans as the best way to grow the overall economy. Short-term deficits would create a stronger economy and in the long term generate balanced budgets. Like President Theodore Roosevelt, Kemp seemed to be the kind of "big idea" Republican who Gingrich believed was needed to save the party from obscurity.[52]

Gingrich got on board with conservative movement politics. Environmentalists and younger students were gone from his campaign headquarters, replaced by staunch conservative Republicans and professional party activists. He aligned himself with the movement by emphasizing supply-side tax cuts and deregulation, combating inflation, eliminating bureaucratic waste, and enacting welfare reform, as well as opposing the ERA.

Foreign policy was not as important in local elections, but Gingrich did make clear his support for higher defense spending, and he lambasted President Carter for agreeing to treaties that relinquished control of the Panama Canal to the Panamanians.[53] Gingrich easily won the Republican primary.

For the general election, he crafted a tough campaign against the Democratic nominee, the Georgia state senator Virginia Shapard, a moderate. His rightward policy promises always came back to a defining theme: Gingrich, the fighter, was going to bring down the entire corrupt political establishment. "Tip O'Neill's title should be changed from Speaker to Dictator of the House," he proclaimed.[54] One of his campaign flyers, titled NEWT GINGRICH—HIS ONLY SPECIAL INTEREST IS YOU!, featured a photograph of the young renegade with his sleeves rolled up and right arm bent in the air with his hand clenched tight in a defiant fist.[55]

Tactically, a now-seasoned Gingrich demonstrated exceptional skill when it came to framing how voters perceived his opponent, no matter how distorted the charges. Gingrich hired Deno Seder, a notorious advertising man from Shreveport, Louisiana, who produced ads that made Shapard look more liberal than she was. He unleashed advertisements that painted her as a ruthless feminist willing to destroy her family in pursuit of power. Shapard made the mistake of telling a reporter that she would commute to Washington so that her husband could keep his job in Georgia and her kids could stay in their school. "When elected Newt will keep his family together," Gingrich cheekily countered in a campaign flyer. Perhaps with little sense of the irony involved, Gingrich's self-published tabloid, the *New Georgia Leader*, part political information and part campaign propaganda, featured numerous stories highlighting the wonderfulness of his churchgoing family—with one article in October titled NEWT'S FAMILY IS LIKE YOUR FAMILY—to disparage his "home-wrecking" opponent.[56] "Newt knows the problems families face—but he also knows the joys and rewards of strong family life," read the copy of a newspaper ad.[57] Jackie abetted her husband by sending personal letters to fellow schoolteachers reiterating the same message.[58]

In this campaign, Gingrich embraced the bare-knuckle approach that would become a model for his future electoral runs and his congressional conduct. Speaking to a group of College Republicans at the Atlanta Airport Holiday Inn, Gingrich said that the next generation of Republicans couldn't speak like Boy Scouts, the way that the elders in the GOP liked to do: "neat, obedient, and loyal and faithful" were "lousy" attributes in politics. He told his enthralled young audience that when they saw someone doing "something dumb," they should "say it, say it in the press, say it loud, fight, scrap, issue a press release, go make a speech." Republicans, Gingrich concluded, do "not need another generation of cautious, prudent, careful, bland, irrelevant, quasi-leaders who are willing as people to drift into positions because nobody else is available." They needed energetic candidates ready for a "slug fest."[59]

Some of Gingrich's supporters heeded his words immediately, surreptitiously distributing a racially tinged flyer that featured a photograph of Shapard standing next to Julian Bond, the black civil rights leader and state senator, with text that read, "If you like welfare cheaters, you'll love Virginia Shapard." Gingrich denied having anything to do with this incident, though some Democrats didn't believe him.

By the final days of the campaign, Shapard's staff was so angry about their opponent's underhanded tactics that they took to calling Gingrich "s.o.b.," refusing to even utter his name.[60] Shapard charged that Gingrich's misleading ads were tantamount to "political pornography."[61] With a few days to go, Shapard was taken aback once again when Gingrich unleashed a torrent of unfounded accusations that she had violated campaign-finance laws.[62] This time, *The Atlanta Constitution*, which had twice endorsed Gingrich, backed Shapard, concluding that the Republican had plainly lied and engaged in dirty politics. But he didn't need these endorsements anymore.

At 11:30 on a rainy election night, Carlyle Gregory called Gingrich to let him know that he had won. Running as a rock-ribbed Republican, Gingrich defeated Shapard by eight points, with a 54.4 percent majority. Before a cheering crowd at the election-night celebration at the Atlanta Airport Holiday Inn, he declared victory ten minutes after receiving the news. Gingrich instructed the crowd, "I want you to force us to be accountable. Stay alive. Call and raise Cain. We need you to be an angry customer just like you would in any business."[63] As one long-term supporter watched her new congressman stand victoriously on the podium alongside his daughters, Jackie Sue (eleven) and Kathy (fifteen), as well as his beaming wife, Jackie, she broke down into uncontrollable tears and shouted at the top of her lungs, "It sho' is nice after so many times!"[64]

Gingrich's campaign team clapped and hollered for the victor, but Gingrich remained strikingly calm. He spent the winning hours working the room, shaking hands and schmoozing with people about the next steps in his political career. On Wednesday morning, he met with airport workers and then crews at a Ford Motor plant to let them know how much he appreciated their support. "I am fairly unique. I am a strange guy named Newt Gingrich who was born in Pennsylvania and grew up everywhere," he said, adding that he was "a college teacher who is a Republican who was willing to run three times, and I think that makes me weird."[65]

Republicans throughout the country were feeling good, even though Democrats retained control of Congress. In the Senate, Republicans had defeated five Democrats in high-profile races, including Iowa's Dick Clark and New Hampshire's Thomas McIntyre. In the House, Gingrich was just one member in a rambunctious new class of Republicans who leaned to the right. The GOP picked up fifteen House seats, with an especially strong showing in the Sunbelt and the Midwest.[66] "You're going to have a skittish Congress," one adviser warned President Carter.[67]

The election celebration had barely died down when Gingrich flew to Washington to meet Guy Vander Jagt, the chairman of the National Republican Congressional Committee. Gingrich told Vander Jagt, a Michigan representative, that their party needed a bold plan to win a majority in the House of Representatives. Three hours later, when the meeting finally ended, an admiring Vander Jagt decided to appoint Gingrich to head a task force for the GOP to map out a strategy. He recalled, "I skipped him over about 155 sitting Republicans to do it, and from that moment on he has been planning for a Republican majority."[68]

Gingrich was suddenly a player on the national stage. When thirty-five new Republicans gathered for a celebratory weekend freshman orientation at a Virginia hotel in early December, Saul Friedman of *The Charlotte Observer* ran into Gingrich, who was bouncing around the hallway like the big man on campus. The thirty-five-year-old politician jumped at the opportunity to speak to a reporter from outside Georgia. With a wide smile, Gingrich proudly whipped out his new congressional identification card and told Friedman, "Here's how it starts." The reporter glanced at the card, which read, HONORABLE NEWT GINGRICH. Taking a look for himself, as if still almost in disbelief about his victory, Gingrich said, "Until November 8 (the day after the election), I had never been honorable in my life. It's the office that's honorable, not the man. But when they hang such titles on you and a staff trails you everywhere, it's so easy to . . . take yourself seriously."[69]

The humility was feigned. Gingrich's ambitions were almost visibly bursting at the seams, his inner grandiosity latched to a sense of purpose now unleashed. He arrived in Washington with three goals in mind: to "defeat the Soviet empire, replace the welfare state, and replace the Democrats as the majority party in the House. . . . I spent my days on those three goals."[70]

This new congressman was on his way to something big.

His first target would be an African American congressman named Charles Diggs.

Two

A POLITICAL
WRECKING BALL

The new congressman sprang into action. Gingrich stormed Capitol Hill with a plan to clean house, calling out corruption wherever he saw it. This would be the best way to take on the Democrats and catapult himself into the press—and into the growing ranks of young Republicans who shared his desire to challenge Democratic rule. Having run as an outsider, the junior congressman now embraced the message of good-government reform to pursue his bolder partisan objectives. He hit Congress like a human wrecking ball, shattering norms and customs that senior legislators thought were bedrocks to good governance. Nothing was inviolate, including decorum and civility; these, Gingrich insisted, were merely tools that Democrats used to preserve their power.

Gingrich ignored the traditional paths to congressional power: doing committee work while moving up the ladder of seniority or taking a high-profile role on legislation. He was not going to "carve out a subcommittee to dominate," he told *The Atlanta Constitution*.[1] Instead, he would prove himself to his colleagues through high-profile attacks on the majority Democrats that he knew would rile Washington. Gingrich would be the

Republican attack dog with the mind of a policy intellectual, constantly testing the limits of what was possible.

Gingrich spotted an enticing target before he and his family had even settled in Washington. Congressman Charles Diggs, a Democrat from Detroit first elected in 1954, was a prominent civil rights leader and a founding member of the Congressional Black Caucus. In March 1978, a grand jury indicted the fifty-five-year-old Diggs on several charges, including accepting $60,000 in kickbacks from his staff. A jury convicted him approximately six months later on eleven counts of mail fraud and for having filed false payroll forms. His constituents were more forgiving. While he awaited sentencing and planned his appeal, Diggs's district reelected him in November with 79 percent of the vote. Given the legal jeopardy he faced, Diggs agreed to voluntarily relinquish the chairmanship of the House District of Columbia Committee, though he insisted on keeping hold of the chairmanship of the International Relations Subcommittee on Africa so that he could continue working on vital issues such as the fight against apartheid in South Africa.

Gingrich, who had been in Washington for only a few weeks and was not yet formally seated, immediately called on Diggs to step down. He smelled blood when he read in the newspapers that the Democrats, sensing that Diggs could be a liability, had approved rules in early December mandating that the caucus would vote on the subcommittee chairmanship of any member who had been convicted of a felony that included a sentence of at least two years. Emboldened by the fact that Democrats were uneasy about their situation, Gingrich kept up the drumbeat when he organized fourteen House Republicans to demand that the House Ethics Committee investigate.

The young congressman caught the attention of Minority Leader John Rhodes. In 1976, the Arizona Republican had published a book titled *The Futile System*, in which he argued that the Democratic majority would never be willing to reform itself. Rhodes was one of those Republicans whom Gingrich kept writing about in his strategic memos to colleagues, a representative who had served all but two years of his frustrating term on the losing side of the aisle. Rhodes planned to retire after November 1980 unless the nation voted in a Republican majority that could elect him Speaker of the House. Rhodes worried that Gingrich was being too aggressive with Diggs and should let the Democrats clean up their own mess, as was traditional.[2]

Notwithstanding his concerns, Rhodes announced on January 9 that a group of Republicans would move to expel Diggs when the session started. Under Article I, Section 5 of the Constitution, by a two-thirds vote the House had the right to expel a member from his or her seat. This was a serious and seldom-used punishment against a colleague; only three members had been expelled in the history of the House, all of them after being accused of treason during the Civil War.

On January 11, Gingrich wrote to the Illinois congressman John Anderson, a reform-minded Republican, that he was "morally repulsed" to be serving in a government body whose member had "committed a series of crimes against" that very body. If Diggs voted on any substantive matter before the Ethics Committee had completed its investigation, Gingrich warned, he would be "compelled" to take the steps needed to have him expelled from the House.[3] "While I'm pleased the Republican leadership is going to file a complaint with the Ethics Committee on this matter," Gingrich said a few days later to the press, "I'd request that you go one step further. We should insure that Mr. Diggs doesn't vote until the report from the Ethics Committee is acted upon by the House."[4] While the House rule recommended that convicted members not vote (unless they were elected after conviction), Democrats were not prepared to enforce that prohibition. As Republicans ramped up their efforts, House Democrats were able to pressure Diggs into stepping down from his subcommittee chairmanship on January 23 to avoid a direct confrontation with the party.

Fourteen junior House Republicans, with Gingrich as the main signatory, followed through on their promise. On February 2, they sent a letter to the House Ethics Committee requesting that an investigation into

Diggs start "as expeditiously as possible." In a strategic move, Gingrich dropped the demand for the specific punishment of expulsion so that he could win the support of the Missouri Democrat Richard Gephardt, a second termer who hoped to burnish his credentials as a reform-oriented leader and position himself as a key member of the new generation of "Atari Democrats." After the letter was submitted, Indiana's Philip Sharp, one of the Democrats from the class of '74, announced his support, bringing the total number of Democrats to two.

Five days later, the House Ethics Committee launched its preliminary investigation. Putting aside Gephardt's and Sharp's bipartisan support, Gingrich decried the "double standard of justice" that he said existed among the twenty-seven Democrats who in 1976 had voted to investigate Florida's Bob Sikes, a southern conservative accused of financial misconduct, but now sat in total silence. "In essence," Gingrich wrote in *Human Events*, "we should have one standard of justice for all Americans—and for all Congressmen—for white conservative Southerners and for black Northern liberals."[5]

The Illinois Republican Robert Michel, a believer in civility, was expected to replace John Rhodes as minority leader if the Arizonan retired. Michel privately told Gingrich that he supported his effort but worried that going after a prominent black congressman would reinforce the image that the GOP was hostile to minority groups, if not outright racist.[6] Michel was old enough to remember the backlash that took place over the Harlem congressman Adam Clayton Powell. The first African American from New York to be elected to the House, Powell had been an ardent champion of civil rights. But his work on civil rights was often overshadowed by countless stories about egregious financial and personal misconduct, such as tax evasion and using public funds to pay for junkets with his girlfriends. While there were liberals who supported an investigation, Powell argued that the Dixiecrats—many of whom were guilty of much worse—were targeting him because of his work on racial justice. In January 1967, the House voted to prevent Powell from being seated while a bipartisan special committee investigated his case. When the committee recommended that punishment was warranted, his opponents secured a

307–116 vote to "exclude" him on March 1, which meant keeping him out of his seat for technical violations of the requirements needed to serve in the House. The punishment, which required only a majority vote (in contrast with the two-thirds requirement needed for expulsion), enraged his constituents. The NAACP warned that the punishment could be "interpreted as tailor made to apply to him and to no other member of Congress [and] will be fuel for appeals based on prejudice rather than reason."[7] Powell's district overwhelmingly voted for him in a special election held a few weeks later. Because of the standoff, the seat remained empty until June 1969, when the Supreme Court ruled that the House did not have the constitutional right to exclude Powell because he met every technical requirement in the Constitution. While Gingrich distinguished the two cases by saying that Diggs had been convicted of a crime against the House and the Supreme Court had specifically ruled against excluding Powell (saying that expulsion would have been legitimate),[8] senior legislators in both parties saw the racially tinged Diggs case through the same political prism. As a result, most Democrats believed that voters should have the ultimate say to decide on his fate. "I don't think he should be expelled from the House," argued Majority Leader Jim Wright from Texas. "Membership in the House is not ours to bestow. We can't give that to anybody. The constituents are entitled to have the representatives of their own choice."[9]

There was another, more recent scandal that also inhibited Democrats from joining Gingrich's crusade. Koreagate, a scandal that unfolded between 1976 and 1978, involved a South Korean lobbyist named Tongsun Park who made more than $800,000 in donations to Democrats and held lavish dinner parties in his Georgetown town house attended by such powerhouses as Speaker Tip O'Neill. Although a number of major legislators were caught up in the story, in the end the only punishment taken by the House was to reprimand the California representatives Edward Roybal, John McFall, and Charlie Wilson, a mild punishment considered even less severe than censure (the toughest punishment came through the courts; the former California congressman Richard Hanna went to jail). The New Jersey congressman Andrew Maguire's staffer privately confided to Gingrich's assistants that with regards to Diggs they were "very concerned about racism—Koreagate people get their hands slapped and now a black gets more than that."[10]

Gingrich was not concerned about the racial overtones with Diggs. His supporters had dabbled with the politics of race during his 1978 congressional campaign, but in his view he was no old-school southern racist. Gingrich bragged that he was one of a handful of Republicans in favor of creating a national holiday and monument in honor of Martin Luther King Jr. He also liked to say that he was going after corrupt white legislators, such as Pennsylvania's Daniel Flood, a Democrat under investigation for misusing federal money.[11]

The stage was set for a showdown. Gingrich sent a letter directly to Diggs explaining that he would call for expulsion should the congressman take any votes before the investigation ended. On February 28, when Diggs exercised his right to vote on a routine measure, Gingrich followed through on his threat by walking to the well of the House chamber and proposing a resolution—his first official act as a congressman—to expel his Democratic colleague to protect the "honor and dignity of the House." Fellow representatives were taken aback by the severity of the proposal and the fact that a Republican was leading the charge.

Opposing Gingrich was Wright, whose job it was as majority leader to quash the motion and put the GOP upstart in his place. Wright reminded the young firebrand that historically it was up to each caucus to discipline its own members. The Democrats would do with Diggs as they saw fit, Wright said; that's the way it was, and even after Watergate that's the way it remained. Wright walked to the lectern on his side of the aisle and offered a counter-motion that referred Gingrich's proposal to the Ethics Committee, which everyone on the floor understood would bury it.[12]

Most members of the House thought that Gingrich was going too far. Wright's proposal passed by a vote of 322 to 77. Wright dismissed Gingrich's motion as a stunt by someone new to Washington who did not understand how politics worked. "Surely the membership is not prepared to take action expelling a member of the House pending the exercise of his legal and constitutional rights under the law," Wright said in his slow Texas drawl.[13]

The defeat didn't bother Gingrich a bit. After all, as he boasted to his staff in a memo revealing his true strategy, "I was in the Washington news media enough to be a very well-known Freshman. The country is now much more aware that a convicted felon is voting in Congress."[14]

Gingrich felt vindicated on April 4, when the members of the Ethics Committee charged they had "reason to believe" that Diggs was guilty of eighteen violations of House rules. The committee would soon begin the second stage of its investigatory process to see whether the evidence met the highest standards and, if it did, how it should punish Diggs. After a few months of a humiliating investigation scrutinized by the media, Diggs's lawyers reached a deal with the committee. In exchange for dropping the rest of the investigation and settling on censure—the mildest form of punishment—Diggs agreed to pay the government $40,031 that he had obtained from kickbacks and padding the payroll. "I sincerely regret the errors in judgment which led to this proceeding," he wrote.

On July 31, a somber-looking Diggs, wearing a patterned tie and light blue jacket, was the first to enter the chamber. He walked to the front row and sat down by himself, awaiting his punishment. Once the other representatives filled up the room, many stood up to offer their thoughts on what the House should do about Diggs's wrongdoing. The congressman dutifully listened to half an hour of floor speeches in which no one came to his defense. The Wyoming Republican Richard "Dick" Cheney said that Diggs should have resigned "long ago," given the "dishonor" he had brought on the House.

Once the speeches were done, Speaker O'Neill called on Diggs to approach the front of the chamber and remain at the rostrum as he read out loud the language of the censure. Although they stood just inches apart, Diggs looked down and showed barely any emotion as the Speaker mechanically and uncomfortably recited the words off a two-page resolution. O'Neill banged his gavel, proclaiming "the matter" closed. Members crowded around the humiliated Diggs, patting him on the back and whispering words of support before he bolted to the sanctuary of his office.

The House proceeded to vote almost unanimously in favor of the committee's recommendation to censure Diggs.

A jubilant Gingrich told the horde of reporters who met him near his office that he accepted the verdict as "realistically the strongest thing we can hope for."[15] Gingrich realized that expulsion would have been a step too far for most members. And he was savvy enough to understand that he needed to at least act in a statesmanlike fashion as he spoke to the journalists, making it seem as if he were primarily concerned about the fate of his colleague and the health of the institution. Diggs's downfall was Gingrich's first major political victory as a House member. This was Gingrich's first at bat in his effort to paint the entire Democratic Party as fundamentally corrupt, and he had hit a home run. Diggs would resign from the House on June 3, 1980, after the Supreme Court rejected his criminal appeal; he would serve seven months of a three-year prison sentence.

The disgraced Detroit legislator was small potatoes in the larger scope of party politics, but his defeat felt like a big event to Washington insiders. Several news organizations, including *The New York Times*, featured Gingrich in stories about the fresh voices of the GOP. Major print editors, such as Meg Greenfield of *The Washington Post*, who had previously rejected Gingrich's pitches, now solicited his writing. The editor of the *Conservative Digest*, John Lofton, called Gingrich's office to say that he wanted to "give Newt more ink." *Human Events*, the conservative magazine that had ignored Gingrich's congressional campaigns, expanded its coverage of the congressman as a result of his role in the Diggs case. "Newt is now on very good terms with Bob Novak and David Broder," the staffer Frank Gregorsky, on loan from the National Republican Congressional Committee, observed in his private notes, "he is becoming friends with George Will and Morton Kondracke. An A.P. reporter who covered Newt and another freshman in 1979 told him last week that there are about six Representatives whose phone numbers reporters know by heart, and Newt's was now one of them—because they thought Newt understood what was happening and would play it straight with the press."[16]

Gingrich's focus on congressional corruption turned out to be well timed. As the Diggs saga unfolded, another major scandal rocked Capitol Hill that seemed to confirm Gingrich's basic point about Democratic Washington. On February 20, 1980, NBC reported the shocking news that the FBI had been conducting a sting operation on several members of Congress who had allegedly accepted bribes from undercover agents dressed as Arab sheikhs in exchange for influence. The first story about the Abscam scandal to hit the airwaves featured grainy, night-vision videos, filmed by network cameramen, of legislators entering and exiting the town house that the FBI used for its operation. The theme of congressional corruption took on new valence. Just a few weeks after NBC broadcast its report on the scandal, Gingrich convened a news conference at the Atlanta Air Center, where he unveiled a seven-point plan to clean up Congress. His proposal included suspending legislators from committee service if they had admitted to taking money from FBI agents, pushing the House to use more subpoenas to investigate corruption, and having the media establish an ethics watch monitor to cover this beat. "Many people in this country are now saying that all this is just politics, and politics is dirty," Gingrich pontificated to the journalists who had gathered to hear him. "I disagree. Politics doesn't have to be corrupt. In fact, in a free society, it can't be allowed to be corrupt. I think the House can and must do a great deal to clean up government and restore people's faith in Congress."[17]

In September 1980, not even two years since his election to Congress, the Georgian felt as if he had already arrived in Washington as he stood beside the Republican presidential candidate, Ronald Reagan, at a photo session that Gingrich largely organized, joining 150 Senate and House challengers and 23 Senate and 115 House incumbents on the steps of the Capitol to pledge their support for spending cuts, tax cuts, and a hard-line foreign policy. The point of the photo op was to show that electing Reagan would be part of a larger political revolution. Reagan was not a one-man show; he was part of a team. "Yes it's a media event," Gingrich admitted, but it would signal to voters that the party could be held accountable should they be successful in November.[18] The picture was meant to show that the decision on Election Day would be about the direction of the entire Republican Party. *Project Majority*, a report that Gingrich had completed for the National Republican Congressional Committee, which was circulating around Capitol Hill, had recommended that the party act in more "synergistic fashion."[19] This event with Reagan fulfilled that exact objective. Reagan and Republicans like Gingrich were part of a movement seeking to transform American politics. They sought to bring down the entire establishment along the way.

Gingrich's elation about his success with Diggs was nothing compared with the thrill he felt on election night, November 4, 1980. At 8:15 P.M. eastern standard time, NBC News flashed the words across the screen that Republicans had been waiting for: "Reagan Wins!" Just four years earlier, Ronald Reagan had been dismissed by most pundits as an extremist. Now, on CBS, the network displayed a national map of the United States that showed the dramatic sweep of his victory, taking all but six states and the District of Columbia. "Reagan Democrats" had not only helped Republicans carry the day but signaled the possibility of a genuine partisan realignment. Reagan won nearly nine million more votes than Carter and took 489 electoral votes to Carter's 49. And for the first time since 1954, Republicans secured control of the Senate, with a majority of fifty-three to forty-six (Virginia's Harry Byrd Jr. was an independent but caucused with Democrats)—not sufficient to kill a sixty-vote filibuster but enough to set the agenda.

Back in Georgia, Gingrich slowly absorbed the enormity of the result as he and his advisers celebrated his own reelection, taking 59 percent of the vote in a district that had once been solidly Democratic. As a student of history, Gingrich understood the larger implications of the national results. He found Reagan inspirational and had praised his 1976 primary challenge to President Gerald Ford. Although Gingrich's own positions were more nuanced and eclectic than the president-elect's, drawing as much from futurists like Alvin Toffler as from conservative ideologues such as Friedrich Hayek, Gingrich understood Reagan to be the type of transformative figure needed to make conservatism into a governing doctrine.

Having spent decades marginalized in Washington, forced to live in the shadows of American liberalism, conservatives could barely contain their joy that a champion of their cause would soon assume the highest office in the land. Gingrich was twenty-one years old when Senator Goldwater failed spectacularly in 1964. It had taken a generation for right-wing conservatism to triumph as Dixiecrats and Rust Belt Democrats—weary of the lagging economy under President Carter and the ongoing American hostage crisis in Iran—broke for the former actor turned California governor. Reagan's election had only been possible after fifteen years of a brewing political backlash toward the Democratic embrace of civil rights in 1964 and 1965—as President Johnson had famously predicted—finally allowed the GOP to start dominating the South.

Republicans were feeling triumphant on Inauguration Day, January 20, 1981. Breaking precedent, Reagan was sworn in as the nation's fortieth president from the west side of the Capitol, a change that meshed with his sense of American's manifest destiny and endless possibility. All morning, the skies had been overcast. As if on cue, the sun came out when Reagan walked up to deliver his speech to the nation.

Gingrich, standing alongside his Republican colleagues and watching his first inauguration in person, saw the clearing skies as a sign of things to come. In his stirring inaugural address, Reagan uttered the words that would become Gingrich's political fuel: "In this present crisis, government is not the solution to our problem; government is the problem." Standing fifteen feet away from the crooner Frank Sinatra and directly behind the former chairman of the Joint Chiefs of Staff General Omar Bradley, the starstruck Gingrich felt that Reagan's oration "was a pretty darn good speech."[20] Making the moment even sweeter was the surprise release of the fifty-two American hostages after 444 days in Iranian captivity; conservatives crowed that Reagan had achieved what President Carter could not. (In fact, Carter had negotiated the release, but the Iranians spitefully held on to the hostages until he left office.) The television networks covering the postinaugural procession switched back and forth between the celebration in Washington and the news out of Iran.

Gingrich's celebratory mood was tempered by the fact that almost nothing had changed in the House of Representatives. Democrats remained in full control, just as they had for the previous twenty-six years. A few days after the election, when David Broder of *The Washington Post* contacted the congressman to ask him what he thought about the Republican triumph, Gingrich replied bluntly, "We are not in power. If the Reagan people let that idea get abroad, we are in real trouble. We do not control the senior bureaucracy as yet and we do not control the House of Representatives."[21] Republicans had picked up thirty-five House seats and expanded the size of the conservative coalition of southern Democrats and Republicans, but Democrats retained a formidable 243–192 majority, enough to sink Reagan's legislative agenda and neutralize much of his victory. Many Republicans gloried in the fantasy of the ideological shift that Reagan's victory portended, but Gingrich thought only of the continued control of the House Democrats. In the House, only a simple majority was needed to move or stifle a bill; the minority was virtually powerless.

Speaker Tip O'Neill was not eager to play ball with the new administration. He believed that government was a good thing, and he would never abandon the fight to defend the legacies of Franklin Roosevelt and Lyndon Johnson. Nor did O'Neill share Reagan's hawkish outlook on international relations. Facing one of Washington's last "unreconstructed liberals," Gingrich mounted a letter-writing campaign to his fellow Republicans arguing that they should replace O'Neill with a more conservative Democrat who would better reflect the tenor of the election. Democrats would retain control of the office, but a leader from the shrinking southern conservative wing of the party would be more prone toward compromise with the GOP. The Republicans would need to persuade twenty-six conservative Democrats to desert their party during the vote to select the next Speaker. "There is a media conspiracy to assign conservatives responsibility for the U.S. House of Representatives. Well, it's not really a conspiracy. Just a case of the establishment echo chamber at work. . . . Conservatives cannot afford to believe they run the U.S. House," Gingrich warned his colleagues. He also proposed that O'Neill voluntarily agree to make committee appointments that were equally divided between Republicans and conservative Democrats—a total nonstarter.[22] He enlisted conservative activists like Terry Dolan and Richard Scaife to lobby members of Congress to support this cause. It didn't work, although it did give O'Neill the message that liberals would be blamed if Reagan's agenda was blocked. Gingrich was savvy enough to know that the campaign was unrealistic. But he believed that its mere undertaking would remind reporters that liberals controlled the House of Representatives. He wanted to generate enough "noise and energy," one staffer admitted, to send a message to the public and lethargic members of his party that without full control of Congress, the Reagan Revolution was dead on arrival.[23]

That message seemed much more urgent to Gingrich after House Republicans voted to replace John Rhodes with Robert Michel, as much of a middle-of-the-roader as one could find. To Gingrich, Michel's selection as minority leader signaled that his party remained resigned to the life of a permanent minority.

For his part, Michel disliked Gingrich's attention-grabbing antics. Elected to the House in 1956 in a solidly Republican Illinois district, Michel opposed much of the Great Society and older liberal programs but concluded that the GOP would have to work with Democrats to keep a place at the table. Otherwise, he feared, the party would be rendered irrelevant.

Gingrich did not accept this logic. With Michel lecturing his Republican family about the need to be practical and to accept the reality that Democrats still ran the show, Gingrich acted like a petulant child who refused to take no for an answer. Here was another authority figure who made him mad. Gingrich respected Michel's career in Congress, but he didn't like his strategy for the party.

Instead, Gingrich wanted to create a new and lasting majority—one that replicated the New Deal coalition that dominated American politics for more than four decades, but this time from the right. Gingrich believed that the Republicans had honed in on a powerful set of issues—supply-side tax cuts, balanced budgets, higher military budgets, welfare, and fighting the ERA—that every faction of the conservative movement agreed on. While some of his own particular interests, like urban enterprise zones, did not yet command widespread support, there were enough points of commonality among all members of the party to keep the GOP on the same page. The main challenge thus revolved around winning greater control over the levers of power. No one else would have believed that a durable Republican majority was possible, but Gingrich had played and replayed the strategy in his mind for years, perfecting the campaign to tarnish the Democratic majority as corrupt and build a broad electoral coalition that would make Congress Republican.

It all came down to this: for Republicans to dislodge House Democrats from power, they would have to be ruthless. Democrats didn't play fair, Gingrich believed. He said that incumbents rigged elections through gerrymandering and campaign money; they relied on arcane procedures, such as imposing rules that prevented floor amendments to bills, that disempowered the minority party; and they solidified their public support through corrupt pork-barrel spending and favors for business leaders in their districts. "There's a sense that this (the Capitol) is a neighborhood designed to secure congressmen's feelings. That's very, very dangerous," according to the Georgian.[24] If the GOP adhered to the old rules of politics by being civil and bipartisan, it would simply allow the Democrats to keep winning.

As the Ninety-seventh Congress opened for business at noon on January 5, 1981, Gingrich set out to pull the House Democrats from power. The opening day was always festive. Members brought friends and families to the chamber to watch the start of the new session. The House relaxed its rules requiring visitors in the galleries to be silent when members convened so that they could cheer and clap.

The chamber was magnificent. First opened in 1857 as part of the expansion of the Capitol, the grand room had housed quintessentially historic moments: the passage of President Franklin Roosevelt's Hundred Days program that began to claw the nation out of the Great Depression; the declaration of war against Japan after Pearl Harbor; President Harry Truman outlining the new policy of containment against Soviet communism in 1947.

The chamber had been thoroughly renovated in the late 1940s.

Congress abandoned the Victorian, marble-heavy style for decor from the Federalist era. An interior, soundproofed room, the chamber featured a ceiling replicating the stained glass of an earlier period, while the carpet had a design of golden wreaths on a field of royal blue. A huge American flag hung along the wall. Carved into the marble of the top tier of the rostrum were four laurel branches signifying longevity. On the bottom tier, members saw inscriptions that captured the goals of post–World War II America: "Union," "Justice," "Tolerance," "Liberty," and "Peace." Below the rostrum were rows of dense books, such as *Cannon's Precedents* and *Deschler's Precedents*, explaining the rules of the chamber, esoteric technicalities to outsiders but the lifeblood of the institution to its initiates. Light beamed in from the artificial skylight, and relief sculptures of deceased lawmakers decorated the walls.[25]

Gingrich could embrace the history of the moment. Despite the small children who scampered in the aisles, partisan tensions were running high. The House clerk called the roll alphabetically so that the vote on electing Tip O'Neill as Speaker for another term could begin. Majority Leader Jim Wright said, "Just as the American people chose a Republican to sit in the White House, so the American people chose a Democratic majority in the House." Wright delivered these words as a warning to the GOP that the Democrats would not allow the president to do whatever he wanted. But Gingrich heard them as an opportunity. Voters' antiestablishment memories of Vietnam and Watergate remained fresh, and their distrust of government institutions had not yet been cauterized. With the House Democrats clinging to the rules of old Washington, this attack dog was determined to expose them as the epitome of all that was broken in the nation's capital.

Gingrich found his early years in Washington personally difficult. He worked brutal hours in his cluttered office in the Rayburn Building. He didn't like to sit at a desk, preferring to pace while speaking to colleagues or to sit comfortably on his navy-blue couch while crafting pithy memos. He sometimes looked for solace at the single portrait in the room, of the former president and military hero Dwight Eisenhower. Ike too had come to power after years of Democratic dominance.

Gingrich's marriage to Jackie had fallen apart. Repeated attempts at marriage counseling had failed. Jackie had been diagnosed with uterine cancer and was hospitalized several times. This didn't make Gingrich more sympathetic toward her. Instead, he started struggling with feelings of depression and anger. The two separated, sitting down with their girls, then sixteen and thirteen, in their home in Fairfax, Virginia, to explain their decision.

Gingrich acquired a reputation for sleeping around. In January 1980, at a fund-raiser in Ohio, he met an attractive twenty-eight-year-old county planner named Marianne Ginther. The tall, blue-eyed brunette found Gingrich intellectually stimulating, and they spent the evening discussing his ideas for reviving the moribund midwestern economy. They continued speaking on the phone over the next few weeks in late-night calls, and then much more. Some of his closest advisers worried that reporters would overhear them chatting on a pay phone when Gingrich ducked away to speak in the middle of well-covered events. Gingrich loved the fact that Marianne believed everything he said, finding his promises to remake American politics persuasive and exciting. They began to seriously date within a few months. Reflecting his impatience and self-centeredness, Newt discussed divorce terms with the cancer-stricken Jackie during one of her hospital stays.

The personal turbulence took a toll on the new congressman. He had gained considerable weight binge eating and began a diet, which made him, in his own words, "moody and grumpy."[26] He had surrounded himself with an office of sycophantic staffers who treated his theories and slogans, no matter how thin, with the seriousness of a Nobel Prize–winning professor's pronouncements, but even they could grow tired of his tantrums. He frequently sent apologetic notes to his aides, only to lash out at them again.

Gingrich would marry Marianne about a year and a half after they met, just six months after his divorce from Jackie. But this new marriage did not restore his tranquility. Newt was frenetic, moving from one idea to the next, unconcerned with pushing any notable legislation. He was in constant conversation with everyone but intimate with almost no one. He found it easier to speak in slogans than to relate to the person in front of him. He knew that he had an explosive temper and the only way he could contain it was to stay on script, perpetually acting as if he were before the cameras or addressing a large audience so that he wouldn't let his temper flare.

Aside from his personal struggles, Gingrich was happy that Reagan's first year as president had produced some triumphant moments. When the air-traffic controllers' union, which had endorsed him in the campaign, went on strike, Reagan summarily fired them. The president proposed a massive supply-side tax cut, an idea that Gingrich had been supporting since 1978, premised on the belief that the benefits to upper-income Americans would trickle down to the rest of the country. Following the horrific assassination attempt on Reagan's life that March, the president saw his approval ratings soar when he returned to work. Congress passed the tax cut, and it was a big one. The administration used executive orders to deregulate energy markets and dramatically increase military spending. These were significant victories for conservatives eager to shift away from the New Deal order. "We have a chance to bring about a half-century of right-of-center government," Gingrich predicted.[27]

In other respects, however, Gingrich's warnings about the House Democrats' obduracy played out as he expected. Despite his frontal assault on federal spending, Reagan was unable to slash domestic programs such as Aid to Families with Dependent Children, the signature welfare program from the 1930s, and the president backpedaled when his plan to cut Social Security benefits stimulated fierce opposition. In 1982, Senate Republicans joined Democrats to enact tax increases to reduce ballooning federal deficits, a decision that was anathema to the tax-cutting Gingrich. Furious with Reagan and his congressional colleagues for abandoning their orthodoxy of lower federal income taxes, Gingrich criticized those who had capitulated in the "fight for the soul of the Republican Party."[28] The "political establishment in Washington," he lamented, had defeated the ordinary citizens.[29] And while House Democrats were willing to agree to spend more on the general defense budget, they wouldn't go along with the president's proposals to boost military and financial assistance for anticommunist forces in Central America. Meanwhile, social conservatives complained bitterly that the administration was giving up on their entire agenda.

In March 1982, Gingrich wrote a letter to all of his fellow Republicans urging them to develop a better, more coordinated message to use in front of the media—a lecture much like the one he'd delivered to Paul Weyrich at their first meeting in Milwaukee in 1975. After reviewing twelve Sunday television interview shows, Gingrich came away impressed by how much attention congressional Democrats devoted to perfecting and repeating their message. Republicans were far less polished, Gingrich thought. "A political party which focuses on the management and allocation of campaign resources, and neglects political strategy, is a party that loses," Gingrich warned. "Two minutes on the evening news is watched by more people, believed by more of them, and, politically has a greater multiplier effect than paid political advertising." Gingrich implored House Republicans to pay more attention to their media appearances. "Republicans tend to have blurred and unfocused opening statements while Democrats tend to focus effectively and persuasively."[30]

Gingrich urged his party to embrace more radical tactics to achieve their goals. In an effort to win support for a constitutional balanced budget amendment, Gingrich proposed that Republicans ally with conservative Democrats to shut down the federal government for as long as necessary by refusing to pass appropriations bills. The congressman also floated the possibility of refusing to raise the federal debt ceiling, a decision that would send the entire government into financial default. "We want to force a crisis," Gingrich admitted in full candor.[31] Neither threat came to fruition, but like so much of what Gingrich did, he normalized conversations about radical procedural tactics that would have at one time been considered off-limits.

Gingrich was catching fire. In May, the *Conservative Digest* featured him on its cover, an honor for anyone who identified with the Right. In "Rep. Newt Gingrich: A New Conservative Leader for the '80s," Steven

Beckner explained to readers that the "word on Newt Gingrich was that he was a bright, energetic innovator on both the legislative and political fronts—in short, a man with a future." The piece was sprinkled with glowing praise from prominent Republicans. "A key intellectual figure within the Republican Party," said Jack Kemp. Robert Michel told Beckner, "If there was ever a champion of positive thought and positive action in the development and execution of Republican policy, Newt is the one." After reviewing his rise to power and outlining his key policy positions, Beckner ended the article with Paul Weyrich's predicting Gingrich would be a "very important conservative leader" for a "long time to come."[32]

Gingrich was also becoming a familiar voice inside the Washington Beltway through talk radio. Members, staffers, and reporters frequently heard him as a guest host on one of the most popular drive-time radio talk shows, *Confrontation*. The show, co-hosted by the liberal syndicated columnist Tom Braden and the conservative speechwriter and pundit Pat Buchanan, featured liberal-conservative debates on the issues of the day and live calls from listeners. When the producers were having some contract problems with Buchanan, they invited Gingrich to fill in as a voice of the Right (for free because he was a legislator). The gig gave Gingrich a platform to reach some of the most powerful figures in the city as they became familiar with his name and point of view (CNN picked up the show and turned it into *Crossfire* in 1982).[33]

In the fall of 1982, he and Marianne met with Richard Nixon at the Mayflower Hotel in New York. Gingrich had contacted Nixon for advice, and the former president proved happy to meet with an ambitious Republican seeking to create the kind of majority Nixon had envisioned back in 1972. Nixon, the most disgraced figure in American politics at the time, also felt flattered that a younger Republican looked up to him as a legitimate party elder. At one point during their three-hour dinner meeting, Nixon counseled, "If you really want to become the majority, you have to fill the place with ideas." Gingrich left feeling flushed and emboldened—and blind to the irony that one of the most vocal "anticorruption" warriors in Washington was now taking lessons from the disgraced president at the center of the worst political scandal in American history. Gingrich was always comfortable with such contradictions.[34]

Newt's hopes for quickly turning his caucus into the majority grew dimmer in November 1982 when Republicans endured devastating midterm elections. He won reelection, but many of his GOP colleagues were not so lucky. A recession had begun in late 1981, hitting hardest in Rust Belt states where Reagan had sold blue-collar workers on his political vision, which left him particularly vulnerable to Democrats labeling the economic downturn the Reagan Recession. Democrats picked up twenty-six seats in the House, strengthening their position just two years into the Reagan Revolution.

The midterms stirred within Gingrich an even greater sense of urgency about the need for Republicans to undertake dramatic actions to topple Democratic control of the House. Otherwise, as the disastrous midterms proved, conservatives would miss the chance to enact their agenda.

By early 1983, Gingrich had crafted the message that would shape the rest of his career. He would brand the Democratic Party the symbol of Washington's corruption in the post-Watergate era. The marching orders for his GOP allies were simple. Congressional Republicans would drive a wedge between the Democratic Party and the American people by taking on the political *establishment*—that is, the House Democratic Party. What made the strategy so compelling was the steady erosion of the trust of American voters in government institutions since Vietnam and Watergate. Poll after poll revealed that Americans had negative feelings about all parts of government, especially Congress. Gingrich was taking a match to a pile of dry wood. He was offering his colleagues a strategy for insurgency, suggesting that Republicans put aside their concern for governance until they regained power. Undermining the political standing of the Democratic majority needed to be the party's top and singular priority for the time being.

Congress's good-government reforms in the 1970s had also left elected officials more vulnerable than ever. The reforms had primarily focused on weakening the authority of the existing leaders to create more room for rank-and-file members to influence debates. Committees were forced to hold public hearings, and the House began to televise its proceedings. The reforms the Democrats enacted had created more weapons for Gingrich to use to go after corruption.

The Democratic Congress was susceptible to his offensive. Party leaders had responded to the post-Watergate fury, but within certain limits. Many of the practices that had angered voters remained unaddressed, leaving Democrats open to Republican attacks. Congress had failed to substantially reform its own campaign-finance system, and the stench of private money in the political system remained pungent. The complex nexus of lobbyists and legislators also remained as problematic as ever. And the pork-barrel spending that had repeatedly returned Gingrich's former opponent John Flynt to Washington remained commonplace. While both parties engaged in questionable behavior, Democrats were the ones with the power, so voters would hold them more accountable than the invisible Republican minority.

Gingrich understood the need for organization to take on the Democrats. He would also have to outflank the leadership of his own party, which had accommodated itself to life in opposition, with a determined circle of the like-minded. Gingrich formed a caucus of insurgents that would be modeled after the Democratic Study Group, a caucus of northern liberals formed in 1959 to challenge the senior southern Dixiecrats. Gingrich called his new base of operations the Conservative Opportunity Society, or COS. From within the House, the small caucus would start its own revolution, and—to borrow a phrase from the journalist Gail Sheehy after Gingrich was elected Speaker in 1994—he would be the "Che Guevara of conservatism."[35]

Gingrich chose the name "Conservative Opportunity Society" to signal an alternative to the "Liberal Welfare State." Just as he had seen the world divided between black and white as a youth living in West Germany, he now drew American politics into Manichaean opposites of good and evil. Outlining the group's principles for his staff, Gingrich wrote that the Conservative Opportunity Society represented "honest money without inflation" while the "Liberal Welfare State" stood for "a return to double-digit inflation." The Conservative Opportunity Society stood for "no tax increases, and tax cuts whenever possible"; the "Liberal Welfare State" represented "higher taxes on almost everything." Proponents of the Conservative Opportunity Society believed that "people are responsible for what they do whether it's good or bad"; supporters of the "Liberal Welfare State" believed that "society is ultimately responsible for everything that happens." The Conservative Opportunity Society was about "traditional family values," while the "Liberal Welfare State" supported "radical lifestyles." The Conservative Opportunity Society defended "equality of opportunity," while the "Liberal Welfare State" endorsed "equality of result."[36]

In crafting this political manifesto, Gingrich had turned to books about futurism, organizational culture, and institutional transformation, subjects that appealed to his restless boundary pushing and spurred his optimism about political change. He urged his colleagues to read Alvin Toffler's *Third Wave*, John Naisbitt's *Megatrends*, Peter Drucker's *Effective Executive*, and Thomas Peters and Robert Waterman's *In Search of Excellence*[37]—bestsellers by futurists and management consultants who were in vogue as thought leaders. These books claimed that the pace of change was accelerating so rapidly that the older hierarchies of power from the industrial age were breaking down and giving way to new freedoms and choices. Gingrich saw in these books arguments that meshed with his personal mission and explained why the political institutions that had dominated government for so long were bound to end. Democrats were locked into using a government, he said, that would not be a central component of the next stage of society. It would take political visionaries to complete the transformation, leaders willing to break with longstanding conventions to move the nation into a new political era. "We need large-scale, radical change," Gingrich wrote to fellow House Republicans.[38]

The Democratic majority was Goliath; Gingrich was David. The changes he sought necessitated defying political conventions and ignoring norms of government. If there was one popular Washington truism that

Gingrich couldn't stand, it was the ongoing appeal to bipartisanship—a political trap, he thought, that only benefited the Democrats. Early in 1983, just as the new Congress convened, Gingrich warned that "liberal Democrats intend to act bipartisan before the news media while acting ruthlessly partisan in changing the rules of the House, stacking committees, apportioning staff and questioning the administration." After doing all that, he added, they would "use a spirit of bipartisanship and harmony as a polite cover to attract sympathy if we disagree with their version of 'reasonable, responsible compromises'—all of which happen to be liberal and increase spending, weaken defense, increase bureaucracy and raise taxes." Democrats wouldn't even consult Republicans about which issues should be addressed, and so, when the GOP said no to a deal, Speaker O'Neill could turn to the public and say that partisan Republicans were to blame for the failures of Congress. Democrats would use "every possible institutional resource to dominate us and reach out to the country."[39]

Gingrich lobbied hard to win over Robert Michel, the new minority leader. Michel viewed Gingrich as a piece of forbidden fruit.[40] Like almost every Republican, he was intrigued by Gingrich's promise to make Republicans a majority again. Any Republican who had been in the House since the end of the Korean War had never experienced what it was like to be in the majority. Republicans had worse office space, they were ignored at, if not barred from, committee meetings, and they had almost no say in crafting legislation.

Yet Michel saw Gingrich as quixotic. By seeking hard-to-imagine goals and using what he called "parliamentary pyrotechnics,"[41] the party would lose whatever access it had been able to gain through negotiation. Worse, Michel thought Gingrich's methods were dangerous to the health of the institution. Gingrich and COS, who met every Wednesday in an empty room in the House office buildings without staff, sounded like a group who would do anything necessary to win, even at the risk of tearing Congress apart.

In an effort to show Michel that his plan was viable, Gingrich wrote him a letter outlining an alternative way to deal with his party, one that reflected the philosophy of COS rather than the Old Guard Republicans.

Michel needed to encourage the "next generation" of Republican members to get into a tougher stance with the Democrats: "If you teach them how to be aggressive and confrontational, you will increase their abilities to fight Democrats on the floor. If you teach them to avoid argument and smother dissent, then they will be crippled on the floor." Gingrich charged, "We have the habits and demeanor of a minority party." And those habits, he argued, "help keep us in the minority."[42]

Gingrich's strategic thoughts coalesced in an even more unorthodox think piece produced by one of his informal advisers, the Republican consultant Bill Lee. The memo, written six days after Reagan's 1984 State of the Union address, likened COS to the crafty and impossible-to-defeat Vietcong, while comparing the Democrats to the bloated, slow-witted, U.S.-backed South Vietnamese government. COS, Lee argued, had to think harder about what it was and how it would act. "We exist with some support from North Vietnam (the formal Republican Party, the Senate, and the Presidency) on the basis of larger shared goals, but we live under the domination and corruption of the Republic of South Vietnam (the Democrats in the House, and in the majority of the 50 state legislatures, local officials and Governors)." Moving forward with the increasingly contorted historical comparison, Lee concluded, "One of these enemies, the South Vietnamese government, we must destroy. The other, the North Vietnamese government, we must take advantage of, lie to, sidetrack, confound, and possess by recruitment and propaganda until the two are one."[43]

Lee reminded Gingrich that "radical political factions" in the United States were "ultimately diluted and absorbed by larger factions or parties, and thus disappear, along with their ideals and ideas." The premise of COS was that the group "can and must be a revolutionary guerilla *movement*." To this end, Lee argued, COS must find "confrontational means to assure the publicity which indicates our viewpoint that the Democratic Party is the oppressor." "Confrontation and conflict," Lee added, "are the means to the end—the creation of a new definition of a Republican Party that shares the specific goals of the populace." Lee warned Gingrich that it was essential that COS remained autonomous and did not turn into a "tool" of the Republican leadership or they could become "pawns" in destructive bipartisan compromise.[44]

Gingrich loved Lee's memorandum, which became his road map for how he would direct COS. Gingrich would bring his battle to the floor of the House of Representatives—and before the television cameras that post-Watergate reforms had introduced in 1977 to film daily proceedings. The effort to reform government had resulted in the creation in 1979 of a new cable network called C-SPAN, founded by the former Nixon official Brian Lamb. Gingrich was thrilled that any member could deliver speeches to his or her constituents as part of a live feed at the start and end of each day. On C-SPAN, legislators could speak without the filter of network news reporters, who in Gingrich's mind were all too liberal. The cable network offered an electronic "town hall meeting."[45] Now, he enthused, "on the floor, we have the chance to present our views not only to our colleagues, but to the nation." He continued, "C-SPAN permits us to communicate those views without having them digested or reinterpreted by unfriendlies within the media. And C-SPAN's audience would swell if confrontation rather than capitulation characterized the GOP stance in all House debate."[46]

Gingrich liked to say, "You don't get on TV with cars that get home safely," which meant that you needed to give the press more "Indiana Jones than the Philharmonic." Politicians had to feed the appetites of audiences seeking to be "voyeurs" watching "reality happen." Though C-SPAN's audience share paled in comparison to the major networks', Gingrich reminded his colleagues that the station still offered members "200,000 potential viewers" at any given moment.[47] "Most members will travel pretty far," he said, "to talk to 200 people. When I stand up on the floor, the audience might be 1,000 times that."[48] Gingrich, who would later call himself the "first leader of the C-SPAN generation,"[49] realized that provocative statements made on the floor would be picked up by a national press that thrived on controversy. This new cable television medium, a press without sentries, created opportunities to communicate with mass audiences that older Republicans didn't understand and senior

Democrats couldn't handle. Through cable television, Gingrich would be able to carry out the guerrilla tactics his adviser Bill Lee had proposed.

When COS met for a special Saturday session to make plans before the Christmas break, everyone in the room seemed to be on the same page as to what needed to happen in the coming year. COS would have to undertake a "radical strategy," according to the minutes, because Democrats would be doing everything possible to boost their party's standing in a "political year." Even when White House and Republican leaders started feeling pressure to compromise, which they would, COS agreed that there could be no common ground with Democrats. COS would devote every day to driving a "wedge between the Democratic Party and the American people."[50]

With the 1984 election season under way, "the young red hot," as Wright began to call him, smelled opportunity. The national media would be looking for stories of partisan warfare, and Gingrich planned to deliver.

So did his COS colleagues, twelve partisans who shared his goals. The Minnesota Republican Vin Weber, elected in 1982 and always by Gingrich's side, was a hard-line conservative who championed term limits and deep spending cuts. Robert Dornan, a fire-breathing right-winger from California, was enthralled by Gingrich's in-your-face approach. Connie Mack from Florida, Indiana's Dan Coats, and California's Duncan Hunter were ready to follow Gingrich's commands whenever he said that it was time to attack. The lanky Robert Walker of Pennsylvania, elected in 1976, was a former political-science teacher who had spent much of his career scouring arcane House rules to master the art of procedural warfare. The spotlight-seeking Walker, one of the most disliked members of the House, clad in unflattering and cheap three-piece suits, reveled in the fact that he was developing a following among C-SPAN aficionados. Nobody had ever predicted that he would be a television star of any sort.

COS counted on Trent Lott, a five-term Republican from Mississippi, who remained on the "fringes" of the conservative caucus and served as a bridge to the party leadership.[51] Lott, who always managed to keep his blow-dried bowl haircut meticulously in place, had started his political career as the administrative assistant for William Colmer, an ardent Democratic racist and the chief ally of Howard "Judge" Smith, the conservative chairman of the House Rules Committee, who spent most of his career blocking liberal legislation. He had become the minority whip in 1981. Filled with ambition to become a party leader, Lott offered Republicans the rare breed of legislator who could forge pragmatic, bipartisan compromises while maintaining the image of an unfaltering, ideological conservative.[52] While working for Colmer, Lott learned that the House rules could be a brutal cudgel against almost any proposal. Along with Congressman Kemp, Lott helped Gingrich's renegades gain some kind of sway within the party caucus.[53]

The House minority leader, Michel, talked often about civility but did little to stop COS, hoping to incorporate their energy and ideas into the party without allowing Gingrich to take it over. In a Faustian bargain, trading away the norms of good governance for a more potent form of partisan warfare, Michel reached out to all Republicans, urging them to use floor speeches, op-eds, and national press appearances to issue Gingrich-like warnings about how Democrats were manipulating their authority. His staff met regularly with COS to work on strategy.[54]

Gingrich and COS took aim at the hot-button policy issue of the moment: the fight against communism in Central America. The Reagan administration wanted to expand support for rebels in Nicaragua who were battling the socialist Sandinista government that had taken power in 1979, in addition to funding the autocratic government of El Salvador that was fighting against an insurgency. Under Reagan, the CIA was providing financial and military support to a counterrevolutionary group called the contras, a ragtag collection of guerrillas who lived in the jungles while trying to bring down the Sandinista regime. But House Democrats feared that Nicaragua would turn into another Vietnam. To check the president, Democrats had passed a series of amendments starting in 1982 to limit support to the contras.

Congressional Republicans were eager to focus on foreign policy as the presidential election season started. Even though polls showed that a majority of the public did not support U.S. military intervention in Central America, Republicans believed that national security remained a winning issue. Since World War II, Republicans had used the argument that Democrats were "weak on defense" to great political effect. In 1952, the GOP campaigned on this theme to regain control of the White House and Congress for the first time since FDR was elected president. In 1972, President Nixon pilloried Senator George McGovern, a decorated World War II veteran and liberal internationalist, for allegedly ushering the Democrats down the path of isolationism in response to Vietnam. Most recently, Republicans had seen how Reagan used national security to batter President Carter in the 1980 election when his administration was struggling with the Iranian hostage crisis and the Soviet invasion of Afghanistan.[55]

In 1984, Reagan was determined to shift the terms of the public debate and move Central America toward the front lines of the nation's cold war strategy. In February, he proposed an $8 billion, five-year program to fight communism in Central America, including in El Salvador, where the administration wanted to help the U.S.-friendly government beat back left-wing rebels. Although the president excluded Nicaragua from the package in order to avoid an unnecessary controversy, he did seek a $21 million increase in aid for the Nicaraguan contras as an amendment to a separate Senate bill. When pushing for both of these measures, Reagan faced an uphill battle because polls still showed consistently low approval ratings for U.S. efforts in the region.

The Conservative Opportunity Society took up the cause. Gingrich didn't agree with everything that President Reagan had to say, but when it came to cutting taxes and fighting communism, he was all in. The importance of ramping up the war against communism in Central America made sense to Gingrich, who still vividly remembered seeing remnants of the aftermath from the world wars in Europe. "The Soviets are essentially the Nazis of the left," he said.[56] In Gingrich's mind, the basic problem was that too many Americans didn't understand the urgency of the dangers outside Eastern Europe. They had bought into the Democratic arguments that American support in Central America would turn into another quagmire like Southeast Asia and that the region was not essential to national interests. Gingrich compared Reagan's situation in Nicaragua—as well as in El Salvador—to President Lyndon Johnson and Vietnam. This junior member of the House had no problem pontificating to President Reagan about his history lessons. In one of his many letters to the president, Gingrich told Reagan that in 1965 and 1966 Johnson had failed to "rally the American people, to educate them, and to insure there was strong popular support for the war." Johnson had left a "vacuum of leadership into which the Jane Fondas and George McGoverns poured,"[57] and the same thing was happening now to Reagan.

When it came to Central America, Republican policy preferences neatly aligned with their political strategy. As the House considered the administration's Central America package and the Senate legislation that included money for the contras, Gingrich also saw the fight as a chance to wound Jim Wright as he campaigned for federal funds that were urgently needed. The majority leader was an inviting target. The Texan was hawkish on most foreign policy questions—including U.S. support to the right-wing El Salvador government—and had been participating in diplomatic overtures to end the civil war in Nicaragua, hoping that Washington could pressure the Sandinistas into adopting democratic reforms without using military force. Reagan officials, who had often worked cordially with Wright on foreign policy, warned that he was being pushed to the left on this issue by his caucus.

Gingrich began his ambush by talking informally to reporters about a letter that the majority leader and nine other Democrats had sent to the Nicaraguan president, Daniel Ortega, to pressure him to hold free elections. The letter started by addressing Ortega as "Dear Comandante," proof, Gingrich claimed, that congressional Democrats were cozily willing to appease the Marxists and give them legitimacy. With the reporters leaning in, Gingrich denounced Wright and condemned the decision to contact Ortega as a violation of the Constitution's separation of powers. He repeated these charges on the House floor. "It's at best unwise, and at worst illegal," he said, pausing before unleashing his final piece of mischief. Congress, Gingrich said, ought to consider whether the Logan Act, which forbade U.S. citizens to negotiate with foreign governments that were in conflict with the United States, should now apply to Wright and the other Democrats.

Wright, who was serving as Speaker while O'Neill was out of the country, was furious. "Newt Gingrich, the gadfly Georgia Republican, is pursuing a vendetta aimed at discrediting me and nine other Democrats" by insisting that "we were interfering with and undermining official U.S. foreign policy by corresponding directly with an 'enemy' of the U.S.," he wrote in his diary on April 24. "It is sheer McCarthyism of the very rankest order." Wright was shocked that Gingrich had portrayed this letter as an act of support for the Sandinista government rather than an effort to pressure it to institute democratic reforms. "Gingrich knows all of this," Wright wrote, "but he is trying to qualify as a junior grade Joe McCarthy. Ever since his coming to Congress, he has sought opportunities to build himself by attacking others. The little rascal feels no compunction about deliberately distorting this so as to make it appear that Democrats are un-American types who delight in undermining U.S. policy."[58]

Democrats could complain all they wanted to, but Gingrich's plan worked. "Conflict equals exposure equals power," Gingrich liked to say.[59] He was right. The media soaked up the story. *The Wall Street Journal*, *The Washington Post*, and *The Atlanta Constitution* all covered Gingrich's speech. The ferociously anticommunist editorial page of *The Wall Street Journal* speculated that the "Comandante must find this amusing, since the Sandinistas have repeatedly disavowed any intention of holding to a 'bourgeois' conception of elections or democracy."[60] As with Gingrich's attacks on Congressman Diggs, the media liked covering the feisty Georgia congressman and provided oxygen for his provocative assertions.

Wright understood that Gingrich wanted to goad the Democrats into responding. "The silly little devil is like a small swarm of gnats. He hasn't the capacity to inflict injury on anyone unless he makes you lose control of the steering wheel while swatting the gnats. He is a self-appointed pest," Wright lamented.[61] Wright kept downplaying the impact that the televised tirades on C-SPAN would have. "If a fellow wants to waste the time of the television audience with bombast, the rules permit it," he said in dismissive fashion. "But I suggest that the public knows it's phony as a $3 bill."[62] But with a national audience watching, Gingrich was difficult to ignore.

Gingrich and his allies were just getting started. Now Republicans had a taste of the kind of chaos that Bill Lee's guerrilla politics could create and the bonanza of media coverage it could yield. They had no intention of slowing down. COS intended to re-create the kind of constant mayhem that was common in the nineteenth-century House, not necessarily the fisticuffs, but rather the intense partisan conflict that guided all business on the chamber floor. The main goal was to persuade Republican legislators to see every decision through the lens of raw partisan interest. According to what Gingrich called the "floor strategy," COS would move the deliberations out of the committee rooms and into the public eye. The caucus would employ uncomfortable, confrontational tactics with the sole purpose of exposing how Democrats stifled the minority. COS would coerce Democrats into responding to them in aggressive fashion, and Republicans would then use the Speaker's retaliation as a dramatic talking point in their campaign against the "abuse of power."[63] As Bill Lee had written to Gingrich, "Any guerilla worth his powder understands that one of his guiding principles is to drive authority (read democrats) to excess that will anger the people and spark a popular uprising."[64] The setting for this plan would be the most seemingly innocuous routine of the congressional day.

The House's "Special Order" speeches always started at 5:00 P.M., when most members were no longer in the chamber or their offices. Traditionally, they were a time for legislators to read from newspaper articles or deliver local-interest speeches as a favor for constituents. Gingrich would weaponize the speeches.

As Democrats and Republicans left their "office work" to attend fund-raisers, join ceremonies, or gather in Capitol Hill bars to talk strategy over aged bourbon and steak, COS would go to work. During the previous few months, the subjects of their speeches had been picked haphazardly—sometimes in the office of Congressman Walker, more often than not while members of COS, still numbering only about a dozen (though they claimed the "hard" support of forty members), were milling around in the back of the chamber. In May 1984, knowing they would have the C-SPAN cameras largely to themselves, the process was different. This time, they had a coordinated game plan.[65]

On May 8, at 7:30 P.M., one day before President Reagan was scheduled to address Congress to urge it to pass an $8 billion military and financial assistance package to support anticommunist forces in Central America, Walker and Gingrich approached the front row of their party's side of the aisle and sat down, armed with a bulky report.

When the young Republicans were recognized by the chair, the New York representative Ted Weiss, Walker walked up to the lectern with fire in his eye. He started to enthusiastically read a document written by Frank Gregorsky titled *What's the Matter with Democratic Foreign Policy?* The report blamed a number of prominent Democrats, including Congressman Edward Boland of Massachusetts, the well-liked Washington roommate of Speaker O'Neill, for his role in authoring the amendments that had until now thwarted President Reagan's heroic efforts to defeat communism in Central America.

Walker warned that the "radical wing" of the Democratic Party had taken over its foreign policy, abandoning Harry Truman's muscular liberal internationalism for the anti-interventionist ideas of Senator George McGovern. And Jim Wright, Walker said, had allowed this to happen. The majority leader, who had once been among the party's hawks, had joined the radicals, flipping on issues like funding for the MX missile and military assistance to anticommunist forces in Central America. Names were named: Democrats including Thomas Downey of New York, Stephen Solarz of New York, Barbara Boxer of California, and Robert Torricelli of New Jersey were all accused of playing footsie with communist-allied forces.

This was only the beginning. When Walker's time ran out, Gingrich kept on hammering. The Democratic worldview, Gingrich read, was "rigid, unyielding and skewed." Firing off facts and figures, Gingrich told

C-SPAN viewers that Democrats were afraid to stand up to communism. Gingrich closed his binder and sauntered back to his seat, deeply pleased with his performance.

Members of COS had been making these speeches since January, but Speaker O'Neill had not been paying close attention and had allowed them to continue. Chris Matthews, one of the Speaker's top spokesmen and a future cable television news host, said that "Gingrich's Guerrillas" (as some colleagues called them) were an "embarrassment to their own leadership." As he put it, "They're making fools of themselves. The more exposure they get, the better it is for the Democrats, that's how the speaker feels."[66] Agreeing with Matthews in a different interview, O'Neill told a reporter that the "Special Order" speeches "showed a meanness, because they showed an unfairness. . . . Our polls show they helped us."[67]

That changed on May 8, with its climactic flurry of visceral, coordinated speeches. No viewer watching C-SPAN would have known that Walker and Gingrich were speaking to an essentially empty chamber. All that a viewer could see was the upper half of the body of the person speaking, thanks to the House rules adopted in 1977, which stipulated that the in-house cameras for C-SPAN broadcasts could film only the person standing at the rostrum. The rationale had been to avoid embarrassing members who might not realize that they were on camera as they schmoozed with friends or quietly dozed. But Walker and Gingrich had realized that as they accused specific Democrats of failing to support their country, C-SPAN viewers would be left to think that the Democrats had no response.

Congressman David Obey of Wisconsin heard about what was happening from a staffer watching the floor feed from an office television. Stunned and angered, Obey rushed to the chamber to defend his colleagues and himself. Seizing the rostrum, he attempted to explain to "those who might be watching" that "from time to time" in the House, members "more interested in making a political point than seeking truth" decide to "follow an approach which brings into question not only members' judgment but patriotism." Fidgeting with the pen in his shirt pocket and twisting his wedding ring to contain his outrage, Obey condemned

Gingrich and his crew as "descendants of Joe McCarthy." They "may be a bit prettier and a bit more skilled in the use of television, but they are certainly no less comfortable in the use of innuendo."

The evening ended in a tense standoff. A handful of other Democrats ran into the chamber to support Obey, and they marched out steaming about what had gone down. Meanwhile, Gingrich sauntered toward the Rayburn Building feeling confident about the response he had triggered. The Hill's watering holes were packed late into the night with legislators and staffers talking animatedly about what had happened.

On May 9, with this turbulence in the House behind the scenes, Reagan delivered a nationally televised address from the Oval Office urging Congress to pass his bill. "Central America is a region of great importance to the United States," Reagan said. "And it is so close: San Salvador is closer to Houston, Texas, than Houston is to Washington, D.C." Even without explicit coordination, the president and the Republican renegades were heading in the same direction.

The next night, an emboldened COS returned to the floor to resume their attacks on the Democrats, and on Congressman Boland in particular. The self-effacing representative who had authored the amendments prohibiting military or economic assistance to the Nicaraguan contras was reviled in Republican circles for concluding that Reagan's wars in Central America were counterproductive and damaging.

This time, Tip O'Neill was in the chamber, having heard what had happened two nights earlier. He took the bait. Unable to contain himself as he listened to the Republicans pillory his friend, the Speaker extemporaneously instructed the technician controlling the camera to pan across the empty chamber, revealing to C-SPAN viewers the dirty trick that Gingrich's forces were playing.

All hell broke loose. Democrats scrambled back into the chamber to take their seats, some with their jackets hastily tossed on, eager to challenge Gingrich, who insisted in his speech that he had given them fair warning that he was going to read from this study and had invited them to respond. One Watergate Baby, Tom Downey of New York, said that he had never received any such letter. Charles Rangel of New York stood up to denounce Gingrich. Jim Wright warned, "When we begin impugning one another's patriotism, then we cross a bar that should not be crossed!" Republicans booed and hissed as the Democrats spoke, then hollered for Speaker O'Neill to restore order on the floor. The following morning, Michel wrote O'Neill to complain: "This was an act of dictatorial retribution against a Member of the United States Congress. It was deplorable."[68]

The televised fighting continued over the next few evenings. The more the media covered the controversy, the more Gingrich got what he wanted: a televised platform to underline his claims about Democratic weakness on foreign policy.

Finally, on May 15, regular order totally broke down. While Gingrich was reading from a text claiming that Democrats were always ready to tarnish the United States but not the communists, Wright leaped up from his seat to ask, "Would the gentleman yield for a question?" Gingrich refused.

Sick of his Republican colleagues, O'Neill dropped his gavel and turned the Speaker's chair over to Representative Joe Moakley of Massachusetts. O'Neill had already been nearing a tipping point as he and other Democrats saw Republicans abuse good-government reforms they had helped pass in the 1970s, and they started to clamp down.[69] Now members of both parties sat on edge as O'Neill stormed down from the podium to the floor so that he could deliver a speech as a regular member.

"Will the gentleman yield?" O'Neill now bellowed. Gingrich yielded. In his thick New England accent, his face bright red, O'Neill removed his glasses and chastised the Republicans for misrepresenting the facts and making false allegations. O'Neill wagged his finger at Gingrich, who was sitting just a few feet away, and raised his voice: "You deliberately stood in that well before an empty House and challenged these people and challenged their Americanism, and it is the lowest thing that I've ever seen in my thirty-two years in Congress."

There was stunned silence, like the moment after a parent loses his temper with poorly behaved kids. The rebels had been waiting for just this sort of dressing-down and turned the Speaker's attack against him.

Here was the essence of the Gingrich playbook: everything could be turned to his advantage. Flout institutional norms and then, when criticized for doing so, cry foul.

A Republican staffer informed Trent Lott that Speaker O'Neill's comments violated the rules prohibiting personal attacks against fellow members. Lott asked that O'Neill's comments be immediately "taken down," or struck from the record.[70] This was a daring move for a Republican in the era of Democratic dominance. As everyone anxiously waited to see what would happen next, like kids glancing after the first blow had been struck in a schoolyard fight, Weber quietly walked up to Gingrich and whispered in his ear to stay calm in front of the television cameras because "we're winning."[71] Gingrich thought of the advice his wife had offered earlier that week—to employ the principles of judo by provoking a stronger opponent and putting them off-balance, remaining calm the madder they got—and contained his anger.[72] After what one journalist called a "painful silence," the House parliamentarian, William Brown, meekly leaned over to inform Moakley that Lott was correct. Moakley had to strike the Speaker's comments from the *Congressional Record* and then formally rebuke him for being out of order. O'Neill lost the privilege of speaking in the chamber for twenty-four hours. The two-hour fight aired on live television, and a humiliated O'Neill entered the history books as the first Speaker of the House to be officially punished for his own words.[73] Gingrich, who complained to the cameras that it was his patriotism being "impugned" by a "McCarthyism of the left," beamed. Some of his colleagues patted him on the back; others burst out in applause.[74]

The House Republicans kept attacking, using the O'Neill rebuke to exemplify the Democratic majority's flagrant violation of the rules to hold on to power. Congressman Dick Cheney, a Wyoming conservative and former chief of staff to President Gerald Ford, charged that the Speaker had not been playing fair when he flipped around the camera. Cheney was taken more seriously than Gingrich. Unlike his renegade colleague, Cheney was a cerebral levelheaded conservative with an impressive résumé, and he was not known for hyperbole. With his wife, Lynne, who had a Ph.D. in nineteenth-century British literature from the University of Wisconsin, he had coauthored a history of how Speakers had attempted to dominate the House through personal and procedural force with mixed success.[75] House Republicans were grooming Cheney, who was described by one reporter as having an "unsettling calm,"[76] to be the Speaker of the House one day. Although not a member of Gingrich's coterie or an admirer of his fire-breathing methods, Cheney now joined Gingrich in declaring that O'Neill's "repeated attacks" were "damaging the House as an institution."

Cheney tossed the ball downfield to Jack Kemp, the charismatic former football player who championed supply-side economics. The New York congressman claimed that the Speaker had "altered procedure and tried to use the televising of the House to embarrass the Republicans." O'Neill, chimed in Vin Weber, "is one of the cheapest, meanest politicians to occupy that office in this century." Even the docile Michel piled on: "I'll have to agree with you. To have this man act the way this one has is unheard of."[77] Republicans painted O'Neill as nothing more than an old-school corrupt Boston-style Tammany Hall politician who abused his power. "Thanks to C-SPAN," Gingrich said, "we can appeal to the country so people can see how phony the arguments are. We want to convict the Democrats in the court of opinion."[78]

"Camscam," as The Washington Post's T. R. Reid called it, became national news, just as Gingrich hoped.[79] "I'm famous," Gingrich boasted to one reporter.[80] The networks were playing footage of Republicans on the evening news, a rare occurrence in those days. Billy Pitts, Michel's top staffer, believed that O'Neill made "Gingrich a household name" through his response.[81] "The number-one fact about the news media is they love fights," Gingrich would say later. "The minute Tip O'Neill attacked me, he and I got 90 seconds at the close of all three network news shows." You have to give the media packaged confrontations, he added: "When you give them confrontations, you get attention; when you get attention you can educate."[82] Brian Lamb, the founder and president of C-SPAN, admitted, "We've never had any more visibility than this. Forget about whether the argument is right or wrong. It's been on the front pages of every newspaper in the country."[83] Surveying the damage, Congressman Daniel Lungren of California praised COS for having "captured the attention of many Washington reporters, political analysts and the general public."[84]

The way that Gingrich used the medium of television against the Democrats was as important as the specific debate over funding the contras and anticommunism. O'Neill, Wright, and the rest of the Democratic leadership were caught flat-footed. "This is the beginning of the post-Rayburn House," Gingrich observed. "It's like the transition from vaudeville to television, like going from being a Broadway actor to being a television star. O'Neill and others are pre-TV, pre-confrontational."[85]

Wright, who felt that the House had become so tense that it was wound tighter than a "cotton clothesline after a rain," could not have known that Gingrich would soon be coming for him. For now, the majority leader thought that O'Neill had done the right thing by taking on Gingrich, though he realized the Democrats were paying a steep political price. "Yesterday's contretemps between silly little Newt Gingrich and the Speaker should not have happened," Wright wrote in his diary. Gingrich "really is a shrill and shameless little demagogue."[86]

The final results were mixed for Reagan and Gingrich. Majority Leader Wright and fifty-five other Democrats supported the administration's Central America package, allowing it to move through the House successfully. This constituted a notable victory, even though the Senate ended up voting for only a limited package of $1.4 billion for one year. But the proposed assistance for the contras went down in defeat as the House instead imposed tighter restrictions on what kind of money could be given to the rebels, although Congress agreed to resume some kinds of funding in 1985.

But in certain respects, the legislation was beside the point. Republicans were playing the long game. Gingrich, who believed that it was necessary to change the terms of the debate if Republicans ever wanted to be in the majority and actually have the opportunity to enact transformative legislation, had capitalized on this dramatic floor debate to describe the opposition as weak on defense, to make a strong case before the media about why fighting communism in Central America mattered, and to continue painting Democrats as a corrupt party that relied on brute procedural force.

Gingrich's rising stature was on full display at the 1984 Republican National Convention in Dallas. Gingrich had secured a role on the platform committee because he had served on an informal advisory panel with Reagan's deputy campaign director, Lee Atwater, campaign director, Ed Rollins, and political adviser Lyn Nofziger. This kitchen cabinet had been responsible, Rollins said, for "planning themes, tactics, messages, just the overall campaign strategy."[87] From their post on the platform committee, Gingrich and Weber pressured the GOP into adopting right-wing positions such as school prayer, requiring judicial nominees to oppose abortion, and a flat ban against tax increases. Gingrich's "firebrands," according to *Newsweek*'s Jonathan Alter, "took over the platform committee, ramming through a document so close to the fringe that many Republicans— including Senator Dole—felt obliged to condemn it."[88] "We got everything we wanted," Gingrich crowed.[89] With the congressman conducting dozens of interviews in the convention hall, and with his photograph showcased on campaign buttons and in local newspaper ads, one reporter observed, "Newt Gingrich is a hot item here, and he loves it."[90]

As Gingrich kept gaining prominence, reporters started to take a closer look at the aggressive young Georgian. On November 1, 1984, the left-wing magazine *Mother Jones* published a blistering exposé of his personal life by David Osborne, a liberal freelance journalist who had become intrigued with Gingrich, the "intellectual phenomenon." Osborne's editor at *Mother Jones*, David Talbot, agreed that a profile of Gingrich might help explain the freshly assertive Republican Party.

When Osborne interviewed Gingrich in D.C., Gingrich struck Osborne as being skilled, articulate, and willing to "lie all the time." Osborne had to bite his tongue when Gingrich told him things about the budget that he knew to be untrue—such as the effects that cuts would have on domestic programs. It was apparent to Osborne that Gingrich had the power to persuade but lacked a moral core. The reporter flew down to Carrollton to interview voters and staffers in the confident Georgian's district. To his surprise, people started talking to him about Gingrich's womanizing, mistreatment of colleagues, nasty temper, and more. Some of his disillusioned former staffers couldn't help themselves. Lee Howell, who had been Gingrich's press secretary in 1974, arrived at his interview with cuts on his face after surviving a serious car accident that very morning and was still eager to talk. When Osborne called Gingrich to ask him for a comment, the congressman initially did not answer, then finally called and offered a vague statement about not being a perfect man.[91]

The *Mother Jones* article appeared in November 1984, shortly before that year's election. It was shocking. "One former aide," Osborne wrote, "describes approaching a car with Gingrich's daughter in hand, only to find the candidate with a woman, her head buried in his lap." The story included tales about Gingrich's infidelity, his unbearable arrogance, and the coolness with which his close associates viewed him. The hubris and personal distance did not come as news to most, but the infidelity surprised those outside his inner circle who thought of him as one of the moral warriors of the Right. Osborne wrote about Gingrich negotiating divorce terms with his first wife in her hospital room as she recovered from surgery for cancer, exposing a level of selfish callousness not readily apparent in his public persona. Osborne quoted L. H. Carter, a former friend and adviser until 1979: "The important thing you have to understand about Newt Gingrich is that he is amoral. There isn't any kind of right or wrong, there isn't any conservative or liberal. There's only what will work best for Newt Gingrich."[92]

The personal attack stung. The California Democrat Tony Coelho, the influential head of the Democratic Congressional Campaign Committee, sent out copies to 252 members of the House, both as a warning and as a gesture of satisfaction. The article gained more attention when the *Doonesbury* cartoonist, Garry Trudeau, published a strip about the coldhearted encounter in the hospital room. Gingrich would only admit that he had difficult moments in his personal life and that those trying to capitalize on the *Mother Jones* piece didn't like him anyway.

Gingrich was far happier to focus on the 1984 election. President Reagan's resounding victory over the former vice president Walter Mondale offered vindication to his admirers (Mondale's only victories came in D.C. and his home state of Minnesota) and made continued Democratic control of the House even more infuriating to Republicans. Although his staff had worried about the fallout from the *Mother Jones* article, the story had little immediate effect in the Sixth District.[93] Gingrich, who was now being called in the press the "darling of the New Right,"[94] warned that Democratic leaders were planning to marginalize House Republicans to stifle Reagan's voice in the lower chamber despite his historic reelection victory. He wrote to his colleagues to sound his familiar warning, namely that "we have a newly-reelected President, fresh from a campaign for tax reform and economic growth, facing a House skewed to the left by a series of corrupt bargains—corrupt bargains between national Democrats and their liberal welfare state allies who don't particularly understand popular mandates and don't particularly want to."[95]

The predictions seemed to be coming true when a debate immediately unfolded over Indiana's Eighth Congressional District, where Frank McCloskey, a forty-five-year-old first-term Democrat and former Bloomington mayor, was in a too-close-to-call election against the Republican Richard McIntyre, a twenty-eight-year-old conservative state legislator. The "Bloody Eighth" of Indiana, as it was known, was a notoriously competitive swing district in which politics often turned ugly. Indiana Republicans challenged the results, and the recount, conducted by Republican officials, gave the win to McIntyre by 418 votes. Indiana's Republican secretary of state certified McIntyre as the victor by 34 out of the 234,000 votes cast, based on a recount in just one district in one county, over protests from angry Democrats demanding broader recounts.

When McIntyre arrived on Capitol Hill on January 3, 1985, Democrats refused to seat him. They argued that reports of widespread Election Day irregularities were concerning and that state Republicans were trying to take this election without an honest recount. Reports coming out of Indiana claimed that Republicans had unfairly disqualified a sizable number of African American voters in the urban parts of the district. "I'm not going to sit back and let one Republican secretary of state from Indiana dictate to the House who will or will not be seated," said Tony Coelho, who controlled the purse strings for all Democratic candidates.[96] Wright agreed, as did Speaker O'Neill, who administered a collective oath to every member other than McIntyre. The House voted 238 to 177, along strict party lines, to keep the seat vacant pending an investigation. In turn, the Republicans cried that the majority was trying to steal the election. Even the Minnesota Republican Bill Frenzel, a Gingrich ally who was nonetheless known as moderate in his disposition and politics, called the process a "rape" of the voters and the "ultimate abuse" of government.[97]

Such comments convinced Gingrich that his party could make the Indiana brawl look like a full-blown constitutional crisis and compelling evidence of Democratic corruption. On a chilly late January day, with freezing rain pouring down on the capital, Gingrich tried to convince legislators and reporters that this was a scandal of epic proportions.[98]

After the weekly Wednesday morning COS meeting, Gingrich walked back to his office alongside one of his newest recruits, the thirty-five-year-old Joe Barton, a conservative firebrand who had just been elected from Texas. As the two commiserated over the situation in Indiana, the admiring Barton jotted down notes so that he wouldn't forget a thing. "Look up the Wilkes case in the 1770s," Gingrich instructed, referring to a member of Parliament who had been expelled after having been reelected despite a conviction of seditious libel. "This is a constitutional issue! We have to make the press understand that. Now, when you deal with these people, you have to remember two things: absolute certainty and knowledge of detail. That's what these reporters and editors want."[99]

Gingrich was feeling good about himself these days. When he returned to his office after lunch, as he was coming to expect, he was greeted by a crew from *NBC Nightly News* who had come this time to interview him about the story of the day: Reagan's hard-line UN ambassador, Jeane Kirkpatrick, had announced that she was returning to Georgetown University. "It's a decisive defeat for the conservative movement in trying to effect a more realistic foreign policy and a more realistic approach to the Soviet Union," trilled Gingrich. "There's in effect been a bureaucratic coup d'état in foreign policy." When the interviewer, pleased with the sound bite, asked Gingrich if he wanted to add anything else, Gingrich returned to the Indiana showdown. "The thing that's gonna blow this House open," he said, "is the McIntyre thing in Indiana. We have no record of a certified congressman not being seated." When one member of the camera crew asked Gingrich to sit quietly for a second so that they could record a response shot of him nodding, Gingrich gladly obliged (for television, Gingrich would even tolerate being told to stop talking). When the cameraman signaled to Gingrich that he could start speaking again, the congressman jumped right back into his soliloquy. He warned, "We will make it impossible for this House to function. You'll see literal war in the House. This is a constitutional issue, not a political issue. This is not a game. This is like Watergate in the House."[100]

Gingrich had come to believe that the best way to attract attention for an issue was to keep speaking about it over and over again. "We are engaged in reshaping a whole nation through the news media," he crowed.[101] He called the executive director of the National Republican Congressional Committee, Joe Gaylord, and vented about how, the previous day, Coelho had distributed a chart to reporters showing that the Republicans had stolen the seat from McCloskey. "We should take Coelho's chart," Gingrich explained, "and redo it as our own chart showing what really happened. I think the press is beginning to pick up the scent that this is a constitutional issue, not a political issue. But we've got to really break Coelho's believability with the national press and many Democrats."[102]

His next call was to Gaylord's boss, Guy Vander Jagt, the prolific Republican fund-raiser, to whom he delivered a similarly stern message about Coelho's chart and suggested that Cheney, whom many reporters saw as a nonpartisan figure, brief the press about the severity of what the Democrats were threatening to do. Vander Jagt, in his deep, calming voice, lectured Gingrich about how the party leaders preferred to work cautiously on such issues behind the scenes. Gingrich rolled his eyes at this.[103]

Later that day, Gingrich called Minority Whip Trent Lott to let his best contact to the Republican leadership know what he was thinking. Lott was skeptical, telling his colleague that it was not clear whether

McIntyre actually won. "Yeah, I understand what you're saying," Gingrich replied, sensing he needed to at least sound reasonable. "You're right. Yes sir. If we're not on full ground, we won't ask Michel to seat him. I'll check it out. I'll accept it if McIntyre lost, but if he won it's a constitutional issue."[104]

The Republican leadership didn't have to be dragged into Gingrich's world kicking and screaming. Notwithstanding all the televised reverence for congressional civility, many Republicans found Gingrich's partisan approach highly seductive. Over the next month, they joined him in denouncing the contested election as a full-blown constitutional crisis. Wright noted that even his Republican counterpart, Robert Michel, had "succumbed to the coterie of noisy young red hots in his party. It is a ploy wholly uncharacteristic of Bob." It was an ominous sign, Wright noted in his diary. Michel had put "us on notice . . . that we no longer can rely upon the gentlemen's rules which have prevailed for all of my 30 years in Congress."[105]

Although Wright was a firsthand witness as the Republican renegades dictated the party strategy during the battle over the Bloody Eighth, he and other Democrats were not motivated to mobilize a full-throated response. The party was not even remotely scared about losing its power to the GOP. Controlling the House for more than three decades had left the Democratic majority overly confident that Republicans would never be anything but a permanent minority. The working assumption for Wright was that at some point the GOP leaders would contain their red hots and that Republicans would return to a strategy of compromise and civility. House Democrats possessed so many tools, from campaign money to procedural rules, that Wright reasonably imagined that after the smoke settled from Indiana, his party would be able to stamp out the Gingrich problem, with the assistance of senior Republicans like Michel, when the time came to return to "regular" business.

But in the short term there were no signs of calm on Capitol Hill. The distance between the Republican leaders and the Republican insurgents kept diminishing because of the Bloody Eighth. At a press conference on April 16, Guy Vander Jagt complained that Coelho was the "architect of the Democratic Majority's blatant travesty against the people of the Eighth District of Indiana; a travesty against the State of Indiana, its laws, and its elected officials; and even more important, their travesty against the Constitution, and two hundred years of precedents and traditions in the U.S. House of Representatives." He warned reporters that House Democrats had "run roughshod over the facts, the truth, the law, and the precedents in this case by innuendo, by misrepresentation, by distortion. . . ."[106]

Partisan tensions boiled over when a special election-review task force, set up by the House Administration Committee, determined in late April that the seat should go to the Democrat, McCloskey. When Republicans protested, the task-force chairman, Leon Panetta, snapped, "No matter how you break this, your candidate didn't win."[107] By a vote of two to one, the committee decided that McCloskey had won by four votes, 116,645 to 116,641. "The level of rage is so deep," Gingrich told the press, "I think it is conceivable that almost anything could happen. If getting arrested for South Africa is noble, then getting arrested for Indiana is more noble."[108]

Seeking retribution, Republicans kept their colleagues in session all night and prevented the House from conducting any business for three days. Republicans started a talkathon, carried live on C-SPAN to an empty chamber, delivering one tirade after another, about how Democrats were stealing an election. Lott capped off the event by warning, "I don't see much hope for a budget. I'm not sure a budget can get through the House."

Gingrich was like a shark circling its prey. The outcome of the Indiana election was less important than the perception of how Democrats handled the situation. Gingrich called the decision a product of the "Democratic Dictatorship of the House."[109]

"You will see a greatly tougher and more combative Republican Party coming out of this," Gingrich told reporters.[110] As he walked through the Rayburn Building, he smiled as he passed the offices of House Republicans who displayed posters of an empty chair on their doors that read, SEAT MCINTYRE. HE WON! Calling Democratic dominance "thug rule," Gingrich explained to the press that before his arrival "the Democrats and Republicans played golf, and the Democrats came off the course and beat [their] brains out. Now Republicans feel it is legitimate for them to do the same."[111]

Even Michel jumped into the fray. Sounding uncannily like Gingrich, the minority leader, along with Trent Lott, Jack Kemp, Guy Vander Jagt, Dick Cheney, and a few other members of his party, wrote to members that the Republican House leadership "has decided on a series of tactics to be implemented during the next three days to dramatize our case on the issue of the seating of a Member from the 8th Congressional District of Indiana."[112] When Cheney took to the floor, he urged Wright to think about whether he, in line to be the next Speaker of the House, really believed that "the interest of the House and your party" was best served by accepting the "questionable" judgment of Panetta's committee.[113]

On April 31, by a vote of 229 to 200, the House then rejected a Republican proposal to hold a new special election to settle the matter. With dramatic flair, Republicans stormed out of the chamber two days later, refusing to be present when O'Neill officially seated the Democrat. Gingrich went so far as to write a newspaper column connecting the Democratic actions over the Indiana seat, the communist threat in Central America, and the Holocaust. "In a sense, there's a real threat to freedom in the possibility of this becoming precedent."[114] The next day, May 1, the House voted 236 to 190 to seat McCloskey along party lines, with a surprising ten Democrats joining the unanimous Republican opposition.

Democrats clapped and cheered as members of the Indiana delegation presented McCloskey to the House and Speaker O'Neill administered the oath of office. Michel returned to the chamber and shook McCloskey's hand and was "shocked" to hear fellow Republicans criticize the handshake: "When acrimony becomes that bad among members, that really bothers me."[115]

As O'Neill swore in McCloskey, the Republicans stood side by side on the steps leading out of the House chamber to speak with reporters. "This has united the Republican Party as nothing else," McIntyre told the press. "This will live on after Rick McIntyre goes back home to his family this evening. The American people are not going to forget."[116] Abandoning congressional decorum, the Republicans used explosive terms to describe the Democrats like "slime" and "corrupt."[117] Republicans produced a seventeen-minute film about how Democrats had handled the Indiana election that they distributed for members to show in their districts.[118] There were a few Republicans, according to Gingrich, who went so far as to consider chaining themselves to Speaker O'Neill's chair in the House chamber to express their outrage at the situation.[119]

In his diary, Wright noted, "Now there is a deep schism within the GOP ranks. I surely don't envy Bob Michel. His problems are far more severe than mine. Neither he nor Trent Lott can make a commitment with any faith in its fulfillment. The Young Turks, [with] a thirst for revenge and retribution, have the Republican leaders at their mercy. The lunatics have taken over the asylum. One mature Republican said to me, 'We might as well install a sandbox for them to play in.'"[120]

By the end of the conflict over the Bloody Eighth, Gingrich was reviled by many of his colleagues on the Hill, but he was also someone to be feared. He could not be swatted away like a gnat, as Wright once suggested. He was keen to make attacking what he saw as the corrupt Democratic establishment the GOP's defining theme, and he had revealed the multiple opportunities the post-Watergate political system offered for a backbencher to inflict serious damage.

In the summer of 1986, Gingrich took over a political action committee called GOPAC, a relatively unknown outfit that Governor Pierre "Pete" DuPont IV of Delaware and twelve fellow Republican governors had established in 1978 to train promising state and local Republican candidates. Gingrich, who was always on the lookout for unorthodox ways to obtain power, jumped at the chance to manage the moribund PAC and immediately saw how it could expand his influence. GOPAC gave him a tool to start influencing Republican candidates. He used the millions that GOPAC collected to finance audiocassettes of himself speaking about strategy like a general in the middle of a war, tapes that were distributed to thousands of candidates and proved an effective promotional tool for Gingrich. In seminars that he arranged for candidates and donors, Gingrich stressed that the path to political victory in the House rested on the ability to shape public perceptions and influence the language that politicians and reporters used.

Still, many Republican leaders continued to keep Gingrich at a distance. They admired his ambition, and they thirsted for the majority that he promised. But even as they dabbled in some of his techniques, Gingrich's tactics felt too dangerous to be used on a full-time basis. His unconventional ways made some older Republicans feel uncomfortable. His willingness to ignore convention was unsettling in an era when most members still prided themselves on being loyal to the institution above all else. Gingrich needed to prove his value to the party elders if he wanted to obtain a formal position of leadership from which he could have much greater influence on the decisions of the caucus. One path to power was to take down a major Democratic target, someone with more stature than a Charlie Diggs and someone whose downfall would shock Washington and place the Democrats at risk.

His moment arrived a few months later, in December 1986, when the Democrats voted for a new Speaker of the House and gave Gingrich just the target he had been seeking.

Three

THE PERFECT FOIL

O n December 8, 1986, Jim Wright was elated. The Democratic majority leader was proudly walking around the House chamber, shaking hands and slapping backs. Democrats had unanimously voted for him to replace the retiring Speaker, Tip O'Neill, who had announced in March 1984 that he would step down when the Congress ended.

Even if he had not been the center of attention on this mild winter morning, Wright would have been easy to spot. He was a burly five feet eleven inches and looked like a cartoon character with his slicked-back reddish-brown hair parted down the center and bushy owl eyebrows that moved up and down depending on his mood.

On this day, his eyebrows were pointed straight toward the ceiling in the shape of the letter V. Becoming Speaker of the House was a lifetime achievement for the sixty-four-year-old Texan. Although earlier in his career, he had flirted with the dream of being elected president or senator, the House was now his permanent home. Newt Gingrich had arrived in Washington determined to tear down the entire congressional order, but Wright loved the Hill just the way it was. For him, the House of Representatives was an inspiring institution that fulfilled the democratic dreams of the founders. If anything, he thought that the House should be using its power more forcefully to counteract Reagan's imperial presidency.

As the forty-eighth Speaker, Wright would be third in line to the presidency. He would also be the de facto spokesman for the entire Democratic Party. When the president wanted to launch a new domestic initiative or send troops into combat, Wright would be guaranteed a seat at the table.

Few legislators felt much personal kinship with Wright; he was widely seen as a cold, tightly wound, short-tempered person, with a demeanor reminiscent of a slick used-car salesman. But they respected the way he had performed as majority leader between 1977 and 1986. Wright worked to represent the increasingly liberal post-Watergate direction of the party's congressional wing and to ensure that moderates or mavericks didn't defect on critical votes. He was also a workhorse. The folksy O'Neill might have known the names of everyone in the House cloakroom, but the frosty Wright had demonstrated a driving commitment to legislating and leadership that suited his fellow Democrats' mood.

Wright's elevation did not come as much of a surprise: the majority leader was traditionally next in line when a Speaker retired or resigned. Just to be safe, Wright had been rounding up commitments for more than a year to make certain that nobody challenged him when the time came. Cagey and knowing, Wright wanted to preempt any effort by the savvy younger Democrats to make a surprise push for someone from their generation who was more attuned to the winds of reform or more liberal on foreign policy. He also kept an eye on his colleague and friend Dan Rostenkowski, who had coveted the speakership as well. By February 1985, Wright announced to a press conference that the votes were "in my pocket."

"The Reagan era is ending," Democrat Dick Gephardt predicted as he saw Wright take the helm.[1] As the president's second term rounded its final lap, success in public policy and in the midterm elections mattered more than anything else to congressional Democrats, even more than good-government reform.

When Wright walked out of the chamber victorious, he half joked to reporters that he was happy to have Washington State's low-key, reliably calm Tom Foley as the new majority leader. "Sometimes, I'm too prone to shoot from the hip," Wright admitted. House Democrats in the corridor chuckled; most of his colleagues had experienced his explosive temper.[2]

Now Wright was up against another temperamental, ambitious man. An unrepentant New Dealer and Great Society Democrat, Wright was on track for a massive clash with Newt Gingrich that would reshape American politics. Gingrich saw himself as a guerrilla willing to fight dirty for the Reagan Revolution; Wright saw himself as a seasoned defender of the social safety net and a centrist on foreign policy who would not be easy to dismiss as "soft on defense."

Remembering his mentors, Sam Rayburn and Lyndon Johnson, Wright believed that success required cunning, arm-twisting, and hardball politics in pursuit of worthy objectives. He was precisely the kind of Democrat that Gingrich was always complaining about. Because Wright assumed that the Democrats' hold on power would not weaken anytime soon, he was prepared to act aggressively, even if his actions triggered a backlash. With Reagan in the White House and the GOP holding the Senate, Wright felt that his job required him to be tough with the opposition, keep Republicans in line, and prevent anyone within his own party from causing trouble.

Gingrich did not scare the Speaker-elect. It was not that Wright didn't understand how destructive Gingrich could be. Wright had confidence that, as so often occurred in the history of this venerable institution, a troublemaking, headline-grabbing provocateur such as Gingrich would eventually be brought down by the chamber's better angels. After all, this was what happened to the red-baiting senator Joseph McCarthy in 1954, the year Wright first won election to Congress.

As Speaker, Wright planned to be even tougher with Gingrich than O'Neill had been. He would not give Gingrich or his allies an inch. He would render the red hots powerless by excluding them from legislative debates, committee deliberations, and serious negotiations. He remained optimistic that he could persuade the House minority leader, Robert

Michel, whom he respected as a civil colleague, to keep working with the Democrats rather than falling for Gingrich's seductive promises of achieving a Republican majority by blowing up the House. As a Democratic Speaker facing a Republican president, Wright was determined to keep the chamber focused on meaningful policy debates. Congress, he believed, would ultimately cleanse itself of destructive forces that could rip the institution apart.

Gingrich could sense what Wright had in store for him. He would be an incredibly tough partisan adversary for the Republicans. Gingrich told C-SPAN's Brian Lamb that the Speaker-elect was a "more active adversary" than O'Neill, and he was going to be "tough for the Republicans to cope with for a while, to figure out." Wright was like a "first class NFL quarterback who knows his game and is at the peak of his form," Gingrich predicted. Wright would have "all the weapons: he could run, he could pass, he could kick."[3]

W right and Gingrich both came from hardscrabble beginnings. Wright was born on December 22, 1922. His parents—James, a working-class traveling salesman and former boxer, and Marie Lyster, a debutante drama teacher—raised him in Weatherford, Texas, forty miles west of the mobbed-up gambling city of Fort Worth. Ever since the railroad came to town in 1880, Weatherford had been a vibrant town with a bustling outdoor market, an ornate courthouse, and a handsome opera house.[4] Wright, along with his two sisters, spent his childhood moving from town to town as his father searched for work.

Wright was first exposed to politics by his father, a World War I veteran with a populist streak. James Wright signed letters condemning the Ku Klux Klan in the local newspaper, spoke out against powerful economic elites, and became an early advocate for women's rights.[5] Jim's parents nurtured his self-confidence; his mother loved to bring him into rooms of adults during social events to boast about how many grades he had skipped.[6]

Like millions of Americans, the Wright family suffered during the

Great Depression. James had quit his sales job to launch a new advertising business right before the economy collapsed. Without a regular income to count on, the family burned through what money Marie had inherited. As their circumstances worsened, James started drinking heavily. Marie, humbled from her affluent beginnings, now sold eggs at the local market to cover the utility bills. The family pawned most of their treasured belongings to cover the rest. Wright remembered 1931 as the year they "ate the piano."[7] The Wrights were forced to sell Marie's treasured piano, around which the family loved to gather each night.[8]

In 1933, James accepted an attractive business opportunity in Duncan, Oklahoma, the hometown of Halliburton Oil Company. Local officials hired him to help revive the economic well-being of the town as the director of the Chamber of Commerce. His salary allowed the Wrights to live in a decent-sized family home with an attractive backyard. After about one year of proving himself, when Jim was in the eighth grade, James moved the family to Seminole, Oklahoma, where he accepted the better-paying directorship of its Chamber of Commerce. Later in the 1930s, James decided to move the family to Dallas, where the bigger city offered even greater opportunities.[9]

The thin, young Jim Wright demonstrated his fierce determination by boxing and playing football at the segregated Adamson High School in the Oak Cliff neighborhood of Dallas, where the family found their new home. He excelled in the classroom, with a special fascination with American history.

Jim got his first real taste of politics when he volunteered in the 1938 campaign of the Texas gubernatorial candidate Ernest Thompson, a progressive who ran on regulating the oil industry. During one of Thompson's rallies, the candidate called on the fifteen-year-old to join him on the stage. Jim flashed his crocodile grin and made a passionate speech about why Thompson was the right candidate for the job. "He turned me loose for ten minutes," Wright recalled, "It was heady wine to make them whoop and holler and respond."[10] Jim wowed the crowd and Thompson. The boy was disappointed when Thompson lost, but the experience left an indelible mark. When he graduated from high school in 1939, most of

Wright's friends sensed that he was destined for a career in politics. His classmates nicknamed him "the Senator" and predicted in his high school yearbook that he would be elected to Congress by his mid-thirties.

Jim attended Weatherford College, a small, affordable junior college with about three hundred students. To save money, he lived at home. While writing for the school paper and participating in student government, he met Mary "Mab" Lemons, an actress on campus, and they started to date. Upon finishing the two-year program, he transferred to the University of Texas at Austin. Mab moved 250 miles from Austin to attend Texas Woman's University in Denton, but they kept the romance intact.

Jim continued to dip his toes in politics. While campaigning for the Texas attorney general, Gerald Mann, he met Lyndon Johnson for the first time.[11] When Japan bombed Pearl Harbor in December 1941, Wright left college in the middle of his coursework to volunteer in the Army Air Corps. He married Mab on Christmas Day 1942, right before going overseas. He had just turned twenty. During the war, Wright flew more than thirty combat missions and thirty combat flying hours in the South Pacific on a B-24 bomber, for which he was awarded a Distinguished Flying Cross.

When he returned to Texas, Wright found work as a salesman, but he never forgot the thrill he felt as part of Thompson's campaign. A committed liberal with some of his father's doggedness, Wright would speak to the Veterans of Foreign Wars, which veered to the right.[12] Wright proved to be a fearsome counterpuncher. His hair-trigger temper could quickly get away from him. One day, while he was attending a VFW meeting, an oversized and drunken veteran named Dub Tucker purposely brushed into his shoulder while passing him in the hall. Tucker, a bellicose conservative, had heard some of Wright's speeches and called him a "chickenshit sonofabitch," slurring his words. When Wright told Tucker that he had done nothing to him personally, Tucker only grew more belligerent. "You're a damn sissy," he said. Wright calmly reminded his fellow veteran that they didn't even know each other. "I know you alright," Tucker responded. "You're a commie sonofabitch!" Tucker took a swing at Wright.

The future Speaker swiftly turned to avoid the punch, then landed a left hook right into Tucker's stomach. His anger unleashed, Wright pounded Tucker until he fell to the floor bloodied and bruised. The other veterans, watching in stunned silence, were impressed. The young man might have been a liberal, but he sure knew how to throw a punch.[13]

At only twenty-three, Wright won an election to fill an open seat in the Texas state legislature. His first term was rough. Conservative Democrats branded him a radical leftist for proposing to tax the oil industry to help pay for government services, and he caused a stir by calling for higher welfare payments, more education spending, and increased funding for road projects. His critics derided the cabal of liberals with whom he associated as the "Russian embassy."

In his 1948 reelection bid, he faced Eugene Miller, a former state legislator with massive gambling debts and alleged ties to organized crime. Miller spread slanderous rumors throughout the district accusing Wright of being a communist. On July 7, just days before the primary, all hell broke loose. On a hot evening, Miller was rushed to a hospital after being shot by a gunman, with one bullet lodged underneath his heart and another settled in his right leg. Miller muttered to the hospital staff that the shooting had been retribution from a "commie" for having attacked his left-wing opponent. Within hours, Miller died from his wounds.

Miller's advisers unleashed a whispering campaign accusing Wright of being the gunman and waging a pattern of intimidation. Floyd Bradshaw, a schoolteacher who was the third candidate alongside Wright and Miller, capitalized on the situation by proclaiming that he had received a death threat ordering him to withdraw from the race.

In an act of desperation, Wright turned to the issue of race in a state where poll taxes and all-white primaries had disenfranchised black Americans since Reconstruction. Wright announced his opposition to civil rights legislation and defended the principle of "states' rights." That stance sat well with many of his white constituents,[14] but the craven strategy would forever haunt Wright.

But even that last-minute gambit didn't work. The rumors and red-baiting had taken their toll. Wright lost to Bradshaw by thirty-nine votes.

A Texas Ranger who would spend the rest of his career searching for Miller's killer found no evidence connecting Wright to the murder.[15]

In 1950, Wright bounced back by winning election as the mayor of Weatherford, and he soon proved his knack for constituent service. One morning, a woman called his office to complain that boys near her house were shooting at birds with their BB guns, and another called to warn Wright that grackles, those ubiquitous yellow-eyed Texas feeding birds, were ruining her trees. The mayor almost literally killed two birds with one stone: he went to the home of the first caller, picked up the boys firing off guns, drove them to the second house, and had them shoot the bothersome birds.[16]

Four years after being elected mayor, Wright decided to challenge the four-term House incumbent Wingate Lucas. Amon Carter, the powerful publisher of the *Fort Worth Star-Telegram*, stood squarely behind the incumbent, who had done well for the district. Carter published an editorial on the front page of his newspaper attacking Wright for lacking "any well-defined ideas."[17] Wright mounted a populist campaign that targeted incumbency, the political establishment, and Carter. "A place in Congress wasn't meant to be a lifetime job," he argued.[18] Declaring himself a "people's candidate" fighting the "local kingmakers," Wright refused to take contributions of more than $100. He campaigned at such a grueling pace that he lost twenty pounds over just a few weeks.

In the final days of the campaign, in a Hail Mary move, Wright paid $974.40 for a three-quarter-page ad in the *Star-Telegram*. The publisher, who in his old age was less temperamental than in his youth, proved willing to print anything if the check was good—even a personal attack against himself—for the right price.[19] Early in his political career, outside the halls of power, Wright saw how one could topple a political figure by arguing that he embodied a corrupt system. "You have just met a man," Wright now warned in an open letter to Carter, "who is not afraid of you." The letter claimed that the entire newspaper was biased and its coverage of the campaign was illegitimate. The reporters, he said, failed to write stories on most of Wright's campaign events, while they had published politically biased information that had no basis in fact. "It is unhealthy for anyone to become too powerful, too influential, too dominating," Wright asserted. "The people are tired of 'One-Man Rule.' This is a New Day." To Carter's surprise, the young upstart's strategy worked. Wright won every major county in Texas's Twelfth District.

Wright entered the U.S. House of Representatives in an era when it took a long time for members to obtain substantial power. Freshmen could expect to wait their turn in the seniority system, slowly advancing in their committee assignments the longer they remained in office.

Speaker Sam Rayburn advised freshmen "to get along, go along." He adopted his young fellow Texan as a protégé. Young Democrats admired Rayburn, who seemed to have an uncanny feel for how the House worked and could lead a party deeply divided between southerners and northerners who disagreed on civil rights and other key policies. Wright felt frustrated with having to serve his time and wait; he once complained to his other Texas mentor, Lyndon Johnson, who advised him to just be patient. Because Rayburn liked Wright, the Democrats placed him on the Public Works Committee—a plum assignment that controlled huge budgetary resources that were always in demand by legislators.

Determined not to repeat the kind of brutal defeat that took him out of the Texas state legislature in 1948, Wright became a master of pork-barrel spending. He secured lucrative military contracts for companies like General Dynamics and Bell Helicopter that had sizable factories in his burgeoning district.

In the 1950s and 1960s, legislators were expected to deliver as much money to their districts as was politically possible. With a booming economy, higher tax revenue kept flowing into the U.S. Treasury during these decades, which meant that legislators like Wright had a lot of easy money to spend without worrying about growing debt. Political scientists later called it the electoral connection—fighting for your district so that all voters understood they could count on you to be their voice in Washington.[20] Wright was able to "drag . . . every last slab of bacon he could from the congressional smokehouse to his constituents in Tarrant County," noted *The Texas Observer*.[21] Moreover, his Public Works Committee assignment allowed him to help other Democrats do the same by directing earmarked spending their way.

The first few decades of Wright's legislative career were as exciting and challenging as he could have imagined. The entrance of a dynamic group of liberal legislators into Congress in the 1956 and 1958 elections energized the Democrats even with a Republican president, Dwight Eisenhower, in office. During the 1960s, with Lyndon Johnson as president, Wright was proud to be part of the passage of the Great Society, which he saw as a second New Deal. The Great Society included a huge slate of programs, such as federal aid for secondary and elementary schools, student loans and research funds for higher education, Medicaid and the War on Poverty, consumer protection, immigration reform, environmental regulations, and more. Johnson found that he could usually count on Wright as a reliable vote on most issues, even on bills such as Medicare in 1965 that stirred controversy in his district, because he was part of an emerging cohort of moderate southerners distinct from the old Dixiecrats who chaired the committees.

The only time that Wright refused to join the majority of his party on a major bill and bowed to the reactionary elements of his district came in 1964, when he voted against the landmark Civil Rights Act. He later regretted the decision and tried to partially make up for the mistake by supporting the Voting Rights Act one year later. On another core 1960s controversy, Wright—a staunch anticommunist—had backed the Vietnam War.

Throughout the political ups and downs of these years, Wright loved the challenge of whipping up votes on a bill, whether that meant intimidating a colleague to say no or seducing him through promises of appropriations to say yes. He found the process as exhilarating as the final product: when things worked well, laws were enacted that made a huge difference in the lives of average Americans. Wright was consumed with the life of the legislator, always thinking up some new procedural trick or working some new angle. His passion for legislating was on full display during a program that aired in 1965 on the National Educational Television

Network. In *The Changing Congress*, the cameramen shadowed Wright during the workday as he tried to move a water pollution bill through the House and the Senate. The thirty-minute cinema-verité-style documentary provided viewers with a firsthand look at the real textbook Congress as Wright navigated different political land mines—such as the southern conservative Howard Smith, chairman of the House Rules Committee. The program ended with Wright telling the audience in a voice-over, "Somewhere along the line if you're gonna to do your job up here, you develop a healthy respect, and even a passion, for the game as it's played on the Hill. It really doesn't make a lot of difference whether the rules are exactly as you would have written them. If you are going to succeed in Congress, you learn to deal with them, and to win with them."[22] He and Mab reveled during the evening soirees at their home, where they hosted Texas friends and U.S. representatives to dine, smoke, and schmooze after a long day of work. The evenings culminated in Wright sitting at a small round wooden table in the back room by the pantry, where he leaned on the key guests to give him their commitment to a bill. Like his heroes Henry Clay and Sam Rayburn, he could be extraordinarily tough in his one-on-one meetings with colleagues. Unlike them, Wright was known for letting his temper get the best of him, just as it had back in the VFW in 1946. In the middle of a conversation, Wright would cock his eyebrows as he dropped his shoulders. "He looks like he could choke you," said one official.[23]

Wright hated the demands of the press, especially for short, TV-tailored sound bites, which didn't suit his overflowing rhetorical style. But he shone when giving floor speeches, which felt more natural to him than almost anything else. He loved to fill the grand space of the House chamber with booming oratory, controlling his cadence and selecting each word and pause with great care. And as the system promised, Wright's patience was rewarded: slowly but assuredly, he made his inexorable climb up the seniority ladder.

Wright was not deaf to public frustration with Congress. He understood in the 1960s that many reporters and public intellectuals thought that the House and the Senate didn't work well and that many legislators were corrupt. He often complained about sensational media coverage of Congress, but he supported 1960s reforms such as tougher financial-disclosure rules and limits on the business activities of legislators.[24]

Politics back in Fort Worth was as satisfying to him as life in Washington. Wright delighted in feeling like the big man on campus when spending time in his district. When he walked the streets of north Texas, every person he passed seemed to have voted for him or been indebted to him for something. Wright's closest personal friendships were not in Washington, where colleagues continued to see him as aloof and temperamental, but in Texas, where people seemed to understand him. Wright was personally isolated on Capitol Hill. He didn't have many close friends in Congress, just trusted colleagues. One reporter called him an "enigmatic loner." "You don't chew the fat with Jim Wright," a Democratic colleague said.[25]

Wright's personal life suffered from his total devotion to politics, just as Gingrich's would. In 1958, Wright and Mab's relationship was strained when their fourth child, Parker Stephen, died as an infant because of complications from Down syndrome. For once, Wright's tight public grip on his emotions cracked in the hospital parking lot as he told his three daughters about their brother's death.

Mab had disliked life in Washington from the moment they arrived. Now Wright faced steep debts from the accumulated cost of the treatments used to keep Parker alive. Eleven years later, in 1969, he and Mab began a two-year legal separation that would end in a no-fault divorce. Wright was forty-six. He agreed to give her their home and most of their possessions, as well as $950 a month in alimony.

Living in a modest downtown basement apartment in Washington, Wright started dating a woman named Betty Hay. She became the love of his life. They met when she worked as a secretary and then as a staffer on the Public Works Committee. Some in Washington suspected that the two had an affair, resenting Betty for having stolen Wright from Mab, who had moved to Virginia and taken a job as a tour guide on Capitol Hill.[26]

By 1971, the rising star within the Democratic caucus was scrambling to pay his bills. "My finances are in shambles," Wright confided to his diary. "With what unbelievable folly I have so long ignored them and let them drift. In my 30th year I was the richest young man in town [while] in my 50th—well I'm driving a ten-year-old car, owe so God-awful much money that I'll need luck to pay it off."[27] Despite the popular image of fat cats working in Congress, public service did not bring much lucre, and the dual life of living in Washington and one's district was costly. The alimony payments to Mab also added up.

Soon after his second marriage, Wright was again implicated in a scandalous story when Jack Anderson, a legendary muckraker syndicated in hundreds of papers, including *The Washington Post*, published a column titled SHOOTING AT FISH IN THE PORK BARREL. Anderson recounted the details of a secret session of the Public Works Committee during which several committee Democrats who "in public, pay lip service to the environmental movement" complained "bitterly" about the impact that environmental policies were having on public-works programs and construction. Upon reviewing the fifty-six-page meeting transcript, Anderson wrote that Wright had begun "to assault the environmental acts. Dams and buildings had been 'brought to a screeching halt,' he snorted, while the federal government weighed the effects on the environment. 'That is just a monstrous thing,' he huffed. He was willing to see people protected by the laws, he said, but 'the hell with the fish!'"[28]

Wright resented the piece, which he insisted was based on a fabricated account of the conversation. "The Anderson treatment," Wright noted to himself, "is so very typical of the growing irresponsibility of sensational 'expose' type journalism that increasingly appalls, angers and even frightens a lot of conscientious public officials." He bristled at reporters who became overzealous in their desire to expose corruption and carefully parsed the suggestive language that Anderson used: "It demonstrates quite clearly how the selective use of a verb is employed to convey to the reader a predetermined impression of character." The objects of Anderson's opprobrium, Wright continued, "'huffed,' 'groused,' 'blurted,' 'snorted,' or 'whined,'" while sources the journalist liked "explained" or "pointed out." Wright didn't share his private frustration beyond his diary, but the anger hardened within him and cooled his interactions with reporters.[29]

Nor did Wright think much of the good-government reformers of the early 1970s who promised to clean up the way that "corrupt" politicians conducted their business. On June 22, 1972, he reluctantly agreed to meet with Ralph Nader, the consumer activist who was canvassing Democratic members with lengthy questionnaires about their districts, interest-group support, and voting records. Nader hoped to publish a booklet for voters and the press offering a fuller portrait of who their representatives were. Wright agreed with a colleague who asked, "Who the hell elected or appointed Ralph Nader as the judge and the custodian of my conscience?"[30] But Wright, who thought his colleague raised a "good question," had enough sense to fill out the papers.

The Watergate scandal shocked and saddened Wright. He feared that Watergate would confirm to Americans that the entire city of Washington was broken, not just the president. Citizens would now have good reason to believe what muckrakers like Jack Anderson were writing about elected officials.

After Nixon waved goodbye to the nation, a coalition of good-government organizations and liberal Democrats pushed congressional reforms that centralized power in the Speaker's hands, rather than dispersing authority to autonomous committee chairmen as before. Wright, a curmudgeon with a deep reverence for Congress and its work, watched nervously. The goal of the post-Watergate reforms was to take power away from the conservative southern barons who chaired most of the major committees. Seniority was no longer sacrosanct: the Speaker and the majority leader could insist on the appointment of committee chairs who would support the party agenda. Meanwhile, other reforms provided rank-and-file members with new tools to keep their leaders accountable. The Democratic caucus started to vote on committee chairmen and leadership positions; nothing would be automatic anymore.

The Speaker of the House was one of the main beneficiaries of these changes. The House Rules Committee, which had been an independent fiefdom controlled by conservative southern Democrats until the end of the Nixon presidency, now served as a direct arm of the Speaker. To check the Speaker's new power, the reformist Democrats simultaneously created new rules and norms—such as stricter ethics regulations—that would allow them to depose a leader who became autocratic or corrupt.

Moreover, technical changes like recorded votes meant that the public could see where each member stood on a given issue. Wright realized that the ironclad security that legislative leaders had enjoyed during the early decades of his political career, when they could avoid challenges to their posts and horse-trade in secrecy, would soon disappear. Sacred political spaces—such as the famous "Board of Education," where Speaker Rayburn met privately with invited Democrats over bourbon and cards in a small room on the first floor of the Capitol—would no longer be tolerated. And all this was taking place at a time when a young Newt Gingrich, still a college professor at West Georgia College, was sensing the possibilities that the growing public distrust generated and the opportunities that might open up for new leadership in Washington. "From now on," the Wisconsin Democrat Henry Reuss predicted as he watched the reformers, "the sword of Damocles will be hanging over every chairman."[31]

Younger Democrats were willing to shake things up within their own party—ousting powerful committee chairs and enacting procedural reforms—based on the assumption that regardless of what they did, Democrats would retain their power. The "permanent Republican minority" did not appear to pose a serious threat at the time. Reform, in the minds of the Young Turks, would make Congress more responsive and eventually more liberal. "It was the furthest thing from Democrats' minds that [the reforms] would help Republicans," one Democratic staffer admitted.[32]

In this atmosphere, nobody expected Jim Wright to be part of the Democrats' new cohort of leaders. He was not a legislator who had shown any serious interest in congressional reform. While he respected the growing pressure to make the legislative process as democratic and accountable as possible, he was still more at home with the insular committee system that he had mastered under the tutelage of Lyndon Johnson and

Sam Rayburn. But on December 6, 1976, Democrats elected him their new majority leader, the person next in line to be Speaker.

For the first time, as a result of the post-Watergate reforms, Democrats could vote for their majority leader. The campaign was brutal, with four candidates—the favorite was Phil Burton of California, followed by Richard Bolling of Missouri, John McFall of California, and Wright—whipping votes and leaning on colleagues who owed them favors. On the final, tense day, with cigarette smoke filling the air and Democrats huddled into competing camps, the two champions of reform, Burton and Bolling, split the vote. McFall, the majority whip, was embroiled in the Koreagate scandal. Wright defeated Burton on the third roll call—by one vote.[33] The outcome shocked everyone in the chamber. Burton glanced up toward the galleries to catch a glimpse of his wife, Sala, who looked at her husband despondently and shrugged, realizing they had been outmaneuvered.[34] When the ebullient Texas congressman Charlie Wilson learned that Wright had won, he said, "I damn near soiled myself."[35]

Wright, who had chain-smoked Winstons throughout the voting, "shook his head and rubbed his chin in disbelief" when the outcome was clear.[36] Recalling Lyndon Johnson, who won his 1948 election to the Senate by just eighty-seven votes and earned the nickname "Landslide Lyndon," Wright joked, "We Texans are not new to landslides." He added, "I'm fully aware this is not a mandate."[37] But it did put him next in line to be Speaker of the House.

This result, an accident of fate in an unusual race, had come in the middle of a great transition, when the old power structures of Congress fell. But a plurality of Democrats had chosen one of the most traditional politicians to be first in line to the most powerful post in the House. "No institution can function if a substantial number of members work against it," Wright warned the newcomers.[38] The outcome was bitterly disappointing for Burton's and Bolling's supporters. They had not risked so much political capital battling against the old southern committee barons just to see a traditional pol like Jim Wright ascend by one measly vote. The resentment and distrust of Wright among younger Democrats would never disappear.

Wright might not have been a reformer, but he was willing to be an aggressive partisan. He wasn't convinced that Democrats needed to change the way they did their business. The aftermath of Reagan's devastating 1980 victory was no time to play nice. Wright didn't fear that Democrats could lose control of the House anytime soon, but he now faced a conservative Republican president who was intent on shifting policy sharply to the right and a sympathetic Republican Senate. House Democrats were in the thick of a historic rearguard battle to protect the legacies of the New Deal and the Great Society.

As a leader of his party, Wright concluded that Democrats had to use every tool at their disposal to check the Republicans. His vision of strengthening the Democrats was not reforming the political process but using old-fashioned techniques, like fund-raising and logrolling, to build up the party. By the early 1980s, Republicans had started to outpace the Democrats in fund-raising as the corporate lobbyists who had come to Washington to fight regulations sent more of their money to the Reagan-led GOP.[39]

Wright worked with Tony Coelho, the feisty Californian, to respond to the influx of corporate funds into Republican coffers. That would prove to be one of Wright's most consequential decisions. Coelho didn't mind skating close to controversy or testing the limits of ethical behavior. When it came to money and campaigns, he saw few boundaries to what the parties could do. When Wright empowered him to handle campaign finance for their party, Coelho opened the floodgates. Coelho, who became chairman of the Democratic Congressional Campaign Committee in 1981, sought to mimic the results of its Republican counterpart and fostered much closer ties between House Democrats and corporate interest groups.[40]

Making money for Democrats turned out to be Coelho's greatest skill. Wright soon gave him the go-ahead to aggressively court new donors. The year before Coelho started, the DCCC raised $1.8 million; six years later, that figure reached $15 million. (That was still half of what its Republican counterpart raised).[41] For too long, Coelho argued, the Democrats had relied on organized labor, whose power was steadily declining. Meanwhile, business and financial communities seeking deregulation had expanded their political operations.[42] Coelho wanted some of those corporate dollars for Democrats.

Coelho declared that "special interest is not a nasty word." He once spotted the Texas businessman James Devlin, chairman of U.S. Telephone, in the House dining room waiting for someone to join him for breakfast. Coelho walked up to him and pushed him to join his elite council of donors for $5,000, which would give him instant access to Speaker O'Neill. Before Devlin could reply, Coelho scribbled his name down on an index card and muttered, "I'll just put you down for $5,000."[43]

Coelho's juiciest target was the savings and loan industry, which was desperate for federal assistance. Savings and loan thrifts had traditionally operated as small savings banks that served homeowners. The government tightly regulated the interest that the banks could pay on deposits so that rates did not go too high for borrowers; Washington also allowed these lending institutions to make only home mortgage and other personal loans. In turn, the federal government had insured deposits in these banks since the New Deal. During the 1970s, these banks were suffering due to stagflation. With the banks paying out higher interest rates on deposits, many of them struggled to survive. Reagan, with the support of many congressional Democrats, crafted a law that deregulated the thrifts, allowing them to invest 40 percent of their holdings in commercial loans and 30 percent in consumer loans. Right away, bank executives used their money in ventures from high-risk commercial real estate to junk bonds. For a time, many of the thrifts did well, and their executives enjoyed high-flying lifestyles. But when real estate markets collapsed in the mid-1980s in states like Texas and Arizona, the thrifts went broke.

When the banks came running to Congress for help, Coelho stood ready to oblige—with the understanding that savings and loan officials would help Democrats in return. One such executive was the Texas entrepreneur Thomas Gaubert, a boisterous, cigar-smoking Dallas native who had purchased a savings and loan thrift for $1 million and within one year increased its net worth from $40 million to $223 million. Now, like most of the other big players, his bank was struggling as a result of bad investments. Coelho brought Gaubert into the DCCC, and the former Republican donor became one of the House Democrats' biggest check writers.

Such efforts looked sordid to campaign-finance watchdogs, but the leaders of both parties were impressed with what Wright accomplished, with Coelho's help. Wright and Coelho had refilled Democratic campaign coffers, even with Reagan in the White House. Wright and Speaker O'Neill had kept House Democrats disciplined on almost every key issue. Few Democrats defected from the party line after 1982, which created an enormous obstacle to the Reagan Revolution, and House Republicans were pushed aside in policy debates. Democrats also cheered Wright on when he helped Speaker O'Neill respond to the Republican C-SPAN tirades and defend the Democrat Frank McCloskey's right to the contested Indiana seat. Wright made no bones about his opposition to Reagan and his record. On the eve of the president's 1984 State of the Union address, Wright called for legislation to reverse the president's "cruelly deranged" policies so as to "revive the American dream, to renew the American spirit, to rekindle America's faith in our future."[44]

Wright's emotions became so intense at times that they almost devolved into violence. In July 1985, the Republican COS members Daniel Lungren and Robert Walker approached Wright on the floor of the House to complain about the way he had used parliamentary procedures to block Republican participation. When the two COS members threatened to tie up the business of the House through procedural tricks of their own, Wright unexpectedly broke into a smile. According to Lungren, seeing the confusion on his colleague's face, Wright coldly explained, "I am smiling because I am trying to hold inside how I feel. I want to come down here and punch you and Mr. Walker in the mouth."[45] Lungren told reporters that Wright then walked up and forcefully grabbed him by the arm, repeating the threat until the congressman insisted that he let go right away. Wright's spokeswoman admitted that the two legislators had exchanged "intemperate words."[46] Wright apologized, though the sixty-two-year-old majority leader insisted that he had been joking about hitting his thirty-eight-year-old weight-lifting conservative colleague.[47] On another occasion, colleagues had to physically hold Wright back after the California Democrat Pete Stark called him a "cocksucker" during a heated exchange on the floor. "I remember thinking I'm about to be hit in the face and I think it's going to hurt a lot," Stark said.[48]

When it was Wright's turn to become Speaker in 1987, not everyone thought he was the best face for the Democratic Party. In *The New Republic*, Paul West recounted the Texan's penchant for pork and decried the shady figures who had surrounded him during much of his career. At heart, West noted, "Wright remains a deal-making, big-spending Texas pol—hair trigger and all. . . . Not a few of his colleagues wonder whether the last of the old-time Democrats is the right leader for the House and the Democratic Party." Elevating "an old-line politician with more than a hint of the snake-oil salesman about him as your national spokesman is no way to win the hearts and minds of tomorrow's voters."[49] There was no evidence or rumor of any kind of serious wrongdoing, just countless stories about the shadier people whom he associated with in his home district and the fact that he was not a strong champion of reform.

As Wright prepared to take over from O'Neill, Republicans were surprisingly gloomy. The 1986 midterm elections had been tough for Reagan's party: Democrats had recaptured the Senate with a 55 to 45 majority. "We took a bath in the Senate," said the Senate minority leader, Robert Dole of Kansas.[50] "We had a fine victory yesterday," a gleeful Wright reported in his diary. "I won by 69% and we gained the Senate, along with some modest gains in House numbers. Everywhere Reagan went asking for a referendum on his policies, the voters elected a Democrat. Even in Indiana, where the president tried to purge Frank McClosky, we won."[51] The retiring Speaker, O'Neill, announced, "If there was a Reagan Revolution, it's over."[52]

A scandal in the weeks following the midterms rocked the White House further. The press and Congress discovered that members of the National Security Council and the CIA had secretly sold arms to Iran. The notion that Reagan had authorized the sale of weapons to Ayatollah

Khomeini's Iran, in exchange for assistance in freeing American hostages being held in Lebanon by the terrorist group Hezbollah, contradicted everything that he stood for in foreign policy. It also appeared to violate a U.S. ban on selling military hardware to Iran.

Much worse was to come. On November 24, Attorney General Edwin Meese, who had conducted a top secret internal fact-finding mission for the president, revealed to Reagan's high-ranking advisers that funds from the weapons sales to Iran had been diverted to the Nicaraguan contras—violating the 1982 and 1984 Boland Amendments, which expressly prohibited military and economic assistance to the right-leaning rebels.[53]

In private, the president was shaken by Meese's report. Reagan recorded in his diary, "This was a violation of the law against giving the Contras money without an authorization by Congress." Lieutenant Colonel Oliver North, the National Security Council staffer who had been the point man for the operation, "didn't tell me about this. Worst of all," Reagan continued, National Security Adviser John Poindexter "found out about it & didn't tell me. This may call for resignations."[54]

The Iran-contra scandal, as it was soon called, kept growing. By the time that Democrats voted for Wright as Speaker, the Reagan administration was in a full-blown political crisis. Congress was preparing to set up a Watergate-style select committee to investigate the scandal, while Reagan appointed the conservative senator John Tower to head a bipartisan commission to do the same. By mid-December, Reagan's public-approval ratings had plummeted from 67 percent to 46—the worst one-month drop ever since Gallup had started recording approval ratings in 1936. It wasn't Watergate, at least not yet, but the White House was bleeding heavily.

Wright publicly questioned whether Reagan had been telling the truth when he insisted that he didn't know of the funds transfer before Meese's discovery. It "defies logic," Wright argued to the press, that lower-level officials had made these crucial decisions. "The president should have been aware. If nobody knew of it, that in itself is a confession of a great void in the execution of our foreign policy."[55]

When the One Hundredth Congress convened on January 6, 1987, Wright delivered a stirring opening speech calling Congress the "highest theater that anyone plays upon this earth today." The chamber was particularly crowded with guests, with people sitting in the aisles. Joseph Kennedy, Robert's son, was being sworn in for his first term in the House—an emotional moment for those who remembered the tragedies that had befallen the Kennedys. Joseph's mother, Ethel, couldn't find a seat in the members' gallery until Wright's sister, Betty Lee, offered her one.

Plenty of Texans were on hand to celebrate the new Speaker as well. At a party in the Cannon Caucus Room after his swearing in, Wright's successor as mayor of Weatherford, Sherry Watson, handed him a handsome wood carving of a witty caricature created by a local artist. Back in Fort Worth, thousands of residents watched on satellite television in the Will Rogers Coliseum.[56]

While Wright reveled in his moment of victory, Gingrich prepared to go on the attack. Gingrich had started his congressional career by bringing down Charles Diggs, and he believed that he could do the same to the new Speaker. As one Gingrich staffer wrote, the evidence of ethical problems among Democrats was "clear and well-documented."

Six months into Wright's tenure as Speaker, Gingrich pounced. At the same time he was peddling an unpopular plan to privatize Social Security, Gingrich proposed an amendment to a $1.4 billion appropriations bill to tackle corruption in the House. His amendment would establish a special independent commission to investigate a "pattern of corruption" in the House; a commission was needed because the House Ethics Committee "seems to protect the institution rather than police it."

Most journalists knew that this ploy would not get far, but they covered Gingrich's proposed amendment nonetheless. The amendment went down to defeat by 297 to 77, but Gingrich and his cosponsors were undeterred. According to the minutes of a COS meeting that took place on July 1, Bob Walker said they lost the vote, but "we won in the press."[57]

Wright began to draw more critical attention. *The New York Times* published a tough editorial on June 24, asking, "Does Jim Wright want to be known as the Speaker of the House or as the defender of some Texas banking hustlers?"[58] Writing in *Newsweek*, the correspondents Rich Thomas and David Pauly half joked that Wright was a great believer in Tip O'Neill's maxim that all politics is local, given that "three times recently he intervened with federal regulators on behalf of Texas real-estate men, all of whom have run into legal problems."[59]

Gingrich sent newspaper clippings to reporters and policy makers that questioned Wright's ethics.[60] The Georgian assigned Karen Van Brocklin, his legislative assistant, to search newspaper archives for articles he could circulate.[61] Van Brocklin, a tough-minded Minnesotan with a knack for full-contact partisan politics, scoured microfiches and pulled stories from the Fort Worth press that spattered mud across Wright's image. The adversarial style of journalism that Wright hated in the Washington press corps had seeped down into local newspapers such as the *Fort Worth Star-Telegram*. A New York–based company, Capital Cities Communications, had purchased the *Fort Worth Star-Telegram* and two radio stations in November 1974, and it wanted to turn the newspaper into a hard-hitting publication with national appeal and the style of high-quality investigative reporting that could sell subscriptions. "The Speaker still has difficulty understanding the new and modern press," one of his staffers admitted.[62]

Reporters now looked at the underside of Wright's fierce loyalty to constituents. The *Fort Worth Star-Telegram* reporter David Montgomery wrote articles populated by colorful and disreputable characters living in Wright's district, all of whom seemed to have unusually close relationships with their congressman. In need of money, Wright had entered into a series of investments back in Texas, all of which were legal but most of which involved him with figures and financial deals that didn't look good on the front page.[63]

One of Montgomery's most provocative stories revolved around a Fort Worth real estate developer named George Mallick. A self-made success, the grandson of a Lebanese peddler and son of the owner of a chain of meat markets, Mallick turned some of his savings into investments, gradually growing his capital into a profitable real estate development operation.[64] Despite his Texas twang, Mallick always felt like an outsider in Fort Worth. His father had made his own way in this country, and George had worked his way up, starting as a gofer for his dad at eight years old and then making money on the streets by selling snow cones near the bus stop with a fifty-pound ice shaver he purchased with his savings. By his late twenties, he had worked his way up in the world and raised enough capital to build and sell apartment and office buildings. His own development company handled all aspects of each project: purchasing the land, constructing the property, and managing rental units. He also rubbed some people the wrong way, coming off as crass even as he yearned to be seen as a man of stature.

Wright had been friendly with Mallick since 1963, when they met at a ribbon-cutting ceremony for the opening of one of the developer's Fort Worth shopping centers. In 1979, along with their wives, Wright and Mallick formed a company called Mallightco, a combination of their two names. Betty worked as the vice president. Mallick's investments soon expanded into the oil industry and other kinds of businesses.

Wright, according to Montgomery's reporting, secured $30 million in federal development grants to revitalize the stockyards in Fort Worth in 1985 and 1986. The stockyards were located by a major railway line, but by the 1970s the streets in the area were dead. To improve the neighborhood, some local residents planned to lure in restaurants, nightclubs, museums, apartments, and offices.

In 1981, the revitalization moved into high gear when Billy Bob Barnett—a former football player turned bar owner and beer distributor—purchased a massive building to launch Billy Bob's Texas, a honky-tonk spanning over two acres, with everything from a rodeo to live music. From his Fort Worth office, according to the stories, Mallick mapped out his plans to save the city, much of which depended on an infusion of federal funds. By 1986, Barnett's honky-tonk bar was struggling, and he approached Mallick for help. Mallick, according to Montgomery, offered to find Barnett $27 million in financing in return for a stake in the business. The

Fort Worth papers published stories about the negotiations, suggesting that the proposed deal reflected untoward political relationships in the district. Additional stories reported that Betty, who regularly used the company Cadillac, earned a salary of $18,000 a year with Mallightco until two years before Wright was elected Speaker.

None of these small-bore stories worried the Speaker. Not only did it seem as if they would be uninteresting to most readers, but Wright insisted that they were not true or misconstrued the facts. While Mallick had dabbled with investing in the Fort Worth redevelopment neighborhood, Wright reminded his friends and staff that nothing had come of the efforts. Although it was true that Billy Bob Barnett offered Mallick 17 percent ownership in his bar in exchange for $27 million to get him out of bankruptcy, Mallick was unable to raise the funds.[65] His friend and partner didn't have any "direct interest" in federal legislation. Nor had George and his wife, Marlene, given the Wrights any gifts of over $100 (the maximum limit according to the ethics rules). Betty was in fact a legitimate co-owner of Mallightco, which owned the company car, and she earned her salary (half of what she earned in the job that she quit when her husband became majority leader) by making most of the investment decisions for the couples. Upon reading the press clippings, Wright brushed aside any concern that anything would come of the pieces.

Believing that the sensational stories would damage Wright, Gingrich distributed these and other stories, including another series from the *Dallas Times Herald* that centered on a colorful Fort Worth oilman named Monty Moncrief who had business dealings with celebrities like Bob Hope. Wright had known Moncrief and his family for most of his adult life. Moncrief allegedly turned to Wright in 1979 for help when an overseas investment was threatened, involving a commercial oil well in Egyptian water right off the Sinai coast—territory that Israel controlled after the Six-Day War in 1967 but returned to the Egyptians after the 1979 Israel-Egypt peace deal. According to the *Times Herald*, then majority leader Wright wrote to President Carter, Secretary of State Cyrus Vance, and even the Egyptian president, Anwar Sadat, in March 1979 to prevent Moncrief from losing the lease, worth over $100 million. And Wright allegedly obtained an exceptionally good, risk-free deal for an investment in an east Texas oil well that earned him between $70,000 and $220,500. As with the stories about Mallick, Wright didn't panic. While he had tried to help Moncrief, unsuccessfully, he didn't do anything he wouldn't do for other Texas constituents with problems that impacted his state. Moncrief and Wright had invested money in the same manner, and they had taken the same financial risks. There were no favors granted by anyone. Nor could Wright help but chortle at the fact that with other stories reporters didn't even have their facts straight. Gingrich had circulated a provocative news account documenting how Wright had contacted the secretary of the interior to protect the Texas Oil and Gas Corporation's right to drill on federal lands in Arkansas. The reporter alleged that Wright owned stock in the company and was protecting his economic interests. Wright noted to his staff that the story was entirely wrong. He never owned stock in the company, plain and simple. And though the newspaper had published a second story correcting itself, Gingrich handed out only the first.[66]

Several articles reported that Wright had struggled to make ends meet despite his political power. Between 1984 and 1987, Wright's personal investments had plummeted by almost 75 percent.[67] In addition to the ongoing costs from his divorce and mismanaged investments, some reporters suggested that his wife, Betty—who usually looked as if she had just walked out of a salon and had developed a penchant for lynx coats and fancy cars—had an expensive lifestyle. In 1983, they had purchased a handsome brick home in McLean, Virginia, adding on a sunroom large enough to seat three tables of ten so Wright could do more entertaining. The house was decorated with crystal chandeliers, an inlaid Chinese table, and a large portrait of Betty.[68]

Thanks to Gingrich's footwork, these and other pieces from the Texas press began to circulate around Washington, leading more national reporters to pay closer attention to Wright.

Hot on Wright's trail was Brooks Jackson, a dogged and methodical investigator whose work examining how lobbyists influenced politicians had made him a trailblazer on what was becoming the "money and politics" beat. He tended to see politics through a moralistic lens, a tale of good and evil rather than a complex, nuanced process. Although his claim to fame was a humorous story about President Carter batting away a swamp rabbit during a fishing expedition in Georgia, Jackson's work usually revolved around dollars and decision making. By 1980, he was covering the savings and loan industry for *The Wall Street Journal*, which led him to Wright, Coelho, and the congressional Democrats. In 1986, Jackson took a leave of absence from the paper to write a book about the upcoming midterm elections. As part of his research, he followed the chairmen of both parties' campaign committees in the House. Because Coelho gave him unlimited access, Jackson saw firsthand how the Californian was orchestrating a revolution in party finances by raising extraordinary amounts of money from the savings and loan industry in a sprint to catch up to Republican corporate fund-raising.[69]

His first big article about the Speaker was published on August 5, 1987, titled HOUSE SPEAKER WRIGHT'S DEALINGS WITH DEVELOPER REVIVE QUESTIONS ABOUT HIS ETHICS AND JUDGMENT. Jackson examined Wright's relationship with Mallick, writing that he helped Wright "earn tens of thousands of dollars from real estate, oil wells and imported rubies." Jackson quickly picked up on the national implications. The ties between the two men, he said, threatened "to mar the Texan's auspicious start as a strong Democratic leader of the House." Jackson recounted allegations about Wright's Fort Worth friends and repeated Gingrich's accusation, frequently made in private with colleagues as well as to reporters, that Wright was "the least ethical speaker in the 20th century."[70]

These pieces, like larvae, hatched a swarm of pesky new reporting. Like Jackson, Charles Babcock of *The Washington Post* was one of the post-Watergate reporters interested in exposing the ways in which politicians abused their authority. In September, Babcock reported that Wright had earned a substantial amount of income through his relationship with William Carlos Moore, a printer and political consultant in Fort Worth. Moore helped the Texan find unsavory ways to make almost $55,000 between 1985 and 1987 by selling a slender book by Wright titled *Reflections of a Public Man*. The slapdash, 117-page volume, padded with blank spaces and empty pages, was composed of excerpts of Wright's speeches, writing, and notes.[71] As *The Washington Post* put it, "House Speaker Jim Wright (D-TX) has received almost $55,000 over the past two years as 'royalties' on a book he wrote in 1984 that was published by a longtime friend whose printing company was paid $265,000 for services to Wright's campaign committee last year."

Moore published the book himself and gave Wright royalties of 55 percent, far above the conventional rate of 10 percent earned by most authors. Babcock recounted to his readers the trouble that he had tracking down where any sales actually took place. The manager of the big downtown bookstore in Fort Worth, Barber's, reported having sold about a hundred books. Four other local merchants in the city had never stocked them. Moore explained that most of the copies were sold at "political rallies." Moore's background appeared to underscore the deal's corrupt character: years earlier, the consultant had worked in Washington as political director for the scandal-tainted Teamsters' union then led by Jimmy Hoffa. Wright fumed about Babcock's story because he never had staffers work on the project during their official time. Nor had he requested a large advance, he said, because he wanted the book to be sold at an affordable price. But none of that mattered. Now it was in *The Washington Post*. WRIGHT-GATE, blared the editorial headline in *The Detroit News*.[72]

Such stories convinced Republicans that Gingrich's strategy could work. During a series of closed-door September meetings, members of the Conservative Opportunity Society agreed that ethics—not such conservative chestnuts as anticommunism and dismantling the welfare state—would be the key theme of their plan to topple the Democratic majority.

At a September 9 meeting, Gingrich, Walker, and Bob Smith boasted about how positive the press had been "over the August break with regards to the recent ethics initiatives."[73] Just as he had in high school, Gingrich carried around an overflowing binder, now filled with press clippings of ethics stories about Wright and other members that he could hand out. He hoped to persuade the *700 Club*, a show on the Christian Broadcasting Network, to start broadcasting a regular feature called

"Ethics Watch."[74] On September 16, Gingrich told his closest allies that besides Wright sixteen other Democrats were being investigated by the Ethics Committee or the media, which proved "that this is a real and institutional fight, not a right-wing political vendetta."[75] One member, after listening to Gingrich, succinctly summarized the strategy: "If the Democrats can be made to be illegitimate ethically, they may be perceived as illegitimate politically."[76]

Gingrich sent out a letter to GOPAC members listing ten House Democrats who had been indicted or investigated for legal or ethics violations over the previous year (including Wright). "Together," Gingrich wrote, "we'll force the media to focus on this unprecedented partisan corruption of Congress, which I'm calling 'Sleaze-gate.' Gingrich anticipated that "by forcing the Ethics Committee to act, we can bring the media down on Democrats."[77]

The New Right was girding for the battle to challenge Wright's legitimacy. Ethics was Gingrich's battle ax, but he also had daggers and arrows in his arsenal. Whenever the Speaker appeared to overstep his authority, Gingrich would call him a tyrant, redefining the assertion of leadership as the abuse of power. As Gingrich hustled daily to attach a target to Wright's back by sending local press clippings to national reporters or calling them directly with tales of the latest misdeeds he'd discovered, the Speaker himself would come to embody the rampant partisanship of the Democratic Party.

One of the most dramatic early skirmishes involved a budget battle in October 1987. On October 19, the Dow Jones plunged 508 points after the preceding week set records for one-day losses. On the nineteenth, the Dow fell by 22.6 percent (this would be between 5,000 and 6,000 points today). "Really, it's a blood bath," one investment executive despaired.[78] Worried congressional leaders and White House officials, shocked by the enormity of the drop, convened an emergency summit on October 26 to reach a deal on a budget package that would reduce the $148 billion deficit and calm the markets. The president met with the "Big Five" leaders in Congress, including Wright, Tom Foley, the Senate majority leader, Robert Byrd, the Senate minority leader, Bob Dole, and Bob Michel. Secretary of the Treasury James Baker, the White House chief of staff, Howard Baker, and the White House budget director, James Miller, were there to be the president's eyes and ears. As the Oval Office summit got under way, Wright proposed a deficit-cutting reconciliation bill with $12 billion in higher revenues. Reagan suggested he might be open to raising taxes as part of a deal with the Democrats, but congressional Republicans refused to compromise.

Wright brought the deal to the floor without an agreement from the GOP. On October 29, he suffered a stinging defeat: a coalition of 169 Republicans and 48 Democrats voted against allowing his version of the budget legislation to come up for a vote. Conservatives hated the proposed higher taxes as well as a watered-down welfare reform program that Wright had included in the measure. Liberals were upset that he included higher defense spending to placate southern conservative Democrats. Wright desperately needed another round of voting to avoid a total defeat.[79]

The House rules stipulated that without unanimous consent Wright could not ask for another vote on a bill the same day that it was defeated. So Wright turned to a parliamentary trick and simply declared it a new legislative day—even holding a "morning prayer"—so that the House could vote again on the deficit-reduction measure before the actual day ended. Visibly outraged and outmaneuvered, Gingrich accused the Speaker of violating the will of the House by holding a second vote, wagging his finger at Wright before the C-SPAN cameras.

The situation only got worse when the House actually voted. According to a rule adopted in 1973, every recorded vote was supposed to last a minimum of fifteen minutes and then come to a close. However, the Speaker did have the discretion to keep the vote open longer, which many often had. But Republicans were going to be Talmudic about interpreting the rule. As Wright's team monitored the votes on the electronic board behind the rostrum, which listed each representative's name next to green or red lights for yes or no, the Speaker saw that he was about to lose again. The California Democrat George Miller, who was holding a grudge against the Speaker over an unrelated matter, voted no and left. Tom

Foley tried to stop him as he walked into the elevator, but Miller said nothing they could do would change his mind.

Desperate, Wright sent Coelho out to find the Texas congressman Jim Chapman, who had voted no but promised that he would switch if truly necessary. Coelho found Chapman sitting on a couch in a darkened area of the cloakroom and tried to call in that chit. But Chapman refused, saying he didn't want to risk his seat on this controversial decision. John Paul Mack, one of Wright's most trusted advisers, let Chapman know that he really didn't have the option.[80] He reminded Chapman how indebted he was to Wright, who had helped him win a special election two years earlier and steered the donations of savings and loan executives his way. Now was the time to return the favor.

As the clock reached the fifteen-minute mark, and as Gingrich and his comrades fretted on their backbench, Wright refused to state the results, even though the time for voting had expired. He was still one vote down. Members huddled in small groups trying to figure out what was going on, looking up at the clock, then down at Wright. Wright kept gently tapping his gavel against the lectern, delaying as long as possible. Republicans screamed at the Speaker to call the final results.

Wright announced that a member wanted to switch his vote. Chaos ensued. "Can we lock the damn door?" Trent Lott yelled, pounding the lectern in the well so hard that it bent.[81] Coelho appeared at the door to signal to Wright that the member in question was on the way.[82] Wright glanced at Coelho, and Republicans glared back at him. With tempers flaring, Mack escorted a sullen-looking Chapman back into the chamber. Republicans watched in shock as Chapman signed a card officially switching his vote from a nay to an aye, with Mack standing intimidatingly behind him in what looked to angry conservatives like a scene out of *The Godfather*. Ten minutes after the vote should have ended, Wright announced that the bill had passed, 206 to 205. Only one Republican—Jim Jeffords, a Watergate Baby from Vermont—had voted for it.

Republicans were livid. With C-SPAN covering the proceedings, viewers watched as their elected officials booed and hissed, making a spectacle reminiscent of the popular afternoon interview shows of the era, the crass brawls of *The Morton Downey Jr. Show*. Springing from his chair like a jack-in-the-box, Gingrich demanded that the House parliamentarian explain how Chapman could change his mind after Wright had announced that the vote was officially closed. Gingrich continued to protest, his nasal, high-pitched voice escalating and accusatory. Wright responded that he had the full authority to allow any member to change his vote as long as he was standing in the chamber—and then brought the discussion to a close. "He is a ruthless left-wing Democratic partisan imposing his will on the House," Gingrich told reporters as his closing statement.[83]

This overheated procedural brawl fit Gingrich's narrative. In a memo to colleagues, quoting Winston Churchill's "war is horrible, slavery is worse," Gingrich ominously proclaimed, "Given Wright-Foley-Coelho arrogance (and that of their party) we have no choice."[84] Ironically, Wright had swung his partisan fist so hard at the GOP that he ended up fomenting a backlash among a broader pool of Republicans against the old ways of doing business. More members of the GOP were starting to come around to Gingrich's point of view. Even Wright privately realized that he might have gone too far. "It has totally broken down cooperation between Democrats and Republicans. I have absolutely no respect for Jim Wright," said the Florida Republican Connie Mack. Dick Cheney growled to the *National Journal* that the Speaker had proven he was a "heavy-handed son of a bitch."[85]

A few weeks later, foreign policy provided the next partisan battleground between Wright and the Republicans. President Reagan had survived the congressional investigation into Iran-contra; the probe found extensive evidence that National Security Council and Pentagon officials had violated the law, but Congress found no "smoking gun" directly connecting Reagan to the secret assistance for the contras. The hearings unexpectedly turned one of the scheme's architects, the telegenic and entirely unapologetic Lieutenant Colonel Oliver North, into a hero. As "Olliemania" swept the country, with admirers buying T-shirts, posters, and pins of the document-shredding marine and National Security Council aide, Gingrich led Republicans in defending North and attacking the investigation as a partisan witch hunt.[86] "I do have some difficulty with those of our friends on the Left," Gingrich said at a speech in Williamsburg, "who are always sure America's wrong, and are always willing to humiliate America, and to weaken America, on the premise that we may become a wreck, but at least they'll own the wreckage."[87]

As Reagan's fortunes rebounded, Speaker Wright began promoting a peace plan for Nicaragua developed by the Costa Rican president, Oscar Arias. Democrats were excited to see the Speaker step into the fray. Nicaragua was a vital conflict where their party sought to take a stand on foreign policy by pushing back against the militaristic impulses of a conservative president who had forgotten the lessons of Vietnam. The Speaker's intervention posed a serious threat to Reagan, who was determined to rebuild political support for sending more U.S. assistance to the contras. Wright was doubly problematic for the White House because he was not an easy Democrat to attack as "soft on defense." Even Reagan administration officials had to admit that Wright had strongly supported their policies in El Salvador, even as liberals had blasted the administration for supporting a brutal right-wing regime. Wright had also backed the administration's requests for several high-cost weapon systems. Reagan had agreed to the Arias plan, which Wright also supported, back in August, before the Black Monday market crash. The Wright-Reagan agreement stipulated that the United States would temporarily withhold military assistance from the contras if the Nicaraguan government made concrete progress on a series of democratic reforms by a deadline of November 7.

Liberal Democrats felt Wright betrayed them by making a deal with the hawkish president, and Reagan hoped the tentative agreement would fall apart because his preference was to provide arms to the rebels. Much of the country, however, saw the deal as a stunning success for the Speaker, who had reached a compromise with the hawkish Reagan that advanced an objective—peace in Central America—that Democrats desired. "That's a real leadership thing Wright did," Gingrich later recalled thinking to himself. "We may be about to lock horns savagely over ethics, but that was real gutsy."[88]

To Wright, the biggest obstacle to implementing the plan was Reagan's refusal to speak with anyone from the Sandinista government. "How do you negotiate a cease-fire," Wright asked, "when the Sandinistas would talk to nobody but Reagan, and Reagan and the White House were saying there could be no talks between the Sandinistas directly and the contras?"[89] Having read extensively about South and Central American politics since his childhood in Texas, Wright believed that the United States had been too imperial in the region and Reagan needed to respect the regional governments, even the Sandinistas, to achieve peace. A U.S. president dictating the terms would never work.

Feeling intense pressure as the November deadline approached with no resolution in sight, the Sandinistas decided to open their own dialogue with the contras. Wright agreed to meet with the Nicaraguan president, Daniel Ortega, in his Capitol Hill office, without anyone from the administration present, on Wednesday, November 11. This was a bold move in a country where international diplomacy was usually handled by the executive branch. As snow fell over the city, Wright and Ortega met for an hour to discuss a fifteen-point cease-fire agreement. The Speaker told Ortega that he would need to avoid using confrontational language and to do more to guarantee political freedom for the opposition if he wanted the plan to succeed. Everyone understood that Wright was a huge risk taker, but an apparently unauthorized diplomatic meeting with one of Reagan's prime international adversaries seemed extraordinarily defiant.

Three days later, Wright met with Ortega again, this time for almost ninety minutes, and completed the outlines of a peace deal. With international observers looking on, the contras would desist from fighting, be granted amnesty, and be allowed to fully participate in Nicaragua's new democracy. Wright met with the visiting cardinal Miguel Obando y Bravo, the widely respected Catholic prelate of Nicaragua whom he had befriended during his trips to the region on congressional delegations, who told his old friend that upon his return he would be pleased to present the plan to the contra leaders.

At a November 13 press conference in the elegant Rayburn Room, Wright announced that these discussions had taken place. Standing before a copy of Gilbert Stuart's striking portrait of George Washington, Wright made his case calmly, insisting he was no Lone Ranger and claiming that he had told Secretary of State George Shultz about the ongoing discussions several times, including "last night" on the telephone.

Wright then flew back to his district for some scheduled events. When he landed in Meacham Field, the producers of *NBC Nightly News*, whose newscast was about to start, rushed Wright to a small, cramped airport office in which cameramen had already set up their equipment. The crew scrambled to clip a microphone onto Wright's tie, and the camera went live to a national audience. The anchor, Tom Brokaw, peppered Wright with hard-hitting questions, including whether Shultz had formally agreed to specific meetings with Ortega. Cool and composed, the Speaker reminded Brokaw that he did "not have to ask permission" to speak to anyone. Nevertheless, Wright said, neither Reagan nor Shultz expressed hesitation about his assisting on this matter.[90]

White House and State Department officials sent a very different message, making it clear that they did not approve of the Speaker's diplomacy.[91] The administration now said that Wright's actions had endangered the peace process: as a result of the Speaker's overreach, the State Department said, the Sandinistas felt less pressure to concede to democratic reforms.

The Speaker was furious: the White House was leaking comments about tensions between him and the president, and the story was featured in the Sunday newspapers and television talk shows. Wright had no doubt that Shultz knew about his negotiations and bristled that he was facing a made-up scandal orchestrated by his opponents.

With attacks raining down, Wright requested an immediate meeting with the president. By Wright's account, the forty-minute session on November 16 was tense. When the Speaker arrived at the Oval Office, Reagan "was angrier than I had ever seen him, stiff, and unbending." The president criticized Ortega as untrustworthy and complained that they now had a "Wright-Ortega plan."[92] He then walked out of the room without saying any more.

Reagan's team admonished Wright for talking to Ortega without knowing all the facts. "We let him have it pretty good," Reagan recounted in his diary.[93] A joke made its way around the White House: "Where are President Ortega and the Nicaraguan rebels going to meet? Speaker Wright's embassy."[94]

The situation deteriorated so badly that the Democratic power broker Robert Strauss, a Texan like Wright and a close friend of Shultz's, stepped in to negotiate a peace agreement between the two men. The resulting document, signed by both men on November 17, outlined a six-point agreement on how the peace process in Nicaragua should be handled by U.S. policy makers. The pact stipulated that the peace deal would be crafted by the Central American presidents rather than imposed on them by the United States and that negotiations would be handled by Central American officials without U.S. involvement unless requested. The United States would meet with the Sandinistas once it was clear that serious negotiations were under way. Wright convened a press conference alongside Shultz, with Strauss standing between them.[95] "The war is over," the White House spokesperson Marlin Fitzwater proclaimed.[96]

Brooding from his office in the Rayburn Building, Gingrich worried that Wright had gotten the upper hand. "Mr. Speaker," began a press statement by Gingrich, "your secret meeting with the Communist dictator on Veterans' Day was the most destructive undermining of U.S. foreign policy by a Speaker in our country's history."[97] During a speech to a group of Florida Republicans who were visiting Washington, Gingrich grew even more belligerent. He charged that the Speaker was "systematically undermining the foreign policy of the United States" and said that he was "so consumed by his own power that he is like Mussolini, believing he can redefine the game to suit his own needs."[98] When asked on CNN's *Larry King Live* about Gingrich's ire, Wright dismissed the irritating Georgian: "I don't pay too much attention to what Congressman Gingrich says. He says that kind of thing about Tip. He says it about me. He says it about all kinds of Democrats. That's his profession, and that's all right. I don't pay much attention to it."[99]

The White House might have agreed to a truce, but Wright's opponents had not. The Texas Republican Congressional Committee warned that Wright was "implementing his own personal foreign policy" and saw "no difference between fighting Communism and spreading Communism."[100] On one conservative talk radio show in Chicago, a listener called in to say that "somebody should blow [Wright] away."[101]

Something had clearly shifted in the 315 days since Wright first took up the Speaker's gavel. Every time he tried to do something bold, Republicans had used his actions as proof that Democrats were constantly abusing their power. "Wright's a useful keystone to a much bigger structure," Gingrich privately acknowledged to one reporter. "I'll just keep pounding and pounding on his ethics. There comes a point where it comes together and the media takes off on it, or it dies."[102] Toward the end of the year, Gingrich wrote to Ralph Nader, "We are now in the most frightening period in the history of the House of Representatives. If the current mood of 'acceptance corruption' is tolerated, it will grow into an ugly and destructive system of corrupt behavior. This pattern is ultimately a threat to the process of democracy."[103] Several major newspapers were working on stories about the Speaker's relationship to the savings and loan industry and other tales of alleged greed and poor judgment.[104] Little stories—such as the fact that Wright and a top Democratic campaign official had gone to meet with the New York City real estate developer Donald Trump in Trump Tower to try, unsuccessfully, to persuade the registered Republican to chair a major fund-raising event for the Democrats—were being picked up by journalists like Brooks Jackson as part of a bigger pattern.[105] "The allegations against Wright have been mounting for months," wrote Cort Kirkwood, author of the column Sleazewatch for the Washington-based wire service American Press International, "and they are now echoed not only by partisan opponents but in establishment organs like the *New York Times* and *Newsweek*."[106]

Wright and many other Democrats remained confident that they could swat away any threat posed by Gingrich. During a meeting with the editorial board of *USA Today*, Wright responded to a question from reporter Tracey Lyons about Gingrich's charges by explaining that he had learned that these kinds of investigations were now part and parcel of being Speaker. Party leaders had to expect to be the "target for poisoned arrows" from the partisan opposition. Gingrich had harassed Speaker O'Neill as well. Wright, who had "accepted that as part of the price you have to pay," indicated he was not very concerned. Using a sports metaphor, he reminisced about a friend who compared partisan politics to the game of "sack the quarterback." When a quarterback won nine games in a row, as Democrats had in Wright's first year as Speaker, the opposing team would send in its most "ugly, active, vicious, mean" tackle in the tenth game to try knocking the quarterback out of the game. The purpose was either to sideline the quarterback by injuring him or to incite him into an altercation so that the referee threw him off the field.[107] None of the stories floated by Gingrich involved serious matters, and in Wright's mind they weren't even true. Wright's friend Steve Jost of the Democratic Congressional Campaign Committee advised him to simply ignore the attacks from the arrogant little Georgian: "If you were not hitting the right chords, the hogs would not be howling so!"[108]

But other Democrats were starting to worry. Gingrich seemed to be gaining support from his party. The line that separated mainstream congressional Republicans from the Gingrich faction was getting harder to discern. House Republicans established a task force, headed by Dick Cheney, to map out a strategy for counteracting Wright's crushing tactics.[109] Gingrich didn't feel any pressure from his party to stop. "They were quite willing for *me* to do this. No one asked me to stop."[110] Almost everyone in the GOP, from President Reagan to the lowest-ranking House backbencher, was complaining about Democratic corruption and abuse of power. The whispers were becoming a roar. And none of them favored Speaker Wright.

Nor did many Democrats love the Speaker. Plenty of younger Democrats who'd cut their teeth in the post-Watergate era preferred a more reform-oriented leader. Other Democrats feared that Wright was far too hawkish on foreign policy. And most Democrats agreed, at least privately, that Wright had surrounded himself with too many shady people for his own good.

"There is a good feeling about success for the party," Representative Tim Penny, a moderate Democrat from Minnesota, told *The New York Times*, "but it's tempered by a nervousness about potential embarrassments."[111] A shared feeling began to take root among Democrats: if this wildfire continued to spread, the Speaker—and the entire party—could get badly burned.

Four

LEGITIMATING GINGRICH

In mid-December 1987, as Speaker Wright's first session came to an end, Gingrich asked his personal secretary, Laurie James, to step into his office. James had been feeling the tension around the watercooler as the holidays approached and the atmosphere in the House heated up. Always alert to Gingrich's moods, she sensed that her boss was getting ready to escalate. Now Gingrich surprised her with a dangerous gambit: he planned to file an ethics complaint against the Speaker.

Taking a second before responding, James shot Gingrich the kind of nervous look that a Hill staffer occasionally gives to a boss toying with a seemingly bad idea. Delicately, James asked Gingrich if he was concerned about the possible fallout from such a dramatic step. Gingrich compared himself to Martin Luther confronting the Diet of Worms in 1521. With righteous zeal, he said he needed to move against the Speaker, with or without his colleagues: "Here I stand. I can do no other. God help me."[1]

Gingrich knew that the Washington intelligentsia still dismissed him as a radical operating far outside the accepted norms of polite politics. He didn't care much about what they thought; he cared far more about getting them on board. He was a man on a mission, and he was certain that he knew better. When he looked around the House chamber at the senior

Democrats and Republicans, he did so with disdain, pleased to have gotten under their skin.

Gingrich felt good about the progress he'd made in diminishing the space that separated him from the rest of the Republican pack. Speaker Wright took solace in knowing that most of their colleagues remained skeptical about anything the baby-faced Georgian had to say. Gingrich knew that many in his caucus deplored his antics. But he also knew, absolutely knew, that being a provocateur, playing for the television cameras, deploying exaggerated rhetoric, goading his opponents into appearing to abuse their authority, and keeping the media focused squarely on him benefited all Republicans, even if they couldn't quite see it yet. If he became the prime driver behind ethics accusations against the Speaker, Democrats would expect the scandal to fizzle. They were wrong.

The major question facing Gingrich at the start of 1988 was how to persuade some of Washington's most prominent Republican officials— the Bushes, the Michels, the Cheneys—to go all in for his fiery campaign against Speaker Wright, even if they would have to hold their noses to do it. In February, Michel asked two Republican House members, Robert Livingston and Jim Sensenbrenner, to look into the stories contained in Gingrich's thick binder of newspaper clippings. They reported to the minority leader—and a livid Gingrich—that there was no basis for a formal complaint with the Ethics Committee.[2]

The media spotlight on Wright's missteps and relationships had drawn blood, but it had not been enough to sway the Republican Party's power brokers. Gingrich had them on board for his campaign against Democratic corruption and Wright's autocratic methods, but not for a historic effort to force the Speaker of the House from office. This, Gingrich understood, was an entirely different ball game.

And then he hit on his Big Idea.

The key to Gingrich's strategy would be winning support for his anti-Wright campaign from the reform-oriented institutions that had emerged after Watergate. He would go further than he had with Charlie Diggs in co-opting the government reforms of the 1970s for crass partisan objectives. If he could get respectable groups fighting for accountability in politics to enlist in his cause—making that the high road—then mainstream elected officials would have little choice but to follow. Without these reformers, Gingrich looked as if he were orchestrating a shabby partisan coup. They would offer reluctant Republicans the cover they needed to get behind him. This would be his masterstroke, and it would capitalize on the Democrats' shortsightedness.

The good-government organizations, ironically, were mostly liberal and thus usually disliked by Gingrich, their new suitor. They believed that the central lesson from Watergate was that politicians must be held accountable by rules and oversight. If the political process was not made to be more democratic and accountable, the good-government types argued, then politicians would never produce good policy. The reformist groups were usually worlds apart from Gingrich on policy questions. But Gingrich clearly saw the common ground on the issue of whether the political process was broken, especially with the growing clamor from post-Watergate journalists looking for official malfeasance. The reform organizations had the Washington clout to give credibility to Gingrich's allegations and the power to do real harm.

As Gingrich embarked on his quest for broader support, Wright kept bungling his responses. The Speaker's first major effort to quash the emerging ethics scandal took place through George Mair, an award-winning reporter whom Wright's chief of staff, Marshall Lynam, had brought on in December 1987 as the Speaker's chief press officer. Mair had been a respected syndicated columnist for the *Los Angeles Times* and the editor in chief and publisher of the *Alexandria Gazette*, as well as the author of ten books. Seasoned political hands such as Kirk O'Donnell, the former chief aide to Speaker O'Neill, told Wright that he should ignore the swirl of accusations. Wright decided to follow that advice, but in the meantime he hoped that Mair would swat away some of the charges and work behind the scenes to slow down the disparaging media coverage.

Unfortunately for Wright, Mair went too far in his first weeks on the job. The press officer sat at his typewriter and sent off blistering letters to the publishers of major newspapers and magazines in which he accused their reporters of falling back on slander and innuendo, even plagiarizing material, to make their case. Mair wrote to Mortimer Zuckerman, the editor of *U.S. News & World Report*, that his writers should get "their facts straight and deep-sixed [*sic*] the stereotypes." In response to a scathing article that appeared on December 21, 1987, Mair charged that a number of claims made about Wright's relationship with the "high-rolling Texans in the S&L business" were "flat-out wrong." Another *U.S. News* article about Wright's role in the negotiations with Nicaragua were "so totally without foundation that it boggles the mind to grasp." Mair was not diplomatic. To Robert Bartley, editor of *The Wall Street Journal*, he complained that he was surprised to see an article about the Speaker that was "marbled through with innuendo that is so far beneath the professional standards one used to expect from the Wall Street Journal." He wrote to the editor in chief of *Newsweek*, Richard Smith, "I know *NEWSWEEK* is in a circulation and advertising fight for its survival and that you're having to hype your sagging publication with stories on bra museums, angels of death and semi-nude female movie stars." Mair also accused two top *Los Angeles Times* reporters of writing an article that was "badly researched, poorly written and possibly plagiarized." On and on the letters went, volcanic eruptions that did little to aid the Speaker's case.[3]

Directly attacking the press was a dangerous strategy. They had a big platform from which to respond. And they did. The editors of these powerful publications were not going to sit by quietly as Mair delivered these reprimands and smeared the reputations of their top journalists. So, the editors exposed Mair's campaign by speaking to reporters. The story looked to many Americans like an effort to intimidate and harass honest journalists investigating potential corruption. Lynam reassigned Mair, and Wright convened a private luncheon with several of those directly maligned to apologize for Mair's actions. When the waiter came to serve the meal, Wright tried to lighten the mood by asking, "Is this crow? I'll ask for a generous serving."[4]

Gingrich used all of this as political fuel to keep the scandal going as nonpartisan voices took up the cause. Speaker Wright drew the critical eye of the most prestigious good-government reform group, Common Cause, in early March after *Bankers Monthly* published a bombshell about his relationships with shady savings and loan officials.[5] (The story had originally appeared in *Regardie's*, a local business magazine.) The scathing article from the muckraking journalists William Adler and Michael Binstein probed the nature of the Speaker's close relationship with an official named Donald Dixon. The allegations about the connections between two "good old boys" from Texas were shocking. Dixon had grown the Vernon Savings and Loan Association in Dallas from a thrift with holdings of $82 million in 1982 to an institution that was worth $1.4 billion a scant four years later. At the heart of this expansion were a series of high-risk construction loans that Dixon resold to smaller financial institutions. Then, like so many of these banks in the mid-1980s, Dixon's business crashed and burned in 1987 with the collapse of oil prices and the Texas economy. Wright, according to the authors, provided federal support to the Vernon Savings and Loan Association that allowed the unlikable Dixon to continue living an opulent lifestyle despite his business having gone bust.

The article opened with the tale of a February 1987 meeting where Wright allegedly appalled three high-level officials of the Federal Home Loan Bank Board. The board planned to shut down Dixon's failing thrift until the Speaker demanded, through a "string of colorful expletives," that they keep the institution up and running. They "sat tight-lipped, their expressions frozen," as the Speaker threatened to withhold his support for pending legislation to bail out struggling savings and loans unless the regulators took it easy on Dixon. "They were astonished that the Speaker," the authors said, "one of the most important people in American politics, was going to bat for a sleaze ball like Dixon, who exemplified an industry run amok." This, the journalists concluded, was nothing less than a morality tale "of greed and selfishness, of the abuse of power and wealth, of the perversion of democracy. It's another example of how Texas politicians carry the water for the state's business tycoons."

This story about the Speaker of the House caught the attention of Washington's pundits. When the piece appeared, Wright's allies realized that they had a serious political problem on their hands. It was the most highly charged accusation about Wright yet.

The reason the story instantly caught the attention of Common Cause was that it directly linked Congress's highest-ranking member to one of the biggest policy scandals of the era: the deregulation, collapse, and federal bailout of the savings and loan industry. Investigative reporters were discovering just how disastrous the deregulation of the early 1980s had been and how Congress was spending billions of dollars to save failed institutions in their states and districts. Democrats and Republicans had kept their mouths shut about what happened, because both parties were implicated in the fiasco. The federal bailouts had further supported many high-paid executives who had made extraordinarily risky investments and taken gratuitous, even obscenely high compensation. In March, a federal court indicted Thomas Gaubert, the savings and loan official who was Coelho's ally in Democratic fund-raising, for fraudulently using $8 million in federal loans as part of an elaborate deal to "flip" land. According to the indictment, Gaubert had purchased commercial land for less than fifty cents a square foot, financed through the Capitol Savings & Loan of Mount Pleasant, Iowa, and then sold the land to a company for $5.25 a square foot on the same day. The deal totaled $5.6 million. HOUSE SPEAKER'S ALLY IS INDICTED IN TEXAS LAND DEAL, blared The Wall Street Journal. If convicted, Gaubert would face up to twenty-seven years in prison.

After reading the Bankers Monthly story, Marshall Lynam gathered information from Wright's staff to poke holes in the narrative, even enlisting John Barry, a sharp Washington reporter then shadowing Wright as he researched a book about the Speaker. The Speaker and his staff were furious, alleging that the article was based on the outright manipulation of facts and false claims. Barry thought the piece, for which Adler and Binstein had not even conducted interviews, was shoddy, irresponsible, and flat-out wrong. He had written a letter to the editor of Regardie's rebutting the article and defending the integrity of a New York Times profile of Wright that he had published in November 1986,[6] from which the authors had borrowed heavily and cited incorrectly. Barry had been in the meeting with the federal regulators described in the article and insisted to Lynam, based on his handwritten notes, that their conversations with Wright had focused on the health of the regional economy of Texas and that there was never any discussion of a specific bank or individual until the regulators themselves brought it up. The Democratic power broker and fellow Texan Robert Strauss called for the meeting, not Wright. The only reason Wright agreed to meet with Dixon—who, Barry said, contacted the congressman himself—was the important role of the savings and loan industry in the Texas economy and the troubling complaints that Republican regulators were targeting them for partisan purposes.[7] As Barry explained, Vernon S&L was mentioned only when the regulators turned to Dixon's situation. In Barry's account, Wright didn't even seem to know who Dixon was. "At no time," Barry wrote, "did Wright ask anyone in the room to do anything whatsoever, of any kind, for any individual, or any individual company." Barry added that the profile was not accurate about the "facts of that meeting" and "distorted and misrepresented" quotations that they had "plagiarized" from his piece in *The New York Times*.[8]

Armed with this information, Lynam wrote to the board chairman of *Bankers Monthly*, the publisher Theodore Cross, to say that the piece was based on "grotesque distortions and deliberately contrived innuendo."[9] Hoping to prevent the publication of a second installment of the story promised for the next month, Robert Strauss burst unannounced into the meeting of the magazine's board of directors in their New York offices. Strauss threatened to sue Cross, Adler, and the entire organization for libel if they didn't destroy the remaining copies of the first issue and abandon their plans to publish the second installment, which evidently had already come off the press. The board sat in stunned silence listening to Strauss's tirade. Though Adler and Binstein insisted that their article was accurate, the publishers reprinted the April issue without the offending second installment.

But the damage was done. Since the article had first appeared, Gingrich had been carrying it around in his show-and-tell binder of clippings and sharing the piece with reporters. "I think you will find the material very disturbing," he warned Michael Barone of *The Washington Post*.[10] He wrote David Gergen, a former Reagan communications advisor who had started writing for *U.S. News & World Report*, to complain that his recent article about Attorney General Meese did not mention Wright's troubles. As a refresher, Gingrich attached two troubling articles about the Speaker. "I need your help and the help of *U.S. News and World Report*," in the fight against corruption, Gingrich proclaimed.[11] "The need to reveal to the public the corrupt nature of the Speaker of the House of Representatives," Gingrich wrote to Abe Rosenthal, associate editor of *The New York Times*, "is necessary if we are ever going to clean" up Washington. "Should a reporter be assigned to cover the story, may I suggest that they contact Karen Van Brocklin on my staff."[12] When he had sent a letter to every member of Congress explaining why Wright should be formally investigated, Adler and Binstein's work, with its eye-grabbing headline, THE SPEAKER AND THE SLEAZY BANKER, had been one of the key articles he attached to support his case. With the eye of a trained historian, Gingrich had a knack for framing the information in the most grandiose terms possible. He warned fellow legislators that the stories revealed they were facing an "ethics crisis" that "threatens the freedom and liberty of every American" and they had to act.[13] The respected *Los Angeles Times* correspondents Karen Tumulty and Sara Fritz also mentioned the piece in an article, giving the charges even more lift.

Until the *Bankers Monthly* article appeared, Common Cause had remained notably silent about Speaker Wright. As Gingrich emerged, predictably chasing and chastising, the leaders of the celebrated watchdog group worried about lending support to an investigation that was so rabidly partisan. The founders of Common Cause had worked hard to avoid anything that could justify the claim that government reform was a political issue as opposed to a bipartisan cause in the public interest. Though Gingrich had repeatedly pestered the organization's president, Fred Wertheimer, to take action against the Speaker,[14] Common Cause had ignored his pleas. Wertheimer didn't like Gingrich, and avoided his calls and shoved aside his letters. But Gingrich pressed on. "Given the key role

Common Cause has played on ethics," Gingrich complained to Wertheimer in a pointed letter about his silence, "your advice on which path to take is vital. Your silence in this matter weakens the cause of honest government."[15] Wertheimer didn't place much faith in Gingrich, feeling that the legislator pursued "situational ethics," using the House rules as a partisan bludgeon rather than as a "means to protect the integrity of the institution."[16] He wrote Gingrich that their efforts to strengthen congressional ethics "would be undertaken separately and independently of your own efforts."[17] But by the spring of 1988, the pressure on Wertheimer to request an investigation from the House Ethics Committee was becoming unbearable. The stream of news stories about Wright's sordid relationship with book publishers, Texas oil executives, and now savings and loan officials all made it hard for Common Cause to ignore the brewing scandal. On May 10, Wertheimer was particularly upset when *The Wall Street Journal* published a caustic editorial asking why Congress did not receive the same ethical scrutiny as the Reagan administration, which he read as a veiled attack on his organization.[18]

Common Cause's chairman, Archibald Cox, a hero from the Watergate scandal who had been the righteous victim of the Saturday Night Massacre, and Wertheimer decided shortly after the *Journal*'s editorial appeared that it was time to act.[19] Cox's decision to sign on with Wertheimer was significant. The former Watergate prosecutor and Harvard Law School professor stood for many Americans as the embodiment of political accountability. Cox's opinions carried substantial weight in any debate over political reform, given the experience that he had suffered through.

On May 18, Wertheimer sent a letter to the House Ethics Committee calling on Chairman Julian Dixon to launch a formal investigation into Wright. The letter to the California Democrat did not proclaim that Wright was guilty of any infraction, but citing the savings and loan stories as well as the *Washington Post* articles about Wright's book, Wertheimer explained, "Common Cause believes that it is in the best interests of the public, the House of Representatives, and of Speaker Wright for the House Ethics Committee to examine and resolve these matters."[20]

Wright was savvy enough to understand that Common Cause's letter would propel the story like a booster rocket, making it appear to be much more than partisan slander. The letter brought the full weight of the reform world, which was usually seen as a force of good to those who lived outside Washington. One Democrat confidentially admitted, "The fact that an 'objective' public interest group has taken the step gives some greater credibility to what has been a partisan effort."[21] Wright tried to assure House Democrats in a closed-door meeting that this scandal would not be a serious problem for the party, arguing that this was all a grandstanding Republican effort to shift public attention away from the scandals plaguing the Reagan administration itself. Wright's colleagues—moved by his persuasive powers or their feelings of kinship—showed their support by giving him a standing ovation at the conclusion of his speech.

On May 24, Wright took his case to the public by appearing on CNN's *Larry King Live*. When King asked the Speaker about the ethics charges, Wright was ready: "I have written to the Chairman of the Ethics Committee and have said to him that, in light of all this public talk, if he wants to look into it, fine. He will have my full cooperation." Common Cause's Wertheimer responded to Wright's remarks by going even further. He called on the Ethics Committee to appoint an independent prosecutor to ensure a fair investigation.[22]

The Common Cause report had changed everything. For while it was possible that Common Cause could keep politics out of its own internal decision-making process, it was illusory for it to think it could prevent government reform from becoming weaponized in the partisan wars of Washington. Within an instant of the letter going public, Gingrich sent a missive of his own asking colleagues, "How much evidence does it take to 'merit further inquiry' by the House Ethics Committee?" In addition to four editorials from *The Wall Street Journal*, *The Atlanta Constitution*, the *Fort Worth Star-Telegram*, and *The Dallas Morning News* supporting an investigation, Gingrich attached the letter from Common Cause, the gold standard of good-government reform.[23]

The dominoes started to fall. The scandal gained national visibility when Republicans entered it into the presidential election. In the summer of 1988, Vice President George H. W. Bush, the Republican nominee for president, joined the campaign against the Speaker. Unlike Robert Michel, a figure largely unknown to the American public, Bush could sway the national debate with a mere utterance. And Speaker Wright's problems were politically attractive to the GOP standard-bearer because his opponent in the presidential race was going to be the Massachusetts governor, Michael Dukakis, a liberal technocrat who promised that under his watch he would hold the federal government accountable. A central line of attack for the squeaky-clean Dukakis was the ethical baggage that Vice President Bush carried from his time in the Reagan administration.

Republicans were worried. Dukakis was polling extremely well in April and May. Very few vice presidential candidates had been elected to succeed two-term presidents, and Bush seemed like a weak candidate, despite his unexpectedly strong performance in the Republican primaries. The silver-spooned vice president had shortcomings as a leader (*Newsweek* featured a story about what it called his "wimp factor"). Although he had held a seat in Congress, led the Republican National Committee, and directed the CIA, he struggled to articulate his vision in front of television cameras. A *Doonesbury* comic strip teased him for "placing his political manhood in a blind trust." Bush struggled to shed his patrician image, botching carefully choreographed photo ops. His aides winced at a New Hampshire truck stop when the candidate asked for a "splash" of coffee. His sojourns to the massive Bush family compound in Maine didn't help matters with middle-class Americans.[24] Wright once joked that Bush was "the only Texan I know who eats lobster with his chili."[25] Even President Reagan was lukewarm about Bush. He worried, as many on the Right did, about how committed Bush would be to the conservative cause.

Republicans grew more anxious when Dukakis focused in early May on what he called the "sleaze factor" in the executive branch. For the Massachusetts governor, Iran-contra proved that the Republicans could not be trusted with power.[26] Dukakis hammered away at the point at every campaign stop: White House operatives had intentionally subverted the law, abused their authority, and hidden their actions with the intention of evading congressional restrictions. Moreover, the vice president was directly implicated in the scandal. There was documented evidence that he knew about the operations. After Oliver North and the former national security adviser John Poindexter were indicted on charges of conspiracy, he had declared that he was friends with both men. As the venerable conservative *Wall Street Journal* concluded, Bush could not "dispel his Iran contra problems."[27]

Dukakis also pointed to other controversies in the Reagan administration that were producing a "cloud of corruption" over the executive branch. These included a scandal surrounding Attorney General Edwin Meese, who was being investigated by an independent prosecutor for alleged financial improprieties involving a pipeline construction deal in the Middle East, and an ongoing investigation in the Pentagon involving billions of dollars in fraudulent contracts. The Pentagon had spent a stunning $640 each on aircraft toilet seats and more than $400 each on basic wrenches—high-priced payoffs to loyal contractors. Republicans, including Gingrich, were desperate to turn attention toward other issues as soon as possible. The opinion that Reagan had run the "most corrupt administration" in American history was prevalent in Democratic circles. When Dukakis brought the sleaze factor up in his stump speeches, the attacks ignited the crowds.

Bush's campaign adviser Roger Ailes, who had started his career in politics through advising President Nixon, urged Vice President Bush to go on the offensive. He needed to start delivering tougher campaign speeches and airing attack ads to cut Dukakis down to size. When Bush confessed that he worried these tactics would make him look desperate, Ailes responded, "We *are* desperate."[28]

Bush knew that he had to respond before his opponent cemented this perception of him in the public imagination. The task fell on the shoulders of his campaign manager, the hard-hitting, street-brawling South Carolinian Lee Atwater, a veteran of Reagan's 1980 campaign. When Atwater had a politician in his crosshairs, he could be extremely dangerous. Atwater was to presidential campaigns what the anti-establishment Gingrich was to Congress. One mentor described him as having the "eyes of a killer," and another observer described him as the "Babe Ruth of negative politics."[29] Atwater practiced a no-holds-barred style, where the goal was to destroy the reputation of an opponent. Rip apart his character, Atwater argued, and then what an opponent said simply wouldn't matter. Atwater often compared politics to his favorite form of entertainment— professional wrestling.

Gingrich and Atwater could have been brothers born to different mothers. Atwater had first brought Gingrich to the attention of high-level Reagan officials in 1981, describing him as one of the rising congressional stars taking over from the vanishing Dixiecrats.[30] The two men, along with Ed Rollins and Lyn Nofziger, had served on the informal advisory group that helped Reagan plan for his reelection campaign. Like Gingrich, Atwater believed in a vicious approach to politics and saw the media as the central arena through which electoral struggles played out. The art of politics, in their minds, was as much about the theater of partisanship as about policy. Although Gingrich was much more serious than the frathouse, rock-'n'-roll-loving Atwater, they were kindred spirits in their tactics for how Republicans could gain power.

Now the shrewd campaign manager thought about how to get his mild and diffident patrician into the cutthroat mentality that he needed to combat Dukakis. With Dukakis up by seventeen points in mid-May, Atwater responded by trying to make the Democrat look guilty by association. While it was difficult for Bush or Atwater to tar and feather Dukakis, given that his personal and professional record was as clean as a whistle, they did see an opening to connect the candidate to a corrupt Democratic Party, which was headed by Speaker Wright. As Speaker, Wright would be in the television spotlight as he chaired the Democratic convention in Atlanta. If the Republicans played their cards right, seeing the Speaker on-screen would remind voters about the corruption of the Democratic

Party at a pivotal moment in Dukakis's campaign. With Atwater at the helm in the Bush campaign, Gingrich could sit back and watch the presidential candidate do the damage for him.

Maybe it was the influence of Atwater, or perhaps it was the pressure to prove his grit, but Vice President Bush decided to jump in headfirst. Wright didn't see this coming, nor did most Democrats or Republicans. Bush was not known for making the kinds of slash-and-burn attacks that were becoming popular in the House. And as fellow Texans, Bush and Wright had enjoyed cordial relations until that point.

At an appearance in New Jersey, the gentle scion of the "civil" Republican establishment seized the opportunity to change the conversation: "I wonder if Michael Dukakis and Jesse Jackson will join me in calling for the House of Representatives to appoint a special prosecutor to look into its own troubles, starting with the Speaker of the House of Representatives."[31] Bush repeated the challenge in the coming weeks. "Talk about ethics. You talk about Ed Meese?" Bush pondered. "How about talking about what Common Cause raised about the Speaker the other day? Are they going to look into it? Are they going to go for an independent counsel so the nation will have this full investigation? Why don't people call out for that? I will right now. I think they ought to."[32]

Like many Republican leaders at the time, Bush knew that the charges against his colleague from the Lone Star State were based on flimsy evidence—speculative media pieces that alleged technical violations of ethics rules that few members of Congress followed. Nothing that Wright was accused of rose to the level of high crimes and misdemeanors. The worst allegations, regarding Wright's relationship to the savings and loan industry, were based on hearsay and questionable journalism. But the vice president sensed that there was enough "there there" to make the rhetoric stick. And in fact, the tactic succeeded insofar as it took the focus off Republican wrongdoings. One top aide to Michel, Johanna Schneider, believed that Wright's predicament "minimizes the ability of Democrats to use the 'sleaze factor' against George Bush."[33]

Gingrich felt that it was time to make the investigation official. On the morning of May 26, after giving the press advance notice, Gingrich took a stroll on the first floor of the Capitol toward the office of the sergeant at arms. Tailed by reporters throwing out questions, a somber Gingrich walked past the Board of Education room, where Wright was having a breakfast meeting, oblivious to what was happening outside. Gingrich entered the office of the sergeant at arms, where members could deposit checks and notarize documents. The office looked like a small-town bank, with chipped paint on the walls and a long counter of teller windows. Secretarial staff were on hand to help members with everything from parking to security to office support, and Gingrich asked a clerk to notarize his complaint against Wright. Then, with the document in hand, Gingrich headed directly to the reception room for the Ethics Committee. He had engaged in a lot of hijinks since coming to Washington, but now he was filing formal ethics charges against the most powerful person in Congress.

Signed by 72 out of 177 House Republicans, the official ethics complaint that Gingrich submitted alleged "highly questionable conduct" and enumerated four major "areas" that he said warranted investigation. The first charged that Wright had written to the Egyptian president, Anwar Sadat, in March 1979 requesting assistance in relation to the investments in Egypt that had allegedly been made by Neptune Oil. The complaint suggested that Wright did this in exchange for a favorable deal on an investment in a Texas oil well. This would have been a violation of a House rule that prohibited members of Congress from receiving compensation from any private individual who could directly benefit from their position of power.

The second charge revolved around another oil deal. Wright sent a letter to Secretary of the Interior Cecil Andrus in September 1979 requesting help in an oil lease dispute in Arkansas. Gingrich claimed that Wright's goal was to use his influence to assist Texas Oil, a company in which he had, according to the news stories, purchased stock.

The third accusation from the Republicans centered on the book deal with William Carlos Moore that had been reported in *The Washington Post*. If this story was true, Gingrich charged, Wright violated another House rule. Gingrich noted that normal book royalties were about 10 to

20 percent, far below the 55 percent the congressman received from Moore. Furthermore, the royalty deal was given to Wright by a person who had been convicted for tax fraud. Gingrich also alleged that Wright used some of the royalties to pay for services performed by companies owned by Moore that had been involved in Wright's campaigns, a clear ethics violation. Because Moore received payment for campaign work in 1985 and 1986, Gingrich saw this all as a "thinly disguised way to launder campaign funds."

The final charge Gingrich raised in his letter was that one of Wright's speechwriters, Matthew Cossolotto, worked on the book. Ethics rules strictly prohibited staff from performing private work for members. This rule was the vaguest of all, because staffers commonly helped produce these kinds of publications. Politicians claimed that some of these books were not "private" work at all but rather a mechanism for them to convey their message to the public as legislators.

All of the accusations were based on thin evidence from the newspaper clippings that had been collected by Karen Van Brocklin, which Gingrich's office nonetheless claimed met the "evidence standard" to trigger an investigation. "We are not an investigative team," Van Brocklin slyly said to reporters, "so we have to rely on the press for a lot of information. That's what they're there for. And we believe there's enough stuff out there that looks funny."[34] Yet Gingrich was remarkably candid about how speculative the evidence was. Pressed by *New York Times* reporter Jeff Gerth, who had cut his teeth investigating Watergate for George McGovern's 1972 campaign, Gingrich admitted that the charges about the oil investments, for instance, were not "actionable." He conceded that by the time he had sent his letter to the Ethics Committee, journalists had already confirmed that Wright never purchased any stock in Texas Oil. And Gingrich freely acknowledged that he had no evidence for his claim that the investment with Neptune Oil was risk-free. Jeffrey Smith, a lawyer who helped to draft Gingrich's complaint, stated publicly that the House rules on outside income were not intended to apply to book royalties, and even Gingrich granted that he had no firm evidence that there had been a scheme to launder the book royalties into campaign activities.[35] But none of this stopped him from formally injecting the charges into the record. Given that the accused was the House Speaker, Gingrich knew it would create a media frenzy, something that was far too tempting to pass up, and the accusations themselves, opaque as an oil slick, would be difficult for Wright to clean up.

Even the editors of *The New York Times* now agreed that the complaints about Wright had for too long been "dismissed" as "politically inspired." Ever suspicious about the motivations of the GOP, the *Times* editors concluded that "a credible investigation is needed. . . . There's no taking politics out of ethics accusations in this election year, but the time has come to get the facts—and get them out."[36]

Conservative organizations were enthralled by this turn of events. Citizens for Reagan, a grassroots organization that had been hounding Wright in his home district since the 1980 election, sent out a press release to its seventy thousand members urging, "Your help needed to expose most corrupt Speaker in history," a phrase that borrowed directly from Gingrich's rhetoric. The Citizens for Reagan letter also spoke about Wright's dealings with Nicaragua and claimed that "his Speakership has been marked by dishonesty, lying, intimidation, and the use of a host of anti-democratic practices" like the budget reconciliation vote. The broadsheet concluded by asking citizens to alert their representatives and to write to the Ethics Committee, as well as the editors of their local newspapers.[37] The next morning, Dick Cheney walked over to Gingrich while they were in the middle of a quorum call to whisper, "You're not alone."[38]

Now Wright was starting to worry. He had seen how the winds of reform could fundamentally shake Capitol Hill. The Speaker would sit in front of his stately wood desk overflowing with memoranda, handwritten messages, and letters from constituents and colleagues, trying to figure out what he could do to make Gingrich disappear. He didn't want to focus on this. Yet he had no choice. The aura of power that emanated from the Speaker's suite could not displace the threat of an opponent who was aiming for his head.[39]

Michel was isolated, too. The rest of the Republican leadership had signed on with Gingrich. Michel was now calling himself the "Republican" rather than "minority" leader because, as Wright later recalled, "he was being driven by an insistent, vocal band of mostly younger Republican members to act in a more vigorously partisan way. I always felt it went against the grain of his nature, but he had been slowly yielding to their demands with increasingly forceful and partisan statements."[40]

The question on Speaker Wright's mind was this: What would Sam Rayburn have done? Unfortunately for Wright, his mentor was no longer alive to guide him toward political safety. Lyndon Johnson would surely have known how to crush an antagonist like Gingrich, but he had passed away in 1973. Most of the Democratic members in the Texas delegation, one of the most sizable in the House, who would ordinarily be expected to serve as Wright's most powerful allies, were relative newcomers to Capitol Hill—a result of the turnover the Texas Democratic delegation experienced in the mid-1970s. Many of the delegation's giants, like William R. Poage, had been swept away by the post-Watergate reforms. Most Texans in the House lacked the institutional know-how or gravitas to offer their fellow Texan much support. Unfortunately for Wright, he and the irascible Jack Brooks—the one Texan with the muscle and knowledge to offer guidance—had a lukewarm relationship. Wright had never forgiven Brooks for voting for another candidate for majority leader in 1976.[41]

To survive this investigation, Wright would need to find a good attorney. A few weeks earlier, Marshall Lynam had invited the forty-seven-year-old William Oldaker, a veteran at one of Washington's most prestigious law firms, to discuss a number of issues. Their conversation quickly turned to ethics. Oldaker's last major job had been working on the 1987 presidential campaign of Delaware senator Joe Biden, whose candidacy crashed as a result of a plagiarism scandal. Satisfied with what he heard, Lynam ushered Oldaker into Wright's office. The two men spoke for another half an hour, and the Speaker hired him on the spot.

Oldaker seemed like a good choice. He was one of those Washington insiders who knew the key players in town and had a sense of just how rough partisan politics could become—or so he thought. Oldaker had his work cut out for him. Wright made it clear he would spend as little time as possible on this matter, believing it to be a distraction. He hoped that simply lawyering up would quash the problem.[42]

Julian Dixon, the affable fifty-three-year-old California congressman, was in an uncomfortable position for a Democrat. Being the chairman of the House Committee on Standards of Official Conduct, known as the House Ethics Committee, was a thankless job. Nobody wanted to sit in judgment of the colleagues they ate with in the Members' Dining Room, worked out next to in the basement gym, and deliberated with in committee rooms and the House chamber. Dixon had been closely following Speaker Wright's case in the newspapers, hoping that the issue would be resolved before it ever reached the Ethics Committee. When he learned about the request from Common Cause, his hope was gone. The Wright saga had fallen directly into his lap.

The House Ethics Committee had earned a bad reputation since its creation in 1967. The solution for previous chairmen of this panel, like John Flynt, had been to do nothing when a complaint was made. With Democrats in perpetual control of the House, Republicans saw the committee as one more example of how the opposition abused their power to protect their own members, regardless of the sordid behavior that ethics investigations turned up. And yet the committee's ineffectualness was appreciated by many Republicans who took comfort that the committee was hesitant to police its fellow members. An investigation would barely produce a shudder from the accused member. For years, an assignment on the Ethics Committee had been regarded as a demotion or, at best, an easy job that freed up a member to spend time working on other issues.

One of the most egregious examples of committee inaction—especially in the minds of critics like Newt Gingrich—had taken place right after Dixon took over the chairmanship in 1985. The Rhode Island Democrat Fernand "Freddie" St. Germain was the focus of a high-profile ethics inquiry related to the savings and loan industry. St. Germain, the chairman of the House Banking, Finance, and Urban Affairs Committee, was accused of accepting thousands of dollars in dinners, entertainment, and travel from savings and loan officials in exchange for his authorship of the 1982 legislation that deregulated the industry.[43] A fourteen-month investigation produced a fourteen-hundred-page report, yet the committee did not recommend punishment. No action was taken, Dixon explained, because there wasn't sufficient evidence that St. Germain had broken any of the congressional ethics rules. His only proven sin, based on the months-long investigation, was doing a sloppy job filling out the financial disclosure forms, which, in Dixon's mind, was not deserving of punishment. If the Democrats wanted to strip St. Germain of his chairmanship or other privileges, that was their prerogative, not his. Dixon did not feel that the committee could go beyond the House rules in dictating behavior, no matter how noxious it seemed, particularly if the Ethics Committee was going to avoid misusing its authority. Critics called the decision an outrage, and Dixon was badly stung by the affair.[44]

After this controversial decision, Dixon was desperate to improve the reputation of the Ethics Committee. He respected Wright as a legislator's legislator, yet understood that investigating the Speaker could lead citizens to believe committee members were serious about doing their job. Dixon could not risk giving Gingrich even the slightest opening that he was not conducting a tough inquiry. Nothing short of a thorough investigation was required.

The action now shifted to one of the more inauspicious spaces in Washington, room HT-2N, a cramped basement chamber in the west front of the Capitol that housed the House Ethics Committee. To get to HT-2N, legislators had to take an elevator down to an unmarked and darkened corridor, devoid of artwork or the tourists who enlivened the rest of the building. Buckets lined the barely lit hallways to catch water dripping down from leaking pipes.[45]

On June 9, the committee met in a closed session for eight and a half hours. The twelve members, the only committee designed to be equally divided between Democrats and Republicans, huddled around a narrow wooden conference table, engaged in what an anonymous source called a "grueling discourse" about all of the charges Gingrich had raised.[46] The committee's Republicans did not hesitate to vote in favor of a formal investigation, but Democrats were loath to open the door to a politically damaging process. The meeting took hours because Dixon refused to conclude until he had a unanimous decision. One Democrat held out until the very end. A bleary-eyed Dixon, sensing that he was on the cusp of turning him in favor of a yes, popped his head out of the room to tell the reporters that they were still working on their decision and would issue a "statement or a status report" the following day. Speaker Wright, eager to know the outcome, was back home with Betty in McLean, Virginia, while Gingrich finished up dinner at a Capitol Hill eatery where he spent the evening enjoying the attention of a reporter.

At noon on June 10, Dixon emerged from the cloistered committee room to make his announcement. As reporters flocked around him, he began with a warning that his statement would be short and that he would take no questions. His staffer would handle the rest. Looking tired from the long deliberations of the previous day, he stated without emotion that the committee had voted unanimously in favor of a formal investigation into whether Speaker Wright violated the House rules. Wright, he said, had been informed about the decision and promised to cooperate. "I'm sorry I can't answer any questions," he said as he walked away, turning the press over to his aide. Dixon wanted to make it crystal clear that he was taking on this responsibility as his obligation to the House rather than out of any craving for media attention.

Dixon's senior staffer jumped into the horde. There would first be a "preliminary inquiry" by the committee, the aide explained in clinical fashion, something along the lines of a grand jury investigation, into six of the accusations raised by Gingrich and Common Cause. The burden of proof was relatively low at this stage, because the committee was charged only with determining whether there was reason to believe a legislator was guilty. Once they concluded this stage of the process, the committee would issue a report outlining their findings. If there was sufficient reason to believe that the Speaker had violated the rules, the committee would begin a second stage, more like a legal trial, where the standards of evidence would be much higher and where Wright would have an opportunity to present his case to the committee.

As Dixon retreated from the harsh glare of the cameras into the committee room, Wright and Gingrich, who had been watching on television sets in their respective offices, absorbed the news. For Gingrich, it was an exquisite validation. The unanimous decision vastly diminished the ability of Wright's supporters to claim this was all about politics. This outcome could not have gone better for the Gingrich camp.

The Speaker responded to Dixon's announcement by convening a press conference. With reporters clamoring, Wright said that he welcomed the investigation and wanted to appear before the committee as soon as possible; he had nothing to hide. Standing behind a lectern and in front of an elegant, packed bookshelf with bound volumes of the *Congressional Record*, Wright acted as if he were in good spirits. But C-SPAN viewers could see the beads of sweat trickling down his forehead under the glare of the lights. With William Oldaker and Tom Foley, the Democrat majority leader, flanking him, Wright insisted he was confident that the committee would see that he had not violated any rule. Oldaker had already given the press a twenty-three-page narrative rebutting every charge. When one reporter asked Wright to walk them through the various charges, the Speaker did so without any appearance of guilt or shame. He spoke slowly and with the same modulated cadence in which he delivered his floor oratory. Straining to show a tense smile, Wright explained why each charge was dead wrong. He would occasionally glance over to Oldaker as he spoke, pausing as if to seek confirmation that his answer was on point. Each accusation, in his account, was either bogus, a gross misreading of the ethics rules, or a total misrepresentation of the facts.

The most difficult question came toward the end, when one reporter pressed the Speaker on having his staffer work on his book. Wright first responded that it was always hard for members to determine what was public versus private business. When a reporter asked in disbelief if he didn't see a problem with a publicly paid staffer working on a book that brought the Speaker personal profit, Wright struggled with his response, talking about how proud he was to write this book and how he had done all the work on it by himself. Profit, he insisted, was not his motive. The reporter pressed him further on the staff member's work, suggesting that there would be a "howl" around the Hill if Ronald Reagan's beleaguered attorney general Edwin Meese had done this. "Perhaps," Wright admitted, it might be good if Congress imposed a tighter standard. He had made a few mistakes in judgment, he acknowledged. Still he insisted, shaking his head, he had broken no rules. When a reporter yelled out a question if all of this was retribution for the scandals that dogged Meese, the Speaker couldn't help himself. He turned around before walking out the door, saying, "I think you answered your own question." Then he disappeared into the dark of the adjoining room.

Wright was all over the Sunday morning talk shows a few days later, although his feigned, made-for-television charm was absent. He bridled with anger when the anchor on *Face the Nation,* Phil Jones, questioned whether it would be right for him to chair the Democratic National Convention in July with "this cloud over your head." "There is no cloud over my head," Wright responded indignantly. "No sir, I don't accept that one second."[47] On ABC's *This Week* the Speaker insisted, "I have violated no rule, I'm certain. I may have done some things one time and another in my career that were bad judgment, but whatever mistakes I made have not been dishonest."[48]

Joining Gingrich, who favored strengthening the investigation with the appointment of an independent prosecutor, the most prominent Republican figure of all stepped in to share his opinion. Although presidents traditionally stayed out of the internal affairs of Congress, at least in public, on June 15, President Reagan told a group of reporters that he supported such a move. "I think everyone would feel that it was more proper if it was done by an investigator outside, an appointed investigator," the president said in an interview with a gaggle of reporters.[49]

The press corps wasn't buying Speaker Wright's side of the story. A torrent of articles followed, all of them raising the new question about whether Wright was the best face for the Democratic Party. The editorial pages of the local press were brutal—with headlines like SPEAKERGATE, CONTD. in the *Boston Herald* and LET THE INQUIRY BEGIN in *The Albuquerque Tribune*—while the national media coverage was not much better.[50] "Sleaze is a word the Republicans have had to live with for much of

Ronald Reagan's second term. Now Edwin Meese will have some Democratic company in the public dock," according to a piece in *Time*.[51] A particularly blistering article appeared in the June 20 issue of *The New Republic* titled ALBATROSS. Robert Wright, one of the liberal magazine's editors, wrote, "Since coming to Washington 34 years ago, he's done a number of things that belong somewhere on the ethics spectrum between shady and criminal." The magazine, which prided itself on being the voice of post-Reagan liberalism, called on Democrats to embrace the investigation and concluded by saying that "the post-Watergate world calls for party leaders who are cleaner than tradition dictates." The editors of the magazine, through this piece, were publicly calling on Democrats to consider a new leader, a stunning legitimization of the investigation.[52]

Moreover, the *New Republic* piece captured the generational tensions that were unfolding as the press tried to make sense of the Speaker and the deeper issues the widening scandal laid bare. Robert Wright, who was thirty-one, stepped into this partisan tempest not fully aware of the implications of what he wrote. New to political reporting, he had just moved to Washington from New York, where the editorial staff assigned him this story because nobody else was available that week. He later said that the assignment was "an aberration." He didn't have any expertise in congressional politics, and his opinions were based primarily on gut-level conclusions he drew during his reporting.

The influx of young journalists like Wright, eager to replicate the kind of hard-hitting work of Woodward and Bernstein in the 1970s, created a massive opportunity for renegades like Gingrich. Well intentioned and often well educated, most of the up-and-coming stars of the media didn't have a strong grasp of how politics worked in Washington. They arrived with strong convictions about government and political ethics. But they weren't fully prepared for the ways in which savvy politicians could play them for their own partisan purposes. Gingrich instinctively grasped the possibilities for taking advantage of their idealism; he would throw gasoline onto the fire with one accusation after the other, knowing that the press would eat it up and respond with genuine investigative concerns or for good copy. As a result, the scandal kept growing. "I've had two investigative reporters tell me," Gingrich said, "that when you get involved in this kind of process, it just accelerates—the more you find out, the more damaging it is. I think we might see the end of Wright as speaker before the end of the year."[53]

In an interview with C-SPAN soon after publication, the clean-cut Robert Wright, who dressed true to type by wearing a tweed jacket, appeared nervous and was uncertain about some of the basic information asked of him on live television. His fresh face and meticulous grooming made him look extraordinarily young, reminding viewers that this was not a journalist with deep experience covering Washington. On camera he backpedaled. With a slight hint of an Oklahoma accent, Wright acknowledged that the Speaker didn't do anything illegal. Nor was it clear, he said, that the Speaker had technically violated any ethics rules, other than the most recent allegation that a staffer might have helped with the book while being paid by taxpayers (though he acknowledged that other legislators did the same). Throughout the discussion, the editor displayed a precarious grasp of the congressional rules at the heart of the case and the history of other leaders who had struggled with comparable challenges.

Robert Wright felt that he knew enough to understand that something was wrong. Watergate taught the nation that you didn't need to be an expert to spot an abuse of power. In fact, many of the experts had missed the story, the same way they had with Vietnam. Younger reporters felt that they had to be willing to analyze what they were seeing in politics with their own eyes without being scared off by the conventional wisdom of Washington. The *New Republic* editor told C-SPAN that the political class had been "playing fast and loose with ethics for a long time now" and that these kinds of questions had become more prominent and relevant since Watergate.[54] His bigger point was that the Speaker was not the best voice for Democrats post-Watergate, even if his actions were "hardly unheard of in politics." Justifying one's behavior as part of the status quo was no longer tolerable for many reporters when the status quo didn't work.

From Wright's perspective during that summer of 1988, his biggest advantage was the composition of the Ethics Committee. None of the twelve members, not even the six Republicans, seemed especially eager to take on this challenge. Moreover, Wright knew each panel member fairly well; he had been responsible for the appointments of the Democrats, and he was confident that when they heard the facts, they would not produce a negative report. And fortunately for him, even the committee's Republicans were not the most partisan in the GOP. He would keep appealing to the committee members throughout the process, on the assumption they agreed with him, that nobody wanted the kind of impediment or distraction to the serious business of legislating that an investigation would inevitably produce. Most of the committee members would be reluctant to take on someone as powerful as the Speaker, fearing the inevitable fallout that would result if they missed their target. Journalists tended to agree. In *Newsweek*, reporters noted that the committee "rarely votes to censure." The idea of a punishment more severe than that was beyond the realm of possibility.[55]

To an extent, Wright had correctly sized up his jury. The Republican side of the committee seemed like a relatively tame bunch. The member most likely to be a problem was George "Hank" Brown from Colorado. A fiscal hawk who had served in Vietnam, Brown had broken with President Reagan in the early 1980s after concluding that the administration was spending too much. As a Coloradoan, he was an advocate of environmental programs, for which the Reagan administration had little appetite. Brown, whom one reporter described as the "picture of distilled earnestness," developed close ties with Gingrich and his campaign against corruption. Another potential warning sign was that Brown took the responsibilities of the committee very seriously.[56] He wanted to demonstrate that the Ethics Committee could take action, because he believed that it tended to "bend over backward" to help fellow members, even when they acted in "egregious ways."[57] Brown also had a personal vendetta against Wright for having short-circuited his welfare reform package during the budget reconciliation battle in October 1987.

Another staunchly conservative GOP member, Larry Craig, seemed to be compromised. A lanky right-winger with a self-righteous streak, Craig had become embroiled in a scandal in 1982 when his name surfaced amid accusations that there was a drug and prostitution ring involving underage pages serving members in the House.

From Wright's perspective, the other Republicans were more moderate and malleable. Utah's James Hansen and Wisconsin's Tom Petri were middle-of-the-road conservatives. Each represented a district with enough Democratic voters to dissuade them from being seen as Gingrich's handmaidens. The other two Republicans were insiders who were practiced distributors of congressional pork, something that would be a major issue in this investigation. California's Charles "Chip" Pashayan, who liked to demonstrate that he was a tough interrogator of witnesses coming before his committees, had nurtured strong support from agribusiness and defense contractors in his home district, and through his position on the Interior and Insular Affairs Committee he had become legendary for doling out congressional funds. And perhaps most crucially for Wright, the ranking member of the Republican cohort, John Myers, was the kind of Republican Gingrich didn't like or trust. A genial World War II veteran first elected in 1966, Myers believed in bipartisan compromises and maintained terrific relations with members of both parties. The Indiana legislator was described as "a very silent mover in Washington. He didn't make great waves. He was very effective behind the scenes."[58]

The Democratic lineup, likewise, looked relatively good for the Speaker's case. The committee was stacked with Democrats who were quintessential insiders with little thirst for reform. Although the Democrats had learned the lessons of Watergate, almost none of them were good-government zealots. These were Democrats who revered FDR—not Ralph Nader—and who were more focused on defending the New Deal and Great Society legacies than in fighting for ethical purity.

The California Democrat Vic Fazio enjoyed a personally close relationship with Wright. Elected in 1978, Fazio quickly solidified his district's support when, after obtaining an appointment on the Armed Services Committee, he directed huge amounts of money to local defense contractors.[59] If the committee was concerned about the relationships between House members and lobbyists, Fazio was not going to be the person to sound the alarm. Fazio was also an intensely political person with huge ambitions. He was not about to take on the leaders who could later block his ascent. Some Republicans wanted Fazio to take himself off the committee because he had invited Wright to a Democratic fund-raiser in California and he frequently dined with the Speaker while he was the subject of this investigation, which didn't sit well with many in the GOP.

The Speaker had another fan in Alan Mollohan, an evenhanded forty-five-year-old Washington-bred corporate lawyer elected in 1982, the son of a former representative, and a member of the Ethics Committee since 1985 who had openly opposed the Wright investigation. A loyal liberal Democrat from a poor West Virginia district, Mollohan had come to appreciate Wright's leadership, which he saw as an antidote to Reagan's trickle-down presidency. Moreover, he had no appetite for destroying a colleague's career. As a moderate force, he was joined by New Jersey's Bernard Dwyer, a sixty-seven-year-old inside player who avoided the television cameras and usually voted with the leadership. The other senior Democrat was Pennsylvania's Joseph Gaydos, who was against bringing charges against Wright. Gaydos was so loyal to the Speaker that he refused to attend the press conference when Dixon outlined the charges.

The land mine waiting for Wright was the sixth Democratic member, Chester Atkins from Massachusetts. Elected to Congress in 1984 and only forty years old, Atkins had a pedigree very different from those of his committee colleagues: he was a Brahmin baby boomer with a reputation for integrity and honesty. Atkins had a maverick streak dating back to his undergraduate antiwar-activist years in the late 1960s. He had a healthy dose of distrust for politicians, regardless of what party they came from. Wright's allies were uneasy about where Atkins would come down on the final ethics vote.[60]

Then came the wild card. On July 26, the Ethics Committee unanimously voted to appoint a special prosecutor to assist them with the case. In making his formal announcement, Chairman Dixon assented to the wishes of Gingrich and Common Cause but noted that the special prosecutor would work "at the direction of the committee," could only subpoena witnesses with their approval, and would be limited to investigating the six allegations the committee had voted on.

The decision to hire a special prosecutor was shrewd. The committee believed that a special prosecutor, a hallmark of post-Watergate political reform, would grant legitimacy to their final verdict. Appointing a special prosecutor would insulate Democrats from the inevitable charges that they were too loyal to the Speaker, while it promised Republicans a tough investigation that would not cast them as the villains.

Dixon named Richard Phelan for the job on the recommendation of the ranking minority member, Myers. Phelan, who was planning to run for governor of Illinois on a reform platform, had sought out the job from Congressman Myers through intermediaries, realizing that this would be a high-profile opportunity. The ginger-haired Chicago native was a hard-hitting civil litigator who earned a lucrative $450,000 a year with the fifty-person law firm Phelan, Pope & John. Tall, handsome, and dynamic, Phelan was called "the Presence" by his colleagues;[61] he was everything a defendant might fear. One reporter described Phelan as "equally adept at seducing a jury and sacking a hostile witness." In the courtroom, a reporter observed, "he likes to toss out theories, occasionally wild ones—while associates search for the case law to support them."[62] This wide-angled approach to bringing down his targets suited his ambition to eventually run for office.

Republicans ought to have been jubilant, but outside the Ethics Committee they were concerned. They questioned Phelan's experience, asking how a lawyer who specialized in liability cases would handle a highly charged investigation into political corruption. Other Republicans knew that Phelan had been named as a delegate to the most recent Democratic convention (although he had not attended) and had raised $100,000 for the primary candidate Paul Simon, a well-respected senator from Illinois. DEMOCRATIC ACTIVIST TO PROBE WRIGHT, complained the conservative

Chicago Tribune in its headline. Peter Flaherty, chair of Citizens for Reagan, expressed to Gingrich "deep alarm" over the possibility that Phelan's appointment would be a "whitewash of the Speaker's corrupt actions."[63] Gingrich griped that Phelan was the equivalent of the Justice Department hiring a conservative midwestern Republican who had donated $100,000 to Senator Robert Dole to investigate Reagan. "Every Democrat would be up in arms."[64] Paul Weyrich had been proposing a different set of possibilities, such as New Mexico attorney general Hal Stratton, who was close to the "movement," or Judge Robert Bork, Reagan's extremely conservative Supreme Court nominee, whose confirmation had been defeated by Senate Democrats in 1987.[65]

Phelan, with his eye on the 1990 Illinois gubernatorial campaign, sensed that this appointment could be career making. As he went to work, he was eager to prove that being a Democrat had nothing to do with the way he would handle this case. Yet, despite his assurances to the committee, his political ambitions became evident. This was an era of heroic political litigators who were intent on cleaning up Washington. Phelan wanted to join the ranks of legends like Archibald Cox, Leon Jaworski, and, more recently, Lawrence Walsh. This post would allow Phelan to embellish his bona fides by displaying an unwavering sense of indignation about corruption and a conviction that public officials should be more accountable.

The energetic Phelan immediately assembled a talented team of eight litigators to scour the public record for information about every single accusation that had been made against the Speaker. As he had always done in preparing his cases, he wanted to look at as much evidence as possible. This, he said, would be the only way to understand Wright's intentions in the different relationships being examined, given that the cases were not themselves about explicit corruption. Though the formal scope of the committee investigation revolved around the six major charges, Phelan felt it was essential to understand how Wright viewed the world so that his actions made sense. Phelan ordered his staff not to leave any stone unturned.

The appointment of Phelan coincided with the publication of Brooks

Jackson's *Honest Graft: Big Money and the American Political Process*, a searing account of the former DCCC chair Tony Coelho's seedy fundraising efforts that garnered widespread attention. The timing of the book's release could not have been worse for Wright, with its attendant follow-up reporting in several major newspapers about the ties between House Democrats and the savings and loan industry. The publicity delighted Gingrich. He wrote to Republicans in one of his lengthy memos, "*Honest Graft* and the continued editorials in *The Wall Street Journal*, *Washington Times*, *New York Times*, and *Washington Post* are all bringing into focus the sickness of the current House elections' and ethics' system."[66]

The House Republican leadership and Gingrich were singing the same tune. Even the House minority leader, Michel, stoked the flames of scandal. His office sent the media and House Republicans a provocative report titled *The Broken Branch of the Federal Government*, an account of the "real crisis of corruption." The report, which Gingrich had no hand in writing, accused the Democratic leadership of abusing its power by isolating and marginalizing their opponents. The rules, the report said, had been turned into a weapon of the majority. The document reiterated many of the points Gingrich had made and employed the same vituperative language that was regularly featured in COS speeches. It highlighted three issues. First, there was a singular difference between the two parties because "Democrats have been in power 34 years. The power has corrupted their party." Second, House Republicans had a duty "to expose corruption and the incumbent advantages which make corruption more and more a danger." Finally, the report called corruption a "growing cancer" that threatened the House.[67] House Republicans, including Michel, Cheney, and Lott, celebrated the study for C-SPAN viewers on May 24 by coordinating special order floor speeches to discuss their findings.[68]

If there was still any daylight between Gingrich and the Republican leadership on the matter of the Democratic majority or Speaker Wright, it was becoming hard to see it. The GOP seemed to be rapidly converging around the Georgian's message about the corruption of the Democratic Party.

Gingrich was pleased to see Michel on board. But he was experienced enough to know that releasing a report to legislators and reporters was not enough. The GOP would have to sell these ideas to the public and relentlessly beat the drum in front of television cameras, on the radio, and to print reporters to do so. Gingrich told his fellow Republicans that they needed to give the news media "a specific hard-hitting critique of what's wrong with the House Democrats' machine" and to "force a series of votes on specific ethics problems so [they are] forced to pay attention to the issue every week we are in session." Because Democrats would never reform themselves and the news media could not be expected to "function as an opposition party," it was incumbent on House Republicans to "make news by investigating, exposing, and confronting an increasingly arrogant, corrupt, and entrenched House Democratic Party," Gingrich advised.[69] Besides Wright, Gingrich targeted nineteen other Democrats who were working under an ethical cloud.[70] He kept reiterating the point that ethics reform and the Democratic monopoly on power were as potent issues as the war on drugs, cutting taxes, or fighting communism. "An honest self-government versus Jim Wright and the corrupt House Democrats project will enthuse our activists, focus the news media and the public, and keep the left on the defensive," Gingrich promised Republicans as he rallied them to his side.[71] Congressional corruption under the Democrats, Gingrich went on to say, as he harkened back to John Dean's famous diagnosis about Nixon and the presidency, "was a growing cancer, threatening the very essence of representative freedom."[72]

A copy of the Republican report had come across Speaker Wright's desk, but he took comfort in the strength of Congress as an institution, and the Republicans as a party, and this led him to believe that the accusations about Democratic corruption or the investigation into his own career would not become the focus of his counterparts in the GOP. Cooler heads would prevail. His stubborn faith in the better angels of the GOP and his preference for keeping his head buried in the work of governance blinded him to the change in tides. He was now swimming against a political rip current.

Wright did not have time to concern himself with the big picture in

American politics, because his most pressing need was to mount a personal defense. On September 14, he appeared before the House Ethics Committee to testify for the first time. While he walked through the murky hallway toward the committee room entrance, a staffer wheeled a hand truck behind him that bore fifty books written by other members of Congress. The Speaker exuded a sense of confidence and displayed his saccharine smile. He was in good spirits for someone who was about to face a congressional inquisition. His attitude was genuine; he believed he had nothing to worry about and nothing to hide. Once his colleagues heard his version of the story, they would understand that the charges were spurious.

As the committee met in their dark basement room for five long hours, Wright reviewed each accusation, explaining to the members in detail why it was either factually wrong or the result of the truth being twisted in such a way that suggested wrongdoing when there was none. He handed out mimeographed copies of press statements distributed by conservative organizations seeking to take advantage of his problems to rile up their base. Turning to the cart that was stacked with books by other public officials, including the volume that Newt Gingrich had coauthored with ten other Republicans, *A House of Ill Repute*, the Speaker read out loud snippets from the acknowledgments sections to show that they too had received assistance from staffers. Even in the case of Gingrich's coauthored work, Katherine Watson, his executive assistant, and Sheila Ward, his press secretary, had helped. Wright wagged his finger and shook his fist: "The longer the proceeding goes on, given the desire and the intense attempt of the committee to keep it professional and to keep it in a dignified process, I think you saw from those things [the letters from conservative organizations] that I handed out to you that there is agitative, active effort to use this investigation to engender hate and bitterness. Congress, as an institution, doesn't need that."[73]

Since Gingrich had begun promoting his corruption narrative nine years earlier against Congressman Diggs, many House members believed the Republican opposition was attempting to score political points by criminalizing the normal responsibilities of a legislator. This was not a belief shared by the special prosecutor, Richard Phelan. Despite the committee's instructions, the restraints on Phelan's investigation were not followed. As Phelan dug deeper into Wright's past, looking into all sorts of stories that had surfaced in the press, his investigation widened to include old canards like the 1948 state election story alleging that Wright might have been involved in his opponent's murder.[74] As Phelan's work stretched into weeks and then months, the stain on Wright's character remained fresh in people's minds.

A short-lived national security scandal added to the circus surrounding Wright when the conservative *Washington Times* reported that he had shared classified information with its journalists about a CIA operation to foment opposition against the Sandinista government. The Chicago-area Republican Henry Hyde, the ranking minority member of the Intelligence Committee, slammed Wright's comments to the newspaper as "Sandinista propaganda," calling it "appalling" that the Speaker made these statements.[75] The Speaker responded that all of the information came directly from newspaper stories about the Iran-contra hearings. Republicans, he said, were manufacturing a fake crisis. There were also rumors circulating on Capitol Hill that the news stories were being spread around Washington by high-level national security officials who were still fuming about Iran-contra as well as Wright's efforts to prevent Reagan from sending assistance to anticommunist forces in Central America. The scandal faded quickly when the Intelligence Committee concluded that Wright had done nothing untoward. Still, the episode was unnerving to Democrats, who saw the intensity of anger brewing against Wright within the GOP.

Anonymous quotations started to appear in the press from Democrats speculating about the Speaker's future. Talk of the possibility of some kind of punishment, which still seemed far-fetched, hung in the air.[76] Referring to incidents like the battles over Indiana's Bloody Eighth and the previous year's dramatic intervention in the Nicaraguan peace negotiations, Tom Kenworthy of *The Washington Post* concluded that the Speaker's "fiery partisanship and hell-for-leadership style already have polarized the House, and some Democrats believe the speaker could be vulnerable to a challenge if the House ethics committee investigation were to result in a harsh report or recommendation for punishment." There were a few whispers about who might replace him, with stories that Democratic leaders like Coelho and the Ways and Means Committee chairman, Dan Rostenkowski, were meeting more and more with their colleagues as this scandal unfolded. "There's a lot of group dining going on," Kenworthy reported one member saying.[77] "Behind the scenes," wrote Steve Roberts in *The New York Times*, "some aspiring power brokers are sniffing the political winds, taking younger members out to dinner and quietly preparing the way for a possible challenge, should Mr. Wright falter."[78]

Still, there was some reason for optimism among Democrats even after Bush overwhelmingly defeated Dukakis in the November election with 426 electoral college votes. The election marked the first time since 1908 when the party that would be out of power in the White House—the Democrats—had increased the size of its majorities in both chambers. Despite his calls in the summer for an investigation into Wright, Bush maintained a collegial relationship with Wright dating back to their days in Texas, so it was questionable whether the president-elect would support an effort to remove him. Democrats still perceived Bush as being committed to bipartisanship. Once the campaign was over, he would not have the same impetus to continue a witch hunt. Politics would go back to normal. And Wright had offered an olive branch after the results were in. Seeing how the electorate voted for divided government, the Speaker promised to work with Bush on issues like the federal deficit, education reform, and protecting the environment. "If there is a mandate, it clearly is for Bush as president and a Democratic Congress to build upon the constructive program we embarked on last year," he said.

Bush appeared to share this enthusiasm. The president-elect was eager to soften some of the harder edges of the Reagan Revolution by finding areas of possible agreement with Democrats, such as protections for Americans with disabilities, without alienating the Republican base. As a sign of respect to the congressional Democrats, he went to meet with Wright for a ninety-minute lunch at the Speaker's office on November 18. When Bush walked in, one reporter blurted out the question whether this was a peace mission. Smiling, the president-elect asked how you can "make peace when there is no war" before ducking into the room.[79] Following the meeting, Wright told reporters, "He was willing to come halfway, rather than asking me to go down to the White House—if you're looking for symbolism. I think it shows a willingness to work with us."[80]

Things were looking up for Wright when he received a vote of confidence from his caucus on December 5; the Democrats unanimously nominated him to serve another two-year term as Speaker. At sixty-five years old, Wright still believed he had years of service ahead of him and promised his colleagues to work closely with the Republican president on legislation to reform elections in order to reduce the power of private money and to push for federal regulations that would curb the corporate consolidations that were leaving many Americans without jobs.

But the House Republicans were having none of this bipartisan celebration. "You cannot govern from the left in this country. And you cannot govern against the right if you're a Republican," Gingrich said.[81] Many in the GOP had coalesced around Gingrich's position.[82] Bush's kumbaya overtures to the Democratic Speaker seemed ridiculous to nearly all of the congressional Republicans, especially after what they had witnessed during Wright's first term as Speaker. No one in the GOP believed that Wright would change his stripes.

The party lines were hardening in the House of Representatives, where Gingrich's army gathered momentum. Movement activists were hailing Gingrich as a hero. The Eagle Forum founder, Phyllis Schlafly, told her followers that he "is a real leader. He did what no other Republican Congressman seemed willing or able to do—expose Jim Wright. . . . Gingrich is one of the top strategists of the conservative movement."[83] House Republicans appeared to be more like Gingrich than like Bush when talking about partisan politics. And with a smaller minority, they felt even more desperate. On the same day that Democrats voted for Wright to serve another term, Michel, doing his best impression of Gingrich, stood before his Republican colleagues to announce that ethics rules needed to be stringently enforced and that the lower chamber must be cleaned up soon, starting with the Speaker. "The reputation of this institution has been smeared by members who blatantly break our rules and mock the institution's inability to enforce a penalty," the GOP leader asserted.[84] Without uttering Wright's name, Michel made his goal clear. Confirming his shift in tone was the news that a top counsel working for the House Republicans, Hyde Murray, who had been viewed by COS as insufficiently combative, resigned. After affirming a newly combative Michel as their leader, Republicans elected the COS member Vin Weber as secretary of the House GOP Conference. Dick Cheney, now a vocal supporter of Gingrich's fusillades against Wright, would be the Republican whip. Whatever President-elect Bush said over lunch didn't matter. The Republican Party had the Speaker in its crosshairs.

Wright went back to Texas to spend Christmas with family and friends. The presidential election had been disappointing, and the tenor of Republican rhetoric was ominous. But his fellow House Democrats were pleased with his performance. He had taken on President Reagan, and he wasn't showing signs of letting up. The Democrats would certainly have his back. Gingrich and the Republicans might be griping, and the good-government reformers might be making some noise, but from the Democratic perspective in 1988, there was no reason to panic. Not yet.

Five

MISSING THE TEMPEST

S peaker Wright didn't grasp the enormity of the conservative tempest
that was taking shape in the late 1980s. As congressional Republicans started to come to terms with the limits of the Reagan
Revolution—given the continued expansion of the social safety net and
massive deficits—a growing number of them were drawn to the bare-
knuckle legislative style that Newt Gingrich had pioneered.

Though the Speaker and his closest associates continued to think of
Gingrich as a historical outlier, conservatives were becoming more anti-
establishment in their outlook about Washington. Robert Michel loved to
distinguish himself from Gingrich, but in practice the distance between
them was shrinking. The Republicans were determined to tear down
the political status quo by whatever means necessary. Anti-establishment
conservatives were eager to turn the legislative branch into a bastion
against liberalism, just as it had been for southern Dixiecrats and midwestern Republicans between the 1930s and the 1960s. Gingrich offered
the party another direct connection, like Reagan, to conservative movement activists.

The strength of this insurgency within the GOP caught Wright by
surprise. What's more, the limits of Wright's own political prowess increased the friction between him and his party, just when he needed

support the most. The ferocity of the Right in early 1989 transformed the political environment in which the Speaker's case was to be judged. As the House Ethics Committee probed deeper, Democrats started to buckle, while Republicans were looking more and more like the party of Gingrich.

Speaker Wright got a taste of the growing fury in a feud over a proposed congressional pay raise. Almost anytime that legislators had voted to grant themselves higher salaries—a duty that Article I, Section 6 of the Constitution bestowed on them, should they desire it—political fireworks ensued. There was usually some member of Congress and some cluster of voters who saw this decision as yet another example of how politicians abused their power, a story that resonated in a nation that was deeply distrustful of government. Historically, each of the twenty-two times that Congress voted on stand-alone legislation to increase salaries between 1789 and 1968, legislators faced political heat. When Congress voted to give itself a pay raise in 1873, from $5,000 to $7,000 a year, the Ohio Republican William Lawrence observed that the only other events to have "aroused as much indignation" had been the Missouri Compromise and the first shots fired at Fort Sumter.[1]

In 1955, Wright's freshman year, when Congress proposed to raise salaries from $17,500 to $22,000, the young Texan got a mountain of angry mail from his district back home. Unsettled by the response, the newcomer informed his colleagues that he planned to vote against the legislation. It seemed like the safe thing to do. That was until he paid a visit to Speaker Sam Rayburn's office. "Mr. Rayburn frowned that businesslike frown of his and said, 'Jim, if you vote against the pay raise, it's for one of two reasons: either the job you sought isn't that important a job, or you're saying that you aren't a big enough man for the job,'" Wright recalled. He voted for the raise. He also survived politically.[2] But Americans still hated when their representatives jacked up their pay. In 1967, Congress attempted to insulate legislators from this kind of fallout. It established an alternative mechanism by which a presidentially appointed federal salary commission would recommend raises. The raise would automatically take effect unless the House and the Senate both voted against it.

But the reform had not worked as planned. Congressional pay raises remained as unpopular as ever. Post-Watergate Americans believed that their representatives enjoyed a lifetime sinecure embellished by exotic junkets provided by interest groups and extravagant boondoggles paid for by taxpayers, like expensive steak dinners, first-class air travel, and black town cars to shuttle them around. The Abscam scandal, which resulted in the expulsion of the Pennsylvania Democrat Michael "Ozzie" Myers and the resignation of the New Jersey senator Harrison Williams, left the public with indelible images of corrupt congressmen taking bribes. Middle-class Americans struggled to make ends meet while their elected representatives enjoyed perks like gymnasiums and free parking, subsidized health care, and a $3,000 tax deduction to offset their expenses in Washington.[3] In 1987, at the end of Wright's first year as Speaker, after a 2 percent raise automatically went into effect, Congress took a ribbing. As the *Saturday Night Live* comedian A. Whitney Brown joked in the show's "Big Picture" segment, "I'm sure some of them need the money. After all, it's not easy raising a family these days when you are saving up for a legal defense fund. You have to admit $90,000 a year doesn't go far when you are looking at multiple indictments. My question is, though, why can't they get a raise from the military contractors and tobacco lobbyists like they've always done?"

The big challenge came when Ronald Reagan's commission proposed a whopping 50 percent increase for public servants in all branches of government a year later in December 1988. Chaired by the former White House counsel Lloyd Cutler, a well-known Washington insider, the bipartisan commission said that in an age of inflation public pay failed to keep up. The raise would cost Treasury about $300 million. Representatives would receive $135,000 a year instead of $89,500. Speaker Wright's salary would go up to $175,000. The commission reduced the sting for taxpayers by proposing that the generous salary hike be tied to a ban on honoraria and strict limitations on how much federal officials could earn from other kinds of outside income.

Common Cause thought the trade-off was worth it. Fred Wertheimer liked the total ban on honoraria, currently limited to 30 percent of salaries, and saw the package as the first step toward more comprehensive ethics reforms. "Honoraria fees," Wertheimer said in a press release, "represent one of the most insidious ethics problems in government today. In fact . . . there is no 'honor' involved . . . when money is used by special interests to obtain political access and influence and when elected representatives in Congress actively seek and accept the payments."[4] Members of Congress earned $9.8 million in honoraria in 1987, a combination of speaker fees from a range of groups and organizations, the majority of them private, and payments that were offered to legislators in exchange for their attending breakfast meetings, lunches, and retreats. Legislators were even paid to take tours of corporate headquarters. Wertheimer was outraged when interest groups compensated legislators whose support they needed upward of $25,000 (more commonly, $1,000 or $2,000) to participate in some kind of manufactured event.[5] This preeminent reform organization announced its support for the raise.

But the Right smelled blood. On December 14, one day after the commission unveiled its recommendations, David Keating, the executive vice president of the National Taxpayers Union, denounced the hike. The 150,000-member National Taxpayers Union was a conservative organization devoted to low taxes and low spending. Regarding the pay raise, Keating complained, "Is it too much to ask today's Congress and high-ranking government officials to freeze their pay for a few years while the federal budget is being brought into balance?"[6]

Conservative talk radio hosts chimed in to denounce the pay raise as a uniquely bad idea. The pivotal interview took place on WXYT-AM in Detroit on December 6, ten days before the 215th anniversary of the Boston Tea Party. During the discussion with the fiery, red-bearded, flannel-shirt-clad host Roy Fox, a caller named Tony from Roseville, Michigan, chimed in to express his outrage. Fox loved what he heard from Tony. The veteran talk show provocateur, who yelled into the microphone every chance that he could, had spent thirty years on air railing against big government. He had started out when he was eighteen years old at a small station in Henderson, Kentucky, owned by the mayor, where he honed a broadcast mixing news, music, and talk with his pet parakeet, who interjected sounds in the background as he read commercial announcements. Fox had lived the nomad-like existence of radio hosts, moving from one station to the next across the Midwest. While hosting on a small station in Akron, Ohio, Fox mastered a new format of pure talk radio that was being popularized in New York by Bob Grant and in California by Joe Pyne, whose aggressive back-and-forth conversations attracted sizable audiences. Fox imported this provocative style to the Midwest.[7] Fox heard his caller's suggestion that listeners send tea bags to members of Congress with a message, attached on the string, saying, "No pay increase." At first, Fox thought that it was a "moronic idea." But overnight he changed his mind. The next day he instructed his audience to write on tea bags, "Read My Tea Bag: No 50% Raise!" along with their names and home addresses, and then send one to their legislator and another to the president. Fox's wife, Mary, upped the ante by faxing out information to about a dozen hosts in major markets around the country urging them to repeat the message as well.[8] David Keating took a short break from his vacation in San Diego to appear on more than thirty shows.[9]

The conservative opponents of the pay raise found unexpected support from a prominent figure on the left. The consumer advocate Ralph Nader, now a leader of his own nonprofit, Public Citizen, blasted the salary increase proposal as outrageous. In contrast to Fred Wertheimer, Nader was a reformer with far less faith in government. As a product of the 1960s counterculture, he took inspiration from grassroots civil rights and antiwar activists who exposed the hypocrisy of both political parties and the ways that powerful interests tainted democracy. Nader dismissed the commission's recommendations to reporters. Not even a deal that adopted honoraria reform satisfied him. "They don't need it, they don't deserve it and they shouldn't receive it," Nader said.[10] "You don't say, 'Honorariums are bad; stop being bad people and we'll make it up to you.' They're separate reforms."[11]

Like his conservative counterparts, Nader took to the airwaves. He was bemused that the most receptive audiences were the listeners of right-leaning programs such as *The Jerry Williams Show*, a popular Massachusetts radio program. Known as the "Dean of Talk Radio," Williams made his name by attacking Michael Dukakis and championing the kind of blue-collar populist conservatism that Gingrich had been enthralled by ever since his childhood in Harrisburg. As part of his "Stop the Salary Grab" campaign, Nader announced the phone numbers of Speaker Wright and Minority Leader Robert Michel, with both Nader and Williams imploring listeners to call their offices.

This was the precise moment when talk radio was coming into its own. In 1987, under pressure from President Reagan, the Federal Communications Commission stopped enforcing the fairness doctrine, a 1949 regulation that had required television and radio shows to provide equal airtime for all sides of a political debate. Many on the Right opposed the doctrine (though not all, including Gingrich, who thought that the rule should be preserved). Conservatives who were opposed to the doctrine believed that liberal voices dominated television and radio under the guise of objectivity. With the doctrine eliminated, radio and television hosts could opine on anything, and station owners, should they be of a mind to, could promote their particular political views unimpeded, 24/7. Radio and the budding cable industry would never be the same. There was an explosion of conservative talk radio shows after the doctrine was abandoned, with personalities such as Rush Limbaugh, whose show became nationally syndicated in 1988, shaking up the airwaves.[12]

The congressional pay raise was a perfect issue for this new Wild West. Conservative hosts pummeled their opponents without the requirement to be "fair." The impact was immediate. Whenever someone like Roy Fox or Jerry Williams raised the issue, the phone lines lit up. Many other regional hosts picked up on Fox's call for a "Tea Bag Revolution," and within a week a national movement had been launched as thousands upon thousands of tea bags arrived on legislators' desks. "We were on the phone to each other every day," as one radio host described it. "It was like managing a political campaign." At one point, he added, "we got hold of Jim Wright's fax number. I called the other stations, and we *buried* him under a blizzard of paper."[13]

From his regal quarters on Capitol Hill, Speaker Wright was blind-sided by the ferocity of the opposition. Conservative activists were familiar with the world of talk radio, a medium that had been popular for decades as the Right searched for alternatives to the mainstream press.[14] But most of Washington's elected officials had not paid much attention. Neither Wright nor his colleagues believed that talk radio was a serious medium. If it wasn't in *The New York Times* or on the *CBS Evening News*, they thought, it probably didn't matter.

Gingrich, ever alert to trends and opportunities, however, was more attuned to what conservative talk radio had to say. He actually supported the raise, agreeing with the commission that it was needed to recruit good people to public service, but he certainly didn't mind watching the heat it generated for the Speaker. Gingrich remarked that the pay issue had "sparked a level of anti-Congress feeling that is more intense than any other political feeling since Watergate," a comparison that he liked to make whenever possible because it automatically elevated the seriousness of the controversy for the generation who suffered through Nixon's downfall.[15] The pay raise fit his narrative about the heavy-handed Democrats trampling on the will of the people. The California Democrat Vic Fazio, who supported the raise and was one of Wright's top defenders on the Ethics Committee, recalled, "We became cartoon cannon fodder for trash television and for talk radio. . . . We fell prey to the deception of the rabble rousers."[16]

On January 6, President Reagan endorsed the commission report and inserted the pay raise into his budget, likely with the understanding that it would raise hell for Wright. The antiunion president, who famously said that government was the problem, was now on record as favoring paying legislators and civil servants more generously. But he had also laid down a no-win challenge to lawmakers. The decision was theirs. Under pressure, Senator George Mitchell of Maine, a former federal judge and the cerebral new majority leader, with the agreement of Minority Leader Bob Dole, announced that the Senate would vote on the bill. The raise would not go through before each senator stood up to be counted.

The stage was set for a showdown between a Democratic-controlled

Congress and the American public. To many Watergate-era journalists, the right-wingers seemed to have a point. Why should congressmen enrich themselves? They were not Wall Street moguls or real estate investors but rather public servants. Several news magazines declared their opposition to the size of the proposed raise and called for accountability in the House, where Wright had not said yet whether there would be a vote. Without one, the raise would be automatic. *Time* magazine reminded readers that the extra financial benefits that legislators received were "cushy enough to provoke the envy of all but the best compensated private executives." With *Newsweek* using terms like "cowardice" and "duplicitous" in its reporting, it also branded Speaker Wright the "wagon boss of the gravy train" for members who "enjoy a wide range of perks from lavish pensions to cheap haircuts." *The Washington Post* called the raises "too generous" and complained that they were being enacted through a "no-fingerprints" process.[17] According to Gallup, even when Americans were informed that the raise would be connected to a strict ban on honoraria, 82 percent surveyed said they were against the increase.[18] And congressional offices were flooded with negative letters and faxes. One postcard showed a picture of a pig with text that read, "Re: your obscene pay raise—Piggies that do nothing but get fatter and fatter get gobbled up at the next meal."[19]

Members of Congress got an earful whenever they traveled as well. While attending church in his home district of Dorchester, Massachusetts, the Democratic representative Brian Donnelly and a group of other male congregants were preparing to become godfathers. Right in the middle of the service, a fellow godfather-to-be leaned over and hissed in Donnelly's ear, "You better vote on that raise, and do it this week!"[20]

The Colorado Democrat Patricia Schroeder warned the Speaker that he needed to take this uprising very seriously. With 80 percent of Americans "flaming mad" against the measure, the recently departed "Teflon" president, Reagan, would not "take the heat" for the House passing the increase; the Democratic Party would. "Make no mistake about it," Schroeder predicted. "The raise will be blamed on each and every Democratic [*sic*] in the Congress. I suspect Lee Atwater is already cutting the commercials, substituting the 'obscene Democratic pay raise' for Willie Horton."[21] One of the most vicious and infamous ads from Atwater's 1988 Republican campaign focused on a paroled African American named Willie Horton who assaulted and raped a woman while on a weekend furlough.

Caught in a political trap, Wright made matters worse. At the very moment he was counting on his colleagues to beat back the ethics scandal, he deflected responsibility on the pay raise issue. In an unorthodox move, he distributed a survey to House members to see how they felt about the raise, asking whether they would accept a lower amount and whether there should be a vote. In Wright's mind, if the results revealed that a significant number of legislators wanted the raise, he could use the data to make the case that he was simply fulfilling the members' will and take himself off the hook.

Members were furious. By asking for their opinion, he was implicitly putting some of the burden for the decision on the backs of his colleagues. "When you're elected speaker or majority leader or majority whip you are expected to absorb heat on behalf of the members on tough issues," one Democratic staffer bluntly complained. "Everyone understood the questionnaire as an attempt to pluralize the heat. And people felt burned."[22] Republicans could only laugh that Wright had thrown his fellow Democrats under the bus.

On February 2, the Senate voted against the raise by 95 to 5. All eyes were now on Wright. Would he let the raise go through and take the heat? Or would he call for a vote? Wright floated the idea of the House voting for a 30 percent raise, but that would not provide cover for Democrats as the issue continued to simmer. The Democrat Les AuCoin of Oregon said the tension was unlike anything he had seen in his fourteen years in the House. "People are ready to pick up a brick or pick up a rifle. It goes much deeper than the raise, the dollars. This has crystalized a perception [of Congress] that we have the rulers and the ruled," and that citizens felt an "inability to control events."[23]

In Los Angeles, KFI station producers reported that their callers wanted to speak only about the pay raise. "All I have to do is go on the air and say pay raise, and the phones light up, especially now when people sense that we may be close to victory," said the host of a morning talk show in San Diego, Mark Williams. He admitted, "I'm not doing journalism here, I'm doing an activist talk show." The representatives of the Tetley tea company offered Houston listeners a monthlong supply of their product to anyone who joined the Tea Bag Revolution. Talk radio, meanwhile, charged onto the national stage, with Roy Fox, identified as the creator of the Tea Bag Revolution, becoming one of the biggest media sensations in the country.[24] The late-night talk shows piled on. During one monologue, Jay Leno, guest hosting for Johnny Carson on NBC's *Tonight Show*, joked, "Congress said if we give them a 50 percent pay raise they won't go out on the road and give speeches. You know what? Why don't we give them 100 percent pay raise and shut them up altogether!"[25]

Days before the raise would go into effect unless the House voted against it, Democrats handed their opponents more ammunition. On February 3, 140 House Democrats, along with their families, arrived at Washington, D.C.'s Union Station to depart for their annual retreat at the grand Greenbrier resort in West Virginia, their suitcases bulging with vacation clothes and sporting equipment. Lobbyists made $6,000 contributions to subsidize the train that would transport the legislators. When the legislators walked to the track to board their Amtrak train, they were greeted by protesters with posters reading, HOUSE OF GREED! and WRIGHT IS A CROOK! The protesters chanted, "You can run but you can't hide," as the members headed out in their nineteen-car train.[26] Majority Whip Coelho tried to deflect the bad optics by joking, "Once a year, Democrats try to live like Republicans."[27]

Over the next two days, television cameras captured legislators on horseback, playing tennis, and lining up for drinks at a catered dinner as they listened to orchestral music. There was Mississippi's Mike Espy picturesquely ice-skating in the mountains with his two children, while Connecticut's Samuel Gejdenson splashed in the resort's heated pool with his kids. "Around the corner," wrote one reporter, California's Norman Mineta waited "his turn for a bowling lane" while Dan Glickman of Kansas "finished a class of low-impact aerobics. Most of yesterday's appointments for mineral baths, massages and manicures were made long before the 140 House Democrats arrived for their annual retreat. . . . Look for no apologies here from lawmakers enjoying a posh weekend—partly subsidized by lobbyists—at a time when there is an uproar about an impending 50 percent congressional pay raise." Karen Hosler of *The Baltimore Sun* quoted the Maryland Democrat Benjamin Cardin, taking a pause during a tennis match with another Democrat, as saying, "Congress has got to go on doing its business," seemingly oblivious to the irony behind his words.[28] The reporters told readers about the Saturday night diner gala, during which House Democrats dressed up in kitschy 1950s costumes, dancing the Peppermint Twist and the jitterbug—Coelho turned out to be masterful at the latter. The eighty-eight-year-old Claude Pepper was reported to have lit up the dance floor boogying to Jackie Wilson's "Higher and Higher."[29] But the radio show hosts Roy Fox and Mike Siegel certainly understood and gleefully shared the Greenbrier's phone number with listeners, as did other radio hosts. The resort's switchboard lit up with hundreds of calls.[30]

Wright was caught off guard by the tumult. He had been through several pay raise battles throughout his career, starting in his first term. On each occasion, the dynamics had played out the same way. Congress considered a raise, opponents kicked and screamed, and then the salary hike went into effect even if there were a few stumbles along the way. Everyone eventually moved on. Wright learned from Speaker Rayburn in 1955 that the job of the legislator was to be firm when constituents complained. The party leader took the heat while the rank and file stood behind him. Like the other times, Wright assumed that once the pay raise kicked in, Congress would move on to other matters.

What the Speaker didn't grasp was how much had changed in the years since Reagan had become president. The conservative movement was reshaping the political landscape, turning politicians into villains in the public imagination through their campaign to delegitimize the federal government. The movement's allies on Capitol Hill were mobilizing to bring down the Democrats. Every example of the Democratic majority misusing their power—real or perceived—would be paraded around the news media as further evidence of how the party had abused its power.

When the Democrats returned to Washington on February 6, the House Republican minority leader, Michel, teamed up with the new minority whip, Dick Cheney, to propose a resolution opposing a pay raise. Wright was blindsided. The minority leader had previously assured him they would stand together to let the raise happen, but now he sensed that Wright was weak. Michel saw his chance and made a move to openly humiliate him. Wright attempted to dodge the GOP's attack by proposing that the House adjourn, but more than half of the Democratic caucus voted against adjournment and he was defeated. The conservatives had backed the Democrats into a corner, and like their colleagues in the Senate they had to vote the raise down. Without Wright's protection, they scrambled to save their own hides. "That blowtorch was just too hot," quipped Charlie Wilson.[31]

On February 7, with the galleries packed with spectators, the House rejected the pay raise by 380 to 48. "I voted no," the New Mexico Democrat Bill Richardson would later tell a reporter, "because I think I want to be re-elected to Congress. And secondly, because voting no means this gigantic ordeal is now over." Leaving the chamber, the North Dakota Democrat Byron Dorgan observed, "This is everything the Hindenburg was without the gas."[32] Democrats like Vic Fazio, who had been out front defending the pay raise, felt that the Speaker put his colleagues in a dangerous bind and then left them to fend for themselves.

Mary McGrory of *The Washington Post* dubbed the entire sorry incident "Reagan's Revenge."[33] The former president, who had struggled through his final years as he confronted scandal and a liberal rebound, had pushed forward a recommendation that caused chaos for the opposition party.

"Yippee!" Roy Fox screamed on air after hearing the news. "It's terrific . . . the complete turnabout in Congress." Fox told his listeners that it was "like a horse race, like extra innings in baseball."[34]

"I think I had known for perhaps four weeks that the 50 percent thing just wasn't going to wash," Wright told reporters. "By the time I advocated [voting on a smaller increase], it was too late."

Gingrich was uncharacteristically silent about the vote. This was not simply because he supported the raise. Rather, he was enjoying watching from the sidelines as the Speaker took this political blow. His silence ensured that the media would focus on Wright's incompetence instead of turning this into a story about partisan attacks. And Gingrich's tactics were catching on. This skirmish showed that an alternative media world, centered on talk radio, could shape the news narrative. Unlike Wright, Gingrich could see the synergistic power of talk radio and the conservative grass roots. The attacks were effective because they pinpointed and exaggerated real flaws within the political process and then characterized those abuses as problems caused by one party as opposed to being a symptom of a broken system.

The pay raise fiasco left Republicans with yet another issue to use against Speaker Wright and the Democrats. A corrupt party, led by a corrupt Speaker, working in a corrupt institution, had attempted to give themselves an obscene salary increase. The people had fought back and won. And House Democrats felt that they were left to foot the political costs for this fumbled effort, and without an actual raise to show for it.

One of the people most excited about the pay raise fiasco was Lee Atwater, a terrifying prospect to House Democrats. Atwater became the RNC chair after Bush's election, and being in his crosshairs circa 1989 was a serious matter. Notwithstanding his hand-wringing about the slash-and-burn campaign that he put together in 1988 against Governor Dukakis, Bush kept Atwater on his party's political team. It was not that much of a surprise. After all, the new president had shown in the thick of the campaign that he had no problem getting down and dirty. Bush's own background as the former chairman of the RNC—during the height of the Watergate scandal (1973–1974)—encouraged Atwater and other conservative operatives to believe that, unlike Carter or Reagan, Bush would go all in during the midterms. As vice president, he had campaigned in forty-seven states during the 1986 midterms, proving his chops as a politician who loved the game. "I'll bet you dollars to doughnuts he'll be a very active participant in the [1990] off-year elections," predicted the White House press secretary, Marlin Fitzwater.[35] As soon as he took on the position, Atwater transformed the RNC headquarters on First Street in Washington from a sleepy bureaucratic building into a bustling hub of political skullduggery. The RNC had once been, as Atwater's biographer wrote, the type of place where people obtained jobs if their parents had made large donations to the party. Atwater had re-envisioned the RNC, recruiting some of the most talented staffers in the business, young twentysomethings who were hungry, ruthless, and inspired to take action. The atmosphere was now electric.

The charismatic Atwater, arriving at work each morning, would gregariously bark out hellos in his "good old boy" accent while vigorously shaking hands as though he were running for office. Atwater even changed the Muzak system in the elevators, replacing the tired classic pop with gritty rock 'n' roll.[36] From the perch behind his desk, where he usually sat with his feet up as he strummed his electric guitar and drank a can of hyper-caffeinated Jolt soda, Atwater and the Republican National Committee sensed they had the opposition on its heels as the 1990 midterm elections approached. From his methodical reviews of the city newspapers and television broadcasts, Atwater believed that Wright's troubles made for great copy in a media industry that was always searching for another Washington drama. The fact that so many Democrats had voted against Wright on this pay raise indicated to the shrewd Atwater that he was becoming a drag on his party, and the strategist prepared to pounce. "With Atwater at the R.N.C.," one Democrat admitted ruefully, "we expect methodical attacks on Democratic members. Private investigators will be used by Republican challengers, who will be programmed to make Atwater-style campaigns."[37] Wright heard from trusted sources that Atwater fully supported Gingrich's attacks on him.[38] In other words, Gingrich and Atwater were pursuing the same grand strategy: take down Wright, and take back the House.

Atwater had gained a powerful ally when Ed Rollins took over the moribund National Republican Congressional Committee. The first person who called to congratulate Rollins was Gingrich, who appreciated what he had done in Reagan's 1984 campaign. "We'll give you a five-million-dollar bonus if you get us a majority," Gingrich half joked in their brief conversation. "Safe bet," Rollins replied.[39] Atwater, Rollins, and Gingrich fed off one another even if they did not directly coordinate their activities. All of them saw that Speaker Wright was *the* major liability for the Democrats. Rollins, who looked like a bulldog, was the driving force within the GOP to make Wright a centerpiece of the party's midterm campaigns. A populist Democrat turned Republican and the mastermind behind Reagan's 1984 landslide victory against Walter Mondale, Rollins was a tough campaign strategist who knew exactly how to package messages in the new media environment. "The ugly scenes of Capitol Hill," the syndicated *Washington Post* columnist David Broder concluded about this convergence of circumstances—the weakened Democrats, the resurgent GOP, an activist electorate, and a House Ethics Committee deep into its investigation—"could be a prelude to more panic politics to come. A House scared enough of its shadowy reputation to abandon a pay increase is certainly scared enough to ditch a speaker many of its members now regard as a campaign liability."[40]

And so the plan became official on February 22, 1989, when the Republican National Committee announced that Speaker Wright would be the centerpiece of the Republican midterms, still twenty-one months away. "Target No. 1," Rollins said in a simple yet direct statement to reporters. "My responsibility is not governing. My responsibility is to go out and try to knock out as many Democrats as I can. And obviously the guy I'm going to make Target No. 1 is the Speaker," he warned.[41] The findings of a National Republican Congressional Committee poll back in June 1988 had proven to Rollins that targeting Wright and Democratic corruption was a winning strategy. The NRCC pollsters first informed voters that the Democrats controlled the House (45 percent of respondents did not know this) and then explained that Wright and thirteen other Democrats were being investigated by the Ethics Committee. When the NRCC then asked those polled whether they would vote for Republicans to replace the

Democratic leadership, 51 percent said yes.[42] Following Rollins's comment about "Target No. 1," the Democrats immediately felt the shifting winds and the electoral risks they took by defending the Speaker. And the tactics in this political fight were about to get nastier. As the pugnacious Rollins responded to a reporter's question, "I promise you today that I won't steal, murder, lie, cheat or pillage, but other than that I think just about anything goes."[43]

Their commitment to tougher partisan warfare was strengthened in response to the Senate confirmation battle over President Bush's nominee for secretary of defense, John Tower. A former chairman of the Senate Armed Services Committee, the sixty-three-year-old was respected by many on the Right for his hawkish positions on military spending and his strong relationship with the defense community. He was the Republican who had replaced Lyndon Johnson in the Senate in 1961. Since retiring from the Senate in 1985, Tower had been teaching at Southern Methodist University.

Although Sam Nunn, the hawkish Democrat who chaired the Armed Services Committee, predicted a smooth confirmation process, Tower came under fierce attack. With Bush in the White House, Senate Democrats were eager to flex their muscles. They portrayed Tower as a hard-drinking womanizer who could not handle the job and as someone who, as a result of his committee chairmanship, was too close to defense industry contractors to serve as an ethical or effective secretary of defense. Democrats received an assist when the conservative activist Paul Weyrich expressed doubts as to whether the senator possessed the "moral character" necessary for the job. Since his first encounter with Gingrich at the 1975 campaign workshop in Milwaukee, Weyrich had emerged as a towering figure in conservative politics; his Heritage Foundation was one of the most influential right-wing think tanks, and he founded a number of other conservative organizations and campaign operations that supported candidates and pushed social causes. When someone from the Right with Weyrich's stature raised questions about Tower, Republicans and the media listened. The blitzkrieg of attacks that followed—most of them based on rumors coming out of Washington, as well as an FBI background report on Tower that described a "pattern of alcohol abuse," which Senator Ernest Hollings of South Carolina released to the press—killed Tower's nomination. Nunn backed off his support too.

Gingrich could see where this was all heading, and the Georgian had just the right warhead ready to launch. Gingrich warned that "the Sam Nunn rule on the chain of command has to apply" to the Speaker. "One thing you can count on," Gingrich promised. "On the morning after the Tower vote, we are going to ask Nunn, 'If you couldn't stomach Tower at the Department of Defense, how do you feel about Jim Wright being second in line to be president?'"[44]

Just forty-eight days into his presidency, on March 9, President Bush suffered a humiliating blow when the Senate rejected Tower's nomination by a vote largely along party lines. The vote was "conducted in almost funereal calm" as each senator sat silently while the final count was tallied.[45] Everybody wanted the process to end. Fifty-two Democrats and one Republican (Kansas's Nancy Landon Kassebaum) voted against Tower's nomination. Forty-four Republicans and three Democrats (Texas's Lloyd Bentsen, Connecticut's Christopher Dodd, and Alabama's Howell Heflin) voted in favor. "The nomination of John Tower to be Secretary of Defense is not confirmed," announced Vice President Dan Quayle. Only after an uncomfortable silence did the senators stand up and quietly walk to the chamber door.

This was the only time in American history that a new president had seen his cabinet nominee rejected, and the first time in thirty years that a sitting president's cabinet choice had gone down to defeat. Republicans charged—Weyrich and his conservative activists notwithstanding—that Senator Tower had been defeated through a partisan campaign of character assassination. The Senate minority leader, Dole, decried the outcome, saying of Tower, "After what we've done to this good man, maybe we ought to hang our heads. He knows this is politics. He knows he's being shot down because he's a Republican and there are more Democrats than Republicans."[46] John McCain, in the middle of his first Senate term, instantly drew a connection between Tower and the ethics investigation of Wright: "What about the Speaker of the House, what about dealings with savings and loan institutions or book contracts? The specific allegations against Jim Wright are much more specific than they are against John Tower."[47]

Gingrich, viewing all this on his television set, fumed. Senate Republicans had bungled the confirmation, and Democrats had placed another notch in their belt. Now Gingrich was especially eager to see the Ethics Committee report, scheduled to be released soon, so that he could help his party exact its revenge. As one of Gingrich's partisans framed it, "the Tower stuff" will hurt Wright most. "It takes ethics and raises it to a higher level. . . . House Democrats will now have to be as tough on him as Senate Democrats have been on Tower."[48] Senate Democrats had taken out a high-ranking general; now Republican soldiers needed to even the score.

If there had ever been a chance that House Republicans would be merciful to Wright, that time had passed. And with the RNC planning to use the Speaker to drive down Democratic majorities, the decision about Tower motivated many Republicans to accept Gingrich's logic. Why not fight by destroying a person's character? Even Democrats could see what was on the horizon. Speaking to a reporter, the Montana Democrat Pat Williams predicted that "there will be an orchestrated assault on the Speaker and the Democrats by Republicans," because the confirmation fiasco "makes Republicans want to get even."[49]

Enter Gingrich stage right. In the spring of 1989, the Soviet Union was crumbling, and President George H. W. Bush did not feel that he could wait long to fill the post of secretary of defense. He desperately needed to appoint someone whose confirmation would be speedy and successful. He turned to Dick Cheney, who had only recently taken over as minority whip when Trent Lott won election to the Senate. At forty-eight years old, Cheney was the second-highest-ranking figure in the House GOP. Rollins and Atwater had been grooming this tough, right-wing conservative to be the next Speaker of the House. In contrast to Tower, Cheney was known in Washington as a cerebral straight arrow (though he had flunked out of Yale University after partying too much). His hawkish right-leaning political bona fides were unimpeachable, and his defense of the administration's actions during Iran-contra and of officials like Oliver North had permanently endeared him to the conservative sector of the caucus. As word of President Bush's selection reached Capitol Hill, all three Democratic House leaders praised the choice. They were eager to dispel notions that their rejection of Tower had been wholly partisan. "Dick is a very serious and committed conservative and he'll be fairly tough minded about a lot of issues," commented the House majority leader, Tom Foley. "I think it's a splendid choice, a man of great experience and capacity and ability and I would hazard a guess that there'll be an early and unanimous confirmation."[50] Just one week and one day after Tower's rejection, the Senate approved Cheney by a vote of 92 to 0.

The successful appointment of the nation's seventeenth secretary of defense created a big vacancy in the House Republican leadership team. Minority whip was a powerful position, responsible for counting votes, lobbying undecided members to support or reject legislation, and keeping accurate track of the vote count. The majority and minority whips were considered important liaisons between the top party leaders and the rank and file. If you became whip, you joined the inner circle.

With Cheney's seat still warm, Gingrich seized the opportunity to take his job. For years, Gingrich had conducted his attacks from the position of a bomb-throwing maverick. His status had risen much more than Republican leaders were comfortable acknowledging, given that they were echoing his message about the corruption of House Democrats. The campaign against Speaker Wright had boosted his political standing, which was the only reason he had a fighting chance for a leadership position to begin with. Now, after having gained national attention as a result of the Ethics Committee taking up his charges against Wright, the Georgian wanted legitimacy.

But Gingrich would have to compete to win the job. One of the earliest contenders was the California Republican Jerry Lewis, who was a fund-raising juggernaut and a master politician. Lewis had started his career on the San Bernardino School Board, he had recently been elected chairman of the Republican Conference, and he was seen as next in line for the job, given that he was third in the official Republican leadership hierarchy. Moreover, Lewis appealed to a broad coalition of Republicans. He was more moderate than many of his colleagues on social issues like abortion, and he had effectively used his centrist reputation to position himself as an agent of legislative compromise. Like his fellow freshman class member Dick Cheney, Lewis had secured a seat on the powerful Appropriations Committee only two years after being elected to the House in 1978, a position that enabled him to win support from a large number of colleagues who became indebted for his assistance obtaining earmarked funds. His relationships with his fellow Republicans were further strengthened by the committee assignments he arranged for while serving as a member of the "Committee on Committees." Charismatic and handsome, with a great mane of shiny black hair, Lewis was completely at ease in front of the television cameras. Gingrich would have trouble taking him on.

Another candidate for the whip position was the fifty-three-year-old Illinois representative Edward Madigan, who came with a proven conservative track record on domestic issues, such as his staunch opposition to environmental regulation or federal health-care programs. Madigan, who before entering Congress ran his hometown's yellow cab company, was a quintessential Republican insider. At a time when many Republicans were spending their waking hours finding new ways to rail against Washington, Madigan lived and breathed the art of deal making. If Republicans sought to replace the whip with someone cut from the cloth of Minority Leader Michel, Madigan was their man. Already serving as the deputy whip for Michel, Madigan thrived in the messiness of bipartisan negotiation and legislative horse-trading.

With two reliable choices—Gingrich was a nonstarter in his mind—Michel lobbied for Madigan. In public, Michel stayed out of the race, following the custom for the party leader. But behind the scenes, he threw his full weight behind Madigan, not simply because he liked his style or because they came from the same state but also because he owed him a favor. Madigan had agreed to voluntarily step down as ranking member of

Energy and Commerce (moving to Agriculture) so that Michel could prevent the Vermont Republican Jim Jeffords, a liberal Watergate Baby, from obtaining a seat on the panel.[51] In paying him back through his informal backing to be whip, Michel was making the controversial decision to side with Madigan over the Illinois Republican Henry Hyde, a popular dyed-in-the-wool conservative and a serious legislator respected for his parliamentary acumen. Hyde combined the capacity to legislate, more so than Gingrich, with a commitment to the rightward agenda. He had gained national prominence in 1976 when he pushed through an amendment to legislation that imposed stringent restrictions on the use of federal funds to provide abortions to low-income women. This was a landmark victory for conservatives who had been fighting to overturn *Roe v. Wade*, and one with a lasting impact decades later. Michel told Hyde, who was interested in the job, that Madigan would have his support and the final votes.[52] Gingrich breathed a sigh of relief because he felt that Hyde could unite the conservatives and the establishment votes into an unbeatable voting bloc.

That Michel and the deputy whip were both from Illinois posed a problem, because the parties historically tended to distribute leadership positions to legislators from various states, but many Republicans nevertheless believed that Madigan was exactly what the GOP needed at this turbulent moment. For Republicans who disliked Gingrich and his methods, electing Madigan would affirm the kind of civil politics senior House Republicans believed they had practiced for decades.

Madigan even generated enthusiasm from some stout conservatives, including the brash Texan Tom DeLay, who, with ambitions of his own, wanted to show Michel that he could be a team player. Elected in 1984, one year before he became a born-again Christian, DeLay was a proud right-winger with a religious zeal for deregulation. A former owner of a pest extermination company, he had entered politics out of his frustration with environmental rules. In a strategic move, Madigan asked DeLay to run his campaign. The Texan then recruited another solid conservative to assist him, a new Republican congressman from Illinois named Dennis Hastert, a plainspoken and heavyset former high school wrestling coach.

Elected in 1954, Jim Wright came of age in an era of Congress dominated by pork-barrel spending, bipartisan deal making, and closed-room negotiations. Younger members followed Speaker Sam Rayburn's dictate, "to get along, go along." On November 22, 1963, Wright welcomes Vice President Lyndon Johnson and President John F. Kennedy at a rally in Fort Worth. Later that day, Kennedy would travel to Dallas, where he would be assassinated.

Newt Gingrich, who received a Ph.D. from Tulane University, started his career as a history professor at West Georgia College in 1970.

Gingrich speaking during his 1976 campaign for the House of Representatives against Democrat John Flynt—his second attempt—surrounded by his wife Jackie and their two daughters, Jackie Sue and Kathy. He won office two years later when Flynt retired. The first Republican to represent this district, Gingrich shifted to the right and campaigned as part of the growing conservative movement.

Speaker-elect of the House Tip O'Neill and Wright meet with the press on December 6, 1976, after Democrats elected Wright to be majority leader. Given that younger Democrats had been ousting old southern barons in the wake of Vietnam and Watergate, few pundits expected Wright to be victorious. But a four-way race opened up space for him to defeat two prominent reform-oriented colleagues.

President Ronald Reagan delivers his inaugural address from the U.S. Capitol on January 20, 1981. Gingrich, who watched from the crowd, still felt that Democratic control of the House of Representatives meant the "Reagan Revolution" would be stifled, and that the media would blame the president. Reagan's election left him doubly determined to do whatever it took to win majority control.

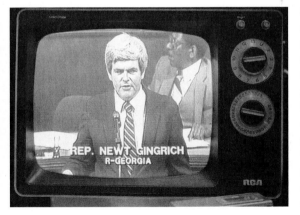

In early May 1984, Gingrich and his allies in the Conservative Opportunity Society (COS) orchestrated a series of blistering attacks on Democrats in front of the C-SPAN cameras. Gingrich, who understood better than most the potential of cable television, read from a report that criticized Democrats for being "weak on defense." Viewers could not see that the chamber was empty when Republicans called on Democrats to respond.

Gingrich's personal life was always problematic. A syndicated Doonesbury cartoon in 1984 popularized the story from the left-wing magazine *Mother Jones*, whose reporter found that Gingrich discussed divorce with his wife while she was in the hospital recovering from cancer surgery.

The Conservative Opportunity Society emerged as the congressional wing of the Reagan Revolution. In 1986, the year that Democrats would retake control of the U.S. Senate, Reagan met Gingrich and Robert Walker (PA) and Connie Mack (FL) of COS. Walker, an unexpected star to conservative C-SPAN viewers, looks toward the camera.

The mood among Republicans was bleak in the weeks that followed the 1986 midterm elections. Not only had Democrats recaptured control of the Senate, but the Iran-contra scandal stoked fears that the president could be impeached. At this cabinet room meeting on November 25, Reagan is in a state of shock as he meets with congressional leaders about the sales of arms to Iran, including Senators Robert Dole and Robert Byrd, as well as Minority Leader Michel and the next Speaker of the House, Wright.

Having reached the pinnacle of power, Wright stands proudly in the doorway of his office in 1987, his first year as Speaker.

Wright's diplomatic efforts in Central America to bring an end to the Nicaraguan civil war angered conservative Republicans. On August 5, 1987, Wright and Robert Michel stood outside the White House following the announcement of a Central American peace plan.

Bipartisan good government organizations created in the 1970s in the wake of Watergate demanded higher standards from politicians. Gingrich and newspaper reporters had raised questions about Wright's behavior. When Fred Wertheimer and his organization Common Cause called on the House Ethics Committee to launch an investigation into Wright in May 1988, Gingrich's campaign against the Speaker gained more legitimacy.

Gingrich turned Wright's legislative work and personal relationships in his district into a political vulnerability. The ethics investigation looked into whether Fort Worth real estate developer George Mallick had given Wright, his long-time friend and investment partner, sizable gifts in exchange for influence over federal legislation that benefited his business.

The redevelopment of the Fort Worth Stock Yards into a major tourist attraction became another part of the investigation. While Wright's supporters praised his success at turning this area of the city into a stretch of town filled with saloons, restaurants, stores, museums, and western heritage celebrations, critics like Gingrich argued that the federal funding used in this project was part of a sordid nexus of government money, real estate developers, and crooked congressmen.

Gingrich found growing support from the Republican establishment, including the 1988 Republican presidential nominee, Vice President George H. W. Bush. South Carolinian Lee Atwater, who ran Bush's 1988 campaign, injected the Wright scandal into "mainstream" Republican politics. Confronted with criticism from Governor Michael Dukakis about the "sleaze factor" in the Reagan White House, Bush pointed to Wright as evidence that Democrats were corrupt. Atwater's hardball style of politics meshed well with the campaign against the Speaker that Gingrich was leading in Congress.

Wright and his wife, Betty, at an event at the Capitol Hilton on December 18, 1988. Betty, who was usually dressed to the nines, also became a focus of the investigation. The Washington rumor mill blamed Wright's need for money on her spending habits. The attacks on his wife were more upsetting to Wright than almost any other part of the saga.

Wright meets with President Bush on Capitol Hill on Tuesday, February 8, 1989, soon after the House rejected the 51 percent pay raise. Wright had been caught off guard by the impact of conservative talk radio, which had been freed from restrictions with the elimination of the fairness doctrine. The poorly handled legislation undermined Wright's standing within the Democratic caucus at the exact moment when he needed stronger support in his party.

Atwater (right), Ed Rollins (center), and Republican operative Roger Stone (left) meeting about GOP strategy. When Rollins, the head of the National Republican Congressional Committee announced that Wright would be "Target No. 1" in the 1990 midterm elections, Democrats ran for cover as they believed that the Speaker was making all of them vulnerable.

When President George H. W. Bush appointed Wyoming representative Dick Cheney, one of Wright's fiercest critics, as secretary of defense one year after the failed confirmation of Senator John Tower, the position of House minority whip suddenly opened up and created a vacancy in the Republican leadership.

Gingrich had the uncanny ability to brush aside his own political scandals, even as he pursued the Speaker. On March 20, 1989, two days before Republicans voted for a new House minority whip, Newt and Marianne, his second wife, spoke to the press about his book deal for *Window of Opportunity* to counter ethics accusations that Democrats had leveled against him.

Because of his role in the Wright investigation, Gingrich gained an official seat in the Republican leadership, a turning point in his career. Robert Michel, a symbol of bipartisan civility who had nonetheless capitalized on his colleague's fierce campaign against the Democratic leadership, congratulated Gingrich when he won the race for minority whip on March 22, 1989.

By the spring of 1989, Democrats felt that the Speaker was under siege as Gingrich escalated his attacks. Flanked by top House Democrats, Wright stands in the Rayburn Room on April 13, in front of a portrait of George Washington (who never told a lie), at a press conference to respond to the ethics charges.

Gingrich walks around the halls of the Capitol carrying the House Ethics Committee report in his arms.

Congressman Julian Dixon (CA), chairman of the House Ethics Committee, directs a hearing on April 20, 1989. Special prosecutor Richard Phelan sits to his left. Phelan's ruthless prosecutorial methods were extremely effective at raising concerns within the Ethics Committee and the media even though Wright's supporters pointed to mistakes, misstatements, and misleading information contained in his lengthy report. Wright's attorneys mounted a legalistic defense of their client while Phelan painted a damning portrait of corruption and scandalous behavior.

On April 21, the day after a last ditch effort to dismiss the charges failed, Wright sits with a forced smile for the cameras in his Capitol Hill office. He was barely containing his frustration that the Ethics Committee was dragging its feet in allowing him to respond to the accusation that he was guilty of sixty-nine violations of House rules.

Wright's standing deteriorated rapidly on May 4, 1989, when journalist Ken Ringle (pictured here at his desk) published a bombshell story in *The Washington Post*. The lengthy piece revolved around a brutal assault that had taken place years earlier on Pamela Small by John Mack, who had gone on to become Speaker Wright's top aide.

Colorado representative Pat Schroeder, who had remained loyal to the Speaker despite her doubts about his liberalism, emerged as one of the most vocal opponents of Mack being able to keep his job. Schroeder was outraged by the story and saw Mack's presence in the leadership as further confirmation of the male culture that dominated Capitol Hill.

When the powerful majority whip Tony Coelho resigned on May 27 because of his own financial ethics scandal, the murmurs about Speaker Wright stepping down intensified.

On May 31, 1989, Wright delivered his resignation speech, in which he warned against "mindless cannibalism." Here he holds up a copy of *Reflections of a Public Man*, a book that became the focus of the scandal.

Gingrich listens angrily to Wright's resignation speech. Gingrich felt that Wright was blaming Republican partisanship rather than taking responsibility for his own actions. At the same time, Gingrich realized that he had become a major political force in Washington.

One of the workers in Jim Wright's district office captures the feeling of many Capitol Hill veterans about the resignation speech.

Wright and his wife depart from the Capitol following the resignation speech. Wright hoped that his stepping down would calm the partisan wars on Capitol Hill. A horde of reporters are on hand to capture this historic moment. Betty's steely glare offers a stark contrast to the Speaker's smile.

Wright's hopes of ending the worsening partisan wars did not come true. Instead, Gingrich went on to become one of the nation's most influential Republicans as a result of his taking down Wright. His style of Republican partisanship prevailed. In November 1994, Republicans would take control of Congress for the first time in forty years and elect Gingrich as Speaker of the House.

Former Speakers Wright, Tom Foley, Gingrich, and Dennis Hastert meet during a tense ceremony on November 12, 2003. Wright forgave Gingrich, but the Georgian never really apologized for what he had done.

Gingrich liked his chances, despite the broad respect his opponents had among the members. He saw himself as the only true "anti-establishment" candidate at a moment when Republicans desperately needed new leadership. He alone had racked up meaningful political victories, not least by bringing Speaker Wright to his knees, as he never failed to remind his colleagues. Ronald Reagan had played the maverick as a presidential contender. Gingrich would fill the same role within Congress.

But he had ground to make up. Gingrich was on his way to his field office in Griffin, Georgia, when President Bush announced the appointment of Cheney. After a *USA Today* reporter informed him what had happened, Gingrich began to frenetically work the phones. "As soon as the receiver hits the cradle of my phone, I know I'm running," Gingrich recalled.[53] For the first time, Gingrich engaged in the kind of old-fashioned political vote gathering he usually abhorred. He knew that he had to reach legislators before they promised their support to one of his opponents, particularly because he was not the obvious choice. He called his chief administrative assistant, Mary Brown, into his office and instructed her to locate where every member would be over the weekend so they could be reached.[54] Two hours after learning of Cheney's nomination, Gingrich had made thirty calls to possible supporters. He spent the entire weekend convincing Republicans that he could handle the nitty-gritty of vote counting and coalition building while touting himself as the only candidate with the vision to seize the House for Republicans for the first time since 1954.

From his cramped field office, Gingrich tapped into his network of allies like Pennsylvania's Robert Walker and Joe Barton of Texas, who spent all of Sunday working the phones to round up votes. Often, Walker recalled, he couldn't keep up with his friend. "I was calling people, who were telling me, oh yeah, I've already had three or four calls about Newt Gingrich. . . . Even people who said they couldn't support Newt were impressed by the fact that the whole organizational thing seemed to come together."

By the time Gingrich returned to Washington on Sunday night, March 12, he had obtained assurances from fifty-five Republicans that they would vote for him. The Republicans who supported Newt were angry, not just about being a permanent minority, but also about the heavy-handed way in which Wright had treated their caucus. Even if they didn't like Gingrich personally, many of them wanted a leader who would play rough with the Democratic majority. Wright's stubbornness with the Bloody Eighth, his brash decision to hold open the vote on the controversial budget bill in 1987, and the struggles over Nicaragua had created a great sense of urgency among Republicans to change the status quo and to revise their tactics. To have a Democratic Speaker take such defiant stands in the midst of the Reagan-led revolution was unbearable.

Gingrich would need another thirty-two votes for a win, so he distributed talking points to his supporters to sway undecided members. His candidacy, the talking points emphasized, was the only one that could give Republicans any chance of controlling the House by the year 2000. At the same time, feigning humility, Gingrich's surrogates were instructed to say that he wanted Michel to become the Speaker and that, until then, he would be "Michel's whip." This message was intended to show concerned Republicans that he would remain subordinate. And, countering Madigan's appeal to moderates, Gingrich stressed that he was not the rabid conservative his opponents painted him as: without much evidence to support his point, he said that he had a good record of working with moderates on environmental and racial issues, as well as with women and, yes, even Democrats.[55]

A few days after Bush announced Cheney's nomination, Gingrich's promised vote total was up to seventy, eighteen short of victory. On Thursday, he looked to seal his victory by circulating the galleys of a forthcoming editorial in William Buckley's *National Review*, the gold standard for conservative opinion, endorsing his candidacy.[56] According to the editors, Gingrich "irradiates energy, rather like the sun, and there is zero ozone layer between him and Speaker Jim Wright, whose progressively deteriorating situation is the result of Newt Gingrich's insistence that if there is to be ethical conduct by members of the House of Representatives, there ought also to be ethical conduct by the Speaker of the House of Representatives." The editors continued, Gingrich "wants to give the House an opportunity to be organized by a Republican majority. To this end, more resourcefully than anyone else whose name comes to mind, he is willing and anxious to work day and night, exploring Democratic techniques for effecting political longevity, shredding the artificial barriers that have been erected to thwart the will of the voters."[57]

But as the campaign pressed on, Gingrich had to contend with bad news. Congressman Lewis announced that he was dropping out of the competition. This was a blow for Gingrich because the non-maverick votes would be united around Madigan.

Then, as quickly as the pool of candidates had shrunk, it expanded again. After making his announcement to a press conference, Lewis started walking toward the exit. Before he left the room, one of his supporters, the New York Republican Gerald Solomon, stormed up to the lectern and yelled to the assembled reporters, many of them already packing up, "Ladies and gentlemen, wait. I have an important announcement! I know you'll be interested!" Although Lewis, who was shocked by his colleague's outburst, continued walking, almost all the reporters turned around to listen. "Henry Hyde [an Illinois representative] will be nominated for whip," Solomon revealed.[58] "Could you identify yourself?" asked one reporter who couldn't recognize the New Yorker. Solomon, without consulting Hyde, made this impromptu announcement after having supported Lewis right until the press conference. Solomon, who agreed with Gingrich on policy and tactics, feared that his colleague from Georgia did not have what it took to serve in a leadership role. He would be unable to control his ego in front of the cameras and ultimately subvert the party's chances of gaining a majority. With this Hail Mary move, Solomon tried to throw Hyde into the competition.

"Everyone in our party says Henry is the best man for the job and I'm going to nominate him," Solomon announced to stunned reporters. From the moment that Solomon shared his plan with the press, Republican support for Hyde as a conservative alternative to Gingrich grew steadily. Those who were wary of Gingrich's tactics were drawn to Hyde's candidacy.

Meanwhile, some Republicans had become frustrated with Michel's aggressive lobbying behind the scenes for Madigan after Hyde entered the race. For instance, Michel placed one of Gingrich's closest allies on the Intelligence Committee, making it clear that he then owed him his vote.[59] On the day that Lewis announced to reporters that he would withdraw, fifteen conservative Republicans paid an unexpected visit to Michel's office to express their anger. They complained that his lieutenants were pressuring members to vote for Madigan by implying that if he won there would be repercussions for anyone who voted against him. The minority leader had control over committee assignments, budgetary resources, and a media platform that could be used against any Republican who stood in his way. The leader from Peoria, who prided himself on being "fair," was upset to see just how visibly disturbed his fellow Republicans were with what they perceived as his bullying tactics. Michel denied that he or his representatives had done anything heavy-handed, and he assured legislators that if what they said was true, he would tell his deputies to stop applying pressure so that everyone could vote his or her conscience.[60]

Gingrich's only hope was to emphasize his vision for winning the House for the GOP. He would never be seen as the insider who would be the best at working the halls of Congress and rounding up votes. Gingrich conceived of the whip's role as also being a master party strategist. "Other than (former Rep. Jack) Kemp," Gingrich boasted in his always confident tone, "I have been the most energetic Republican of my generation."[61]

By defining the decision that House Republicans had to make in these particular terms, Gingrich forced members who normally might lean toward the traditional choice, in this case Madigan, to give him a second look, sensing that there was a real possibility to overtake the Democrats. The humiliation the House GOP had already suffered during Wright's short tenure felt so intense that many were desperate for fundamental—not incremental—change. The success of Ronald Reagan had inspired an entire generation of Republicans to think differently about what was possible in American politics. Gingrich tried to win votes by appealing to those Republicans who were drawn to his overall vision for the party even if they didn't agree with his cutthroat maneuvers. "We have good ideas," said the Rhode Island representative Claudine Schneider, a liberal

Republican, explaining her support, "but they're not coming from the old establishment that has been happy to go along. Newt is a strategist . . . a mover and shaker."[62]

Besides spreading his vision for the party's future, Gingrich continued to throw himself into the job of whipping up his own vote. Gingrich, who woke at 5:30 every morning, met with potential supporters during one-on-one walks at six. Wearing his hiking boots, he strolled with undecided colleagues through the empty National Mall, quoting Machiavelli or Churchill from memory as they passed by the Smithsonian museums and paced toward the Washington Monument, to explain what his party needed to do to finally achieve true political power.[63]

And like both of those tacticians, Gingrich had a knack for goading his opponents into fighting political battles on his terms. Madigan did not shy away from the contrast that Gingrich was trying to make. Instead, he embraced it. Madigan, depicting himself as the "wiser" candidate, warned fellow Republicans of the potential cost of electing someone as erratic as Gingrich to be a leader. "The Whip is the guy who makes things work," Madigan explained. "The job description is coalition building."[64] Although Gingrich might sound exciting to Republicans who were bruised from their battles with Speaker Wright, Madigan warned that he would be disastrous as whip, worsening divisions and discord with the Democrats as well as alienating Republican leadership with his over-the-top personality. Madigan said that Gingrich's fierce partisan schemes would doom the GOP to be even more marginalized and ostracized, because he would burn any lines of communication with Democrats. Of course, these arguments were a harder sell for disillusioned Republicans because Madigan himself, along with the leadership, had repeatedly issued statements declaring that Democrats had rendered the GOP powerless.

Whereas Gingrich wanted Republicans to bet on their ability to become the majority, Madigan claimed that he was offering them the most pragmatic approach for exerting influence as a continued minority. He described Gingrich's promise that the GOP could become a Republican majority in the House in the near future as quixotic. "The important thing for people in a minority is not to cause themselves to become irrelevant. If your minority becomes ineffective through confrontation with the majority," Madigan counseled his fellow Republicans, "then your party is out of the loop. You have to be in a coalition-building posture all the time. That's my forte. That's what I've done."[65]

The media enjoyed the slugfest. When covering the race, reporters adopted Gingrich's framework for the stakes of the leadership race. Previous elections had seemed like an insider's game of musical chairs, and this was more exciting to cover. The press described it as a contest between change and the status quo, or "Newt versus anti-Newt," in the words of the Oklahoma Republican Mickey Edwards. "It's Mr. Inside vs. Mr. Outside; the coalition-builder vs. the confrontationalist." It made for excellent copy and sound bites.

In contrast to Gingrich, Madigan didn't do much to court the media. When the prestigious PBS program *The MacNeil/Lehrer NewsHour* invited him to speak about his campaign, he turned down the invitation in order to use the valuable time remaining to make calls to members. And rather than convening a press conference in the final days of the race, the kind of event Gingrich masterfully used to depict himself as the agent of muscular change, Madigan spent just a few hours informally responding to reporters' queries. He was living in the age of newspapers, and Gingrich understood that this was the era of television. Having bought into Gingrich's characterization of this race as something more grandiose than most thought it would be, the reporters pressed Madigan to outline what he hoped to accomplish for the House Republicans. They wanted evidence that he could do more than count votes. In a somewhat diplomatic manner, Madigan responded by talking about his "special relationship" with Michel and how that would help him get things done. "I do not try to verbally abuse people in an acrimonious way that causes them to feel unable or unwilling to do business with me in the future," Madigan added so that he could get in a bit of a zinger.[66] The reporters' eyes glazed over as he stubbornly refused, or proved unable, to give them much to write about. While Gingrich was talking about revolution, Madigan was talking about competence.

Still, the race wasn't over yet. With only a few days to go before the election, a bombshell report raised questions about Gingrich's ethics. After months of covering Gingrich's charges against Speaker Wright for selling a book to interest groups as a way to circumvent honoraria restrictions, *The Washington Post* now reported that in 1984 Gingrich had a murky book deal of his own, all of which was legally aboveboard but smelled totally rotten. The scheme revolved around *Window of Opportunity: A Blueprint for the Future*.[67] The book, coauthored with his wife, Marianne, and a science fiction writer named David Drake, offered Republicans a familiar manifesto to regain power and transform policy.[68] According to the piece in *The Washington Post*, Gingrich had done something highly unusual to assist with the book's promotion. To supplement the publisher's campaign, he established a nonprofit institute that raised money from Republican donors, most of whom gave to Gingrich's campaigns, to be used for book advertisements in newspapers and the author's promotional travel. The COS Limited Partnership, as Gingrich called it, raised $105,000 in 1984. Each partner contributed $5,000 to the fund. The goal, Gingrich genially acknowledged to a reporter, was a half-baked plan to "force a bestseller," which would of course enhance Gingrich's public standing.

The story took an even more bizarre twist, because *Window of Opportunity* was a commercial failure. Even so, contributors to the COS Limited Partnership somehow managed to each earn a profit because they were eligible to write off their losses on their tax returns, making the story even more scandalous. *Washington Post* reporter Charles Babcock, who had broken the story on Wright's book-buying deal, noted that Newt's wife, Marianne, received $10,000 for her work as a "general partner" in the COS Limited Partnership.

All of the major newspapers picked up on Babcock's story.[69] This was not Gingrich's first brush with scandal. He had survived the *Mother Jones* article in 1984 that exposed the sordid underside of his private life. In the case of that article, Gingrich's response had been to ignore the story. This time the scandal felt very different, more threatening to him and his political agenda. *The Washington Post*'s piece undermined the legitimacy of his attacks on the Speaker, and the accusations tarnished his reputation as a champion of personal ethics. Gingrich understood that the story made him look guilty of the same kind of blatant hypocrisy that he constantly attacked Democrats for. Feeling the urgency of the moment, with the vote for minority whip fast approaching, Gingrich instructed his staff to quickly assemble a press conference to respond to the charges.

When the reporters convened on March 19 in the Radio-Television Gallery on the third floor of the Capitol, the room buzzed with anticipation about how Gingrich would react to the report. Seeming unfazed by the media scrum, Gingrich stepped up to the lectern armed with an explanation. His self-righteous attitude, even at a moment like this, is what made him so dangerous and formidable as a political opponent. With Babcock's report exposing the apparent contradiction between what Gingrich said in public about Wright and what he did in private about his own financial affairs, Gingrich exhibited the demeanor of a person who believed deep down that he was virtuous. He didn't care what the reporters said. They were wrong.

"This was totally legal, totally legitimate," Gingrich began, and it was nothing like what he was accusing Speaker Wright of having done.[70] "We wrote a real book for a real company that was sold in real bookstores," he argued. Gingrich, however, was forced to concede that he tried to delay the story for more than a month, because he knew that it would be a clear "disadvantage" in the whip's race if the press reported that he had arranged for a book deal that, in his words, was "equally as weird as Jim Wright's."[71] His own royalties, Gingrich explained, were reasonable, unlike the 55 percent received by the Speaker for his slapdash work. During the press conference, Marianne Gingrich stood by her husband's side as he swatted away the charges and predicted that this news would have no impact on the race. At one point, trying to maintain a steely demeanor, she held up a copy of *Window of Opportunity* as if to say that the material existence of the book proved its legitimacy. When asked by a reporter if she could furnish a list of the partners, Marianne insisted that nobody had done anything wrong. "One of the reasons they contributed is that they have been active in Republican politics and agreed with Newt's message."[72]

Democrats tried to run with the story as evidence that Gingrich wasn't the choirboy he made himself out to be. Wright couldn't resist saying something to reporters about the breaking scandal. "I find it somewhat remarkable that a fellow would write a book about how the Republicans were going to take over the House, and hire a science fiction writer to help."[73]

The story had an impact in spite of Gingrich's assurances. In the final days of the campaign for minority whip, there was great uncertainty about the outcome. Madigan claimed that he had pledges for ninety-three votes, enough for victory; Gingrich confidently announced that he was sure of at least eighty. Hyde's supporters boasted that they had forty votes. Regardless, it was a number that was high enough to scare both Madigan and Gingrich. Hyde's support would probably have been stronger had he not continually expressed ambivalence about wanting the job, insisting, "I'm not making phone calls or campaigning." He didn't want to run without Michel's support.

The math didn't add up. The estimates totaled 213 endorsements and there were only 175 House Republicans, 174 once Cheney was confirmed.[74] Relationships among Republicans became so strained that Robert Walker blasted Democrats in a floor speech, saying that their party had purposely interfered with the whip vote to trigger internal chaos. In a conspiratorial tone, Walker accused Democrats of planting the false reports in the media about Gingrich's book deal to stir doubts and speculation.[75]

The press favored Madigan. They loved to cover Gingrich in the same way that they liked to cover a good bench-clearing brawl, but most major newspaper editors tended to see Madigan as the "responsible" choice. They were still rooting for the old ways of Washington. A majority of them believed that Gingrich would be bad for the Republic, even if he would make for great stories. He seemed too dangerous to hold power.

The morning of March 22, in the early hours before the vote, Henry Hyde surveyed his diminishing chances and shook the race again by announcing that he did not want to be nominated. Realizing that he'd entered the race too late to amass enough votes to win, Hyde also knew that he had enough support to be the "spoiler" in the race, as he said. This was a role the devout Republican did not wish to play. Michel's good opinion meant a great deal to him, and he was leery of going up against the party leader.

That same morning, Madigan's support further eroded. Pennsylvania's Lawrence Coughlin came to meet with Michel in the minority leader's office. Michel had been counting on Coughlin's vote for Madigan. But Coughlin, averting his eyes, nervously revealed that he would vote for Gingrich. Coughlin justified his change of heart by saying that he wanted a candidate who could promote "a new generation of leadership."[76] In reality, Robert Walker had pressured Coughlin into changing his vote over breakfast.[77] If he didn't support Gingrich, COS would not be there to support him in the future, and if Gingrich won, he would not find a sympathetic ear in the whip's office come April. The news was a blow to Michel, who had just learned that another Madigan supporter, New Jersey's James Courter, wouldn't be showing up for the vote, citing previously scheduled commitments in his home state, where he was running for governor.[78] Though Michel had offered to let him use a personal airplane to fly to D.C., Courter, preferring to stay out of this messy conflict, declined.

Republicans gathered to make their decision in the elegant Capitol Hill Club. Legislators made their way under the green awning that led into the handsome town house, located a little over one block from the U.S. Capitol and next door to the Republican National Committee headquarters. This was one of Washington's most exclusive clubs, prime real estate, where party members spent evenings together drinking scotch, eating steaks, and smoking cigars. When Republicans walked through the front door ready to vote, most of them felt that they were on the verge of a historic decision. With Newt Gingrich in the race, they understood that the outcome could be a game changer. As they gathered in one of the ornate rooms decorated with thick carpets, dark wooden furniture, and walls lined with portraits of the great party leaders, many of whom never imagined that someone like Gingrich could one day represent the GOP, the legislators prepared to cast their votes. Jerry Lewis presided over the secret proceedings. Gingrich had shrewdly persuaded Bill Frenzel, who had been embittered by Wright's actions, to formally nominate him. By doing so, Gingrich hoped the respected senior moderate from Minnesota could help in his effort to win over the support of anyone still worried that Gingrich wouldn't do much more than cause trouble. As expected, Frenzel's words of support, and his urging of others to take some risks, resonated with many legislators in the room. Connecticut's Nancy Johnson, Maine's Olympia Snowe, and Rhode Island's Claudine Schneider were all moderates who supported the nomination and sent a similar message. Johnson called Gingrich a "leader who has the vision to build a majority party and the strength and charisma to do it."[79]

The people who spoke in favor of Madigan only confirmed the impression that he was the candidate of Washington. His key supporters—Kansas's Pat Roberts, New York's Jim Walsh, and New Jersey's Dean Gallo—were all Republicans with reputations for being part of the establishment.

When the votes were counted, Lewis paused to gather his thoughts and then proceeded to inform his colleagues that Gingrich had won. It was an extraordinarily narrow victory: 87 to 85. Just two votes changed the course of the GOP. Chance played a role in the outcome. One of the secret ballots was spoiled so it didn't count; one member also checked a line that said that he or she was voting for "another." But Gingrich's overall tally was coalitional, as he intended, drawing from the approximately thirty members of the Conservative Opportunity Society and more liberal Republicans like Olympia Snowe of Maine and John Paul Hammerschmidt of Arkansas, a good friend of President Bush's. When asked about the strategy of Republican leaders, Snowe admitted, "It's not working for us. We need to do something."

Just outside, waiting to hear about the final tally with a group of reporters, Gingrich thanked moderates in the caucus, as well as his wife, for helping him in the race. Whatever the outcome, he was pleased with how the campaign unfolded. Then the New Hampshire Republican Chuck Douglas, one of the young firebrands who had lobbied for Gingrich, threw open the door and exclaimed, "We did it!" Gingrich's staff and Marianne, with journalists watching the drama, began screaming and crying in jubilation.

Glowing from the tally, the newly designated whip entered the room where his colleagues were gathered and walked to the front as everyone rose to their feet to give him a standing ovation. At Gingrich's request, Michel, Madigan, and Guy Vander Jagt, who was still serving as the chairman of the National Republican Congressional Committee, came up to stand next to the victor as a sign of unity. But conservatives who failed to endorse him, like Tom DeLay, applauded politely, knowing that there would be hell to pay. They now had a thin-skinned enemy in the inner circle of the party leadership.

At the press conference that followed, a somber minority leader appeared beside Jerry Lewis, Marianne, and Gingrich as he stoically announced the results. A few days earlier, Gingrich had appeared at the exact same lectern with his wife trying to stifle a scandal; now he was standing before the same reporters as an official party leader. It was hard for many in the room to believe that Gingrich had prevailed. Standing next to Marianne, an emotionally charged Gingrich could barely contain his distaste for Michel, visibly impatient as he waited to speak, sighing heavily in front of the cameras.

When he walked up to the microphone, Gingrich told Republicans exactly what they needed to hear. The new minority whip gave assurances that he understood the responsibilities of the job. Feigning modesty, he said that the vote had depended on personal relationships and hard vote counting, nothing more. Gingrich rejected the idea that this was a victory for COS or the Right; rather, he said, this was a win for the entire party. "Every element of this party is winning through this process. It's not a COS victory. It is not a conservative activist victory. It is the entire Republican team."[80]

But tensions were palpable. The normally composed Michel revealed his discomfort when he mistakenly called his new partner "Nit" during the question-and-answer period, a slip that drew some chuckles. Closing his eyes, with his arms tensely folded, and shaking his head in embarrassment, Michel looked ahead as Gingrich, who stood there with a poker face and the faintest of smiles, half-laughing and half-mad, uttered from behind him, "It will take a while." The reporters laughed even harder, though they understood that he wasn't joking.

Gingrich couldn't resist an opportunity to declare that he had a mandate. The party was changing. The new minority whip noted, in pointed fashion that, according to Marianne, "had Michel wanted to break COS in the early days, he could have. Had Michel wanted to cripple you in the investigation of Jim Wright, he could have."[81]

This was his turn in the spotlight and he seized on it. "The truth is I represent a general mood and a generation direction [among House Republicans], and a level of energy," Gingrich offered while promising to build a more "aggressive" and "activist" party.[82] And then he trained his sights on Wright. His attack on the Speaker had galvanized his rise to power, and he wasn't going to stop now. When asked about his views on the Speaker, Gingrich assured the press that "if he's totally exonerated," then he would "say I am glad he's exonerated and I'm sorry for any pain I've caused him." If he was not exonerated, Gingrich added, the Speaker would have to leave. A reporter asked what it would mean for Wright to be "exonerated." Gingrich borrowed a famous comment from a Supreme Court case about pornography: you "know it when you see it." As he moved further away from voicing niceties about Michel and spoke more about Speaker Wright and the broken condition of the House, Gingrich came alive. He stepped closer to the microphone, almost as if to push Michel out of the television frame. When asked if he owed his victory to Wright's troubles, Gingrich answered, "No, but he didn't hurt."

Inching his way back into the picture, Michel took up the cudgel. He, too, would be a fighter. When one reporter asked Michel how Gingrich's election changed the institution, he answered, "I'd like to think for the better." Michel added, "They want us to be more activated, and more visible, and more aggressive and we can't be content with business as usual."

The press wasted no time in announcing the changing of the guard. CONFRONTATIONAL CONSERVATIVE WINS PARTY'S NO. 2 POST, the *Los Angeles Times* reported. THE REPUBLICANS WANT TO STRESS OPPOSITION MORE THAN

LOYALTY, according to *The New York Times*. NEW CONFRONTATIONAL STANCE BY PARTY IS PORTENDED BY FIREBRAND'S VICTORY, read *The Wall Street Journal*. One cartoonist depicted a jolted Wright, as if an earthquake had hit, with his coffee cup hovering in midair, with a caption that read, "Newt Gingrich has been elected WHAT?"[83] A reliable barometer of elite conservative opinion, the *Journal* assailed the so-called experts who had missed the shifting direction of the political winds. "The Washington establishment had become comfortable with the House Republicans," the editors noted, "much the way audiences are comfortable with the Washington Generals, the team that serves as the doormat for the Harlem Globetrotters. . . . Mr. Gingrich is likely to keep House Democrats awake and alert."[84] He appeared in as many television interviews as possible to spread his gospel. "I'm the first leader of the C-SPAN generation," Gingrich explained during a C-SPAN call-in show.[85]

President Bush was on the fence about his partner on the Hill. On the day of Gingrich's victory, Bush pondered in his diary, "The question is—will he be confrontational; will he raise hell with the establishment; and will he be difficult for me to work with? I don't think so. I called him and congratulated him. He's going to have to get along in some degree, and moderate his flamboyance. He will be a tough competitor for the Democrats, but I'm convinced I can work with him and I want to work with him. He's a very bright guy, [an] idea a minute, but he hasn't been elected President and I have." The president decided to invite Gingrich, along with Vin Weber, to meet in the White House over beers. After some pleasantries and small talk, Weber, who sensed that the president was holding back, got right to the point. He asked, "Mr. President, you've been very nice to us. Tell us what your biggest fear is about us." Bush responded bluntly, "I'm worried that sometimes your idealism will get in the way of what I think is sound governance."[86]

Wright was a fighter too, and he knew that Gingrich's ascent would cause him trouble. Following Gingrich's election as whip, the Speaker initially didn't give the victor a customary congratulatory call. Instead, the Speaker opted for a little humor as a way to deliver a stern Texas warning. The Speaker sent Gingrich a note that said, "If you think a two-vote victory is thin, try it sometime with one, as I had to settle for in '76"—a reminder that Newt did not have his whole party behind him and that Wright himself had come a long way. To give the Georgian a little taste of his own ethical medicine, the Speaker sent him a Xerox copy of the cover of *Reflections of a Public Man* along with a note, published in the press, that pointedly said, "For Newt, who likes books too."[87]

For his part, Gingrich made it clear that he had no intention of letting up. During the Easter recess, he gathered members of the press who were bored by the inactivity of the holiday. He told them bluntly as he grabbed another headline, "I have placed $1 bets that Foley will be speaker by June."[88]

Six

SCANDAL FRENZY

I n late February, the special counsel Richard Phelan delivered an exhaustive 450-page report on Speaker Wright to the House Ethics Committee, documenting every alleged wrongdoing he had discovered. After nine months and almost $1.5 million, the blistering report made the Speaker look like a petty politician, at best, who routinely abused power for personal gain. Phelan was heavy-handed with the evidence, twisting information in a negative fashion and inserting every charge into the document regardless of its veracity. He claimed that Wright had violated the rules over a hundred times. His report left no doubt of the Speaker's guilt, at least in his opinion.[1] He followed up by testifying, point by point, before the committee during three weeks of hearings.

Phelan's case was at least superficially strengthened by Wright's dough-faced attorney William Oldaker, who tried to bring the controversy to a conclusion with old-fashioned backroom negotiations based on rational appeals to the facts and a measure of good old wheeling and dealing. Oldaker was an expert on election laws and fund-raising rules; he felt at home in the world of cigar-chomping lobbyists and litigators who knew how to make deals when partisan passions flared. As such, he was doing everything possible to refute the accusations in private meetings with members of Congress. But Oldaker was out of his league. He had few tools to counteract the pressure coming from congressional Republicans and investigative reporters, not to mention the histrionics of Phelan.[2]

When the ethics panel heard final arguments from both Phelan and Oldaker, the members found Speaker Wright's defense awkwardly underwhelming. Just as when Wright had spoken to the committee directly, Oldaker parsed legal interpretations of the rules to prove that the Speaker had not technically violated ethics standards. He treated the committee members like a courtroom jury as opposed to a roomful of self-interested politicians. He instructed them, "The obligation here of the committee is only to find a violation where there has been clear and convincing evidence. . . . I ask each Member who has a particular concern on that issue to study the record in detail; and if that determination is going to turn on the interpretation of a rule, I ask you to look at that rule as it is written, as the legislative history would suggest."[3]

Oldaker's opening remarks unintentionally framed the fact-finding stage of the ethics process as more definitive than it really was. The committee's official standard in the preliminary investigation, per the legislation that established it, was low, with the task being to merely determine if there was "reason to believe" that a legislator might have committed ethical improprieties. Deciding whether there was "clear and convincing" evidence of ethics violations would only come in the second stage despite what Oldaker stated. Then the standards of proof would be much closer to those used in a courtroom.

The committee members were seeking a full-throated, emotional defense of the Speaker and his integrity. The low-voltage, passionless Oldaker did not deliver; rather, he gave the impression of a person who just wanted this nonsense over with. He lectured the committee as if they were children who needed to get the facts straight. Crucially, he warned that Phelan, whom Oldaker called an overzealous prosecutor with grandiose political ambitions, was seeking to criminalize normal legislative behavior. If the committee found Wright guilty, every member of Congress would be vulnerable in the future. Where Phelan was supposed to provide the committee with facts, Oldaker argued, he had instead written a speculative, highly opinionated report that implied that the Speaker was guilty. He blamed Phelan for relying on unsubstantiated news articles as the basis of his case. "*Regardie's* and other folks started writing these articles and they made a lot of noise and they stirred up a lot of dust, and a lot of other people threw up a lot of dust, and people said then if there is enough dust in the air, maybe there is smoke, and then maybe there is fire, and let's keep throwing up dust more, and boy have they."[4] None of the accusations, he continued, would stand up as the process continued.

There were a huge number of allegations in which, Oldaker explained to the committee, Phelan had manipulated or misconstrued the truth. Phelan, for example, said Mallightco's payments to Betty were a gift. This claim was hogwash, according to Oldaker, who insisted that Betty had earned her salary by conducting most of the research into potential investments. She was also a co-owner of the company. He provided documentation and statements to support this claim. Nor was there a shred of evidence that Mallick ever benefited economically from federal government funds. Another example of Phelan's taking liberty with the truth, Oldaker continued, had come when he argued that the House ethics rules should be influenced by the Senate floor debate when it created its own stringent ethics code, a perspective that would make Wright's book publication more problematic. In this case, Oldaker insisted that there was no basis for Phelan's assertion. Indeed, the Senate had written its rules *after* the House. And everyone in Washington knew that the two chambers never had much interest in abiding by the rules of the other. All of these were persuasive arguments, but none were a match against Phelan's dramatic oratory.[5]

Before the committee, the sandy-haired Phelan walked up to the lectern with his customary swagger. If Oldaker's demeanor was all business, Phelan acted like a fired-up football coach exhorting his team to go out and win the Super Bowl. His frenetic cadence and the way in which he raised his booming voice while methodically pounding the lectern as if to keep the beat enthralled the committee. Phelan, immaculate in his suave double-breasted suit, reviewed the key points in his report while Oldaker sat on the side of the room watching furiously as he saw how intently the committee members were listening. At the heart of the diatribe was Mallightco, the real estate and energy investment company founded in 1979, which Phelan characterized as an elaborate con designed to funnel money to the Speaker so that George Mallick could gain influence on Capitol Hill.[6] Whereas Oldaker gave the committee members sawdust to chew, Phelan offered them steak and sizzle. He was relentless. Even Betty Wright was tainted, charged Phelan; she had done nothing for the company, yet received an annual salary of $18,000, a free condominium in Fort Worth, and the use of a company Cadillac (including when she was in Washington, where Mallightco didn't do any business). Responding to Oldaker's argument that she worked for the company, Phelan proclaimed that almost all of the evidence was fabricated. "I believe that someone providing a place to live and a salary and a car and a corporation that has 20 transactions is an absolute blatant gift from a person who had direct interest in legislation," Phelan told the committee.[7] Phelan claimed that when "she worked for Mallick Properties, and believe me, we looked at it closely, contrary to others, we concluded that for the first two years there was some, some evidence that she performed some services at some time for Mallick Properties. Again, there was no work product. No one could point to how many days she worked nor could they point to exactly what she did. All they said was that she showed up a couple of times in Austin."[8]

Reflections of a Public Man was another front in Phelan's version of the story. Published by a political hack and a former convict, the book was no more than a means for Wright to circumvent the 1977 ethics rules that strictly limited honoraria.[9] The rules stated that legislators could earn no more than an amount equal to 15 percent of their congressional salary ($72,600 in 1984) through speaking fees, but they placed no limits on book royalties. Phelan had shifted much of his attention away from Moore's role as the book's publisher and allegations that a congressional staffer had worked on the book toward the issue of bulk sales to interest groups and associations. He argued that Wright had intentionally skirted the limits on honoraria by requiring groups to purchase large numbers of books before he spoke to them. Phelan claimed that there was even a "smoking gun" that he had discovered in a series of exchanges written in October 1984. After having reached his earnings limit for honoraria, Jim Wright and his chief of staff, Marshall Lynam, returned a $3,000 honorarium to the Lyndon Baines Johnson Institute at the Southwest Texas State University in San Marcos for a guest lecture he was giving. Wright then recouped the lost money when the president of the university offered to purchase copies of his book to distribute to students, ensuring Wright substantial royalties. The university endorsed the $3,000 check back over to Moore's publishing company. Phelan highlighted specific bulk sales of *Reflections of a Public Man* to organizations with political interests in Washington, such as $2,000 in books to the National Association of Realtors and $1,000 to the Mid-Continent Oil and Gas Association.[10] The fact that the House rules did not cover book royalties had no bearing on how he viewed the earnings or presented these facts. Acting like a hardened Chicago courtroom prosecutor, Phelan would leave it to the defendant's attorneys to knock down his charges.

And then there was the matter of Wright's relationship to the savings and loan industry and whether he had intimidated the chairman of the Federal Home Loan Bank Board, Edwin Gray, into backing away from closing down Texas banks. This was the most disturbing charge of all. Although Phelan made numerous factual errors in his allegations—he alleged, for instance, that Wright had not reported certain income from his gifts when it was shown that he had—the special counsel's claims remained in the record and part of the conversation.[11]

Although the committee conducted these hearings in total secrecy, Gingrich tensely monitored the situation through leaks and whatever information he could obtain. Meanwhile, his staffer Karen Van Brocklin proactively fueled the publication of stories about Wright to keep up the momentum. In late March, for instance, she relayed to *The Wall Street Journal*'s Brooks Jackson a memo from her contact in Fort Worth detailing new allegations about other suspicious investments.[12]

Gingrich predicted that the ethics report would be "devastating."[13] He and Common Cause both applied pressure on Chairman Dixon, who was striving to be fair and judicious, to release Phelan's entire report to the public on the grounds that reporters and citizens should be able to review the findings for themselves. Gingrich threatened to propose a House resolution that would force the Ethics Committee to release all of the information unless the panel did so voluntarily.[14] Republicans circulated a memo that listed over a hundred Democrats who were actively fighting to suppress the unredacted report.[15] Gingrich argued that in this post-Watergate era keeping the report from the public would smack of a cover-up, and he promised that "the radio talk shows will go berserk, the citizen activists will be enraged, [and] the newspaper editorials will pour out."[16] Dixon, however, was reluctant to share the lurid content, given that much of the material was unsubstantiated and went far beyond the scope of the inquiry. He understood that once Phelan's report reached the public, the stories, sound or not, would quickly circulate and it would become more difficult for the House to judge the case in an unbiased manner. Yet Dixon's options were few. The pressure from Gingrich and Common Cause to shine light on the case was difficult to resist. Determined to improve the reputation of his committee, the last thing he wanted to do was to give the impression that it was hiding information to protect the Speaker.

Sensing that the committee's next decision might not go his way, Wright convened an impromptu advisory meeting with Oldaker and a group of high-profile Washington insiders in the first week of April to strategize. The roundtable team consisted of Jack Valenti, the former LBJ adviser and president of the Motion Picture Association of America; Wright's friend Robert Moss, an understated lawyer-lobbyist who had worked for the Democratic National Committee, the House Education and Labor Committee, and the House Administration Committee in the 1970s and now represented the Coastal Corporation, a major oil company, and served as a fund-raiser for political candidates; and John White, the former chairman of the Democratic National Committee, now also employed with Coastal as a consultant. Together they mapped out a game plan for the next stage of the investigatory process.[17] All of them agreed that the best response would be to attack the process rather than litigating the intricate details of the case. Wright would turn the tables and argue that the entire scandal originated with Newt Gingrich, one of the most polarizing figures on Capitol Hill. Wright would also argue that Richard Phelan had exhibited "prosecutorial zeal" by bringing up charges that were not even contained in the original committee report.[18] Both Gingrich and Phelan were using the investigation to further their own ambitions.

Wright's friends knew he had to come out hard and fast. This investigation was neither a joke nor a distraction that would go away. As they packed away their briefing materials to leave, the team's mood was grim. The Speaker had his work cut out for him. After huddling with the Speaker and his staff, Valenti met with reporters to say, "This terrorizing attack on the Speaker is very painful."[19]

After almost ten months, the House Ethics Committee completed the preliminary investigation. The time had finally come to take a vote. Along with their staff, the members had sat in their basement bunker poring over Phelan's lengthy report and reviewing the testimony from their hours and hours of deliberations. What they had seen troubled them enough to move forward to the next stage of the process. The stories might not add up to high crimes and misdemeanors, or even violations of the ethics rules, but they certainly didn't look good for Wright or for the Democrats as a party. Wright's actions had created enough smoke to leave many colleagues, as well as reporters, suspicious of his activities. Even the Speaker's most loyal supporters could see that. Dixon instructed the committee members that they needed to get this case right and with a strong bipartisan imprimatur—either some Republicans would have to vote against further investigation or some Democrats vote in favor of more—so that the decision would be seen as legitimate in the eyes of the public. The Ethics Committee had taken a beating over the years, and now the panel had a chance to demonstrate that Congress could be trusted to clean its own house. Because there was to be a second and more vigorous stage of the investigation, committee Democrats could use the first vote to show constituents—and Washington correspondents—that they were taking the concerns seriously, with the full knowledge that Congress would have an opportunity to exonerate the Speaker within a few weeks.

Speaker Wright's legal team could see political trouble on the horizon. The information coming to Oldaker suggested that the committee was going to vote in favor of proceeding to the next stage of the investigation. The headline of a blockbuster front-page story in the April 5 edition of *The New York Times* read, ETHICS COMMITTEE EXPECTED TO FIND VIOLATIONS BY WRIGHT ON FINANCES.[20] Seeking to head off the damage of an unfavorable vote, Oldaker handed out a forty-two-page briefing book about the case to over fifty key House Democrats and then followed up by meeting with them in small groups to rebut each one of Phelan's charges.[21] The briefing book made a strong and detailed case that Wright had not violated any ethics rules. While he might have acted in ways that the committee thought to be untoward, he always operated within the boundaries of the House rules. Gingrich, who read about these meetings when the *Los Angeles Times* published a story based on a leaked copy of the briefing book, blasted the attorney for violating the trust of the House after the committee had allowed Oldaker to sit in on the closed sessions where Phelan was laying out his case, an unusually generous gesture but one justified by Dixon in order for the committee to be able to hear how the Speaker's team was thinking about the charges. "My reaction is sort of beyond rage, into amazement," Gingrich said.[22] Dixon summarily rejected Gingrich's demand that the committee investigate Oldaker, explaining that the lawyer could defend his client however he saw fit as long as he did not share confidential information, which he had not done. "What do they expect!" demanded John White, who had just advised the Speaker's team to be tougher. "Gingrich has been throwing grenades for 10 months and the Speaker is supposed to sit there and take it? That's nuts."

In the secrecy of the musty basement room in the Rayburn Building on April 12, Dixon looked around the conference table and called for a vote. The results were an endorsement for having undertaken the investigation (though not for a conviction). A majority of the committee concluded that there was reason to believe that several of the charges warranted further investigation. They cited Wright for having potentially violated the rules of conduct sixty-nine times. Voting on the first group of potential violations, the committee concluded that George Mallick might have had a "direct interest" in federal legislation and might have improperly given gifts, packaged as employment compensation, to Wright and his wife. In the second major area of possible violations, the sale of *Reflections of a Public Man*, the committee dropped the original charge that the Speaker used campaign funds to pay for his staffer to work on the book or that he had received inflated compensation due to lack of sufficient evidence. But they replaced those charges with another one just as politically damning. Though the allegation had not appeared in the original report, the sales of the book became the basis of a new conclusion, namely that Wright, as a way to circumvent the honoraria rules, had sold bulk orders to interest groups and organizations.[23] In the committee's view, "the sales demonstrated an overall scheme to evade the outside earned income limitations of House Rule XLVII by re-characterizing such income as royalties."

In the final days of their ten months of deliberations, the committee had decided to drop, for lack of evidence, a number of the biggest charges that Phelan leveled against the Speaker. These concerned the allegations about Wright's unethical relationship with Texas oil companies, which allegedly provided him with favorable treatment on risky investments in exchange for his political support. Nor did a majority of committee members feel that Wright had acted in an unethical manner when discussing with federal regulators the problems that faced Texas savings and loan institutions.[24]

Dismissal of these charges did not lessen the severity of what was to come. All of the committee Republicans voted in favor of the charges. Most of them believed that Wright came from an older world of politics and had failed, or refused, to change with the times. Any sympathy they might have felt for old-school ways receded before the benefits that would accrue to the Republicans from this verdict. But it was also clear to the GOP that Wright had skirted the rules and that he was indeed trying to avoid ethics restrictions. Skeptical that their Democratic colleagues saw this truth, they sensed that the only reason the investigation had moved this far was that Wright's obvious guilt—prodded by the media scrutiny—prevented him from using his power to quash the investigation.[25] Republican members could feel both righteous and pleased.

Many of the committee Democrats, on the other hand, disagreed with most of Phelan's conclusions. They believed that a significant number of the charges were trumped up and that Gingrich had invented the wrongdoing based on made-up and skewed information. The Republicans were weaponizing the inevitable messiness of congressional politics, messiness any working member knew was baked into the job, and had manipulated idealistic journalists to use them as a cudgel to bring down a Speaker who was causing their party problems. Gingrich had a keen sense of how to take elements of legislative life that most politicians saw as benign and to speak about them in ways that created a media frenzy and tainted the reputation of the person he targeted. Just as bad, in their estimation, was the overzealous prosecutor who was interested in running for elected office and determined to win this "case" in the court of public opinion, irrespective of the truth. Speaker Wright might have made some bad choices in his career and associated with the wrong kinds of people, enough to give them concern about a few of the charges that had arisen as a result of the investigation, but nothing in the record yet suggested to them that he should not retain his job as Speaker. Gingrich, now with Phelan's assistance, had turned small piles of petty issues, they said, into a huge mountain of scandal.

Even before the outcome of the vote had been formally announced by Dixon, word quickly spread about what had happened in the damp basement room of the Rayburn Building. Although the committee Democrats had dismissed the bulk of the charges contained in Phelan's report, as well as those in Gingrich's original complaint, there were a few allegations that had emerged during the investigation that concerned them enough to vote in favor of looking further. As each member was polled one by one on each charge, party lines blurred on different votes. Not all of the Democrats reached a conclusion of innocence, and that was a big problem for Speaker Wright. The first piece of information to spread around Congress was that the final committee vote on whether George Mallick might have a "direct interest" in legislation, potentially the most damning charge of all, was 8 to 4, with the Democratic congressman Chester Atkins, the Massachusetts maverick, and Bernard Dwyer, the New Jersey insider, joining the six Republicans.

The bipartisan outcome was politically devastating. Atkins's vote made sense given his countercultural past, but "Dwyer's vote caused the most surprise because he was regarded as a model of party loyalty," correctly judged the *Los Angeles Times*.[26] If Dwyer believed that there was a problem, then there might be something there. The upstanding legislator was sensitive to appearing as if he were lenient on corruption after Abscam swept up two fellow New Jersey legislators, Senator Harrison Williams and Representative Frank Thompson.

The Democratic votes in favor of the charges made it extremely difficult for the Speaker's supporters to summarily dismiss the process as a Republican fabrication. As Common Cause's Fred Wertheimer recalled, "You can't win that fight once you have a unanimous decision."[27] One Democratic aide noted, "You can't bitch that it's a Republican plot that easily anymore. You've got two reputable Democrats who went along."[28]

Atkins was ostracized for his vote and quickly became the loneliest man on the Hill. According to a reporter who was closely following these events, when the Massachusetts congressman "walked onto the House floor . . . it was like the parting of the Red Sea as groups of Democrats wordlessly moved aside as he passed by."[29] Jack Brooks, the crusty, cigar-chomping Texas Democrat, was so angry that he openly threatened retribution against Atkins and Dwyer. He told *The New York Times*'s Robin Toner that he had one word of advice for Democrats who had voted against the Speaker: "pray."[30] Rumors that a corrupt deal had been struck between Phelan and the two Democrats swirled through the building. On the night the committee voted, Phelan and Atkins were mugged while walking in front of the Supreme Court on their way home from dinner together at Adirondacks, an upscale restaurant in Union Station. The mugger fled after both men handed over their wallets. The episode was shocking and upsetting, but for Democrats supporting the Speaker, their main emotion was anger—anger that the prosecutor and this crucial Democratic swing vote had had dinner together. The stories about Phelan's socializing with committee members had bothered House Democrats from the first; now, however, the damage was impossible to ignore as they learned of a critical Democratic legislator blithely walking through the dark streets of Washington after a lavish dinner with the prosecutor right before an Ethics Committee vote.

But some of the heat directed at Atkins and Dwyer started to fade when journalists reported that on different votes other committee Democrats had also joined the Republicans. Dixon himself sided with the Republicans in favor of moving forward with the count about the bulk book sales to interest groups. And only two Democrats, Joseph Gaydos of Pennsylvania and Alan Mollohan of West Virginia, voted against the charge that Betty Wright's salary might have been a "gift" to the Speaker. The committee voted unanimously on some charges, which meant that even stalwart Democrats like Vic Fazio voted in the affirmative on some counts. Karen Van Brocklin, whom Gingrich had assigned the task of trolling for Wright scandals, told reporters with an unmistakable hint of glee, "Consider Vic Fazio. He is very close to Wright. But he could not overlook everything that came before the committee. He could not conscientiously or morally vote against some things, because it is so bad."[31]

The Speaker's staunchest supporters, and there were not many by this point, scrambled to change the conversation. The Arkansas Democrat Bill Alexander feared that his party was being too timid. "Answer Rep. Newt Gingrich's attacks upon our party or be prepared to lose again and again," he warned in a *New York Times* op-ed.[32] Alexander hit back by formally filing charges with the House Ethics Committee accusing Gingrich of having violated House rules with his own book deal in 1984. While the committee remained holed up drafting its official report about their findings on Wright, Alexander laid out a case that included ten different charges about Gingrich's ethical misconduct when, in 1984, he set up a limited partnership of twenty-one conservative figureheads, such as Joseph Coors, the Colorado beer magnate, along with powerful business interests in his district, to finance the promotional efforts for *Window of Opportunity.* "Mr. Gingrich is a congressional Jimmy Swaggart," Alexander said to the press, referring to the televangelist recently exposed for having sex with a prostitute, "who condemns sin while committing hypocrisy."[33]

Wright, who was barely seen these days, felt as though he were fighting for his life. It was one thing to take on Gingrich, quite another to wrestle with an ethics committee that was headed by a respected Democrat. Listening to the advice of his friends from Texas, Wright tried to move out in front of the issue. On April 13, the Speaker, who was now being trailed by a horde of reporters, convened a press conference to address the charges. Democrats from the House leadership, senior committee posts, and top liberals looked on as their boss stood uncomfortably before reporters in the packed room. None of his colleagues knew exactly what to expect because this situation was unfamiliar to the Speaker. He rarely allowed reporters to record anything he did. Here, under the harsh glare of the camera lights, all they could do was to look on nervously, almost painfully, as Wright tried to deflect the specter of another Watergate.

Wright adamantly denied the committee's initial findings and dismissed Phelan's report. There were moments when Democrats familiar with him could see from the way the Speaker's forehead cringed or his skin reddened that rage was bubbling beneath the surface, just as it had when he had been confronted by a drunk veteran decades earlier or when he came close to punching Dan Lungren on the House floor.

The most emotional moment occurred when Wright defended the honor of his wife. Of everything that the committee voted on, what angered him the most was the accusation that Mallick had provided her with a job and fancy benefits as a way to funnel money to him. As his voice trembled and tears welled up in his eyes, Wright blasted Phelan for suggesting that Betty had done anything untoward.[34] His body sagged as he thought about how his political problems were affecting her. It had always bothered Wright that there were rumors in Congress that Betty's expensive tastes, such as the sizable wing they added onto their home in McLean, were to blame for his financial issues. With reporters watching his face quiver, the Speaker vowed to "damn well fight to protect her honor and integrity against any challenge, by any source, whatever the cost." The cynics in the press pool would have known that feminism had never been one of Wright's signature issues, but now the Speaker embraced the cause with a righteous fervor. By defending Betty's professional work, he was standing up for the rights of all Washington spouses to have a career. He brought up the fact that in Washington there were many legislators whose spouses worked and slammed the report as an attack on dual-income families. Wright regained his composure before concluding the press conference, which was punctuated by vigorous applause from his Democratic colleagues. He pleaded for the committee to start the next stage of the ethics process as soon as possible. He was absolutely certain that the committee would find him innocent of all the charges and this would clear his name.

The speech was an ineffective defense and visually reinforced that Wright was a politician under investigation. The press conference resembled the growing list of televised confessionals from troubled politicians. Richard Nixon's 1952 "Checkers" speech or Senator Ted Kennedy's 1969 Chappaquiddick apology could not have been far from viewers' minds. As Margaret Carlson wrote in *Time*, "The ritual is eerily familiar. A public figure under fire for wrongdoing rises to defend himself, proclaiming his honesty, years of service and adherence to the rules. Last Thursday it was Jim Wright's turn before the TV cameras. . . . Like the others, Wright's performance only emphasized how much trouble he was in."[35] Richard Viguerie's United Conservatives of America sent out a fund-raising letter that included a bumper sticker, which read, JIM'S NOT WRIGHT FOR AMERICA, and a missive demanding that a special investigator be appointed to look into the "ultra-liberal Speaker of the House."[36]

Robert Michel instructed his caucus to stand down, saying there was no incentive for them to become part of the story or to give fodder to Democrats who wanted to paint this as a partisan hit job. Let the sixty-nine violations in the report bury him. Republicans were to maintain a posture of restraint while they offered fact-based talking points about the ethics process in their conversations about the case over the Passover recess.[37] Illinois's Henry Hyde warned his colleagues, "I think it really is premature to start dancing on the Speaker's grave. I think we all want to maintain a sense of scrupulous fair play in this highly charged political situation." But the most notable reaction was Gingrich's. The usually voluble Georgian said only that he would wait. "I'm not going to have anything to say until I've read the full report," he told reporters.[38] He was possibly taking a page out of the playbook of Lee Atwater, who said, "We'd be fooling ourselves if we think anyone is going to get elected in 1990 strictly on the Jim Wright issue. But every day the Democratic Party is on the defensive because of Jim Wright is a day we're coming out ahead. In politics, you win when you're on the offensive. We're winning right now."[39]

Meanwhile, Dixon and the Ethics Committee, as well as Phelan, received ample praise from editorial writers who agreed that the right decision would be to continue with the next stage of the investigation. *The New York Times* argued that Wright's defense of having not "knowingly" violated the rules was "off the mark." After all, they said, "even if ordinary members of Congress are held to lower standards, the Speaker, second in line for the Presidency, is required to steer clear of transactions he has reason to believe are improper. Did Mr. Wright do so? The public will be well served if the full House matches the Ethics Committee's example of careful decision and careful explanation."[40]

When the committee made the results official on April 17, the Speaker knew that the walls around him would crumble fast. At the press conference to announce the committee vote and release Phelan's report, Dixon and Myers revealed that the stories about their secret deliberations had been accurate. To the dismay of the Speaker and his counsel, Dixon announced that the committee was also looking into new allegations that emerged about additional investments. Dixon, who promised to expedite the process, cautioned reporters that Wright "has not yet been found guilty of any violation." Wright's supporters were savvy enough to understand that the warning would not be heard; most Americans didn't follow the nuances of the process. Instead, they gravitated toward dramatic

headlines. HOUSE COMMITTEE CHARGES WRIGHT WITH 69 ETHICS-RULES VIOLA-
TIONS, *The Washington Post* proclaimed.[41]

Wright would have twenty-one days to respond. Thereafter, the committee would deliberate for up to thirty days, using stringent standards
of evidence, to decide whether the Speaker was guilty and whether any
kind of punishment was warranted. There would be a floor vote to determine how to respond to the committee's final recommendations. If the
committee did not propose some form of punishment, any member of the
House—such as Gingrich—could bring the issue for a vote on the floor
as a resolution.[42]

On the day following Dixon's press conference, the Speaker addressed
a closed session of 240 Democrats in the House chamber to assure them,
"I have never dishonored this institution and I never will."[43] The speech
lasted for forty minutes, and with glistening eyes he vowed to fight until
the very end. When he finished, they stood and applauded. But the support in that closed room was ephemeral. The loyalty that Democrats were
showing toward the Speaker came out of a sense of respect for his hard
work as a legislator and a clinical feeling of duty to protect the interests of
their party. The California Democrat Ron Dellums admitted to a Knight
Ridder reporter, "It's not going to be about justice. It's going to be about
how it'll play in Peoria."[44] With very few Democrats liking Wright personally, it was now, at the height of this crisis, that his laconic and abrasive personality started to cost him dearly. He had few true friends on
Capitol Hill whose support he could count on. The Speaker's tight circle
in Fort Worth was useless in this fight, and some allies, like Mallick, were
liabilities.

In this atmosphere, members of the committee began to fight back
against their critics. When one hundred Democrats signed a letter stating
that Phelan's report "sets the stage for the ruination of any member's career" and said the ethics process was similar to the one used "during the
Joe McCarthy era," Vic Fazio lashed out. The congressman told reporters
that Phelan's report was "fair and unbiased" and "not McCarthy-like."[45]

Through most of April, Gingrich had remained silent about Wright.

As minority whip, he was finding himself mired in policy issues, and he was increasingly in conflict with President Bush. In late March, Bush had infuriated the Right by announcing an agreement with the Democratic Congress allowing for nonmilitary aid to the contras until the elections of November 1990. As long as the Sandinistas demonstrated they had implemented democratic reforms, the United States would not undertake any further efforts to overthrow them. In the agreement, President Bush agreed to yield power to Congress to terminate nonmilitary aid immediately if the contras engaged in military action. The accord, which was made the same week that Republicans elected Gingrich minority whip, was seen as a blow to hawks like Gingrich who had gone to the mat for Reagan in the 1980s. The agreement poured fuel on his desire to go after the Speaker.[46]

Gingrich also found himself at loggerheads with President Bush over taxes. Eager to reduce the ballooning federal deficit, Bush was toying in mid-April with increasing taxes despite his famous campaign pledge— "Read my lips: no new taxes." When news stories emerged that the president was open to raising the federal gasoline tax, Gingrich pushed him away from the idea by telling reporters, "It raises taxes for working Americans who sit in traffic every day."[47]

Still, legislation remained a secondary concern for Gingrich, who spent most of his first month as minority whip selling his message to reporters. He tested out catchphrases such as the "Looney Left" to describe Democrats to the press.[48] One of his favorite terms was "institutional corruption," which he used to characterize the endemic wrongdoing that he said occurred whenever Democrats held power, from their control of big-city machines to Capitol Hill.[49] In a remarkable op-ed in *The Washington Post* titled THE GINGRICH MANIFESTO, he outlined his strategy and made certain chilling promises. "It's spring; even in Washington that means it's time to clean house. But up on Capitol Hill, spring cleaning involves stirring up more than dust." He reminded those who were "hoping for grenades in the halls, bombs in the Rotunda and mines in the House" that he'd been supported by a broad and influential coalition that included seven New Englanders, seven women, and a sizable contingent of the party's moderates. Gingrich vowed that fighting against corruption in pursuit of a new Republican majority would remain central to his agenda.[50] In an effort to show that his fight was not solely partisan, he personally called out the fourteen-term Republican congressman, Joseph McDade of Pennsylvania, who had been accused of not having disclosed sizable gifts, such as junkets and college scholarships for his child, that were given by companies and individuals who were pursuing government contracts. Gingrich's sporadic jabs at Republicans like McDade helped him to justify making grandiose statements like "We are at the early stages of an era of political reform like the Progressive Era."[51]

Although he had remained silent about Wright for weeks, Gingrich could no longer contain himself once Phelan released his report and the Ethics Committee voted. At a lunch with reporters on April 20, he complained that the committee had brushed aside the savings and loan charges, a massive mistake in his estimation. "The Cadillac is minor compared to the savings and loan question," he told reporters. He broke his silence about Wright's future by offering another bold prediction: "I will be very surprised if the senior members of the Democratic leadership don't try to talk the speaker into stepping down before going through the agony of a public defense, public cross-examination. . . ."[52]

But with the ethical finger-pointing also turned on him, Gingrich sought to hit back hard against Democrats like Congressman Alexander who had embarked on a scorched-earth policy. He sent a list of documents to Dixon to expedite the committee's review of his book. "The entire project was a legitimate effort to publish and promote a real book," he wrote to Dixon, "one that appeared (albeit briefly) on the 'best seller' list."[53] At the House Press Gallery on April 25, Gingrich stood beside Marianne to again refute the charges that his book deal was no better than the Speaker's sordid moneymaking scheme. Gingrich explained that his book was a legitimate publication, written by someone with a Ph.D. in history. "What we did," he said in his prepared statement, "we did legally correct, we did ethically correct, we did it out in the open and it is above board and I think that's a huge difference between us and Jim Wright."[54]

Following his prepared remarks, the reporters started barking out questions about the Gingriches' personal finances and the book arrangements. When one reporter asked if he helped obtain federal funds for a profitable steel cable company in Carrollton called Southwire, Gingrich acknowledged the story was true but explained that his efforts were aimed at helping a major employer in his district. He did not obtain these funds as a payback to James Richards, the company's president, who had invested in the promotional fund for his book.[55] As the aggressive questions kept coming, Marianne Gingrich burst out of the room in tears, muttering that nobody in the press actually had an interest in looking at the evidence. Her dramatic walkout might have been staged political theater, but it had an effect, regardless. "I think she just blew up. . . . She's entitled," Gingrich explained to the reporters as they watched this spectacle unfold.[56] Standing outside in the corridor shaking, Marianne told the reporters who had followed her that "it was awful in there" as her husband remained trapped inside answering the hostile questions.[57] Though neither Gingrich's statements nor her tirade ended the controversy, they were sufficient to temporarily calm the storms and make sure that reporters turned back to the main event: Speaker Wright.

By the end of the month, some Democrats were telling reporters, off the record, that the Speaker would not survive. It seemed as if all the Democrats could do was to wait a few more weeks, when the trial would begin, and just hope that somehow the news stories moved in a different direction. Horace Busby, a longtime aide to Lyndon Johnson who had remained in Washington as a high-powered lobbyist and consultant, sent out a memo to his clients, mostly Democrats, warning that the next stage of the process would be grueling. The Speaker's fate would be "based more on politics than ethics." Busby was an experienced Washingtonian. He dismissed all of the news reports about the gloomy "mood" among legislators about the Speaker's future—including Gingrich's prediction that Wright would be gone by June—as meaningless. The speculation was irrelevant. As of late April, Busby didn't see any chance of Democrats taking action against the Speaker: "There is nowhere near a majority of House Democrats ready to give the GOP its victory." Nor was Wright going to step down, even if establishment figures implored him to do so.

Unlike Nixon in 1974, Wright was a "scrapper." Wright also had a good "chance of winning on a House vote; that could be an incentive for him to force a roll call." The House was under no pressure to act, especially with the "Slo-Pitch Presidency" of George H. W. Bush.[58]

Meanwhile, in preparation for the hard days ahead, the Speaker's office revamped its legal team. The new lineup was meant to bolster the Speaker's ethics defense and send a message to his fellow Democrats that they should not abandon him because he intended to fight until the bitter end. Based on the earlier conversations with his Texas friends who had warned that Oldaker was not up to the job, the Speaker now reached out to some of the most prominent legal names in town. The legendary eighty-two-year-old Clark Clifford, who had advised Democratic presidents since Harry Truman, had been expecting the call. Clifford was the biggest fixer in town, and almost every politician who had ever been in trouble turned to him. When they met in the Speaker's office, Wright asked Clifford to sign on as senior adviser. Without hesitation, Clifford said yes. To join him, the Speaker also brought in Richard Ben-Veniste, the former Watergate assistant special prosecutor, and Stephen Susman, a top national litigator from Houston renowned for his aggressive courtroom style. "If you want to change the rules," as Susman would say, "you don't do it retroactively."[59] The New Jersey representative Robert "the Torch" Torricelli was also invited to join the team; as a voice from the northeastern wing of the party, he was selected to blunt the image of Wright as just an old-fashioned southerner.[60] Though he was a sitting member of the House, the rules did not prohibit him from representing a fellow legislator. By anyone's reckoning, here was a dream team of legal advisers. They relegated Oldaker to a secondary role.

As Wright and his legal team prepared for the fight ahead, the Democratic whip team conducted an informal vote count to see where House Democrats would side on the Ethics Committee report, and the numbers were not good. They concluded that Wright was going to lose. Personally unpopular to begin with, now the Speaker, because of his poor judgment, would potentially cost them seats.

Understandably, none of Wright's colleagues in the leadership wanted to break the news to him, knowing his temper. Tom Foley, the majority leader, asked Dick Gephardt to handle the job. Gephardt turned to Tony Coelho, the majority whip, who in turn asked Robert Torricelli. The thirty-seven-year-old congressman, now part of the new, revamped legal team, obliged. When he entered the ornate Speaker's office, Wright looked up to see what he wanted. The straight-talking Torricelli held his breath for a second and bravely blurted out the news about the whip's count. Standing by the door with trepidation, with a large set of Texas bull-horns hanging over his head, he informed the Speaker that the Democrats would likely vote in favor of the ethics report. After a moment of awkward silence, Wright looked down at the floor and placed one hand on his desk as he slowly leaned over. With the other hand, he reached down to take off his shoe. Then Wright looked up and, in a fury, threw his shoe at Torricelli's face. Torricelli ducked in the nick of time, realizing why none of his colleagues wanted to be the messenger. The Speaker didn't say anything else. Torricelli left the room. Underneath Wright's anger was the unpleasant realization that he was unlikely to survive the vote of his own party.

As if the situation were not bad enough, *The Washington Post* uncovered the criminal past of one of Speaker Wright's top staffers and published the kind of riveting human-interest story its readers devoured, one with violence, physical assault, and attempted murder. Ken Ringle, a *Washington Post* Style section assignment editor, put out a bombshell piece on the troubling personal background of the Speaker's top adviser: John Paul Mack. The story destroyed the last shreds of Wright's reputation, killing any political sympathy that still existed for keeping him on the job.

Ringle was not a journalist whom anyone would have foreseen playing a role in the Speaker's saga. Although he had worked at the *Post* for almost two decades, Ringle, a Democrat, didn't regularly cover Congress or the story currently obsessing his colleagues. He simply had not been "keeping up with Jim Wright."[61] Ringle was a "generalist" who covered "crazy, offbeat" topics in formats ranging from historical essays and book reviews to firsthand accounts of cultural events in the city. While he had covered some presidential and congressional campaigns, he was not very absorbed with the House or Senate on a daily basis. What distinguished his writing was his ability to tune in to the quirky rituals and customs that others didn't notice, and above all he was attracted to the human-interest side of the people who made the government work. Freed from the conventions of "hard news" journalism, and from professional norms about appearing objective, he could write with literary flair and capture the personalities of Washington (practicing what was called the New Journalism, as pioneered by writers like Tom Wolfe). He focused his gaze on the embattled Speaker.

Ringle's interest in Jim Wright originated in his friendship with a woman named Pamela Small. He first encountered Small in the mid-1970s when she was working as a tour guide for the *Post*. The paper's headquarters had become a popular tourist attraction after the Watergate scandal. The two hit it off immediately. Small was outgoing and personable, and they liked to joke around whenever they saw each other. Once, sometime around 1976, Small was giving him a hard time as they traded friendly barbs. Ringle noticed that there was a scar on her neck directly under where her scarf had slipped down. Jokingly, he asked if she got that "falling off her tricycle." Small's face turned somber, and she responded, "No, some guy cut my throat." Stunned, Ringle asked if the assailant had been caught. She said he had, though he got off too easily. Sensing that she didn't want to talk anymore about whatever had taken place, he moved on. Though their friendship continued, neither of them would bring up the issue again for a long time.

Ringle was only vaguely aware that his friend's career had taken off. Small worked for the Hartford Insurance Group Corporation in public relations in Hartford, Connecticut, from 1980 to 1985 before returning to take a job as a public affairs executive at MCI Communications, a major telecommunications firm in Washington. Sometimes her work called for her to attend events on the Hill. Quite accidentally, she learned that her assailant worked in the office of Majority Leader Jim Wright. A friend with a job on the Hill had told her about having dated someone named Mack. Small, who warned her friend to stay away from him, didn't know how significant his job actually was. During her visits to Capitol Hill, she had been fortunate to never encounter him.

One night when Ringle and Small were having dinner, she told him about this and said that he "ought to look into it." After all their years of interactions, Small still had not shared with Ringle what had actually happened to her on that frightening night in August 1973. This was not surprising. She had worked hard to forget about the crime and didn't want it to define how people thought of her. Although Small encouraged Ringle to investigate the story, he hadn't followed up, assuming that the person who attacked her was a low-level office worker—maybe emptying wastebaskets—whom Wright had assisted through a work rehabilitation program. Years later, Ringle admitted that his journalistic instincts had utterly failed him.

But during an editorial meeting of the Style section staff in late February 1989, one of the editors, Mary Hadar, asked if anyone in the room had an interesting angle on the Wright saga that had not yet been explored. Though he still didn't know much about Wright, Ringle remembered what Small once told him over dinner. Raising his hand, Ringle mentioned that he knew someone who "got attacked" by a man now working for the Speaker. When Hadar asked him what this person did for Wright, Ringle admitted he didn't know, nor did he have the details about what happened. Intrigued, Hadar gave him the green light to move forward with the story.

Upon returning to his office, Ringle called Pamela. Until then, Small had refused to share the details of her story with anyone, worried about becoming a media sensation, especially after conservative newspapers had touched on the attack in 1987. She remained fearful of going public. But she had become aware that, in the heat of Wright's political scandal, several major networks and newspapers were snooping around for her side of the story. She decided to share the details with Ringle so that she could explain what happened on her own terms and with a focus on her experience rather than only the political implications for Wright.[62] She gave him her attacker's name: John Mack.

Eager to learn more, Ringle drove back to his office to look through a copy of the *Congressional Directory*, which confirmed the details that Small had told him.[63] Through a little digging, he discovered that the Steering and Policy Committee was a direct arm of the Speaker's office, controlled by Wright, and that it had the power to shape the policy agenda for the entire House Democratic Party and to make committee appointments. Ringle discovered Mack earned a very good salary for a staffer—$89,500. He was officially the "executive director of the Steering and Policy Committee." As the director of this committee, Mack effectively functioned as the Speaker's main assistant, even though his official job title did not reflect this fact. Mack's desk was located in the Speaker's Lobby, close to the office where Wright would hold ceremonial events.[64] When Mack came to visit a legislator, everyone on Capitol Hill knew that he represented Congress's most powerful member. A consigliere of sorts, Mack was known to be thin-skinned and impatient with anyone he suspected of being disloyal to Wright. Ringle was stunned that Mack held a job of this stature given that he had been convicted of a felony. Mack was a power broker with a criminal record. He couldn't legally vote, yet he had immense influence over what legislation the House would consider.

Ringle, who hadn't seen Small in more than a year, asked her once again to dinner to discuss the details of her attack, which took place in the back room of a furniture store, an act so violent that she required several rounds of surgery. Small told Ringle that she didn't want her name used in the story, given that she had kept this information private for most of her adult life, but over the next few days they continued to discuss the gruesome details of what had happened.

Ringle soon learned that a few months after the House officially elected Wright as Speaker in January 1987, members of Congress were alerted to Mack's history of violence. Many legislators and reporters had known about Mack's crime, including Wright, but never appeared to have questioned his holding such a prominent position. The concern about

Mack had begun when members of Congress received an ominous letter that warned that the Speaker's "top aide is [a] violent criminal." Allegedly written by a former Virginia policeman who was "offended" to see Mack holding a position of influence, the telegram stated, "You and the American people should be aware that John Paul Mack, top aide to House Speaker Jim Wright, tried to kill a woman in 1973 and was sentenced to 15 years in the Virginia State Prison system. Despite his brutal crime, John Paul Mack served only 14½ months in prison. He got out so soon because Congressman Jim Wright offered him a job! This was in 1974." The writer added a stunning revelation: "Jim Wright's daughter was married to John Paul Mack's brother at that time."[65]

The Washington press corps largely ignored the story, feeling that the letter had been a smear job from conservative opponents. Several members of the press had come to know Mack personally. He was respected by members of both parties as a dedicated public servant who spent up to thirteen hours a day in the office. It was hard for them to fathom that the person they spoke with regularly had been guilty of a horrendous crime. The deputy national editor of *The Washington Post*, Edward Walsh, concluded there was no reason to run a piece on the story in 1987, fourteen years after the crime, because it would be unfair to Mack.

The only exception had been the *Fort Worth Star-Telegram*'s ace investigative reporter Dave Montgomery, who had long been covering Wright's many connections. In August 1987, he published a lengthy story about Mack titled SHADOW OF VIOLENCE HAUNTS WRIGHT'S TOP AIDE, which included an anonymous quotation from Pamela Small. When Wright had become Speaker, Montgomery decided to take a harder look at the staffers who surrounded the new leader, just as he had been exploring the world of money brokers who inhabited Wright's district. The article recounted how Mack had "clubbed and slashed a woman customer, then left her unconscious and near death in her parked car." Montgomery noted, "With the help of his sister-in-law—Wright's daughter Kay—Mack was given a clerical job in the congressman's office after he was freed on a work release program." The piece went on to cover much of the story of the crime and Mack's life ever since.[66] Mack had offered to resign to save the Speaker any embarrassment, but Wright refused the offer.[67]

Given the meager coverage, it was not that surprising that Ringle didn't know about this open secret. In an era when print publishing still dominated, stories in the small city and state newspapers were easy to miss or could be quickly forgotten unless someone dug around in the microfilm or had a phalanx of research assistants gathering clippings on a daily basis. In a profile of the Speaker's team that Edward Walsh published in *The Washington Post* on March 17, 1987, absolutely no mention was made of the crime.[68]

Many of the staffers and legislators who knew about Mack's background felt that it was fine for him to work on the Hill after being rehabilitated. The most generous explanation was that he had served his time in prison and that people deserved the ability to restart their lives. More problematic was the gendered fault line in Washington that Ringle was confronting. The sexist culture in Washington paid scant attention to the ongoing aggression toward women. Female legislators were accustomed to being considered less formidable than their male peers; female staffers knew whom not to be alone with.[69]

This was a historical moment before the national conversations catalyzed by Anita Hill, Monica Lewinsky, or Christine Blasey Ford. The term "date rape" had only recently gained national attention, and laws combating sexual harassment in the workplace were still relatively new. Congress was exempt from most of the laws that did exist based on the principle that no branch of government could infringe on the prerogatives of the other. Within Congress, there was no such thing as a human relations department. Each member's office was responsible for handling its own workplace, which in practice meant that these issues could be ignored. In this environment, the poor judgment of a few men, who were not sensitive enough to the violence regularly inflicted upon women, could allow for the hiring and promotion of a violent felon. Mack's was the most egregious case imaginable, but it still grew out of the same broken environment on Capitol Hill that disregarded these sorts of workplace gender issues.

When Wright was asked directly on the record about Mack in the first year of his speakership, his response garnered little attention. The host of CBS's *Face the Nation*, Phil Jones, asked him about it in June 1988 while interviewing him about the Ethics Committee investigation. Jones said that various issues had raised questions about the Speaker's judgment, like "one of your top aides, John Mack, is a man who bludgeoned a woman back in the 1970s with a hammer. He left her for dead. He was convicted on this, sent to prison, was later released to his brother and his brother happened to be your son-in-law at the time. And you hired that man." Now he was working, Jones pointed out, on the public payroll. Wright responded that Mack had "problems. I don't know why. It was something that happened before I knew John. The sheriff asked me to give him a chance, give him a job. And I did when he was a young man, still a teenager, maybe twenty, twenty-one, and he has worked admirably well. And I think does a splendid job. I believe in giving people a second chance, Phil. That's my philosophy, and I'm glad I've done it. I've never had occasion to regret that I did."[70] That was enough to end that part of the conversation.

Ringle couldn't afford to take Small's word for what happened. He went to work at a frantic pace to interview all the people who had been involved in the incident and to review any documents that he could find to discern what had taken place.

Deeply appalled that so many evidently knew about but ignored these facts, Ringle resolved not to do the same. He decided to drive to Fairfax to look at the court records from the case. The key to his investigation, Ringle realized, was to obtain the police report and the transcript from the sentencing hearing, which had been transcribed in shorthand but was so ignored by the press that it had never even been written out. Ringle had to find an aging stenographer who knew the shorthand in question, which most court reporters no longer used (this record had never been sealed by the court).

No newsman had ever questioned the doctors who treated her, or the prosecutor who told Ringle that "Mack was lucky. He ended up just one step from murder."[71]

What he read from the transcription astounded him despite everything he already knew. What had not been clear in Pamela Small's own accounts of the night, or even in the stories that followed, was how truly vicious the attack had been. Mack's assault had been much more of an attempted murder than an "altercation."

Mack's tenor during the hearing was also unsettling. The transcript showed that when asked by the prosecutor why he stabbed Small, he answered, "Just blew my cool for a second," stunning even the interrogator. As he read through the sentencing transcript, the savagery of the attack—Mack's "beating her over the head and stabbing her," as the prosecutor described—and its aftermath took Ringle's breath away.

Armed with his interviews with Small, her family, and the hearing transcript, Ringle began to compose his article. He persuaded Small to allow him to use her name in the story and to include a photograph, explaining that the revelation of her identity would bring attention to what happened in a way that hadn't been possible in the previous news accounts, when her identity remained anonymous. Because of their long friendship, Small trusted Ringle and let him move forward with the full story. But she insisted that the picture not make her identifiable.

On the morning of Thursday, May 4, 1989, the four-thousand-word story, MEMORY AND ANGER: A VICTIM'S STORY, landed like "a bomb," one reporter said, "in a capital shaken by the ethics inquiry into Mr. Wright's dealings."[72] The story featured a picture of a grinning John Mack with his round face and blond mustache placed on top of the Capitol dome, next to a photograph of Small contemplatively looking into the distance. Ringle described the slightly overweight Mack as "Wright's right-hand man and, since Wright became speaker of the House, [Mack] has been arguably the most powerful staff member on Capitol Hill."

Ringle recounted a terrifying story that sounded utterly different from an "altercation." In August 1973, Small, then a twenty-year-old college student at American University, had gone to a discount home furnishing store to purchase some items for her new apartment. She was the only customer in the store. When she finished her shopping, Small walked to the cash register to pay for the goods. Mack started to add up the total.

But Small noticed that one of the window blinds she was buying had a small crack. She asked if he could replace it. Mack believed there were more in the storeroom and asked her to go back with him so she could make sure they were the same. Although no one else was in the store, Small felt no reason to be wary because the young sales associate appeared calm and at ease.

When Small entered the room, Mack's entire demeanor changed. He "blocked the door and ordered her to lie face down on the floor." When she refused and attempted to escape, he "grabbed a hammer and slammed it into her skull. She immediately lost consciousness but he continued pounding, exposing the skull in five places. Then he grabbed a steak knife, stabbed her five times in the left breast and shoulder near her heart, and slashed her repeatedly across the throat."

Assuming that she was dead, Mack carried her body into Small's Toyota station wagon parked outside. He drove the car around town for about half an hour, getting rid of her purse and wallet before returning and abandoning the car in a back alley near the store. Leaving the keys in the ignition, Mack walked away to see a movie. He did not return to the store that night.

After lying in the car for eight hours, Small regained consciousness. Feeling the blood dripping down her head, she struggled to save herself. When she spotted the keys in the ignition, Small managed to crawl into the front and miraculously drove the car for a mile to a twenty-four-hour gas station on the Little River Turnpike. The attendant, horrified by the sight of the battered woman, whose body and clothes were drenched in blood, called the police and paramedics. They rushed her to the emergency room, where a general surgeon, a plastic surgeon, a neurosurgeon, and a thoracic surgeon worked frantically to save her life. During the first seven-hour surgery, they reconstructed Small's collapsed lung and covered the exposed parts of her skull with skin.

Mack was arrested on August 19, 1973, the day after the crime took place, and entered a guilty plea. It was difficult to understand the motivation behind his attack. Ringle explained to readers that Mack had been raised by a good family; his father was a navy officer, and he had never had any run-in with the law. Mack's employers called him a conscientious worker. Mack blamed his actions during his sentencing hearing on tensions in a new marriage and the stress of long shifts at work. "I just blew my cool for a second," he said during the sentencing hearing. That vague explanation, which failed to take real responsibility for his actions, would haunt Small.

But everything about how the case was handled seemed odd, Ringle explained. Poring over all the facts that he found in his research and reading of earlier accounts, Ringle spelled out the benefits that might have come from Mack's connection to Wright. To begin, Judge Burch Millsap of the Fairfax County Circuit Court sentenced Mack to fifteen years in the Virginia State Penitentiary for malicious wounding, instead of attempted murder, which would have carried a minimum of twenty years. The judge also suspended seven years of the sentence, a decision that stunned the Fairfax commonwealth attorney, and said that because there was no acceptable psychiatric prison facility available, the court could place Mack in the Southwestern State Hospital for treatment.

As Mack awaited his sentence, he served time in the Fairfax County jail, which was normally reserved for people who had committed minor crimes. He remained in the institution much longer than expected because his sentencing trial was postponed several times. He worked as a cook during the day and took accounting classes at a local college in the evening. When the court finally sentenced him in December 1974, it counted the time served in Fairfax (more than a year) and never moved him to the state hospital but allowed him to remain in the low-security facility. Then he was released in 1976, after just twenty-seven months, for good behavior through the state's rehabilitative program. He left prison with an offer of employment in Congressman Jim Wright's office.

Ringle then turned to the fact that Wright's daughter was married to Mack's brother. They had dated since high school. Wright wrote several letters to the court, all of which remained sealed from public view, even before the sentencing hearing in which he attested to Mack's good character and informed the court that he would be pleased to employ him in his office, despite his having no political experience or college degree, if he were to be released.

Ringle also told readers how Small learned of Mack's release from prison. It was a year after his parole. As she explained, "I was with this girl I knew who worked on the Hill." They had spent the day shopping in Virginia, and the girl "kept talking about this guy she was dating named John who worked in Jim Wright's office. And it was 'John this,' and 'John that.'" Small didn't pay much attention until they drove past the site where Mack had attacked her. And her friend said, "You know we're right around where John used to work," which gave Small a "very eerie feeling. . . . I stopped the car and I said, 'You know, you haven't told me John's last name.' And she said, 'John Mack.'" When Small realized who her friend was dating and that he had been let free, she burst into tears.

And then she said something that was undeniably true. Mack has "got a very powerful, very important job now," Small observed, "and he wouldn't have it if he hadn't tried to kill me. I find that more than a little bizarre." She had "watched with mounting alarm and anger the growing power of the man who tried to kill her." Then Ringle quoted Tony Coelho, the third most powerful Democrat among the House leadership: "Rightly or wrongly under our system of law John Mack owed his debt to society, not to this young woman." Coelho had learned about the crime in 1987 but decided that he would not hold it against Mack. In fact, the men had become friends and had also gone into business together, investing in a computer software company as well as a rental property.

As he ended the story, Ringle described how each of them—assailant and victim—had moved on with their lives. Besides his great job, Mack was enjoying the tenth year of his second marriage to a woman named Kim, the assistant and appointments secretary of the Massachusetts Democrat Nicholas Mavroules. With their two children, the Macks lived in a lovely home in an affluent Virginia suburb. Meanwhile, Small fought back from near death to normal life astonishingly quickly, and refused either to think of herself as a victim or to act like one, but she understandably had emotional struggles, including incidents where she would find herself overwhelmed by a "paralyzing sense of panic . . . of powerlessness." The article noted that Small had not received any financial compensation, as was required after Congress passed the 1982 Victim and Witness Protection Act.

Copies of the *Post* circulated across the capital. "Appearing as it did in a week when Wright's supporters were trying to play down the numerous allegations of his financial irregularities, Small's story had explosive impact on the political world," wrote Eleanor Clift in *Newsweek*.[73]

The Washington talk radio host Diane Rehm, whose popular show on WAMU public radio was a must-listen for politicians and journalists, opened her phone lines late in the morning of publication for discussion. And callers flooded the lines to express their outrage that someone like Mack could be employed in the Speaker's office. Then, with three minutes left before the show went off the air, Rehm took one more call from a man who was extremely upset. The caller told Rehm that Mack had abducted and raped his wife—two years before the Small attack. Rehm's jaw dropped as she listened and then replied that those were "pretty serious" allegations. The caller said that his wife had not followed through on the charges against Mack because she was too scared of him and feared that nobody would believe it was a rape, given that they had been engaged.

After her show was over, Rehm fielded about ninety inquiries from news organizations who had heard about the call and were seeking additional information about the new rape accusation. A subsequent call to the Fairfax County police where the young woman lived at the time confirmed that the incident had been reported to law enforcement officials. The woman's mother also spoke to Rehm and recounted the story in detail. Even before the caller's allegations could be verified—and Ringle and the *Post* never could verify it and didn't run it—the Associated Press put out a story about the radio conversation on its wire.[74]

Members of Congress, their staff, lobbyists, reporters, White House officials, and even foreign ambassadors, meanwhile, read through the piece with meticulous care. Although Ringle framed the piece as relevant to ongoing debates about criminal rehabilitation and the compensation that should be given to crime victims, what fixated readers was Mack's relationship to Speaker Wright. The story was absolutely stunning when told in full detail and on the pages of a prestigious newspaper. There were no denials coming from the Speaker's office about what Ringle reported, only that some top Democrats thought that he had been punished enough for the crime, so his work in Congress was not a problem. Nothing more was offered. The gruesome story quickly sank in.

With a tin ear for the political temperature surrounding Wright, the story, or the charged cultural dynamic of the time, Tony Coelho responded to the article by insisting to reporters that other legislators would "line up" to hire Mack if he was fired.[75] As jaws dropped in Washington, other Wright supporters with tin ears also dug in to insist that the Speaker had done nothing wrong. Mack, they said, had paid his debt to society by serving his jail time, and he had never been obligated to compensate the victim under the existing law. Mack, who believed himself to be rehabilitated, didn't grasp the impact the story was having. "I was flabbergasted," he later told the author Suzanne Garment. "I wasn't accused of anything except rising too high. They never talked about the years I spent as a $9,000-a-year filing clerk, working my way up."[76] Karen Van Brocklin assembled quotations from Democratic leaders that Gingrich shared to convey the party leadership's myopic response.[77]

The erosion of support for Mack rapidly accelerated. Several female legislators, such as Pat Schroeder, co-chairwoman of the Congressional Caucus for Women's Issues, called for Mack's immediate dismissal. Schroeder was outraged upon learning the details. She had experienced Mack to be personally gruff and aggressive, a man who had often yelled at her colleagues in the caucus in public (so much so that once they walked into the women's restroom to avoid his verbal barrage).[78] The *Washington Post* story was a breaking point. "I believe in rehabilitation," she said, after having been one of Wright's supporters throughout the scandal, "but not when it leads to such a high position."[79] Schroeder said she was shocked upon reading the article that Mack "never really said he was sorry. To be forgiven, you have to repent."[80]

She was not alone. A group of congressional Republican women, including the Maine representative Olympia Snowe and the Illinois representative Lynn Martin, drafted a letter requesting that Mack be fired. The Maryland Republican Constance Morella, part of this campaign, explained that it was a "human story. It touched the heart." Morella, whose office received thirty-eight calls about the story, didn't think Mack could continue to hold his position.[81] Female staffers working for both parties also expressed outrage. Letters calling for Mack to be fired filled up legislators' mailboxes.[82] *The Washington Post* likewise received an overwhelming number of letters from readers, many of them women, who saw what happened to Small as a horrendous injustice and questioned the way that the rehabilitation of male aggressors was handled.[83] The Congress-watcher Richard Cohen wrote in his syndicated column, "The stunner is that politicians whose job it is to stay in touch could be so out of touch. . . . These men of the House came pretty close to adopting a boys-will-be-boys defense of Mack. He was hired as if his crime had been tax evasion and not, as women know, one of misogynist rage. Would Mack have been hired had he attempted to lynch a black person? Would he have been one of the most important men in Washington if he had scrawled a swastika on a synagogue or, even, been caught torturing a cat? The answer, thrice over, would be 'no.'"[84]

Standing by his top aide, the Speaker stuck to the explanation he had given reporters when they asked in previous years about the details of the crime. "[I] was not told the details of the crime," he said, an answer that didn't satisfy many people even when he told the same thing to Phil Jones in 1988. Wright insisted that the Fairfax County Sheriff's Office and his daughter had assured him that Mack was fully rehabilitated at the time he was hired. "I was told that he had served some 27 months upon conviction of a crime," Wright declared. "The sheriff told me he had been a model rehabilitative prisoner and recommended him highly." The sheriff, James Swinson, according to the Speaker's recollection, had commended Wright for giving him a chance, although Swinson told Don Phillips of *The Washington Post* that he did not remember ever having spoken to Wright at the time.[85]

Not a single male Democrat publicly condemned Wright, but there was little that could be done to protect him from the fallout. "You could feel the steam go out" of support for the Speaker, Oldaker recalled. The "damage" was done, given how brutal the story was. "It's hard to overstate what an impact that had," Oldaker added, because Mack was known as the Speaker's "alter ego."[86] Clark Clifford was quickly losing confidence in his ability to make Wright's scandal go away now that Mack's criminal background was in the spotlight. Clifford later recalled to a reporter, "The story was so shocking, and it was presented in a manner that it made people withdraw in horror. It was tough, boy it was tough."[87]

Oldaker approached Mack and said that he would have to resign. Given the perilous charges the Speaker faced, there was no way that he could keep Mack on the payroll. Wright, who felt worse for Mack than for himself, wanted him to stay, but Oldaker insisted the situation was too dire. This was no time for personal loyalty. The other attorneys working on the case agreed. Torricelli would later tell a reporter that the Speaker's "primary focus must be on strengthening his legal case. Anything that diverts attention from this is to his detriment."[88] As the Speaker walked through the hallways of Congress, members were turning corners to avoid encountering him.

The media pushed the story out from Washington and into the hinterland. The Los Angeles Times–Washington Post News Service reprinted Ringle's piece in its papers, which included the *St. Paul Pioneer Press*, the *San Jose Mercury-News*, and *The Atlanta Constitution*. *The New York Times* and the *Los Angeles Times* gave the story prominent coverage and added original reporting of their own about the attack. The syndicated columnist Mona Charen asked her readers, "If you heard that a young man who had driven a hammer into a young woman's skull five times, stabbed her and repeatedly cut her throat, later went on to become a senior aide to the Speaker of the House of Representatives what would you say? Sounds like a bad soap opera? Something Aaron Spelling would dream up? Maybe so—but it's true."[89] The network evening news shows aired horrendous black-and-white police images from the attacks, showing huge bloody slashes on Small's back, throat, and even feet. In her report for NBC

News, Andrea Mitchell interviewed one of Small's physicians, Dr. Eugene Stevenson. "She was in pretty bad shape, the attack was pretty brutal," he said as he pursed his lips, remembering the moment.[90] "If Small had the bad fortune to be shopping at World Bazaar that night," noted *Time*, "Mack had the good luck to have a brother married to Congressman Jim Wright's daughter."[91] The same conservative radio talk show hosts who lit up the airwaves telling their listeners to oppose the congressional pay raise now turned their ire toward the Speaker's employment choices.[92] Many congressional staffers, worried about speaking out against a figure as powerful as Mack, refused to answer questions about him when confronted by reporters.[93]

The prominently displayed story in *The Washington Post*, noted the *Chicago Tribune*'s Steve Daley, "caused as much consternation among House Democrats as any element of the 11-month ethics investigation of Wright's personal and financial dealings."[94] Despite all the unease that Democrats felt toward Gingrich's renegade and reckless tactics, the John Mack story was like a punch in the gut. Ringle's story seemed to give credence to the idea that although Gingrich was unsavory, reckless, and unfair, his targets, the Speaker and the Democratic majority, were vulnerable because of the broken ethical culture they had normalized.

In the *Los Angeles Times*, the radical feminist theorist Andrea Dworkin wrote, "There's no way to live with what John Mack did to Pamela Small in 1973." Dworkin argued that Mack thought that "bludgeoning the skull of a woman with a hammer" and "slashing her throat repeatedly with a steak knife" were things that "any man" could do under pressure. And although she took equal aim at a negligent press—"If Wright's time had not come, if he were not under indictment by the House Ethics Committee, the public would not have been told about Mack"—in her mind, Democratic insiders in Congress knew about his crime, and they did not care.[95]

For congressional Republicans, the Mack–Wright saga, as it played out on the airwaves and across the nation's news and opinion pages, could not have come at a better time. Conservative talk radio shows devoted broadcasts to Mack. One caller after another spoke about how angry they felt.

This was like the battle over the pay raise on steroids. Considerable attention was paid to the question of how and why Wright could have decided to hire Mack to begin with. Wright's judgment was questioned, as was his patriotism. The shows, looking to duplicate the results they'd achieved during the pay raise controversy, urged listeners to call their House members.[96]

An elated National Republican Congressional Committee put out a press release containing some of the most controversial lines from Ringle's article. It reminded readers, if they even needed reminding, that Mack, the man who had assaulted a woman and then left her for dead, was executive director of the House Democratic Steering and Policy Committee. He was "Speaker Wright's 'right-hand man'" and had never served a day in a federal penitentiary. The release then asked why Democratic leaders like Coelho had defended him.[97] When Guy Vander Jagt told Ed Rollins, with whom he now cochaired the NRCC, that he thought the statement had gone too far, one of the most brilliant masters of hardball politics responded, "We've got to go after the Tony Coelhos of the world when they give us openings."[98]

The Mack story left Democrats at a loss. They needed to respond to the tsunami of bad press coming their way but had no good options. Their Speaker had once again fumbled the ball and had given their opponents an opportunity to carry it across the goal line.

The Speaker and his staff were learning that once a scandal accelerated, it was difficult to control and, like hot embers jumping a fire wall, could easily burst into new areas that even the original accusers had not anticipated.

The conversations in Washington about Wright's resignation intensified as a result of the Ringle story. *The New Yorker*, the *National Journal*, and *The Washington Post* all ran stories speculating on how Tom Foley would be as the next Speaker of the House. Though Foley refused to talk about the issue and firmly stood by his leader, most of the stories about him were extraordinarily positive, portraying him as someone who was cautious and a skillful agent of compromise without any kinds of skeletons in his political closet. When Dick Gephardt was asked at a breakfast with reporters about the odds that Foley would become the new Speaker if Wright had to step down, the congressman turned visibly uncomfortable as he admitted, "Foley is very, very popular with Democrats in the House. He is a personal friend of mine. He is doing very, very well as majority leader."[99] Gephardt managed to say something without saying anything, intimating that Foley would be good for the job without slamming Wright directly.

When the Speaker returned to Washington from a visit to his district on May 8, just four days after Ringle's story appeared, the swell of reporters following his every move became so intense that he ran into an office to escape. "I am besieged," he complained to his aides. "I'm surrounded, like Travis at the Alamo," a reference to the head of the Texas forces killed by Mexican soldiers at the end of a thirteen-day standoff at the historic fort in 1836.[100] Mack felt the same. He and his wife had sent their children out of town until the storm died down. Their home was perpetually monitored by television cameras and reporters waiting for them to come out, while the family allegedly received threatening calls in response to what he had done.

On May 11, Mack announced that he would resign, one week after the story appeared. "When I was 19 years old, I made a terrible and tragic mistake that caused great harm to another human being. For that I am and always will be full of remorse. I wish I could rewrite the past, but unfortunately I can't," Mack said in his statement. "To Pamela Small, and also to my family, all I can say now is what I have said many times before and to myself every day since this happened. And that is, I am sorry. Truly sorry."[101] The Speaker accepted the resignation with "sadness and regret." In his formal response, Wright repeated what had become his mantra since his original decision to hire Mack back in the 1970s. "I was told that he had served some 27 months upon conviction of a crime but was not told the details of the crime. My heart goes out to the young woman who was the victim of that crime so many years ago, and I wish there was something I might do to be of benefit to her." The Speaker reiterated that

"I was willing to give this young man another chance, and in the interven-ing years I have never had occasion to regret it."[102]

"It is like a never-ending funeral with an open casket," one Democrat admitted, aptly describing the deep dilemma they shared with Wright. The Kansas Democrat Dan Glickman said that the Mack story "personal-ized the Speaker's problems out there [with voters]. The ethics charges were abstract, financial, legal, and complicated. But this thing was some-thing people could relate to."[103] According to the chair of the Democratic Congressional Campaign Committee, Beryl Anthony of Arkansas, "We heard it in the Congressional committee. We got telephone calls. The re-action was a normal emotional outpouring for the victim of an indefensi-ble crime."[104]

The evening of Mack's resignation coincided with the twenty-sixth annual Democratic Congressional Dinner at the Washington Hilton hotel. Wright slipped on his tuxedo jacket, knowing he would be running the gauntlet that night. As the Democrats were gathered for the $1,500-a-plate black-tie fund-raising gala for congressional candidates, the printed pro-grams at each place setting ironically read, TWO HUNDRED YEARS OF GREAT LEADERSHIP. As soon as he and Betty walked into the building, television cameras and photographers swarmed them as they made their way to their table. Reaching to grab his wife's hand while they moved through the media horde, the Speaker mumbled, "We're going to win, we're going to win," when asked about the Ethics Committee. When another reporter called out, asking for Wright's thoughts about John Mack, he said angrily, "I don't know anything."[105]

So uncomfortable were his colleagues that the Oklahoma Democrat Mike Synar stepped in between the press and the Speaker in order to protect him. "You get up off of him. Come on, let him have a break," Synar snapped. The Ways and Means Committee chairman, Dan Rosten-kowski, a tall and imposing Chicago pol, made his position clear by walking away from the reporters as they tried to ask him questions. But he couldn't resist turning around and grumbling at them, "You fellows are trying him and beating the crap out of this guy. I'm going to wait to see what develops. Jesus!" Then he turned back and stomped off.

The Mack scandal undermined any remaining confidence Democrats held with regard to their leader. Without allowing reporters to attribute statements to them, many legislators anonymously told the press that Wright's time was over. A midwestern Democrat ruefully confided to the *Post*, "I would like him to step down. . . . Even if he survives the ethics problem, I don't think he can survive the political problem," while another from the Northeast insisted, "There is nobody who thinks the guy can make it. Nobody." One prominent Washington lawyer acknowledged, "He's a fighter, but even Rocky Marciano went down occasionally. How many body blows can he take?"[106]

Republicans sat back and watched with delight. Gingrich hardly said a word during these tense days, happy to temporarily take himself out of the story as Wright imploded.

And the Democrats really seemed to be destroying themselves. As if the committee report and the Mack scandal weren't enough, yet another scandal connected to the Speaker moved into the spotlight, with devastating effects. Tony Coelho, the Democratic whip whose reputation was already damaged as a result of his close association and strident defense of Mack, suddenly announced that he would resign in mid-June because of ethics problems. Many Democrats had long viewed Coelho with suspicion. His taste for the world of money and lobbyists as well as his extremely aggressive fundraising style didn't feel right in an era of higher political accountability. The rules had changed, but the Californian had not changed with them.

Coelho's ethics scandal started in April when *The Washington Post* reported that he used campaign funds to purchase $100,000 in junk bonds underwritten by the notorious Wall Street firm Drexel Burnham Lambert. With the media investigating how members earned money as a result of Wright's case, Coelho's financial records came under greater scrutiny. Drexel had been at the forefront of the sale of controversial bonds, which were both high yield and high risk, and Coelho's earnings were eye-popping. Moreover, Coelho held the bonds in 1986, when he headed the DCCC and the committee received $100,000 from Drexel's political action committee. The investment banking firm, known for its aggressive political outreach and lobbying, also gave money to Coelho's personal political action committee. Adding to the bad optics, Michael Milken, Drexel's junk bond king and a personal friend to Coelho, was indicted on a securities violation charge. Milken was at the center of a series of high-profile financial scandals then shaking Wall Street. Coelho's team insisted that the majority whip's problems with the firm were the result of a Drexel computer error. The firm had listed the campaign committee as the bonds' purchaser, even though it had really been Coelho personally. Coelho also stood by the claim that he had not consulted with Drexel or Milken about the investment. Common Cause called on the House Ethics Committee to investigate whether the investment was the kind of "favor or benefit" that legislators were prohibited from obtaining.

After just a few weeks of investigation, it had become clear that the original charge, that Coelho had used campaign funds, was false. But on May 14, just three days after his friend and business partner John Mack resigned, Coelho admitted that Thomas Spiegel, a Drexel client and the head of a California savings and loan association, whom Coelho had previously identified as a "friend from southern California," had provided him with the short-term loans that were necessary to finance the deal. COELHO SAYS BONDS WERE BOUGHT FOR HIM, read a *New York Times* headline.[107] Coelho had repaid Spiegel, though he admitted to having failed to list the loan in his financial disclosure forms. Coelho also insisted that his accountant was responsible for the error, that the oversight was not intentional, and that there was no "sweetheart deal here."[108] Nonetheless, on May 20, Republicans demanded that the Ethics Committee launch an investigation into whether the majority whip had violated the ethics rules. Coelho "is vulnerable," one House Democrat admitted in frustration. "People see him as a wheeler dealer. You know, it used to be macho to raise a lot of money and collect a lot of honorariums. Now all those things are seen as negatives instead of positives and Tony is feeling the results of that change in attitude."[109]

Coelho was especially shaken when he learned that Rollins, with whom he had been personal friends since their days in California politics, had authorized a series of fake polls to go out through the phones to six hundred of the top donors in the Fresno area. The robocall asked each donor if he or she would be less inclined to vote for Coelho if a number of alleged scandals turned out to be true. Rollins was licking his chops, sensing that he now had two top Democratic leaders directly in his crosshairs whom he could possibly take out before the 1990 midterms. When an enraged Coelho called Rollins to vent about what the Republicans were doing with the polls, his old friend warned him that much more of this would be coming his way.[110] Coelho understood how ruthless the Rollins-Atwater combination could be. His future was in serious jeopardy.

At the height of the media speculation about Wright's stepping down, the forty-six-year-old Coelho surprised his colleagues on May 26 by announcing that he did not want to become another distraction to the party and so he would be leaving the House. Coelho, looking physically and emotionally worn down, stood in front of a jury of reporters and announced his own verdict. "I want to give my party a chance to move on," he said. "I don't intend to put my party through more turmoil."[111] He warned, "Newt has said the only way for Republicans to get control is to destroy the institution, tear it down and then to rebuild it." Upon stepping down, the congressman implored President Bush to put the brakes on his Republican colleagues immediately. "The president can stop all this if he wants to."[112]

Democrats couldn't believe the news. "House Democrats are in a state of shock today," reported New York's Tom Downey, a member of the class of '74 who had hoped to clean up Washington.[113] Coelho's decision compounded the impression that the party was in a tailspin. It also gave new legs to the possibility that the Speaker might resign too. Now that Coelho had taken this step, it was easy to imagine Wright doing the same. "I've never seen our party in such disarray as it is now. This is scary," said one Democrat who didn't want his name published. "There's going to be a panic." Gingrich boasted over the phone to two reporters from the *Los Angeles Times* that Coelho's downfall confirmed everything that he had been saying about the Democrats, namely that they had become corrupt after having been in power for so long: "I think the fact that the No. 1 and No. 3 Democrats apparently will both leave in June says something about

35 years of monopoly power."[114] Gingrich's master plan seemed to be working.

The curtain was rising on the final act of the drama Gingrich had set in motion. What began with Gingrich's circulating negative stories in the press about Wright and accusing him of being the most corrupt House Speaker in American history was a much bigger story than even Gingrich had contemplated. Good-government organizations and mainstream reporters, not always thinking about how they might be playing into a concerted partisan attack, had moved the investigation forward on their own terms, finding time after time smoke that looked like fire. The media frenzy had produced a devastating portrait of Wright's top staffer and the resignation of one of the most influential members of his leadership circle. Wright's scandal had spiraled out of control before the formal trial had even begun.

Seven

GINGRICH ON TOP

R epublicans smelled blood. The ethics probe had progressed to a full-scale, klieg-lit, lawyered-up, all-hands-on-deck hearing. Pressure was on for the House to televise the hearings so that this stage of the process would not be conducted in secret.[1] Though Dixon didn't enjoy the television spotlight, he felt it essential to maintain the integrity of the committee process. His decision was reinforced when the Speaker himself hesitantly agreed to participate in televised hearings as a way to clear his name. His dirty laundry would be aired on screens across the nation. An emboldened minority was becoming more vocal in its criticism of the Speaker, warning Democrats and the media that Congress was in a state of crisis as a result of this turmoil. Legislating had reached a standstill, they said, because every member was focused on the future of the Speaker and could not devote the attention needed to make sure key policy issues were addressed. And at this historic moment, when the Soviet Union was collapsing, the nation needed a leader of the House who could govern with authority.

The House minority leader, Robert Michel, finally broke his silence about the Wright case when he called a press conference to say that the unfolding scandal had pushed the House of Representatives into a "state of suspended animation." Six days after Mack's resignation, he told reporters that the Speaker's authority had so greatly eroded that Congress could not do its job.[2]

Right-wing organizations turned their full attention to the Speaker. The Conservative Campaign Fund sent out flyers urging their supporters to "help put Jim Wright on trial!" Outlining all of the charges made against him, the organization said that it felt sickened by "Wright's corruption and dishonesty." The pamphlet asked how the national media would react if a conservative Republican was caught "laundering $60,000 in phony book royalties from his campaign chest into his own pocket with the help of a former convict and Jimmy Hoffa bagman," or if that person had "secured $30 million in federal funds for a construction project that his business partner was developing," or put "a relative on the Congressional payroll at $87,500 who served prison time for bludgeoning an innocent woman."[3]

By early May, the question was not whether the Speaker would survive but rather how long he would last. Gingrich's quip in March that he was placing bets as to whether Wright would be gone by June seemed eerily prescient. Almost all of Wright's support within the Democratic caucus seemed to have faded, and his opponents were preparing to deliver the coup de grâce.

On May 18, a group of influential Democrats gathered behind closed doors in the Speaker's dining room to discuss Wright's situation. Iowa's Dave Nagle, a liberal second termer who took great pride in his connections to the leadership, officially called the strategy session with a small group of mainstream Democrats who hesitantly remained supportive of Speaker Wright. His intention was to provide these Democrats with an encouraging update about where things stood with the Wright investigation—both legally and, more important, politically. Nagle felt loyal to the Speaker, who had given him a great assignment on the Agriculture Committee, which played well with the farmers in his district, and Wright also had attended a big steak-fry fund-raiser in his honor.[4] When Nagle entered the dining room, he anticipated a friendly crowd.

All of the attendees, a cautious bunch by nature, had been assured by him that the deliberations would be secret so that they could speak their minds.

With emotions running high, the meeting quickly veered in a very different direction than Nagle anticipated. One member after another stood up to describe his or her concerns about the immense political carnage that the Ethics Committee report would produce within the party and how the scandal might affect the next year's midterms. If the committee concluded that the charges passed muster, Democrats would be in deep trouble. With Lee Atwater and Ed Rollins licking their chops over every piece of bad news about Wright and a bull's-eye hovering over their campaigns, the Democrats feared that Republicans would make deep inroads into their majority. It pained them to watch how that little gadfly Gingrich had successfully made corruption the lever that could enable Republicans to retake control of the House for the first time since 1954. What once seemed fatuous was looking real. And they were angry, bemoaning that if Wright had played it straight all those years, Gingrich would never have had an opening. Wright had enabled Gingrich by lighting multiple fires.

Congressman David Obey, until that point an ardent defender of the Speaker, admitted for the first time that he did not think Wright could last. Obey said that although the Speaker had the right to a proper defense and a full trial, that was different from the very real political challenges confronting the party as a result of the investigation. Or, as the folksy Obey put it, the "tactical problem [Wright] faces is that the actions he takes to defend himself on one battlefield are entirely different from the actions he may need to take to defend himself on another. Sometimes you can't defend yourself against a run and a pass at the same time." The conversation became so contentious that the Connecticut Democrat Barbara Kennelly called for bringing the meeting to an immediate conclusion. And although the meeting was supposed to be confidential, some members leaked to reporters what happened. No one was happy to see the Democrats' misery chorale splashed across the front page of *The New York Times* the next morning.[5]

What might have cheered the Democrats was the fact that their mounting alarm was not driven by actual evidence of electoral unrest. Their fears were entirely propelled by speculation and anxiety; most polling data suggested that there wasn't a big problem, at least not yet. The Gallup numbers indicated that a large majority of Americans were simply not paying close attention to the ethics story. Less than half of those surveyed could even identify who Jim Wright was. The public was much more concerned about the disastrous *Exxon Valdez* oil spill that had taken place in Alaska that March than about whether a Texas congressman had flouted some esoteric rule about honoraria or whether his wife should have been using a company Cadillac. The poll found that a mere 15 percent of respondents had "very closely" followed the issue.[6] "This still remains, relatively, an inside-the-Beltway phenomenon," Nagle assured his colleagues after their disastrous meeting in the Speaker's dining room. "The fact that there is not widespread interest out in the country does strengthen the speaker's position."[7]

Yet the Democrats were scared, as the not-so-secret caucus conducted by Nagle had revealed. Members of Congress worry about their constituents' opinions—about the issues, about their voting records—not only in the moment but in the future. They are deeply wary about possible challengers and what they might do that would come back to haunt them in an opposition ad.[8] Speaker Wright's problems, in other words, were theirs too. Given that nobody had thought that Gingrich's campaign would ever go as far as it had, there was little reason to be confident that the crisis would fizzle. And Wright seemed so irredeemably flawed as a politician and as a person that few of them cared to defend him any longer. The Speaker spent most days holed up in his office talking with his attorneys, another red flag that real trouble was ahead.

There was also growing reason to believe that Gingrich, with his smug, know-it-all posturing, could divine the nation's mood better than any poll. Individual members were starting to panic. On May 19, the seven-person Indiana delegation of Democrats met in the office of Congressman Lee Hamilton for more than an hour. Hoosier Democrats tended to be sensitive to the political winds, given their state's large number of Republican voters.

All of the members who walked into Hamilton's cramped office expressed their feelings of anger about the difficult position the Speaker had put their party in. They feared that there would be terrible ramifications in the midterm elections. There wasn't much more to say. But one congressman who left the room, Philip Sharp, ran into a reporter from a local newspaper who happened to be sitting in the reception area. The reporter asked Sharp what was going on in Hamilton's office. The congressman, still feeling the emotional charge from the meeting, blurted out, "It's time for a leadership change."[9] His statement carried weight. Sharp was a Watergate Baby and a subcommittee chairman widely respected among Democrats.

Sharp's opinion was shared by others who objected to Wright's leadership style. Though he didn't say this to the reporter, Sharp, like most Democrats, believed that Wright had an abrasive personality and didn't always think through his actions. Nor did he surround himself with the best people. Many members of the rank and file felt that Wright didn't give them opportunities to participate in making decisions and that he depended on a top-down leadership model to keep his Democrats in order. By running the caucus with a strong hand, the Speaker rubbed against a desire for participation that had remained strong in the post-reform House. Sharp's statement appeared the next day in an Indiana newspaper that was part of the national Knight Ridder news service, which in turn reprinted the piece all over the country.[10] He was the first Democrat to publicly call on Wright to step down.

By the time Sharp made his statement in mid-May, with the Ethics Committee report and the Mack scandal in the background, several major newspapers were calling on Wright to resign. The conservative *Chicago Tribune*, not surprisingly, was one of the first to make this demand. "Every day brings new evidence of [the Speaker's] financial misconduct," it noted. "Every day also seems to bring a new defense, a new strategy, none of which appears to be working. Meanwhile, the House is paralyzed in much the same way the audience is transfixed during a horror movie as it awaits the final, fatal attack on a character bleeding from a thousand stab wounds."[11] The liberal *Los Angeles Times* editorial page, in a blistering piece titled SUFFICIENT REASON TO GO, acknowledged that Wright deserved a fair trial but concluded that he should no longer serve as leader: the "speakership is different" from an elected seat in the House. "It is a privilege, not a right. Wright sits in the Speaker's chair by virtue of his selection by a majority of his peers in the House." The problem for Wright, wrote the *Times*, was that he could no longer lead by example or serve as an effective voice for the Democratic Party.[12]

The next few days didn't turn out as Wright and his attorneys had hoped or planned.

Wright's attorneys filed motions with the Ethics Committee to dismiss the charges that the Speaker had wrongly taken $145,000 in gifts from George Mallick and intentionally circumvented the honoraria restrictions, a plan to put the whole charade of the hearings to bed.[13]

Dixon and Myers agreed to consider the motion in a committee hearing. They likewise decided that they would begin the televised portion of their deliberations with the motion to dismiss on May 23. All three major broadcast networks—NBC, CBS, and ABC—planned to show clips from the hearings in their nightly newscasts. CNN would provide more extensive live coverage, while C-SPAN planned a gavel-to-gavel broadcast without commentary. Outside Wright's chambers, reporters staked out the Speaker looking for any nugget of news or insight or drama. Eventually, Wright walked out to address the group following Dixon's announcement that the committee would hold one day of hearings on the motion to dismiss. Wright confidently described his case as "very, very strong." When one reporter asked if he would "consider stepping down," as some colleagues wanted, the Speaker predicted there would be no need to do so because he would be successful in making his case to the committee members. As reporters continued to raise questions about other accusations and investigations, he abruptly walked away.[14]

Newt Gingrich coolly took in all the prehearing preparations. He had been voraciously reading through the papers and watching television to see how this unfolded. The minority whip, who was now starting to tackle other issues as Wright's career unraveled, kept up his whisper campaign with reporters and colleagues, spreading word through Karen Van Brocklin of other scandalous allegations about the Speaker that were still being investigated and that would provide even more evidence for the Ethics Committee to reach a damning conclusion.[15] Gingrich didn't think much of the last-ditch effort by Wright's attorneys to stop this process in its tracks. Indeed, on a television talk show, Gingrich gleefully predicted that the Republicans "are looking at the collapse of a left-wing machine."[16]

On May 23, fifty weeks after they voted in favor of moving forward with the investigation, the Ethics Committee convened in a crowded committee room in the Rayburn Building to hear the case. The flashing bulbs that greeted everyone entering the door were a reminder that this was no ordinary meeting. Wright decided that he would not attend, based on the recommendation of his lawyers, who believed his presence would create too much of a distraction. Like most House members, he would watch on a television set in his office.

The cavernous and brightly lit hearing room had been set up like a courtroom. Susman's team sat at one table with Phelan's team poised at a table next to it. There was a lectern separating the two teams, from which the lawyers could address the committee. The committee members sat at a long table on a raised dais in the front of the room, with Dixon seated in the center. In between the committee and the tables where the attorneys sat were cameramen and stenographers. Behind the lawyers there were five rows of chairs, filled with friends and family, mostly of the Speaker, as well as a handful of public spectators who had lined up at 7:30 A.M. to secure one of the limited seats. As the face-off began, Dixon, with his glasses perched on the tip of his nose, asked for quiet in the room and announced that a quorum of the Ethics Committee was present. Dixon drily explained that they had gathered at this hearing to consider the motion to dismiss. While Susman and Phelan looked right at Dixon as he read through each of Wright's assertions in lawyerly fashion, the other lawyers shuffled through their papers preparing for debate. Dixon outlined the schedule for the six-hour proceedings. Each attorney would have a chance to make his oral arguments before the committee asked questions. There would be no second round of questions from the committee. Dixon called on Susman to begin.[17]

With his square muscular body and measured cadence, Susman cultivated the appearance of a tough-talking, straight-shooting good-old-boy lawyer. One journalist compared him to F. Lee Bailey, the renowned criminal defense attorney known for his folksy mannerisms in high-profile cases.[18] As Susman stood before the lectern, wearing a well-pressed navy suit and red power tie, he framed the issue with a kind of "let's get on with it" pragmatism that was notably short on grandiloquence but neatly captured the defense strategy. The question, he said, was not whether Wright's decisions had been morally sound but whether he had broken any rules or laws.[19] "Why worry about due process for a dead man?" Susman asked rhetorically, and why should this committee "stand in the way of a lynch mob" as well as a conviction that was based entirely on allegations of "guilt by association"? His client rejected every single charge that Phelan had leveled against him. How ironic it was, in fact, that Wright, who had no more money in his bank account than when he started his service in the House, was accused of being bought by lobbyists despite a career devoted to fighting for the common man. And if "Jim Wright is driven from office without a chance to respond to the charges against him, without his day in court, then justice delayed will be justice denied, to the discredit of this committee, this Congress and the American people,"[20] Susman said, his deep Texas drawl rising with a sense of indignation.

So why then was an innocent man seeking a dismissal of the charges rather than waiting for his day in court? The answer, Susman continued, was that it was not right to try a member for actions that didn't actually violate any rules. When Wright had stood before the Ethics Committee the previous year, Susman reminded them that the charges being discussed were very different from those he now faced. Those charges *had* been dismissed. But the committee had denied Wright the chance to testify about the new charges emerging from Phelan's report. Nor had he been able to see the evidence collected against him. Wright never had the chance to bring his own witnesses to testify. All of this was inherently unfair, Susman argued. The charges, which were unsubstantiated, had done considerable political damage, even though he was certain that they would never stand up in the second stage of the ethics process. The Speaker was paying a heavy price and had not been proven guilty. As Wright's team had done in their public statements, Susman aimed to raise doubts within the committee about the process. He characterized Phelan's investigation and report as sloppy, inaccurate, and purposely misleading.

Methodically diving into each accusation, Susman sharply criticized the committee, asserting that they lacked any shred of evidence following an investigation that cost $1.5 million. He urged the members to think about how their own relationships could be used against them should they decide that Wright was guilty. By accepting that Wright was guilty, Susman warned, every one of *them*—no, every member of Congress itself— would be vulnerable simply for carrying out the normal business of a legislator. "The very meaning of a line in the law is that you intentionally may go as close to it as you can if you do not pass it," Susman said, citing Justice Oliver Wendell Holmes in a 1930 case. That's the law of the land, he said. It was simply "not fair" to punish a man for going as close to the line as he could.[21]

Susman urged the committee, whom he called "judges," to avoid treating Wright in a different way than they would other legislators. And Republicans should not be allowed to rewrite the ethics rules just to get retribution on Democrats for other controversies that had occurred in recent years. "The desire to pay some Democrats back for Tower, to pay Congress back for North and Meese, to blame the S&L mess on a Texan, to pay the Speaker back for the failure of the congressional pay raise bill to pass," are all "fierce emotions" that fuel interparty "fighting and feuds," Susman argued, but should not be allowed to drive the decisions in this specific case.

But for all of Susman's oratorical skill and carefully crafted arguments, he did not come across as effectively on television as Wright's supporters had hoped. Unused to television cameras, he made a series of tactical errors, such as displaying poster boards that printed portions of the ethics code that defined wrongdoing, timelines of Wright's alleged infractions, and quotations from evidentiary documents about the case. Susman remained in front of the charts while speaking, highlighting the violations that Wright had *not* committed. He recited the quotations about Wright's alleged wrongdoing and then rebutted those charges, all while standing in front of the easel that displayed the ethics rules. Under the harsh glare of the television camera, his visual aids provided an ongoing reminder to viewers of the charges made against the Speaker, like the chyron today on the bottom of a cable news broadcast.

Susman compared Wright's Mallightco business partner George Mallick with a sordid list of lobbyists associated with prior congressional scandals, with the intention of distinguishing the real estate developer's actions from more serious violators, like the notorious Koreagate lobbyist Tongsun Park. But in doing so, he only seemed to underscore to viewers how shady the recent history of the Democratic majority had been. Others were turned off by Susman's appeal to the camaraderie of legislators. Donna Keaton, a member of the public who obtained a seat that morning, recalled what she had seen during the 1973 Watergate hearings and said that Susman's "appeal to the spirit of rapport that the House members feel for each other" was unappealing. "If you play on that," she explained, "you don't have to deal with the issues."[22]

The most dramatic moment took place about thirty-seven minutes into the hearing. All eyes turned to the back of the room when Betty Wright, dressed elegantly in a bright turquoise suit, gracefully walked through the doorway with her chin up as Susman spoke. Before television viewers could see what was happening, the cameras caught heads turning and the photographers on the side eagerly standing up to snap pictures for the papers. Betty wanted to make sure that the committee sensed that she was unafraid and concealing nothing. Just as important, she hoped to provide a human face to the person whom Phelan had characterized as a participant in an elaborate con game. The committee would have to render judgment on a person sitting right behind the lawyers.

After pausing for a moment in order to give the photographers time to finish snapping their pictures, a steely Betty walked briskly, by herself, to the front of the room with the cameras following her. She sat next to one of her daughters in a reserved seat. A lawyer at Wright's table turned and gave her a friendly smile. The camera zoomed in on her face as she caught her breath. She watched and took notes on a yellow tablet that she had brought along. When Susman finished his presentation, Betty stood up to give him an appreciative peck on the cheek as he walked over to greet her, and they shook hands. Always conscious of helping her husband, she gave Susman a kiss a second time to make sure that the photographers caught the moment.[23] "You're wonderful," she whispered just loud enough to be certain everybody heard.[24]

And now it was Phelan's turn. Although the two attorneys were close in age—Susman was forty-five and Phelan fifty-two—their courtroom styles could not have been more divergent. After sitting through Susman's ninety-minute presentation, the tall and lanky Phelan disagreed with everything his opponent said, doing so with a theatricality that might have made Daniel Webster blush. He thrust his arms dramatically into the air as he went over in his booming voice the many ways in which the Speaker had mocked the ethics rules. Susman had used legalisms to hide corruption. "We are dealing with the confidence of the American public," Phelan warned. "Are we to look at the rules through the prism of the most nearsighted, myopic person that we can?" For visual effect, Phelan pounded his hand on the lectern and threw down his papers when he concluded each point.[25]

Susman was no match for the Chicago litigator. Whereas Susman appeared sober, pedantic, and detail oriented, Phelan mesmerized as he sought to focus the committee, and the public, on the big picture. "But what does all this really mean?" he asked, with his voice getting slightly higher with each word, after talking about the legislative history of the honoraria and royalty rules. "Why is such a technical or legal reading really important? Are we really here debating the niceties of a tax code provision that deals with active and passive income?" The answer was no. "What we are dealing with," Phelan said as he peered into the faces of the committee members, willing them to agree with him, "is the integrity of this institution! We are dealing with the confidence of the American public in the members that serve here and the rules that they are obliged to follow!" He urged members to look at the facts of the case rather than accept Susman's scholastic recitation of how and when the various rules should be applied. "Is that what was intended by these rules? Was it intended by these rules that any member of this institution, could, by calling something a book, or an article, change the basic nature of what was done?" Phelan asked. "As one of the bulk purchasers said, 'What we were paying for was the presence of the man.'"

Phelan painted a terrible picture of the Speaker, "James C. Wright," as he kept calling him throughout the presentation. With Susman sitting stiffly through his opponent's recitation, the prosecutor next dismissed the defense's claim that all members of the House would be in danger of investigation themselves as a result of their friendships and ties to their districts. These were simply scare tactics conjured up by Wright to persuade the committee members to ignore his wrongdoing simply out of fear of being ensnared in their own scandals, he said. Phelan belittled Susman's argument that the members should rely on the rules alone to determine what was a proper or improper gift. "We don't need a trial lawyer or a battery of lawyers," he bellowed, to talk about gifts because most people knew exactly what a gift was when they saw one. "Most folks don't get gifts from anybody other than their family, and a close personal friend on occasion," he reminded the panel. He mocked Susman's effort to avoid the basic and obvious issue of a close confidant imparting "$140,000 in gifts" to the Wrights. "To suggest that everybody in Congress has a friend like George Mallick is absolutely wrong . . . and demeaning to this institution." He reminded the assembled that as a real estate developer, Mallick's "livelihood," "investments," and "future" depended in large part "upon the taxing powers of this Congress."

With the camera zoomed in on Betty Wright, who fought to contain her emotions, Phelan charged, "This man was giving money, a home, a car, and loans to the Majority Leader of this body! And he was doing it for over ten years." He questioned with mock amazement that during all those years Wright never once thought to ask of his friend Mallick, "Why are you doing this? What is in it for you? What do you expect from me?"

Phelan's message to the committee was that they should focus on the "intent" and the "spirit" of the laws, not a technical interpretation of the language. "Look at the facts, the relationships . . . the facts here control, they lead in only one direction," Phelan stated with conviction. And he warned that if the committee dismissed this case, every citizen would lose faith in the ability and willingness of the House to monitor ethics. The rules, he finished, his voice softening, perhaps in calculated exhaustion so the members had to lean in to hear, were meant to place limitations on members rather than to provide them a cover to pursue whatever behavior they wanted. The "integrity of this House" was at stake, he said.

Phelan radiated competence and even glamour on the screen. It was as if a director had cast him to play this part. His charming smile and the handsome gray streaks in his hair, along with the signature curl that hung over his forehead, gave him the appearance of a leading man. His baritone conveyed gravitas, a sense of mission. As Phelan drove home his point that this case was about protecting the reputation of Congress, the television camera caught a dismayed Susman sitting in his chair, his face grim and head lowered.

Perhaps it never was a fair fight. Phelan started with a distinct advantage, one that Gingrich had understood perfectly when he ignited this entire campaign. While Susman had to persuade the committee from a defensive crouch, by making arguments about legal technicalities that wouldn't attract the support of many voters, Phelan spun his narrative around *behavior* that sounded highly questionable, regardless of the rules or the specific facts, and in a way that could be easily understood by any person listening.[26] In terms of the book deal, for instance, Phelan depicted a powerful legislator who had required special interest groups to purchase large orders of a hastily patched-together collection of dusty speeches with the single intention of turning a profit and subverting the rules that members were supposed to follow. Even Wright's staunchest supporters admitted that the robust sales for such a book didn't look good on paper. And Susman never denied the charge but rather argued that book royalties were not covered under the honoraria limitations put into the ethics rules in the 1970s before Wright was Speaker. In the nation's post-Watergate political culture, when all politicians were suspect and when the suffix "-gate" was constantly attached to scandalous news coming out of Washington, Phelan was confident that these kinds of stories from Wright's career would not sit well with many Americans.

The Speaker, of course, was nowhere to be seen throughout the day other than for the few minutes when he stepped out of his office to gavel the House to order at midday. When he appeared for this brief spell, reporters followed him every step of the way, shouting out questions with the hope of getting some kind of response to what was taking place. The only thing Wright was willing to say was that he thought his lawyer did an "excellent" job.[27] As soon as he was done in the chamber, the Speaker rushed back to his office, where his wife joined him for a late lunch. His staffers were so glued to the in-house television feed they almost didn't notice that he had returned to the office.

When the hearings resumed at 4:00 P.M., the two lawyers went back and forth, sniping about the details of the case as the committee members asked questions of both of them. By now the niceties from the earlier part of the hearing had faded away. Everyone was tired. Susman and Phelan felt the pressure from the clock ticking down. Congressman Gaydos, who had dozed off at one point in the presentations, perked up for the second round. Susman began his counterattack by saying that a wise lawyer once told him, "When the law is against you, argue about the facts. When the facts are against you, raise your voice, wave your hands, sound convinced, offended. . . . I think we have just seen a demonstration where a lawyer, at a hearing designed to deal with legal issues, tells you, don't worry about the law, focus on the facts. Rather than talking about the facts we have a lot of appeals to emotion." Susman dismissed Phelan as the "special persecutor,"[28] lashing out at him for talking about issues that were not even in the Ethics Committee report. "Forget about the letter of the law," a frustrated Susman accused Phelan of saying. "The American public doesn't like what Jim Wright did . . . so punish him." He charged that Phelan had twisted the ethics rules to serve his own purpose of obtaining a politically motivated conviction. As if to underline just how ridiculous the charges were, the cameras caught Betty laughing when Susman went over the spurious nature of Phelan's accusations regarding her use of a company car. Yet through it all most members of the Ethics Committee sat "stone faced," according to one reporter.[29]

Meanwhile, from their seats alongside Susman right up front, Wright's advisers searched for clues as to whether any members were changing their opinion. There were some glimmers of hope for those still defending the Speaker. The Republican Chip Pashayan, who was perpetually determined to look like the most judicious person in the room, lamented when it came his turn to ask questions, "These were dark days in Washington." He said to the committee, the lawyers, and the cameras that he was unhappy that the defendant had been "prejudged" by many quarters, including by his colleagues on the committee who were supposed to listen impartially. The "cries of resignation" before the Speaker could present his side of the case, Pashayan said to his fellow committee members, the lawyers, and everyone else in the room, were wrong.

But the moments that bolstered Wright's supporters were few and far between. The ranking Republican, the amiable John Myers, indicated he was skeptical of Susman's presentation. He even tripped Susman up when he asked a question about the intention of Rule 47, the ethics rule that placed limitations on members earning outside income, which Susman simply could not answer. Myers read the language of the rule that said it covered "anything of value" in addition to cash earnings, and he wanted to know why that was put in there if book royalties did not count. Susman looked down at his desk, like a student who couldn't answer his teacher's question, stumbling on his own words before falling silent with a downcast face.

Worst of all for the Speaker was the fact that the two members who were seen as crucial swing votes to both counsels, Representatives Dwyer and Atkins, provided no indication that they might switch their votes.[30] Indeed, Atkins did just the opposite. He said that the hearings were the most "difficult and painful experience of my twenty years in public life. I did not seek election to stand in judgment of my peers or bring harm to my colleagues." He was also mindful of the "terrible hurt and hardship" this inquiry had caused Wright and his family. Atkins called Wright an "effective and talented Speaker," and the Massachusetts Democrat predicted that when the history of the House was written, his tenure would be compared to greats such as Henry Clay and Sam Rayburn. But then Atkins continued that the committee's goal was not to judge his speakership but to evaluate the rules of the House and to restore "public confidence" in government. During his turn at questioning, Atkins told Susman that he was struck by the problem of whether Mallick, the commercial real estate developer, had a direct interest in legislation. Atkins's own reading of the evidence suggested that there was truth to the claim that Mallick's projects benefited from federal funds that were earmarked for the Fort Worth Stockyards.

Glancing at the television screens in their offices, congressional staffers on both sides of the aisle muttered comments about the proceedings the same way they would while watching a sports event. "Phelan's losing it," cheered one Democratic staffer to his office mates. "Too histrionic," he continued. Even Senate staffers remained riveted as rumors flew around their offices that Wright might resign.[31] Republicans felt that Phelan was giving Susman a shellacking, responding to his technical legal defense with common sense and clear-eyed moral arguments that seemed hard to refute.

When the hearings ended after eight and a half hours, the committee members packed up their materials knowing they would soon have to decide whether to accept Wright's proposal to dismiss the charges against him. Speaker Wright, sheltered in his office for the day as his lawyers instructed, rushed out of the Capitol with his wife. He paused to speak briefly with the press. "We clearly had the better side of the legal arguments," he insisted. Admitting that it "remains to be seen" whether he would continue as Speaker, Wright said that Phelan was "very bad about distorting the facts." Wright continued to insist that he abided by all of the ethics rules, "as I understand them." But it wasn't pretty. One reporter asked skeptically if he thought he could win with these kinds of legalistic arguments. Another reporter asked if Wright believed in his heart he could survive politically. Yet another asked if he could be an effective Speaker if he managed to stay in power.[32] The Speaker hurried to his car without commenting.

Although each side had faith that it had presented the stronger argument, Democrats were even more shaken than before the televised hearing. The hearing had been a preview of how effective Phelan could be in the next phase of the committee process, and they felt little confidence in how Wright's attorneys would perform. Imagining how this would unfold when the committee heard from the lawyers again, in hearings that would also be televised, many Democrats shuddered to think that the outcome would be the same as, or even worse than, when they voted on the report. It could be the first time in many years, as one Democrat privately told a reporter as he observed Wright's struggles, "that being an incumbent is not an advantage."[33]

What bothered Democrats the most was that Wright's team did not seem to understand the most fundamental point: a technical defense would not work in such a highly politicized environment. Everyone remembered how badly Wright mishandled the pay raise and the way he had missed the underlying conservative discontent in the electorate. The result had been devastating, and it appeared that Wright had not learned from it. The two-stage ethics process was flawed by design because the deliberations took place in a political rather than a legal setting. In Wright's case, the initial findings of guilt, irrespective of the weak standards of evidence, already damaged his standing, which in turn influenced the opinions of fellow legislators who were contemplating the next phase of the investigation. The next trial would not take place in some closed courtroom; the trial would occur on Capitol Hill and on television with even larger numbers of reporters, cameras, and, crucially, viewers. The public didn't trust Congress to begin with, and it was inconceivable that they would give the House leader the benefit of the doubt. Phelan's dramatic and persuasive style, which played well in front of the cameras and made a convincing case as to the muddier side of Wright's interactions, frightened them. It was as though the Speaker's side were defending him with matches while the prosecutor wielded a blowtorch. And the questions from the committee members provided no comforting indications that Atkins or Republicans were going to change their minds in the near future.

From the inner sanctum of his corner Rayburn Building office, just a few floors away from where the Ethics Committee had met, Newt Gingrich savored what he saw on C-SPAN. He had not yet left the city for the Memorial Day break, but would depart now with an extra bounce in his customary swagger.

The minority whip knew enough about Washington to predict that the Wright story would consume the city even as the legislators returned to their districts for the short break. The story seemed as if it were reaching a climax, so the press would not stop its coverage even while the members were gone. For the many staffers, lobbyists, and government workers staying behind, Coelho's stepping aside and the Speaker's travails were the main topic of conversation at the Georgetown parties and the barroom dives around Washington. Even the late-night talk show hosts had taken an interest in the House of Representatives. "Do you believe what's going on in Congress?" the comedian Jay Leno asked his audience during the *Tonight Show* monologue. "Jim Wright is in trouble. This Tony Coelho guy resigns. And this Representative [Donald] Lukens of Ohio is convicted of having sex with a sixteen-year-old girl," Leno chortled, referring to the jury decision just rendered about the Ohio Republican who was friends with Gingrich. "Suddenly, old John Tower is starting to look pretty good!"[34]

On Wednesday, May 24, the day after the hearings, the Ethics Committee met in private to discuss the presentations of the day before. While the committee was deliberating, the lawyers on each side also decided to meet. Sensing that the committee would reject the Speaker's motion, Phelan felt as if he had the upper hand. He arranged to meet with Robert Torricelli in a discreet area outside the Capitol basement offices that was hidden from the press, just a few steps away from where the committee was working. Dixon wanted more than anything to bring this episode to an end, and over the weekend he had sent word to Torricelli through a staffer that the committee was open to discussions about an endgame that fell short of the House voting to expel the Speaker. Torricelli, who was a bit younger than the rest of Wright's team, was savvy enough to understand that the House leader was in serious trouble. He looked Phelan in the eye and heard the offer that the prosecutor wanted to put on the table. Wright, Phelan explained, would resign from the speakership within the next few days and appoint the Speaker pro tempore, in exchange for the committee's dropping the "direct interest" charges involving matters that took place before 1986 (which meant those that would affect Betty). Torricelli said he would take the offer back to Wright. The Speaker was not happy. Upon hearing the terms, he said that he would not let an outsider to Congress dictate his future. He wanted to be present when the House decided on his replacement rather than leave the decision making up to someone with a temporary appointment.[35]

When the Ethics Committee broke for lunch, Republicans walked out to the balcony located next to the committee room in order to mull over the potential for a deal. When they returned without any definitive decision, Dixon announced to the media that they would reconvene at 3:00 P.M. Half an hour before they regrouped, Phelan and Torricelli met again, this time on the terrace where the Republicans had been standing a few hours earlier. The New Jersey native informed the prosecutor that the Speaker was quickly losing interest in a deal because he feared that the press would depict it as an admission of guilt. Phelan made a new proposal, only slightly better, that he hoped would be more palatable to the Speaker. The committee would immediately drop all of the "direct interest" charges if Wright agreed to resign but would give him enough time before stepping down so that he could play a part in the selection of his successor. Phelan added that the committee would want a letter of resignation in hand or some comparable document to assure them Wright would follow through with his end of the bargain. Phelan warned that the window for deal making was closing. If Wright did not agree to these terms, Phelan was confident that he would suffer. He told Torricelli that he had Atkins's vote assured. The Ethics Committee had information about another oil investment near Sabine Lake that Phelan assured Torricelli would blow up in the Speaker's face. The investigation would drag on, more Democratic support would crumble, and the number of Republicans backing expulsion would multiply.[36] Giving Torricelli an icy stare, Phelan warned that this route would destroy Wright's career and his legacy in the history books.

With that warning, both men returned to their respective parties to talk things over. In room 201 of the Speaker's private office suite, surrounded by walls decorated with war medals and photographs from the Speaker's career in politics, Wright's four lawyers slowly explained to their client that this was the committee's final offer. Wright grew redder and his skin tightened as he curtly responded that he couldn't accept it. It was impossible for him to leave the House on these terms. Resignation would still appear like an admission of guilt. Nor would he let an unelected official determine the fate of the House. At 3:30 P.M., the Speaker's office released a statement: "There is no deal now. There will be no deal in the future. I eagerly await the time and opportunity when my side of this whole question may be heard clearly by my colleagues and the American people. To this end, I shall press ahead." Phelan angrily marched over to the Speaker's office to meet with Wright's team at 4:30, only to be told in person that there would be no deal. He bolted out of the Speaker's suite indignant and ready to fight even harder when the next stage of the Ethics Committee investigation began.[37]

Dixon realized that the committee, too, would have to press on. By the end of the day, the frustrated chairman announced to the press that the committee would recess for the holiday without taking any action on Wright's request to dismiss the charges.

Privately, Gingrich delighted in watching the legal noose tightening around his opponent's neck. He believed it was better for the process to drag on to the midterms. Now he decided to come out of the shadows. Appearing on ABC's *Good Morning America*, he told Charles Gibson and Joan Lunden, "As long as he's a member of the House I think our position is that it is totally inappropriate for the Ethics Committee to engage in plea bargaining." If Wright was going to step down, in other words, he wanted him to do it before any kind of deal was made so that the Speaker's disgrace could be maximized.[38]

Democrats were making ominous predictions to the news media. During a breakfast with reporters, the Texas Democrat Mickey Leland said, "I have hope Jim Wright can survive. I'm a Catholic. I believe in miracles." Another Texas Democrat, Charles Stenholm, standing outside the weekly luncheon for the Texas House delegation, was not so jokey. "The speaker is in serious trouble. And the speaker's problems have translated into unfortunate problems for all of us." Members were most concerned about the damage that the scandal would inflict on them in their own midterm campaigns. "What you have is a group of people who live in terror of television ads," according to one Democrat from Illinois. "Every time they get near a tough issue, they start imagining the TV ad some opponent could dream up and use against them."[39]

As the holiday weekend airwaves filled up with vitriol, the Speaker and his wife escaped to a secluded location so that they could have space to think. Leaving without being noticed was not easy. Wright's McLean home had become a permanent stakeout site for reporters looking for pictures and asking for new information, what reporters called a "death watch." To prevent the press knowing that the Speaker would be getting out of town at this critical moment in the story, Betty walked out of the house to pick up the newspaper in order to distract them. As expected, as soon as she came out, the cameras started snapping and reporters barked out their questions. In a scene straight out of a John le Carré thriller, the Speaker, wearing a trench coat and a hat, snuck out the back door and walked across the yard into the home of Vermont senator Patrick Leahy, who lived behind them. Wright's friend, and Washington insider, Bob McCandless was waiting in Leahy's garage to drive him away.[40] They parked their car in the Rayburn Building garage, where they met up with Betty, and then got into a different car to make their escape.[41] The couple drove away from the Capitol, breathing more freely when they left the city, the signs of spring radiating around them. They drove for hours, trying to make sense of what had happened and what came next.

When they arrived at the peace of McCandless's lake house in

Virginia's Shenandoah Valley, they got out of the car and walked in the front door, unpacking their bags as if everything were just as it always was. Almost instantly, the solace enabled Wright to tap into feelings that had eluded him for months.

Unbeknownst to his colleagues, he and Betty had decided the time had come to step down for the good of the institution, his party, and his family. The past few months had been unforgiving. Wright, who had privately mulled over resigning for several weeks, spent most of his time responding to new allegations rather than governing. There was constant dread that another story was around the corner. Legislative plans for a new domestic agenda to revive the economic security of middle-class Americans or initiatives to solidify the peace in Central America lay stuck in the mud of scandal. What bothered the Speaker more than anything else were the charges against Betty, who had done nothing to bring this on. "Beyond that," he later recalled, "it was clear that Congress would have an almost impossible task conducting the nation's important business while this distraction cast a pall over its corridors. And I was tired. Dog tired. Mentally and physically fatigued. My duty seemed clear. If I could not be an *effective* Speaker, providing moral leadership, I had no wish to be Speaker."[42]

After deliberating with his wife and speaking with his children on the phone, the Speaker concluded that the damage being caused to the Democratic Party, as well as to the House, was too great for him to continue. "I looked out on the distant horizon and over the mountains and over a glassy little lake, and I was able to see this through the quiet of nature, the cows and birds and trees. I just decided there's more to life than trying to live in the middle of a whirlwind continuously."[43]

Based on what his lawyers and advisers were telling him, the vote count on the Ethics Committee and in the House looked bad. Phelan warned Wright's team that he had the votes he needed to move forward with the second stage of the investigation, a bloc of six Republicans and at least one Democrat (Atkins). The odds were utterly against him, and Wright was nothing if not a realist. As he sipped a drink and stared into the long shadows of the pines, he knew that barring some dramatic revelation, none of the members would vote to dismiss the charges. That would move the circus right onto the House floor, his beloved House floor, for a full vote. At this point, his colleagues would have a number of options on the table. A majority of the House could vote to censure him, subjecting him to the kind of public shaming that Charles Diggs endured under Speaker O'Neill in 1979. Or, even worse, two-thirds of the House could vote to expel Wright from the chamber, kicking him out of the job. Examples of expulsion were rare, with most of these votes taking place around the time of the Civil War against legislators sympathetic to the Confederacy. However, Wright knew expulsion could happen, even in this modern era. He was a firsthand witness, and a supportive vote, in 1980 when the House expelled the Democrat Michael Myers for accepting bribes in the Abscam sting. Myers, who uttered the memorable phrase "money talks in this business and bullshit walks," was escorted out of his job by a House vote of 376 to 30, marking the first time that the House had taken such an action in over a century. The House could also penalize Wright financially, which would be devastating to someone who had struggled to stay afloat.

Finally, there was the Bush Justice Department, which, according to the *Los Angeles Times*, was ready to conduct a full-scale investigation through its Public Integrity Section into whether Wright was guilty of criminal violations.[44] David Runkel, the spokesman for Attorney General Richard Thornburgh, predicted, "I expect the department will take an independent look."[45] The Internal Revenue Service was ramping up its investigative apparatus to look into possible criminal charges involving the hundreds of thousands of dollars in financial exchanges between Wright and Mallick, which involved possible income-tax improprieties. There were even murmurs among some Republicans of another possible bombshell, suggesting that the Speaker had improperly interfered in the negotiations with Nicaragua.[46] Wright was facing a devastating end to his career as a public servant. He wouldn't take that, and he couldn't handle the thought of Betty suffering through this either.[47]

Wright's children and sisters called to say that he should fight and that they would stand by his side, but he no longer believed that this was the best course of action. If there was a time when the Wrights felt that this would all blow over, that time was gone. Now he and Betty feared that allowing the investigations to drag on would cost him millions in legal fees. He already owed an estimated $500,000 and was working to raise the money to cover the costs. If he continued to fight, he could be left bankrupt, humiliated, and ineffective.

Nor was the decision only about his own future. For all the news stories about Wright's allegedly greedy behavior, the Texan was a politician who loved his party and loved Congress. During the last few weeks of his saga, Wright had been thinking hard about what kinds of troubles he would cause for Democrats as they headed into the midterm elections. The House had been the last bastion for the liberalism that Democrats had championed since FDR. Now that President Bush had defied the odds and succeeded Reagan, it wasn't clear when his party would find its way back into the White House. Ever since Republicans gained control of the Senate in 1980, Democrats were never quite as confident about the permanence of their majority. Wright couldn't bear to think that his scandal would be the issue that finally cost the Democrats majority control over the lower chamber, as Ed Rollins and Lee Atwater were hoping for.

Putting partisanship aside, this was no longer the Congress that he had entered decades earlier. "I loved my job. I love Congress. In the end," he recalled, "I loved it too much to stay." The House had changed insidiously since the days when Sam Rayburn insisted that legislators could disagree without being disagreeable. It "had hardened, elements within it grown cold and vicious, intent on destroying the mutual respect that was its vital fluid. Worse," from his point of view, this had happened "on my watch. I had not been wise enough to prevent it."[48]

Gingrich and his ilk had been emboldened. The minority whip took to the airwaves on the Sunday of Memorial Day weekend to lob out another provocative statement. He said that the Speaker and Coelho were only the tip of the iceberg. Appearing on CBS's *Face the Nation*, Gingrich predicted that the country was "going to be further shocked when the news media digs deeper to discover that it doesn't stop with Coelho and Wright, that it goes on to more and more people." Employing McCarthyite innuendo, he argued that there were "at least I think another 9 or 10, maybe more than that," who would be under serious investigation within the Democratic Party. When Coelho criticized Gingrich for the "smearing of hundreds of people," Gingrich followed up in two additional interviews by naming names: Harold Ford of Tennessee, Gus Savage of Illinois, Robert Garcia of New York, James Traficant of Ohio, Roy Dyson of Maryland, and Walter Fauntroy of the District of Columbia, Gingrich said, were in serious trouble based on the unfavorable news stories he carried around in his binder.[49]

The partisan battles would only intensify. Democratic colleagues were angered and sharpening their daggers to go after the Republicans. They were already proceeding with their ethics complaint against Gingrich as retribution for what had happened to the Speaker. Anticipating the backlash against him, Gingrich told reporters, "I've had six people tell me that the Democrats they have talked to have said, 'We're going to destroy Gingrich.' . . . I knew that sooner or later, the Democratic machine would try to get even."[50] Chief Deputy Majority Whip David Bonior promised, "I suspect that Mr. Gingrich will get at least as fair treatment as others have received recently."[51]

There was no end in sight, and this deeply troubled the Speaker. He didn't want to become an ugly chapter in future history textbooks about how the parties had torn themselves asunder and, in the process, destroyed the Congress he loved so dearly. If Wright sacrificed himself to the institution he'd served for thirty-four years, there was still a chance, in his mind, that the partisan warfare would diminish.

With all of this in mind, Wright drafted a resignation speech. The dramatic oratory flowed out of him and right onto the paper as it had done so many times before, this time with a speech to demarcate his own demise. He jotted down ideas that would combine a vigorous defense against the charges that Phelan had made with a bolder warning against the kind of political damage that would ensue if the parties continued with the ethics battles that had consumed the last few months. When he finished, he put down his pen, turned off the light, and went to join Betty in the comfort of their bed. Having the first draft of a speech in hand was therapeutic for a legislator like Wright. Being able to define the terms of this drama and the endgame, as unpalatable as the outcome would be, still offered him a chance to close the story, to go into the history books defining what this had all been about. Republicans might want to make this a tale about scandal and corruption, but he would rise to the occasion upon his return to Washington and paint his final action as a heroic effort to save Congress. At least that was his plan as the weekend getaway came to a close.

Back in the Capitol on Tuesday, May 30, Speaker Wright would only tell the press, "I think I know what I should do. I think I know what I believe to be in my best interests and the interests of the institution. I want to be fair to myself, my family, my reputation, and I want to be fair to this institution that I've served for 34 years." Reporters turned elsewhere to gain a sense of where this was going.[52] Happy to take the spotlight, the Texan Charlie Wilson told a packed room of reporters that Wright would be ending his career. "He's resigning, that's what he's doing, he's resigning," Wilson bluntly stated. He then went on to complain that his friend was being tossed "under the blowtorch" by "my nervous colleagues."[53] Although Wilson's predictions seemed to be an all-knowing statement from a trusted ally, there was a temporary halt to the circus when the legendary eighty-eight-year-old Democratic representative (and former senator) Claude Pepper of Florida, chairman of the House Rules Committee, passed away in the Walter Reed Army Medical Center. There were plans to have his body lie in state in the Capitol Rotunda. Wright, who participated in the memorial service for Pepper with a moving speech about what he had done for the common man, walked away from the ceremony even more convinced that he had to bring his own scandal to an end so that the party could move forward.

Anticipating that the Ethics Committee was going to meet again on Thursday, the Speaker believed that this was the last possible moment to end the trauma on his own terms, without it appearing that he was stepping down as a result of his guilt.

Around noon on May 31, Wright met with Majority Leader Foley to let him know that he intended to resign later that day.[54] The Speaker didn't say much, but he did want his colleague to know that he was tired of living in this toxic atmosphere. He wanted to take care of his family. He wanted to let the House return to some kind of regular order. He wanted the partisan wars to end. With his reserved demeanor, Foley listened to Wright without revealing any great emotion. He had been expecting this conversation, so he had been prepared to hear that he would have to take on the great responsibility of leading the House, repairing the Democrats, and figuring out a way to stop the destructive warfare between the political parties. Wright said that he would deliver the news to the rest of his colleagues on the floor of the House. He asked Foley and his assistant to keep this information confidential.

After the meeting, Wright went to his weekly lunch with the nineteen Democratic members of the Texas delegation in the Speaker's dining room, where they were scheduled to pose for their annual photograph. The mood in the room, the site of the meeting where Democrats had rejected Nagle's efforts to calm the storm just fifteen days earlier, was somber. As the participants dined on steak and potatoes, the smiles on a handful of faces seemed forced. Even the most loyal Texans like Charlie Wilson understood that the end was near. There was none of the boisterous joking and schmoozing that was familiar at these regular get-togethers. It was difficult for some of them to look Wright in the eye, knowing how bad things had become. Wright didn't tell them what he planned to do, but most of the Texans sensed that a resignation announcement was just a matter of time.[55] When a few Democrats surrounded him to urge that he resist the pressure to leave, the Speaker admitted that the scandal had been tough on him and Betty but then couldn't say any more as he choked up.[56] Wright let them know that he would be making a statement on the floor that afternoon at 4:00, and he hoped that his friends could be in the chamber to watch. After lunch, the Speaker returned to an office on the second floor to put the finishing touches on his speech. He called his most loyal allies in the House and told them his decision.[57]

At 3:00 P.M., revealing just how much tension existed between the parties, Foley met with Robert Michel for twenty minutes to inform him of what was about to happen. The minority leader, visibly upset that the Speaker had not told him of this news personally, sat in stunned silence.

Michel was just about to convene a regularly planned meeting with his leadership. He informed the handful of members who had arrived at his office early that they should head directly over to the floor. For everyone else, his staff hung a sign on the door that read, THE 4 P.M. WHIP MEETING FOR TODAY HAS BEEN CANCELED. Gingrich was reportedly seen "walking jauntily" with his doughboy gait toward Michel's office and didn't seem at all surprised when he read the sign; he seemed to have the information already.[58]

The chamber was already nearly full by 3:30. Ordinarily, members poured in at the last minute before a vote but not on this historic occasion. Expecting that the Speaker was going to resign, everyone wanted to be in the room for one of the most anticipated speeches in years. The high-intensity television lights, usually reserved only for presidential addresses, went on at 3:49.[59] A CNN team was there to carry the speech live, along with the three networks, all of whom were using C-SPAN's feed. Photographers set up their equipment in the chamber and scrambled to find the best angles from which to document the moment.

Right at 3:59, the sound of rumbling and murmurs faded as the Speaker entered the hushed chamber carrying a copy of his book and folders filled with documents. All eyes turned toward the doors, and Democrats and some Republicans stood up to applaud. Wright walked around the front row so that he could shake hands and pat the backs of legislators from both parties before he strode up to the lectern in the well.[60] The members knew this was the end, but they didn't know what he would say. Wright did not smile. Gone was the confident Speaker who had manhandled Republicans over a budget vote and Nicaragua. The Texan looked tired and worn down. For this occasion, Wright wore the kind of black suit that would be fit for a funeral.

Betty sat in the front row of the gallery overlooking the House floor alongside their daughter, Virginia, and Wright's attorneys. Tony Coelho sat with the California delegation, thinking about his own departure, while the Texas senator Lloyd Bentsen found a place among the House Democrats so that he could be present to watch his friend and colleague. Secretary of Defense Dick Cheney, a student of congressional history whose departure from the House earlier in the year had triggered the process resulting in Gingrich's becoming whip, leaned against the back rail.

As Wright began his remarks, viewers saw a "discomforting" close-up, according to one television critic, as he brought his long career in Congress to an end. There was a voyeuristic element for cable viewers, who were looking at the final moments in the political life of a leader who had fallen in partisan battle. Never a fan of television, Wright didn't look into the cameras but focused instead on the people in the room.[61] Unlike Richard Nixon, who had addressed the nation from the quiet of the Oval Office and bade farewell in the East Room before White House friends and staff, Wright played out his moment of public disgrace among his colleagues and opponents.

For a politician who famously shunned the modern news media throughout his career, not even allowing journalists to record their meetings with him, there was something unsettling about watching Jim Wright end his career in front of the television cameras. With a large stack of documents in front of him, he started his speech by thanking his constituents and his colleagues for a wonderful career. Wright noted that just a few days earlier, 78 percent of his district approved of the job he was doing, including 73 percent of Republicans, and he was "very proud of that." Next, with the color returning to his face, he took a moment to boast about all the accomplishments of the One Hundredth Congress. "Together, we made it possible for great leaps forward to be made in such things as our competitiveness in the world. Together, we fashioned the beginnings of a truly effective war on drugs to stamp out that menace to the streets and schools and homes of our nation. We began the effort to help the homeless. We still have work to do to make housing affordable to low income Americans so that there won't be any homeless in this country. We did things to help abate catastrophic illness, and to provide welfare reform legislation, clean water legislation, and a great many other things that I shall not detail."

The Speaker then turned to his troubles, reminding everyone how the original five accusations against him were dismissed before three new charges were raised, noting that the much discussed sixty-nine counts were simply multiple iterations of three questions. Pausing for a moment, he ruminated about how press leaks had tarnished his reputation and that of the institution. He spoke of the horrible ordeal he had suffered, his Texas twang trembling with emotion. The Speaker held tightly onto notes that were both typed and handwritten, trying to use this opportunity to clear his name even if his career was done.[62] He waved his hands in the air as he spoke, occasionally removing his glasses to mop the sweat that was trickling down from his brow as a result of the lights and the stress. The chamber was so silent while he spoke that it was possible to hear the sound of reporters shuffling their notepads and the squeak from the gallery door whenever it opened.[63]

With his soon-to-be successor sitting behind him, much of what the Speaker said was yet another carefully parsed defense of everything he had done. Trying to clear his name, he reviewed each point that the Ethics Committee and Richard Phelan had raised in order to rebut their claims. This was *his* time in court. No one stirred. No one dared. "Let's look at them, one by one," he said, reminding his colleagues that the Ethics Committee only said he *might* have violated the rules, not that he did.

He defended his wife as hardworking and qualified, the only one in their four-person investment company who really had time to do the work. "Betty alone, among all of us, had the time and the opportunity and the experience and the desire to give effort and energy to exploring and promoting investment opportunities." The Speaker pulled out the manila folders that he had carried in with him, swinging his arms and waving affidavits from businesspeople attesting to all the work that she performed for their investments. He castigated Phelan for saying that his wife was paid money without having delivered any "identifiable services or work products." He and Betty co-owned the company from which she received her salary and the car. Exasperated, Wright asked what Phelan wanted: "You want so many pages of cancelled short-hand notes? So many pages of typed manuscript? She wasn't a carpenter. Is a woman's mental study and her time and her advice not to be counted as a work product?" Wright said, as he glowered at his colleagues, that his wife had left her government job to avoid conflict-of-interest accusations. "How many colleagues in the House and the Senate do you know whose wives are on the public payroll doing good work?"

Wright's emotions intensified as he moved through the different sections of the speech, his oratory striking even to the Republicans. One characterized it as being "perfect English, you could almost see the paragraphs and the sentences, perfectly formed as he spoke."[64] The Speaker attempted to maintain a smile, which was so tense it looked as if it were painted on his face, when describing the accusations against him, vigorously shaking his head and waving his index finger as he angrily explained why Phelan and the House Ethics Committee had been so wrong.

Speaking about George Mallick and the benefits he had allegedly received, Wright asked dismissively, "Now, how do they arrive at that suggestion? I've known this man for more than twenty-five years. He's been my friend—[a] good, decent, hard-working man of Lebanese extraction." He never asked him to vote for any bill or to intercede with any agency, he said, "not once." The Speaker mocked the committee's observation that Mallick had a direct interest in federal tax legislation. After all, the charge would apply to almost every citizen. Wright quoted Congressman Obey, looking down at his op-ed and the affidavit in his folder, reminding everyone that his colleague from Wisconsin had drafted the House ethics rules and had said "unequivocally, emphatically, unambiguously, both in an affidavit that he wrote and [in] a report he wrote for *The Washington Post* that [the rule] doesn't fit George Mallick's case. He doesn't have an interest in legislation as defined under the rules, the rules that David and his committee wrote." Wright slowly scanned the chamber as if pleading with his colleagues to agree with how wrongly he had been treated, how unfair his entire situation had been.

And then there was the matter of his book. The goal of publishing *Reflections of a Public Man* was to distribute his ideas to the widest possible group of people, Wright said. His ideals stemmed from a populist ethos, not greed. His only sin was to write for the people. "It's probably not great literature," he admitted, "but I like it." After taking a moment for dramatic effect and leafing through a copy of the book, he asked the members, "If monetary gain had been my primary interest, don't you think I would have gone to one of the big Madison Avenue publications, the houses there that give you a big advance?" Tip O'Neill, Wright reminded his peers, earned a million-dollar advance for his book. "You know maybe—maybe somebody got the impression that buying a book was the price of getting me to make a speech. I never intended that impression. I never suggested that. I hope that friends of mine did not," he added. Even if members of his staff were overeager to sell books, and even if some organizations had the sense that they needed to buy the book if they wanted him to make a speech (which he denied ever requesting), the rules did not prohibit the sales.

To prove that Phelan was the person who lied, Wright pulled from his material an affidavit from Gene Payte, one of the bulk buyers of Wright's book, who claimed that the prosecutor had purposely twisted his testimony that he purchased more books than he received so Phelan could falsely claim that the people who bought the book had no interest in the actual product, just getting money to Wright. The Speaker had been burning up about this story since Dixon and Myers had threatened Payte with contempt of Congress for making public statements about executive session deliberations; Phelan had ignored Payte's statement in his report. "What do you think of that?" Wright asked his colleagues. "A private citizen, a reputable citizen of my community, misquoted in a document published at public expense, sent widely to newspapers throughout the country, widely cited as authority, uncritically, assumed to be accurate. The citizen being misquoted issues an affidavit to straighten it out, so that he is not misquoted in the public record. And then"—Wright leaned in and glared into the chamber before going in for his takedown—Payte is "warned by the committee that he might be held in violation and in contempt of Congress if he doesn't shut up."

The Speaker asked his colleagues to look again at the charges and to see them for the illogical mess they were. He had no problem with rules; indeed he believed they were important, and he valued ethics investigations. But members were "entitled to know what the rules mean" and if they had changed since they were written. If the rules needed to be revised, the House needed to do it the legal way, "to vote" on it. Wright even talked about what changes he thought would be good, such as an outright ban on all honoraria in exchange for the elusive salary increase.

The bright camera lights had raised the temperature at center stage where he stood. As sweat slowly dripped down his forehead, visible on the television screen when he looked down at his notes, about forty-eight minutes into a one-hour speech, Wright seemed to stumble for a moment, teetering on the verge of losing control of his emotions, as he said it was "intolerably hurtful" to the government that federal officials were "resigning" as a result of "ambiguities" and "confusions surrounding the ethics laws." Wiping the sweat off his forehead and neck and blinking away tears, he warned, "It's happening."

Regaining his strength, Wright delivered the most powerful punch of the hour. Pausing from his critique of the specific accusations, he stepped back to make a bigger statement about the direction of congressional politics. It was "grievously hurtful" to all of American society when "vilification" comes at the hands of "self-appointed vigilantes carrying out personal vendettas against members of the other party." Hoping that his resignation might stop the scorched-earth policies that politicians had adopted, Wright insisted it was "unworthy of our institution" for "vengeance" to become "more desirable than vindication." Shaking his left fist in the air, he urged both parties to "bring this period of mindless cannibalism to an end!"

As he paused after uttering these powerful words before the hushed chamber, the camera zoomed out to show the legislators vigorously applauding. Wright remained silent as most of the legislators in the room gave him a standing ovation.

Among those standing was Newt Gingrich, the instigator and object of Wright's fury. Throughout the address, the Georgian, who was about to turn forty-six, had been sitting next to Guy Vander Jagt and Oklahoma Republican Mickey Edwards, attempting to keep a straight face. But his discomfort was palpable. Knowing that reporters were watching his every move, he attempted to find a place for his hands, sometimes stuffing them into his pockets and at other times resting them behind his lower back. Gingrich listened with evident frustration as the Speaker attempted to justify all of his actions. When Wright warned of "mindless cannibalism" and the entire chamber rose to its feet, Gingrich hesitated, unsure what to do, because in his mind the Speaker was guilty and this scandal had not been a product of the warfare Wright suggested. Recognizing that he was the "self-appointed vigilante" to whom Wright referred, Gingrich leaned over to whisper something in Vander Jagt's ear and then decided to join everyone. To show comity, he stood up and clapped, even though he disagreed with everything that was being said. But he knew what Wright's endgame was, and that satisfaction trumped the soon-to-be-departing Speaker's momentary grab for vindication. And, Gingrich felt, he would get the last word once Wright was gone.[65]

After a few moments, the legislators took their seats again. Wright admitted to poor judgment and to making decisions that he wished he could take back. It was a come-to-Jesus moment where he recognized, publicly, why Democrats were so frustrated with his actions. Standing with his hands on his hips and elbows pointed outward, he admitted, "Have I made mistakes? Oh, boy, how many? I made a lot of mistakes. Mistakes in judgement, oh yeah." But making mistakes, as everyone in the room had done, he said, was very different from being a criminal.

Taking off his glasses to emphasize the seriousness of this moment in congressional history, the Speaker now addressed the controversy about John Mack, whose association with him he acknowledged had deeply troubled his supporters. "I didn't know the nature of the crime that he had been convicted of. I knew only that John Mack was a young man who my daughter had known in high school and my daughter was married to his brother, incidentally; that's how she knew about John," Wright said. When his daughter brought the story to him, she knew only that Mack had been convicted of assault and had served twenty-seven months in the Fairfax county jail. Disputing the worst of the story from *The Washington Post*, he said, "I did not interfere with the court. I didn't suggest anything to the court. . . . I didn't inquire, maybe that's bad judgement, I didn't inquire as to the exact nature of the crime." After being told that Mack was a "model rehabilitative prisoner," Wright decided to give him a job as a file clerk for $9,000 a year. To the Speaker, this was an act of altruism and compassion rather than some malicious scheme to set an abuser free. After that, Mack "really blossomed and grew and developed and those of you who know him can't conceive—as I never could conceive when finally just two years ago I read in the newspaper—the precise nature of that crime. It just didn't fit his character." According to Wright. "Now, was that bad judgment? Yeah, maybe so. It doesn't have anything to do with the rules but it's got all mixed up with it, and I don't think, though, that it's bad judgment to try to give a young man a second chance." Doubling down on a defense of what he did, Wright reiterated that America doesn't stand "for the idea that a person should ever—forever be condemned." As Betty listened to her husband's defense from the gallery, tears streamed from her eyes.[66]

"Have I contributed unwittingly to this manic idea of frenzy of feeding on other people's reputations? Have I—have I caused a lot of this? So maybe I have. God, I hope I haven't. But maybe I have. Have I been too partisan? Too insistent? Too abrasive? Too determined to have my way? Perhaps," he confessed. He offered the men and women in the chamber a "proposition," which was the real basis of his decision to resign instead of fight. He said he would "give you back this job you gave to me as a propitiation for all of this season of bad will that has grown among us. Give it back to you. . . . I don't want to be a party to tearing up the institution—I love it." And then, about fifty-seven minutes into the speech, Wright announced in the formal voice he used to read a resolution, with both hands gently tapping the lectern, that he would step down. With his voice trembling, he said, "You need—you need somebody else. So, I want to give you that back. And we'll have a caucus on Tuesday. And then I will offer to resign from the House some time before the end of June."

Before finishing, Wright implored members of both parties to treat his resignation as a "total payment for the anger and hostility we feel toward each other. Let's not try to get even with each other." He ended by assuring the chamber that he was not a "bitter man. I'm not going to be. I'm a lucky man. God has given me the privilege of serving in this greatest institution on earth for a great many years, and I'm grateful to the people of my district in Texas. I'm grateful to you my colleagues—all of you. God bless this institution. God bless the United States." The California Democrat Don Edwards observed, "It was almost like out of Hamlet, a prince on his knees."[67]

As Wright brought this rousing valediction to a conclusion, Gingrich jotted down some notes on a pad of paper to record his thoughts at this critical juncture in the history of the legislative branch. If this result— Wright's exit, the humiliation of the Democratic majority, and the opening created for a Republican takeover of the chamber—had been achieved, Gingrich nonetheless felt extraordinarily unhappy about Wright's main message. The Speaker had attempted to distract the public and his colleagues from the very real offenses he had committed. His speech, Gingrich fumed, was about the dangers of partisanship rather than the problems with his own decisions. The tone of his speech "angered" him. It was insulting to the House Ethics Committee, chaired by an upstanding Democrat, "to talk about the process of standards as mindless cannibalism." Gingrich continued to scribble on his pad: Wright had incorrectly blasted his colleagues over a "feeding frenzy" with Tony Coelho. The majority whip had made *serious* mistakes in failing to disclose financial transactions.[68] Moreover, Gingrich rejected the charge that *he* had been "nitpicking" with the rules in order to find fault with Wright. All that the Speaker had done with this unsatisfactory speech was to blame the institution and blame the press.

Gingrich knew there would be hell to pay and that Democrats in the room would be out to get him when this ended. Yet he was confident that if he was judged by the same standards as Wright, he would be found innocent. And he noted, "Isn't having an honest House the business of the House?" He believed that Wright was "a symbol of how sick the institution has become." The speech, from Gingrich's point of view, "was an insult to the E.C. [Ethics Committee], ethics process, & the whole idea that letting the facts out in the open is better than covering them up." The thin-skinned minority whip could hold up a mirror to his own image and take consolation in the fact that because so much of the focus of the farewell speech was on him, it meant that he had now officially arrived as a major figure in Washington. "Must be doing good at my job," Gingrich thought, his confidence spiking, "for them to come after me like this."[69]

When the Speaker finished, the House burst into another standing ovation. To be polite, Gingrich joined in a show of collegiality. This was not, after all, the time to look like a "red hot." Feeling a sense of relief and sadness, Wright gathered up his notes and walked toward his colleagues, turning back to the lectern to make sure he had not forgotten any of his folders. About a dozen members from both parties walked toward him to express their support. They showered him with handshakes and hugs, whispering words of praise into his ears.[70]

Wright, looking remarkably poised as he turned to exit the floor, continued to accept the good wishes of his peers. Yet no one envied him for a moment. This final walk up the aisle was the longest and saddest Jim Wright had ever made. "Dreams die hard," *The Washington Post*'s Tom Shales wrote, quoting an unnamed network anchor, "and it isn't easy to see somebody's dreams shattered right in front of you."[71]

The House doorkeepers requested that legislators remain in the chamber for a few minutes so that Wright could leave the building in peace. Taking to the floor while everyone waited, most still in a state of disbelief, Jack Brooks had something he wanted to get off his chest in front of his colleagues. He walked to the rostrum and expressed his anger about the damage that Gingrich had wrought: "There's an evil wind blowing in the halls of Congress that's reminiscent of the Spanish Inquisition. It's replacing comity and compassion with hatred and malice. . . . Conviction without trial is a new and dangerous rule for this Congress and this country. This scenario can destroy Congress."[72] Everyone in the chamber knew Gingrich was the target of Brooks's remarks. Once they were allowed to leave, Gingrich took off without speaking to any reporters.

With his career as a legislator now behind him, Wright hurried through the Speaker's Lobby, eager to get out of the spotlight as quickly as possible. He passed the gilded framed portraits of all the Speakers who preceded him in their dark suits and starched collars, most of whom had enjoyed far more robust terms in office than he. The portrait of Speaker

Joe Cannon, who had faced a revolt of progressives who stripped away his power in 1910, loomed largest as Wright walked down the hall. When one staffer walked up to him to say, "Mr. Speaker, that was wonderful," the forlorn Texan tried to crack a smile before ducking into his office.

By now Betty and Virginia had reached his side, and his wife stood by him in his office while he greeted well-wishers as they came to pay their respects. Most of the Texas delegation stopped in, and the Speaker thanked them for standing by him.[73] When the friends finally departed, Wright, Betty, and Virginia left the building, and with his hand lightly touching his wife's back, they climbed into the waiting limousine. He leaned back against the cushions and stared out the window. The car began to pick up speed as they headed to their home in McLean. Wright wasn't sure what would come next. He might teach; he might write. But he felt certain he would never stop loving the institution in which he had served since 1955.

Eight

MINDLESS CANNIBALISM

As legislators milled around Statuary Hall, just outside the chamber, digesting Wright's speech, reporters sought their reactions. Congressman Henry Hyde, who often tussled with Wright from his opposing side of the aisle, agreed with his message and wanted his colleagues to get back to the business of legislation and governance. "I think most of us are weary of inhabiting the congressional Beirut we've been living in," he said.[1] The Texan Martin Frost believed the Speaker did the right thing, and he hoped the "Republicans were listening." It was time "to stop making lists," Frost said, "let's stop all of that and let's get on with the business of the country." Congressman Dan Glickman said it was important to show the public that Congress was a "viable institution" of government. He praised Wright for sacrificing himself, for falling on his sword so that the partisan rancor would end. "There will be no vengeance," promised a shaken California Democrat, Don Edwards. "We are not being paid to fight with each other."[2]

When asked about the impact of the resignation, a testy David Obey, whose ethics rules had been at the heart of his colleague's downfall, predicted it would be "very difficult" for either party to find "quality candidates" to step into this "maelstrom." Bill Richardson said the time had come to heal under the next Speaker, the levelheaded Tom Foley, because

Congress had become "a war zone right now, where you don't know when the next bomb is going to drop." He warned that if Gingrich decided to engage in "open warfare," Democrats would respond. His preference, though, was to start healing.[3]

Not everyone in Congress was in the mood to forgive Gingrich and his allies. When asked about Obey's comment that Foley would be the first Speaker from the reformist generation to come of age after Watergate, Congressman Torricelli pushed back. He argued that legislators were already living with much higher personal ethical standards but "a decidedly lower standard in personal relationships, trust, and individual integrity as people relate to each other. The integrity of important, decent citizens in our country is being questioned by leaks, blind comments, charges without substantiation. That's not integrity. A person who would do that to another, his integrity is no greater than someone who would steal, or rob, or violate rules."[4]

Wright's defender and friend Dave Nagle, whose ill-conceived meeting of Democrats in mid-May had disintegrated into a series of public declarations that Wright needed to go, could not contain his anger. When a reporter identified himself as working for *The Washington Times*, the conservative paper that had recently printed a pointed article about a number of lawmakers being under investigation from the Justice Department for illicit sexual activities, Nagle did not hold back. "Get your goddamn hands off me," the congressman yelled. "Don't pat me on the back when your paper runs crap like that." The Florida Democrat Larry Smith probably came closest to articulating the view of most as he called the entire Wright scandal a successful old-fashioned coup that Republicans orchestrated, trying to "do what they can't do at the ballot box" by "throwing hand grenades."[5]

"It's a stunning event," noted the editors of *The New York Times* as they closed the door on the Wright investigation. "The Speaker of the House, third in line to the Presidency, resigns over charges that he violated House rules. . . . the Speaker, his support virtually vanished, yields his place as a peace offering. Stunning, sobering and sad but also necessary."[6] The evening news anchor Tom Brokaw began his broadcast by telling his audience that Wright turned the floor of the House "into a courtroom, a confessional, a stage, and finally a platform from which to say goodbye."[7] "Jim Wright did the right thing in resigning," chimed in the editors of *The Washington Post*.[8]

Speaking from London, where he had traveled to participate in a NATO summit, President Bush, whose decision to attack Wright during his 1988 campaign had helped to legitimatize Gingrich's crusade, offered some complimentary remarks. "In spite of the present situation," his statement read, "I believe the Wright tenure was one of effectiveness and dedication to the Congress of the United States. And I recognize his distinguished service to the people of his congressional district. Barbara and I wish Jim and Betty well in whatever lies ahead."

The congressional Republicans of course felt differently. Even if they disagreed with the way Gingrich had conducted his business, most of them did not feel guilty about how the process had unfolded. Moderate Republicans expressed their confidence in the system and the outcome. The ethics process had played out, they said, in a bipartisan manner and with a very reasonable committee chair and had determined that Wright had not lived up to the ethical standards the House adopted for itself. This was not partisan politics. This was congressional justice. What Republicans saw as Wright's tyrannical leadership had created a toxic atmosphere that, in their minds, was as responsible for how this had unfolded as anything that Gingrich or the media had done.

Gingrich seethed as the ex-Speaker returned to Capitol Hill during the short transition—his last official day as Speaker was June 6—and enjoyed a White House visit with his fellow Texan. It pained Gingrich to think Wright could shape the history of what had transpired, as if Gingrich and not the former Speaker had stopped the legislative work of Congress in its tracks. Wright was making himself the hero of this story, to Gingrich's utter frustration. Letting his private feelings be known, the minority whip lashed out at his critics who were depicting him as a villain while they were praising the fallen Speaker. "Jim Wright was not the innocent sacrifice to some tribal ritual," Gingrich said at a June 2 lunch that he organized with reporters to set the record straight. After all, it had been his vision, and he had orchestrated its execution. At the lunch, Gingrich radiated the kind of hubris that a person sometimes displays after an unexpected triumph. It was as if he had traveled back to his days as a small-town college professor, standing before mesmerized undergraduates. "Wright and Coelho pulled off this wonderful scam where they are the innocent victims of a mood in Washington. That is baloney. The guy was guilty." While the Democrats were treating him as evil, Gingrich counterpunched: "Mr. Wright resigned because the weight of the evidence was that he had systematically engaged in behaviors unbecoming of the Speaker of the House. And the evidence is overwhelming."[9] Nor did Gingrich have any intention of relenting now that Wright was gone. In his mind, this scandal was not over until he said it was over. He joined the RNC's Lee Atwater in calling on the House to take a straight up-or-down vote on whether Wright and Coelho were guilty of violating the ethics rules, even though both men were leaving. "There are only two ways to proceed," Atwater said. "We need to get it behind us. One way is to sweep it under the rug. I personally am in favor of getting it behind us by getting the facts out on the Wright matter, on the Coelho matter, and on the eight or nine or ten others—Republican and Democratic."[10] The new Speaker, Tom Foley, did not agree with Gingrich and Atwater. After Wright's decision to resign, the Democratic majority dropped any further investigation. Like Wright, the party had paid its price and it was time to move on.

Wright, in turn, hoping to stave off that humiliation, sent out word through his press secretary, Mark Johnson, that his farewell address was not an attack on Gingrich and that his point genuinely was to end the bitterness in Congress.[11] And now Robert Michel, still Gingrich's superior, stepped in to have his own say

Sending a message to his party, Michel had stern words for his minority whip. He warned on *CBS This Morning* that Gingrich has "got to be much more responsible than he was as a junior member of Congress."[12] Of course, Michel was not the innocent he was making himself out to be. He didn't like Gingrich personally, and he often found his political style distasteful. But over the past two years he had been complicit in his colleague's campaign against the "corruption" of House Democrats. They all had been. And soon they would enjoy the spoils.

Wright's parting message had come much too late. The problem was that Wright didn't understand that the debate over ethics was asymmetric. The purification that Gingrich was demanding from Democrats was almost entirely one-sided. Gingrich, who was under an ethics cloud of his own, one eerily similar to the charges he had leveled against the Speaker, had no intention of demanding the same strict standards from his own allies. The campaign against Speaker Wright was all about politics, not good government.

The Speaker's defeat was an unprecedented moment in congressional history and inspired a new confidence in Gingrich's style of tactical warfare. Simply put, his tactics worked.

Spearheading a campaign to bring down the Speaker of the House without clear-cut justification had been a big step for Gingrich to take. There was only one comparable example, the revolt against Speaker Joe Cannon in 1910, which Gingrich could look to. The traditions of Congress had persuaded most legislators to err on the side of caution so that these forms of high-profile takedowns did not become normalized. Ending the career of a major leader could not turn into a regular feature of partisan battles, most members agreed, or the possibility of legislating would become extremely difficult. Opening this door would trigger an unending cycle of retribution and generate a climate of total distrust. Leaders would lose the sense of security that was necessary to push forward controversial decisions.

Because of these calculations, the bar had always been set high by both parties. While it was true that Wright had done some unsavory things in his career, the evidence against him was hardly a smoking gun. In fact, at the moment he resigned, the Ethics Committee had failed to gather the necessary evidence to support claims that he had violated a single ethics rule. The process was never allowed to play out.

The investigation had created such a frenzied political atmosphere that the Speaker had been pressured into stepping down before the Ethics Committee considered the soundness of the charges they had laid out to the House. This was a massive problem for the integrity of the ethics process and the institution because Gingrich had triggered his campaign based on sketchy evidence culled primarily from newspaper stories. A significant number of the original charges had been disproven. The standards for the committee to move forward had been extremely low. Even with Phelan's lengthy report, which also relied heavily on articles and included discredited charges, the committee had not begun the important stage of their process where they would verify that the evidence before them met the highest possible standards.

The Ethics Committee had not yet proven that Wright had broken any House rules or that he had engaged in any kind of extraordinary wrongdoing that went beyond the ethically gray behavior citizens often saw from legislators, including Gingrich himself. The blockbuster allegations were not proving to be true. But Gingrich had moved at such a fast and furious pace that his efforts paid off. He understood from the start that this scandal would be settled in a political arena, and he had figured out how to shift the opinions and the electoral calculations of fellow legislators. Investigative journalists and good-government reformers had provided him with the institutional support that he needed from legitimate, nonpartisan sources. The party guardians in the GOP, despite priding themselves on their civility, had allowed Gingrich to follow this campaign to its logical conclusion, rewarding him with a major leadership position in the process. "Remember when you're kids and there's always some tough-talking little kid, and when somebody stands up to him he caves in?" noted his disillusioned former press secretary, Lee Howell. "Newt's never had anybody stand up to him."[13] President Bush, Minority Leader Michel, and all the others had some blood on their hands. As a result, the moment that Speaker Wright stepped down, the GOP had shown that they could "go there" in fierce partisan combat and get away with it.

Once politicians lowered the bar as to what kinds of actions were permissible in the political arena, it was virtually impossible to restore conditions to where they had been. When politicians see a colleague get away with something, the temptation is strong to replicate what they have witnessed in one form or another. Speaker Wright's belief that there were cycles in American politics—that conditions would swing back to a better time following the turbulence of the moment—was misguided and underestimated how institutions could be permanently degraded. Wright—who resumed life as a professor at Texas Christian University—only slowly came to realize how Gingrich had remade his party. Republicans had proven that the minority party had the ability to demolish a figure of great authority if they wished. They elevated the needs of partisanship over governance. In the process of pushing Wright toward resignation, Gingrich had also introduced, popularized, and refined a potent theme that the GOP could use in the 1990 midterm elections and beyond, while he, once the black sheep, had emerged as a major force in his party.

Gingrich moved quickly to consolidate his power. Immediately after Wright's downfall, the Georgian telegraphed his goals when he announced that the GOP would continue to make congressional ethics a central issue and added that there were nine or ten other Democrats who were already the subjects of fresh investigations. He now reiterated his plan to go after more Democrats and promised that he would push forward a broad "reform package" that would transform the way legislators did business. Not long after, the *CBS Evening News* reported that the FBI had launched an investigation into Congressman William Gray, a third-generation African American Baptist minister and Pennsylvania Democrat who hoped to replace the departed Coelho as majority whip. Gray reported that the charges of corruption were baseless and had Republican fingerprints all over them. "Some on the other side," said Dick Gephardt, whom Democrats elected as majority leader on June 14, "are committed to the dark side of politics—smear, innuendo, rumors, cynical media management, the politics of character assassination." When Democrats selected Gray to be whip, Congressman Barney Frank said that the decision "sends the word to Thornburgh [the attorney general] and Atwater that efforts to smear people in this party aren't going to work."[14]

Gingrich compared his efforts to clean up Capitol Hill to the arrest of five African American and Latino teenage boys in April for having sexually assaulted a jogger in Central Park. "Nobody 40 years ago would have suggested a young woman could have walked through Central Park. I mean, they just sort of understood, at 10 o'clock at night women don't walk through Central Park. We now have a standard that says, By God, in America you ought to be able to walk through Central Park and not be assaulted." The comparison was both ironic and telling because it eventually turned out that the police had arrested the wrong men, coerced their confessions, and sent them to prison for years before they were proven innocent.[15]

After everything that had gone on, Democrats sought revenge. The party was ready to take out their anger on Gingrich, who they felt was a ruthless hypocrite guilty of his own unethical behavior. Though Gingrich continued to dismiss the accusations against him as a deceitful campaign by Wright allies seeking retribution by spreading lies, others were not so sure. The Republican National Committee sought to preempt further debate by sending out an information sheet to Republican leaders, subtitled "No Comparison," explaining why the income Gingrich received from his two books was completely different from Wright's book deal. The Georgian's book was a "serious political work" published by a reputable publisher, whereas the former Speaker's volume was just a bunch of speeches and vignettes published by a "convicted felon." Gingrich's book was sold in bookstores all over the United States, and even reached the bestseller list, whereas approximately 98 percent of Wright's books were sold as bulk orders.[16]

Gingrich must have been smiling when he read in the newspapers how Robert Michel, once called the voice of reason and said to be the polar opposite of Gingrich, dismissed stories suggesting that Republicans were determined to "kiss and make up" with Democrats after Wright's downfall. The "cleansing process must continue," a resolute Michel insisted to the press. After thirty-five years of "corrosive acid" from Democratic rule, there would be no returning to the old ways of Washington.[17] Michel sent a private announcement to every member of the Republican Conference that they would need to balance the requirements of governing with the need to fight back hard against Democrats through "guerrilla warfare." Michel, having had a taste of victory, wanted more.

John Buckley, the conservative spokesperson of the National Republican Congressional Committee, thought that Gingrich was a breath of fresh air within the tired congressional wing of the party. "Gingrich is classic agitprop," he wrote, "great with devising the arguments to forward our revolution. I see him as one-third Thomas Paine, one-third Winston Churchill and one-third Genghis Khan."[18]

On June 12, *The Washington Post* published a feature article about Gingrich, calling him the "point man in a house divided." Myra MacPherson portrayed Gingrich as the "conservatives' prize pit bull" who would "stop at nothing" to bring down the Democrats. The legislator who had once been derided by members on both sides of the aisle, MacPherson noted, was now in the "catbird seat" and being courted by the media. The story was certainly not all sanguine. MacPherson featured comments from Democrats and Republicans who didn't like Gingrich's style. "Newt doesn't take the low road—he takes the tunnel," said a former colleague from West Georgia College. But the piece still presented him as a master of publicity who was expert at manipulating the press. He was shown to be a politician who understood how to use bombastic language to his advantage and a man who grasped better than most that television was the new medium of political exchange: "a politician who knows that contradictions between voting records and words, between reality and a hyped version of reality, scarcely matter in the world of the fifteen-second sound bite." For all of its critical comments, the feature article, along with a huge photo of Gingrich standing in his office, elevated the minority whip by depicting him without reservation as a force to be reckoned with in Washington politics.[19]

On the same day that the *Washington Post* profile appeared, *Newsweek* released a cover story titled ETHICS WARS: FRENZY ON THE HILL, in which Tom Morganthau, Howard Fineman, and Eleanor Clift wrote about the storm sweeping over Capitol Hill. "Wright's disgrace has shaken the Democratic Party," they reported, "like few events since the fall of

Lyndon Johnson," and continued, "The ethics craze and partisan rancor, both volatile in themselves, are now combining to create an explosive political atmosphere in the 101st Congress."[20]

To be sure, there were a few optimists who said that the process could be different. Speaker-elect Foley promised the nation that his number one goal would be to end the toxic environment on Capitol Hill. He explained in his first interview in his new role that he had confidence the new Democratic leaders could work through this transitional moment. "I think we need to work very seriously at restoring a sense of comity and confidence between members of the two parties," he said. Hoping to declare a truce, Foley promised to begin his term by reaching out to Republican leaders and avoiding the ugly tactics that had caused a backlash against Speaker Wright. He acknowledged that there were Democrats who were "very bitter about what they regard as the crucifixion of Jim Wright," but he would not let them take over.[21]

Even Lee Atwater seemed temporarily contrite when he publicly apologized for a Republican National Committee memo, written by the communications director Mark Goodin, titled "Tom Foley: Out of the Liberal Closet."[22] The memo itself focused on Foley's liberal voting record in the House but compared him to Barney Frank, one of the few openly gay politicians at the time. The leaked memo was viewed as an effort to embarrass Foley, who had been married to Heather Strachan since 1968, by depicting him as a homosexual. Karen Van Brocklin, Gingrich's attack dog, had reportedly called journalists urging them to look into Foley's private life after the RNC distributed this memo. Thomas Ashley, a former Democratic congressman, wrote President George H. W. Bush that the insinuations about Foley's sexuality were "unpardonable" and urged his friend to make a strong statement condemning the memo. Despite Van Brocklin's role, Gingrich denied having anything to do with it. "I called Tom last night," he told a reporter, "and said that I apologized personally for any pain we've caused him."[23]

On the heels of Wright's dramatic resignation, Gingrich had no intention of slowing down or letting up. Speaker Foley could wax philosophical about the need for civility, and Republicans, including himself, might admit that the "Out of the Liberal Closet" memo went too far, but the frontal assault on Democratic corruption would continue. This was what had propelled him into the House leadership, and it was the theme he believed would finally bring Republicans control of Congress. There was no way he would give up now when Republicans were so close.

Shortly after the Foley story broke, Gingrich appeared onstage with Senator Bob Dole, who in 1976 gained the moniker "hatchet man" for his ruthless attacks as the vice presidential candidate for Gerald Ford. The occasion was the annual summer meeting of the Republican National Committee on June 16 at a sterile Washington hotel ballroom three blocks from the White House. The main item on the agenda was for the delegates to give a vote of confidence to Atwater in spite of the Foley scandal, which they did. "The Democrats want me out of a job," an exuberant Atwater said as the local and national attendees offered him their thunderous applause. "But the people here today expressed their depth of support."[24] Dole was up next. He started with a joke, before turning serious, mourning the days when Washington was more civil. After acknowledging the "tragedy for John Tower, Robert Bork, and yes, for Tom Foley," Dole said, "I love politics. I know it's rough and tough. I know we can have our differences. And I know we want to win. But it's gotta be based on wanting to win for some good reason." Pushing against the tenor of the room, he mentioned a series of incidents where the partisanship had become too bitter, including with Foley. Gingrich walked up to the stage when Dole finished. Although Dole did shake Gingrich's hand, it was an uncomfortable moment as the senator visibly looked over his shoulder. He was intent on avoiding eye contact with the person he had previously dismissed as the head of the "young hypocrites."

But this was not Dole's moment. As he walked back into the audience, all heads turned toward Gingrich. With the RNC members listening closely, he took a victory lap, reminding them what he had accomplished and how he would use ethics again as the tool to win Republican majorities. He wanted someone like Lee Atwater at the helm. Seeking to whip up his audience, Gingrich warned that the left-wing "machine" would come to get him and Atwater because it was so frightened by the prospect of losing power. "You're gonna see weird things coming out of this city over the next few years," he told the audience as it kept applauding, "because you're watching the death throes of the machine, and you're watching its power to smear, and its power to intimidate. And the next time you hear anyone say, 'Let's fire Lee Atwater,' the first thing you ought to know is . . . they are either left-wingers or they have been intimidated by left-wingers." The crowd started to whoop and holler so loudly that they could barely hear when Gingrich ended his speech. Atwater, who was sitting in the front row, rushed up onto the stage and gave Gingrich a warm embrace. The two pumped their fists into the air as Jeanie Austin, the co-chair of the Republican National Committee, grabbed the microphone and said admiringly of Gingrich, "Isn't he something? Maybe we can all get that on videotape!"[25]

With heated rhetoric like this coming from the GOP, it was not surprising that the truce did not last. Both parties dug much deeper into the trenches of scandal warfare, and despite the initial entreaties for peace, the Wright resignation was a turning point in American politics. "Because he took on Wright and won, [Gingrich] became a serious political figure," the influential New Right conservative activist Paul Weyrich admitted. "Up to that point, he was regarded as an interesting political figure, somebody that was very good for a quote, but not somebody who was perhaps going to be in the power structure. But when he took on Jim Wright and he won, he was regarded very seriously from that moment on."[26] The Speaker's ignominious defeat proved to others in the House that Gingrich was a force to be reckoned with and that he could deliver on his barbed promises.

The shock had been not just that Gingrich and the Republicans had been willing to engage in a full-throated effort to bring down the Speaker of the House before he was proven guilty of any infraction but that Democrats let it happen. Both parties were responsible for the damage. Speaker Wright had proven to be a failed leader for his party. His competence could not be judged simply through policy and his mastery of legislative procedure. Legislative politics by 1989 was about a charged political landscape and being able to survive in an increasingly brutal, polarized world where the parties grew further and further apart with each passing day. Wright's fall from power was remarkably swift. He proved that he couldn't handle the cauldron of partisan warfare. This was perhaps the most important test for a party leader. And his failures had enormous long-term consequences for his party and for the institution of Congress, because his downfall opened the door to the Gingrich generation of Republicans and led the way for the GOP to regain control of the House.

Wright was not the only Democrat to blame. He was just one part of a generation of Democrats in the 1970s who had done too little to fix the nexus between money and politics when a rare window of opportunity for reform had opened in the aftermath of Watergate. The Democrats, who controlled the institution with an iron fist, were reluctant to address a fundamental problem at the heart of our democratic system. Going into the age of Reagan, Congress remained awash in campaign contributions, lobbyists, and shady revolving doors. Private money remained too pervasive in campaigns, lobbyists were all too present in the halls of Capitol Hill, and some legislators were given too much leeway to go as far as they could to make money for themselves and to funnel funds toward their districts. By failing to address these and other problems when the window for reform briefly opened, Democrats made themselves susceptible to being attacked for corruption. While Republicans were guilty of many of these political sins as well, Democrats were the party with power, and they had held that power since 1954, so the overwhelming weight of public blame naturally fell on their shoulders. Although much of Wright's scandal revolved around personal aggrandizement, it unfolded within a system where many Americans did not trust the relationships and connections that tied members of Congress to money. Gingrich's attacks on Wright resonated, regardless of the details, because they were so plausible.

Democrats made a choice with Wright. Their decision to allow their leader to fall so quickly was not a legal decision but a political one. The endless anonymous comments to the press by members saying that he had to step down, and the private conversations Democrats had in the closed room of the caucus, quickly leaked to the press, ratcheted up the pressure on Wright to leave the institution that he loved. For a devout Democrat such as Wright, this betrayal stung more than anything Gingrich could say. Democrats maintained control of the House in the spring of 1989 and, at the time he was under the most intense pressure to step down, polls consistently showed that the public did not know or care about what was going on. Although there was certainly a big political risk for Democrats to use their power to insulate him, in light of the charges that had emerged, the Democrats could have fought back against the Republican efforts—which only a handful of them did—by insisting that the demand for resignation was excessive based on the evidence available to them. Instead, most members of the party decided by the spring of 1989 that Wright was no longer worth the cost of defending, and they let their feelings be known through anonymous interviews to a press eager to stop corruption. They sacrificed their troubled leader for the short-term benefits his removal might provide.

Pressuring Wright to resign offered some insulation for the party in the short term, but failing to stand by him created strong incentives for Republicans to ramp up their efforts and engage in even more brutal fights. Once the Democrats and Wright conceded, there was nothing to disarm the parties or stop Gingrich from again rummaging through his toolbox. It was a compelling, unapologetic example of the ends justifying the means—ends every Republican could get behind.

Too often, we treat partisan polarization in our recent history as an inexorable force that nothing could stop. Because of the large-scale forces of history, the social scientists say, voters have been sorted into "red" and "blue" states by the institutions remade to incentivize partisanship, and politicians can no longer find areas of agreement. But this view of polarization as inevitable denies agency to the politicians and leaders who pushed partisan combat into a deeper abyss at very specific moments. There were important points where American politics took a more destructive turn. There is a history of partisan polarization that we still need to tell. The battle over Speaker Wright in 1989 was one such turning point, a crucial event, from which Washington never recovered.

The downfall of Speaker Wright opened up a new period in American politics, the era of Gingrich. It was notable that the allegations surrounding Wright were not nearly as significant as the allegations surrounding Nixon during Watergate—not even close. In certain respects, this made his decision to resign even more dramatic. At the point when he stepped down, the accusations were still relatively minor in the minds of many experts and involved technical violations of internal ethics codes, not presidential efforts to obstruct the law or even a sex scandal so embarrassing that there was no way to remain in office. Yet this was enough to bring him down. His resignation shaped the way that several generations of legislators and voters would think about governance and politicians.

Gingrich's successful campaign had also tainted the aspirations of good-government reformers and journalists in the aftermath of Watergate. After the Nixon era, reform organizations pushed measures through Congress that increased transparency and created new rules governing behavior, and journalists became more aggressive in uncovering corruption and wrongdoing. In these years, there was hope in Washington that things could be different. Few were so naive as to think that the political system would be governed by angels, but there had been genuine optimism that the changes that occurred after Nixon's disgrace would make things better. That hope faded once Gingrich asserted his power. He had used congressional reforms and an investigative press as weapons to devastate his opponents. He had made Democrats and Republicans see how even the best-intentioned reforms could be turned against a fellow member. Every legislator felt a bit more vulnerable after May 31, 1989.

Wright's dream that the parties' anger would dissipate once he was gone was wildly off the mark. His leaving only whetted the appetite of Republicans like Gingrich for more political takedowns. Over the next decade, the scandal wars escalated to create one of the most contentious periods in the government's history as the needs of governance and of legislating steadily took a back seat to the imperatives of intense partisan warfare where compromise was considered toxic and where almost any threat to destroy another politician's career or hijack the legislative process was permissible if it was legal. The era would be dominated by ongoing accusations, vilification, investigations, resignations, and the forced removal of elected officials from office as Gingrich played Napoleon and Waterloo was not on the horizon. He survived the initial wave of attacks on his own ethics record by simply moving forward in defiant fashion. He kept finding success as he went after the ethical wrongdoing of Democrats— the Ways and Means Committee chairman, Dan Rostenkowski, would be next—and as he did, a growing number of Republicans became increasingly excited about Gingrich's style and message. They believed his promise that the Republicans could gain control of Congress. For a party that had been out of power for so long, the spectacle of what he did to the Speaker energized them.

The gospel of Gingrich kept spreading. He literally shared his rhetorical style through a GOPAC pamphlet first distributed in 1990, titled "Language: A Key Mechanism of Control," that offered a road map to replicate his way with words. Responding to Republican candidates who, GOPAC said, had told them, "I wish I could speak like Newt," the memo recommended using certain words repeatedly like "corruption," "traitors," "sick," "radical," "shame," "pathetic," "steal," and "lie" to describe the Democrats.[27]

And he was still scrapping with members of his own party. Gingrich defiantly walked out of a budget meeting when President George H. W. Bush finally agreed to raise taxes as part of a deficit-reduction package in 1990. He never forgave the president. Because of the showdown over taxes, the Republican consultant Eddie Mahe said, "Newt comes out a big winner with a lot of people in the country who think the agreement is bad, and he has the guts to say so. He has reasserted himself as the natural leader of the conservative movement."[28] For Gingrich, the issue was much bigger than taxes. "The number one thing we had to prove in the fall of '90," Gingrich said, "was that, if you explicitly decided to govern from the center, we could make it so unbelievably expensive you couldn't sustain it."[29] Gingrich's engagement in internecine squabbles, combined with the sizable number of Democratic voters in the suburbs of Atlanta, nearly cost him his seat in 1990, when he beat David Worley, a thirty-two-year-old lawyer, by fewer than a thousand votes. The exuberance that Washington seemed to feel toward Gingrich did not translate to his district, where some wondered why he spent so much time on his national aspirations as opposed to the bread-and-butter needs of his constituents. At one town hall meeting filled with hundreds of constituents, Gingrich heard angry voters complain about his priorities as well as his blind eye to Republican scandals. But despite the complaints from his district, Gingrich won re-election, and for him that was all that mattered.

He staked his entire future on being able to fulfill the promises that he had been making to his fellow party members. He never lost his instinct to go in for the kill in pursuit of his goals. Quoting Mao Zedong, Gingrich liked to say, "Politics is war without blood."[30] Gingrich kept using corruption as the spear to attack the Democrats. In early 1992, he helped to weaken the political standing of many prominent Democrats (and some Republicans, including himself) during the House bank scandal when the media reported that hundreds of members were overdrawing their House checking accounts without any penalty whatsoever. Among those implicated were Henry Waxman, the environmental advocate from California; Ron Dellums, one of the leading African American representatives, who was committed to social justice; and George Miller, one of the most prominent and effective liberal voices in his caucus. When Michel tried to work with Speaker Foley to minimize the disclosure in the press of the names of members implicated in this scandal, because Michel realized that Republicans were vulnerable to the backlash as well, Gingrich exploded. "This is about systematic, institutional corruption, not personality," he said in an interview. "To ask the Democratic leadership to clean things up would be like asking the old Soviet bureaucracy under Brezhnev to reform itself. It ain't going to happen."[31] Gingrich took a big bite of this scandal, and he wouldn't let go. "We don't know what happened. But I don't think you can restore trust in our institution by taking our dirt and sweeping it under the carpet," said Ohio's John Boehner, one of his close allies.[32] Calling themselves the Gang of Seven, Gingrich,

Boehner, Pennsylvania's Rick Santorum, Iowa's Jim Nussle, and three other Republicans relied on made-for-cable television theater pioneered by Camscam to make their point. Nussle wore a brown paper bag over his head in front of the C-SPAN cameras to let voters know how ashamed they all were to be members of the institution. When Democrats pointed out that Gingrich himself had twenty overdrafts, he didn't flinch. Such revelations of hypocrisy never seemed to shake him. He responded by claiming that the Democrats were "rigging" their investigation to "get him." In the aftermath of the cold war, he envisioned himself as a crusader for good, comparing himself to figures such as Václav Havel in Czechoslovakia and Lech Wałęsa in Poland who had brought down communism.[33] The bank scandal was followed by the congressional post office scandal, which was based on an investigation showing that members had misused their franking privileges— their right to send mail to constituents without paying postage—for personal gain. Meanwhile, Gingrich's public anger about President Bush's agreement to raise taxes didn't help Bush's electoral standing on the Right, contributing to Arkansas governor Bill Clinton's victory in the presidential election in November.

With Bill Clinton in the White House, Gingrich broadened his portfolio of issues to include more than corruption. He stood at the center of the partisan maelstrom that formed over the progressive tax increase that the president rammed through the Democratic Congress in 1993 as well as the failed effort to reform the health-care system. Gingrich used both of these measures, the successful bill and the failed proposal, to paint Clinton—and the Democrats—as big-government liberals when the nation had shifted to the right with the Reagan Revolution. In October 1993, Michel, tired of being Gingrich's punching bag, a perpetual symbol on the Right of why the GOP failed to gain power, announced he would retire, placing Gingrich next in line to be the top Republican. Michel knew that if he tried to stay in power, Gingrich was planning to come after his job. At the press conference announcing his retirement, in a thinly veiled shot at Gingrich, Michel complained of members who indulged in "trashing the institution."[34] But his warnings came much too late. Like most gatekeepers who allow insurgents in for their own political purposes,

Michel had been swallowed by the revolution. The barbarians were no longer at the gates because Michel had allowed them to walk right through barriers in the takedown of Speaker Wright: now Gingrich was in control.

Even though Gingrich liked to present himself as a big-idea man, the truth is that his contributions as a partisan tactician were far more important than anything he did in terms of policy. With few exceptions, his policy ideas came directly out of the familiar toolbox of the conservative movement—tax cuts, strong defense, minimal government, limiting bureaucratic power, curbing reproductive rights—with a few original proposals thrown in, such as his passion for the space program and a handful of centrist positions like being pro-environment. Gingrich made his biggest impact on the GOP by defining what partisanship should look like and by expanding the boundaries of what was permissible in the arena of congressional warfare. Washington was becoming a "less civil government, it's becoming more polarized and it's becoming more vicious," Wright told C-SPAN.[35] Gingrich was not responsible for growing partisan polarization on Capitol Hill, but he legitimated ruthless and destructive practices that had once been relegated to the margins.

Following a battle plan similar to the one he gave Paul Weyrich in 1975 when he was still a hungry political striver, Gingrich nationalized the 1994 midterms by drafting his "Contract with America," a slick ten-point plan that combined conservative programmatic goals including a balanced budget amendment, an anticrime package, and higher defense spending with congressional reforms that built on his long-cherished themes. Gingrich proposed subjecting Congress to the laws that applied to the rest of the country, imposing term limits on committee chairs, and requiring that committee meetings be open to the public. Gingrich coordinated with hundreds of campaigns across the nation in order to make sure they delivered a common message. The Contract with America was a key part of the final weeks of Republican campaigns in 1994. They used the "document," distributed as a tear-out page in *TV Guide* that was designed to be placed on Americans' refrigerators, to define their candidacies. The contract offered voters a checklist to monitor after the election, to assure them that the Republicans would keep fighting for the ideals of

Ronald Reagan while changing the broken legislative branch of government. "He is chief cheerleader, chief fund-raiser, chief recruiter and chief message developer," New York's Bill Paxon, the chairman of the National Republican Congressional Committee, said of Gingrich.[36]

Gingrich's plan worked. For the first time in forty years, Republicans took over the House and the Senate. More than thirty-four Democratic incumbents, including Dan Rostenkowski and Jack Brooks, lost their seats. The number of Republicans in the House swelled from 176 to 230. In the Senate, their majority rose to fifty-four. In the Cobb Galleria Centre ballroom in Atlanta, Georgia, embellished with "Newt Blue," Gingrich walked into a room of boisterous supporters who chanted, "Speaker! Speaker! Speaker!" "This is the beginning of the revolution!" proclaimed a young, up-and-coming Sean Hannity on his Georgia radio talk show on WGST. And it surprised no one when House Republicans unanimously elected Newt Gingrich their Speaker, making him the most powerful person in Congress. He replaced Robert Michel, who had retired from the House under relentless pressure from Gingrich. Almost nobody in the GOP had anything bad to say about Gingrich at that moment. Unlike in 1954, after the GOP leadership decided to end its four-year reliance on the controversial renegade senator Joseph McCarthy, whom they had used to attack the Democrats before losing their majority,[37] this time the party elite never put on the brakes. Instead, they made the renegade their leader. Gingrich was the new normal, and he was seen as being good for the party. He promised something and delivered. Whatever they might once have thought about his tactics, they worked. Winning felt good, and for the once-beaten-down GOP it was the best revenge.

More than five years after Wright left Washington and settled into a second act back in Fort Worth, where he wrote and taught courses at Texas Christian University, Gingrich got what he'd come to Washington for sixteen years earlier. The former Speaker watched in dismay as the media showered attention on Gingrich, who treated his perch like the presidency, depicting him as a brilliant political mastermind and the exciting voice of a new generation in the GOP. Gingrich had reached the top of the congressional hierarchy, the post that Wright had once proudly held. Toppling Speaker Wright had been pivotal to his ascent.

After Gingrich took over as Speaker, Wright asked the House Chaplain to deliver a lengthy handwritten note to his successor. (He didn't bring it himself, realizing that the media would turn it into a sensational story.) In the missive, written on February 15, 1995, from his perch in Fort Worth, Wright did what he felt was "one of the most difficult things" in his life—offering Gingrich full forgiveness. His heartfelt letter expressed genuine admiration for Gingrich's "tactical leadership" before explaining that he was "angry and personally offended" that Gingrich had called him a "crook." The language, Wright said, was "inappropriate and uncalled for." Wright believed that Gingrich owed him an apology. "If you are a gentleman, you'll give one." Even though a respected lawyer had encouraged him to "sue you for slander," Wright explained that he didn't want to add that "harassment" and "distraction" to his new job. So, though it was "not easy for me," Wright wrote, "I want you to know that I forgive you. . . . We all have recited: 'Forgive us our trespasses as we forgive those who have trespassed against us.' To repeat the words is easy. To perform the deed is difficult. At least it often is for me. But you are forgiven. Totally. It's wiped out. That and the other hostile things you have said and caused to be done to me and Betsy in the past. We forgive you." In response, Gingrich could barely muster an ounce of sympathy. In a letter that was not written until December 3, the Speaker responded that he "thought and prayed over your personal note," and stated that "I wish you no ill and I will seek to avoid saying anything that would further hurt you or your family." Wishing Wright a good holiday season without "distraction from the news media or me," Gingrich simply thanked him for writing the note, nothing more.[38]

The next four years were a roller coaster in Washington as Gingrich, whom *Time* named its 1995 "Man of the Year," unleashed his style of partisan warfare from the highest levels of power. Facing off against President Clinton, Republicans under Gingrich demonstrated that they would make extreme threats, such as allowing the federal government to shut down over a budget dispute with the White House. If Clinton didn't think Gingrich would go through with this, he did, leaving tourists stranded at the National Zoo in Washington, government workers without paychecks, and Americans hoping to go overseas unable to obtain visas. Republicans suffered a national backlash against their tactics. But Gingrich didn't care. Within the GOP, he was a hero.

From the moment Gingrich had become Speaker, House Republicans had investigated, investigated, and investigated the Clinton administration, doing everything they possibly could to undermine the president's standing. Speaker Gingrich had strengthened the institutional apparatus of Congress to undertake this process by merging a number of committees with oversight power into the Government Reform and Oversight Committee. He stacked this committee, which had more oversight power than any committee in the history of the House, with loyal freshmen and appointed Indiana's Dan Burton as the chair in 1997.[39] Burton, who was known as a "pit bull" and had proposed mandatory AIDS testing for every citizen, was part of Gingrich's rotating cabal of COS members in the 1980s who used C-SPAN as a platform to tarnish the reputation of Democrats. Burton had led the infamous campaign in 1994 challenging the official finding that the White House deputy counsel Vincent Foster had committed suicide, fueling conspiracy theories that he had been murdered.[40]

And yet life at the top, Gingrich would find, was not the smooth sailing he had envisioned. The instability that Gingrich had created for congressional leaders turned against him and the Republicans when they controlled the institution. In 1997, Gingrich became the first Speaker in the history of the institution to be punished for violating the ethics rules. The Connecticut Republican Nancy Johnson, chairwoman of the Ethics Committee, who had once watched in bittersweet dismay at the takedown of Jim Wright, said when presenting the resolution to her colleagues, "The penalty is tough and unprecedented. It is also appropriate. No one is above the rules of the House."[41] Whereas Wright stepped down before the House moved forward with his case, Gingrich remained in place as the House voted 395 to 28 to reprimand him and impose a

$300,000 financial fine for his using tax-exempt contributions to support partisan videos (masked as educational courses) and then misleading the Ethics Committee about what he had done. Still, he held on to his position.

Sitting for an interview in his Texas home, with an artificial log burning in his gas fireplace as his two dogs napped on the floor, Wright told his *New York Times* interviewer, Sam Howe Verhovek, "Here I am determined that I'm going to be statesmanlike, and there you are tempting me" by bringing up Gingrich. With his bushy eyebrows, now totally white, becoming animated, he couldn't resist saying, "McCarthy comes to mind." Wright, who described Gingrich in his memoir as an "arsonist who torches the building without supposing that the flames could consume his own bedroom," continued to maintain hope that the House could change for the better.[42] He was wrong.

Gingrich's ethical problems didn't slow him down one bit. The Speaker forged ahead in going after President Clinton, who was Gingrich's new Jim Wright, just at a grander level. Gingrich never hesitated to say whatever was necessary to tarnish the president's reputation. He poached ideas from conspiracy theorists and repeated them from the post of a party leader. "He took these things that were confined to the margins of the conservative movement and mainstreamed them. What I think he saw was the potential for using them to throw sand in the gears of Clinton's ability to govern," recalled David Brock, a onetime Republican attack dog who had reformed his ways.[43] The House Republican campaign led to President Clinton's impeachment for perjury and obstruction of justice over his sexual relationship with a White House intern named Monica Lewinsky.

The public thought that impeachment was a step too far and punished Republicans in the midterm elections. Gingrich, who had pioneered this partisan warfare, paid the price. He had become a liability. He now had a checkered ethical record and a compromising sexual affair of his own, and Republicans didn't flinch at asking him to step down. Gingrich had no one to blame but himself. Not only did his personal lifestyle expose the hypocrisy of his conservative moralism, but he had been hoisted by his own petard. He set the ground rules whereby political leaders were expendable if they got in the way of partisan needs. In Gingrich's case, the pursuers were members of his own party. Even though they owed their power to him, they would not let him jeopardize their control of the House and use it to block a Democratic president. His presumed successor, Louisiana's Robert Livingston, didn't even make it to the Speaker's chair. In a dramatic moment, Livingston surprised his colleagues during a speech in which he called on Clinton to step down by announcing that he would resign. His former extramarital affairs also made him a liability. Republicans picked the Illinois Republican Dennis Hastert as their Speaker. The low-key Hastert, who seemed squeaky clean, would reestablish some order among Republicans, although years later it would be discovered that he was guilty of the worst crimes in the bunch.

At some level, as painful as Gingrich's downfall was, he might have found some solace in watching his students heed his lessons. Nothing was sacrosanct in Washington. What could be more Gingrich than that?

It was an exhausting era where there were no winners, least of all the American people. An entire generation of Democrats and Republicans came of professional age watching a brutal style of political warfare in the 1980s and 1990s that spared nobody. The kinds of political fights that were once associated with the extreme fringes of democracy entered the mainstream, where they would stay.

Early on, when writing about the dangerous curiosity that the young Newt Gingrich appeared to be, Speaker Wright had been correct in saying that he was like Joseph McCarthy. The difference was that the Wisconsin senator had been quashed within a few years in the early 1950s, whereas Gingrich climbed all the way to the top. His rabid political style became the echo chamber of the Republican Party. Now nothing was out of bounds as to what either party could do to the other in its drive to obtain a majority. Everything and everyone was fair game.

Although politics was always rough in America, and the nostalgia for better times is usually misplaced, the overall level of respect for elected officials and governance rapidly diminished as a result of this era in congressional history. With distrust in government and the willingness to obstruct legislation on the rise, the better angels that were once the staples of our democracy—reasoned opposition, compromise, civil discourse, respect—could no longer keep darker drives or sentiments in check.[44] Under Gingrich, the dark id of democratic politics triumphed in this scorched-earth battle. The Tea Party Republicans elected in 2010 in a backlash to President Barack Obama's first two years in office embodied everything that Gingrich had preached. In the Senate, Kentucky's Mitch McConnell perfected this style of politics in the upper chamber. Their generation assumed that Gingrich's partisanship was the new normal. As Thomas Mann and Norm Ornstein, two beacons of fair-minded Washington punditry, admitted in *The Washington Post*, "The GOP has become an insurgent outlier—ideologically extreme; contemptuous of the inherited social and economic policy regime; scornful of compromise; unpersuaded by conventional understanding of facts, evidence, and science; and dismissive of the legitimacy of its political opposition."[45] Their hostage-taking approach to politics—where legislative norms were shattered and ordinary decisions, such as raising the federal debt ceiling or funding the government, became tools to achieve political power regardless of the costs to the democracy—grew directly out of Gingrich's having made anything permissible by bringing down the Speaker.[46] Whereas individual leaders were expendable in Gingrich's 1989 worldview, routine legislative processes were on the cutting room floor by the time of Obama's presidency.[47]

When Gingrich ran for president in 2012, Wright, who was eighty-nine years old, seemed less reluctant to state his opinion of the former Speaker. Calling Gingrich "very sociopathic" in an interview with *The Dallas Morning News*, he said, "In my view, he's not the kind of person who we should put in a position of authority or responsibility over other people. He has an insatiable desire to attack and scandalize anyone who seems to stand in the way of his own personal desires and ambitions."[48] One of the people whom Gingrich immediately hired to assist him with his campaign was the Republican pollster and strategist Kellyanne Conway, who had built her reputation by working for the Speaker in the 1990s.

Conway sold her client to the public as a politician who offered a unique mix: he was an outsider with "inside knowledge."[49]

Gingrich's presidential campaign was one part Reagan and one part Tea Party. He drew on many of the now traditional goals from the 1980s, including tax cuts, deregulation, and restricting abortion, while also appealing to a new brand of conservatives. He pledged to build a fence along the U.S.–Mexico border and defended the *Apprentice* star Donald Trump's spurious and easily disputed claims that President Obama was not actually born in the United States. "I know that there is a desperate need to attach racism to everything but in fact I think that Donald Trump said what he said because it's the right thing for him to say," the candidate said to reporters in the lobby of a Trump hotel.[50] He couldn't resist championing a few outlandish ideas, such as his belief that child labor laws were outdated. Gone were his moderate positions, including his support for environmentalism and an individual mandate to purchase health care.

Following poor showings in Iowa and New Hampshire, Gingrich surprised the experts as his poll numbers rose. He found success by positioning himself as a conservative populist, attacking the former Massachusetts governor Mitt Romney for having worked at Bain Capital. Gingrich claimed that Romney's cutthroat investment decisions left working-class towns in shambles. When he won the South Carolina primary, some experts started to think that he had a real shot at the nomination. He also used attacks on the news media as a pillar of his message. "The thing that struck me was what conservative audiences reacted to, even more than attacks on Obama, was attacks on the media," Gingrich said.[51] But his campaign lacked discipline. Despite Conway's best efforts, Gingrich kept veering off message, and his management style was a total mess. His moneymaking ventures as a consultant and businessman—more than $100 million earned in his first decade after being Speaker—became problematic for someone who wanted to be seen as a man of the people.[52] As the campaign sputtered in Louisiana, Alabama, Mississippi, and Florida, Gingrich decided to suspend his operations in May and to endorse Romney. Despite his failure to secure the nomination, he proved that he was still a serious presence in national politics. "With this campaign,

Gingrich established himself as someone who has been a serious force in Republican politics in five different decades, a pretty remarkable accomplishment," noted the *National Journal*'s Ronald Brownstein.[53]

But his worldview remained the same as it had been the year that he brought down Speaker Wright. During an interview with the conservative pundit William Kristol in 2014, Gingrich took a look back at his life and career. To sum up his views about the different psychologies within his party, he explained to Kristol that the Republican establishment's goal was to "get as much as it can without being disruptive." The heart of the Republican insurgency, from Goldwater to himself, was "to be as disruptive as necessary to get what you want."[54]

Enter Donald J. Trump. Reflecting on his presidential victory in 2016, the outgoing president, Obama, told his biographer David Remnick just weeks after the election, "We've seen this coming. Donald Trump is not an outlier; he is a culmination, a logical conclusion of the rhetoric and tactics of the Republican Party for the past ten, fifteen, twenty years. What surprised me was the degree to which those tactics and rhetoric completely jumped the rails. There were no governing principles, there was no one to say, 'No, this is going too far, this isn't what we stand for.' But we've seen it for eight years, even with reasonable people like John Boehner, who, when push came to shove, wouldn't push back against these currents."[55]

The forty-fourth president was right. When Tea Party Republicans stormed into town after the 2010 midterm elections, with their nihilistic view of government as well as their insistence on doing whatever was necessary to bring down the status quo, and Donald Trump shocked the nation by winning the 2016 election against one of the most experienced public servants in modern political history, all of them had a debt to the anti-establishment conservative populism pioneered by Newt Gingrich that shaped an entire generation of Republicans. The Wright scandal was the beginning of this end, and its shadow looms large and grows longer with each passing day.

ACKNOWLEDGMENTS

Many colleagues, friends, and family members have made this book possible. As most people who know me understand, I work at a frenetic pace. At Penguin Press, Scott Moyers raised some important questions early that helped me develop my argument, urged me to slow down, and pushed me to use some "intellectual muscle" that had been dormant. My editor, Christopher Richards, offered shrewd editorial comments and guided me through the final stages of turning this manuscript into the book that you have just read. He offered the kinds of careful line edits that are rare in this day and age of publishing. Ryan Boyle, my production editor, and Ingrid Sterner, the copyeditor, brought the book to a smooth conclusion. My agents, Andrew Wylie and Jacqueline Ko, encouraged me to move forward with the book from the moment that I pitched Andrew the idea.

Several colleagues were generous enough to read the manuscript and provide commentary, including Eric Alterman, John Lawrence, and Eric Schickler. Mike Crispin, Mark Schmitt, and Kevin Kruse offered comments on portions of the book. Jake Blumgart assisted me with the final fact-checking, while David Walsh collected the permissions for the photos.

Susan Leon and Madeleine Adams provided excellent editorial assistance. Blynne Olivieri and Michael Camp of the University of West Georgia, Susan Swain of Texas Christian University, and Frank Mackaman of the Dirksen Congressional Center all helped me move through the archival collections that are the foundation of this book. Numerous participants from this saga were generous enough to allow me to interview them about their recollections. Thanks as well to David Murph for taking me to meet with Speaker Wright and sharing his own memories. Norma Ritchson was kind enough to arrange the interview with the Speaker.

Although Newt Gingrich was unfortunately unable to find time for an interview, I was able to use his archives, one of the most comprehensive and thorough collections of congressional papers that I have encountered in my career. While most congressional archives are filled with letters from constituents and copies of public documents, Gingrich's papers include private memoranda, staff memos, taped interviews, and strategy documents that offered me a rare window into the career of a major legislator.

Special thanks to John Barry, who wrote a magnificent book about Speaker Wright the year of his downfall. Not only has John been a friend, generous with his advice and smart suggestions, but he also provided me with many boxes of material that he had collected for his own research years ago. Most important, he gave me the hard-to-get minutes of the closed Ethics Committee hearings about Speaker Wright. The material was wonderful, as was his guidance. He read through the final manuscript with great care, pointing out some errors in the draft and pushing me to refine the narrative. I am grateful for my new friendship with him and his delightful wife, Anne.

Princeton University continues to provide the best intellectual home possible. The deans and department chairs have been strong supporters of my work. Bernadette Yeager kept me organized and handled more paperwork than I can thank her for. New America and the New-York Historical Society also offered me fellowships so that I could spend my sabbatical years working on the book.

My family has been absolutely incredible. My parents, Gerald and Viviana Zelizer, as well as my mother-in-law, Ellie, have been supportive and enthusiastic. My wife, Meg, read through the book, talked over the story many (many!) times, and always provided insightful suggestions. More important, she is my best friend in the world. She keeps us laughing and makes sure that we keep moving forward. We do everything together, we continue to build a wonderful life, and she has created a rock-solid foundation upon which everything else rests. She moved us to our city of dreams, New York, where this book came alive.

Our children, Abigail, Sophia, Nathan, and Claire, make the home magic, and it has been great watching them become young adults in the course of completing this work. One day, I hope that they will see the political world become a little more tempered, and perhaps they can be an essential part of making that true.

NOTES

Abbreviations

CCP Common Cause Papers (Princeton, N.J.)
GHWBP George H. W. Bush Papers (College Station, Tex.)
JWA Jim Wright Papers (Fort Worth, Tex.)
MSP Mel Steely Papers (Carrollton, Ga.)
NGP Newt Gingrich Papers (Carrollton, Ga.)
RMP Robert Michel Papers (Peoria, Ill.)
RRPL Ronald Reagan Presidential Library (Simi Valley, Calif.)
VTA Vanderbilt Television Archives (Nashville, Tenn.)

Oral History Interviews

John Barry, October 30, 2014
George "Hank" Brown, August 4, 2016
Mickey Edwards, July 13, 2015
Vic Fazio, August 3, 2016
Martin Frost, March 2, 2018
Mary Hadar, December 8, 2015
Brooks Jackson, December 17, 2014
Ladonna Lee, April 10, 2017
Fred McClure, September 9, 2016
Ginger McGuire, September 9, 2016, and July 13, 2019
David Montgomery, December 19, 2014
William Oldaker, July 9, 2015
David Osborne, April 17, 2017
Tom Petri, August 1, 2016
Richard Phelan, July 2, 2015
Dan Renberg, May 30, 2018
Kenneth Ringle, November 24, 2015, and June 30, 2015
Ed Rollins, May 29, 2018
Patricia Schroeder, August 17, 2018
Philip Sharp, November 2, 2016
Pamela Small, July 8, 2019

Suzy Smith, December 8, 2015
Robert Torricelli, May 15, 2017
Steve Waldman, May 26, 2015
Fred Wertheimer, July 21, 2015
Jim Wright, February 5, 2015
Robert Wright, April 16, 2015

Prologue: Speak Like Newt

1. McKay Coppins, "The Man Who Broke Politics," *Atlantic*, November 2018.
2. Mara Siegler, "Steve Bannon Almost Appeared in Michael Moore's 'Fahrenheit 9/11,'" *New York Post*, September 14, 2018.
3. The broader impact of this polarization on American life and politics can be found in Kevin Kruse and Julian E. Zelizer, *Fault Lines: A History of the United States Since 1974* (New York: Norton, 2019); Michael Tomasky, *If We Can Keep It: How the Republic Collapsed and How It Might Be Saved* (New York: Liverright, 2019); Steve Kornacki, *The Red and the Blue: The 1990s and the Birth of Political Tribalism* (New York: Ecco, 2018); E. J. Dionne Jr., *Why the Right Went Wrong: Conservatism—from Goldwater to Trump and Beyond* (New York: Simon & Schuster, 2016); Thomas E. Mann and Norman J. Ornstein, *It's Even Worse Than It Looks: How the American Constitutional System Collided with the New Politics of Extremism* (New York: Basic Books, 2012); Ronald Brownstein, *The Second Civil War: How Extreme Partisanship Paralyzed Washington and Polarized America* (New York: Penguin, 2008).
4. Joanne Freeman, *The Field of Blood: Violence in Congress and the Road to the Civil War* (New York: Farrar, Straus and Giroux, 2018).
5. Mann and Ornstein, *It's Even Worse Than It Looks*, 26.
6. Tim Alberta, *American Carnage: On the Front Lines of the Republican Civil War and the Rise of President Trump* (New York: Harper, 2019), 340.
7. Newt Gingrich, "What I Saw at President Trump's Inauguration," Fox News, January 25, 2017, www.foxnews.com/opinion/newt-gingrich-what-i-saw-at-president -trumps-inauguration.
8. Sarah Westwood, "The Expendables," *Washington Examiner*, December 16, 2016.
9. Newt Gingrich, *Understanding Trump* (New York: Hachette, 2017). Gingrich came out with another book in 2018 praising Trump's first year and a half as president. See Gingrich, *Trump's America: The Truth About Our Nation's Great Comeback* (New York: Center Street, 2017).
10. The only other book on this story is John M. Barry, *The Ambition and the Power: A True Story of Washington* (New York: Viking, 1989). Barry's book is outstanding. Writing right as the scandal came to an end, Barry focused on the ability of Gingrich to manipulate a gullible press into being part of his attack. My book, which sees the press and good-government organizations in a more positive light, and Speaker Wright as well as the Democrats in a much more problematic position, builds on Barry's work. More than Barry, I argue that the Democrats played a bigger role in the outcome, both through the limits of the reforms they adopted in the 1970s and through the pressure they decided to put on the Speaker in fear for their political future. I also believe that the entire Republican Party, from the House minority leader, Robert Michel, to Vice President George H. W. Bush, was much more complicit in Gingrich's campaign than previously as-

sumed. Finally, with the perspective of hindsight, I also emphasize how Gingrich's success was part of a much bigger sea change taking place in Republican politics that was not apparent when Barry wrote his book. The best biography of Jim Wright is J. Brooks Flippen, *Speaker Jim Wright: Power, Scandal, and the Birth of Modern Politics* (Austin: University of Texas Press, 2018).

Chapter 1: The Making of a Renegade Republican

1. Fred Gregorsky, Memo, November 20, 1978, box 230, no file, NGP.
2. Connie Bruck, "The Politics of Perception," *New Yorker*, October 9, 1995, 53.
3. Robert Vickers, "Decision 2012: Meet the Newt Gingrich You Never Knew," *Penn Live*, January 30, 2012.
4. Candace Gingrich with Chris Bull, *The Accidental Activist: A Personal and Political Memoir* (New York: Scribner, 1996), 30–31.
5. Gail Sheehy, "The Inner Quest of Newt Gingrich," *Vanity Fair*, September 1995.
6. Mel Steely, *The Gentleman from Georgia: The Biography of Newt Gingrich* (Macon, Ga.: Mercer University Press, 2000), 4; Paul Walker, interview with Mel Steely, June 25, 1984, box 21, audiotapes, MSP.
7. "Ambitious Zoo Keeper," *Daily Boston Globe*, September 1, 1954.
8. "A Conversation with Newt Gingrich," C-SPAN video archives, December 10, 1986. All of the C-SPAN video archives can be found at www.c-span.org.
9. Nancy Gibbs and Karen Tumulty, "Newt Gingrich, Master of the House," *Time*, December 25, 1996.
10. Sheehy, "Inner Quest of Newt Gingrich"; Newt Gingrich, interview with Mel Steely, January 13, 1989, box 21, audiotapes, MSP.
11. Gingrich, interview with Steely, January 13, 1989.
12. Steely, *Gentleman from Georgia*, 10.
13. Steely, *Gentleman from Georgia*, 12.
14. Steely, *Gentleman from Georgia*, 4–5; Walker, interview with Steely, June 25, 1984.
15. Steely, *Gentleman from Georgia*, 5.
16. Newt Gingrich, interview with Morton Kondracke, December 13, 2012, Jack Kemp Oral History Archive, 2; Theodore H. White, *The Making of the President, 1960,* rev. ed. (New York: American Past, 1988), 60–61.
17. Steely, *Gentleman from Georgia*, 15.
18. Steely, *Gentleman from Georgia*, 16–17.
19. Gingrich, interview with Mel Steely, January 13, 1989.
20. Dale Russakoff, "He Knew What He Wanted," *Washington Post*, December 18, 1994.
21. Craig Shirley, *Citizen Newt: The Making of a Reagan Conservative* (Nashville: Nelson Books, 2017), xxi.
22. David Kramer, "The Long March of Newt Gingrich," *Frontline,* PBS, January 16, 1996, www.pbs.org/wgbh/frontline/film/newt.
23. Fred Gregorsky, "The Basics of Newt Gingrich," April–September 1983, box 230, NGP.
24. Gregorsky, "The Basics of Newt Gingrich."
25. Adam Hochschild, "What Gingrich Didn't Learn in Congo," *New York Times*, December 4, 2011; Joshua Keating, "Newt in the Congo," *FP*, November 22, 2011; Newton Leroy Gingrich, "Belgian Education Policy in the Congo, 1945–1960" (Ph.D. diss., Tulane University, 1971).

26. Shirley, *Citizen Newt*, xx–xxi.
27. On the trends that were reshaping the entire Sunbelt, see Bruce J. Schulman, *From Cotton Belt to Sunbelt: Federal Policy, Economic Development, and the Transformation of the South, 1938–1980* (New York: Oxford University Press, 1991).
28. Steely, *Gentleman from Georgia*, 47.
29. Shirley, *Citizen Newt*, 4.
30. "Gingrich Accuses Congress of Incompetency and Indifference," *Atlanta Daily World*, April 18, 1974.
31. "Newt Gingrich," *Atlanta Daily World*, November 3, 1974.
32. Editorial Board, "We Support Gingrich Too," *Atlanta Daily World*, November 5, 1974.
33. Richard D. Lyons, "Charges of Wrongdoing Being Ignored in Congress Races," *New York Times*, October 27, 1976.
34. Newt Gingrich, *Lessons Learned the Hard Way* (New York: HarperCollins, 1998), 85.
35. John Dillin, "How Can Republicans Make a Comeback?," *Christian Science Monitor*, November 7, 1974.
36. Steely, *Gentleman from Georgia*, 64.
37. Gibbs and Tumulty, "Newt Gingrich: Master of the House."
38. Bruck, "Politics of Perception," 55.
39. Shirley, *Citizen Newt*, 15.
40. Lyons, "Charges of Wrongdoing Being Ignored in Congress Races."
41. John A. Lawrence, *The Class of '74: Congress After Watergate and the Roots of Partisanship* (Baltimore: Johns Hopkins University Press, 2018).
42. "Gingrich Speaks to Young Republicans," press release, August 24, 1976, box 38, File: Speeches, NGP.
43. Steely, *Gentleman from Georgia*, 81.
44. "Goldwater to Visit 6th District," *Atlanta Daily World*, October 8, 1976.
45. Shirley, *Citizen Newt*, 15.
46. Editorial Board, "Gingrich Deserves Election," *Atlanta Daily World*, October 31, 1976.
47. Newt Gingrich, "Let's Quit Picking on Jack Flynt," August 24, 1977, box 38, File: Speeches, NGP.
48. Candace Gingrich, *Accidental Activist,* 49–50.
49. Dale Russakoff and Dan Balz, "After Political Victory, a Personal Revolution," *Washington Post*, December 19, 1994.
50. Sheehy, "Inner Quest of Newt Gingrich."
51. Shirley, *Citizen Newt*, 31.
52. Gingrich, interview with Kondracke, December 13, 2012, 4.
53. Frank Gregorsky to Bob Weed, April 2, 1979, box 40, File: What Newt Said in 1980, NGP.
54. Newt Gingrich, "Tip O'Neill Termed Dictator by Gingrich," August 1, 1978, box 25, File: O'Neill Dictator, NGP.
55. Campaign Flyer, 1978, box 17, File: Brochures, Forms, NGP.
56. "Newt's Family Is Like Your Family," *New Georgia Leader*, October 1978, box 24, File: Clippings, NGP.
57. "Two Good Reasons for Newt Gingrich," *Jackson Progress-Argus*, September 7, 1978.

58. Steely, *Gentleman from Georgia*, 100–101.
59. Newt Gingrich, "Speech to the College Republicans at the Atlanta Airport Holiday Inn," June 24, 1978, PBS.org.
60. Laurie James, interview with Frank Gregorsky, October 29, 1980, in *The First Two Years*, box 39, File: The First Two Years, NGP.
61. "Shapard Critical of Opponents' TV Ads," *Baltimore Sun*, October 18, 1978, box 24, File: Clippings October, NGP.
62. "Friends of Newt Gingrich," press release, November 4, 1978, box 25, File: Shapard Violations, NGP.
63. Steely, *Gentleman from Georgia*, 105.
64. Ron Taylor, "At Last, Gingrich Fans Throw a Victory Party," *Atlanta Constitution*, November 7, 1978.
65. Shirley, *Citizen Newt*, 36.
66. Thomas E. Mann and Norman J. Ornstein, *The Broken Branch: How Congress Is Failing America and How to Get It Back on Track* (New York: Oxford University Press, 2006), 64.
67. Laura Kalman, *Right Star Rising: A New Politics, 1974–1980* (New York: Norton, 2010), 311.
68. Russakoff and Balz, "After Political Victory, a Personal Revolution."
69. Saul Friedman, "The Congressional Charm," *Charlotte Observer*, December 7, 1978.
70. "Newt Gingrich on the 1994 Republican Revolution and His Career in Politics," interview with William Kristol, November 21, 2014, conversationswith billkristol.org/video/newt-gingrich.

Chapter 2: A Political Wrecking Ball

1. Ann Woolner, "Gingrich Fights to Build Party," *Atlanta Constitution*, November 25, 1979.
2. Woolner, "Gingrich Fights to Build Party."
3. Gingrich to Anderson, January 11, 1979, box 145, File: Diggs Stuff—RNC Clips, NGP.
4. William J. Mitchell, "GOP Freshman After Diggs," *Detroit Free Press*, January 13, 1979.
5. Newt Gingrich, "Congressional Double Standard," February 22, 1979, box 145, File: Diggs Stuff—RNC Clips, NGP.
6. Newt Gingrich, *Lessons Learned the Hard Way* (New York: HarperCollins, 1998), 87.
7. Julian E. Zelizer, *On Capitol Hill: The Struggle to Reform Congress and Its Consequences, 1948–2000* (New York: Cambridge University Press, 2004), 81.
8. This analysis was based on a memo from David Warnick. See Warnick to Gingrich, January 9, 1979, box 145, File: Master File on Our Stuff, NGP. A better model, in Gingrich's mind, was the Kentucky Republican "Pork Barrel John" Langley, who was convicted of a felony, sentenced to prison, then reelected while on appeal. *Cannon's Precedents* used this case as the basis to conclude that a "member convicted by the courts refrained from participation in the proceedings of the House pending action on his appeal." See Gingrich to Charles Bennett, February 16, 1979, box 145, File: Master File on Our Stuff, NGP.

9. Mary Russell, "Wright Says House Shouldn't Expel Diggs if Courts Uphold His Conviction," *Washington Post*, January 20, 1979.

10. David Warnick to Newt Gingrich, 1979, box 145, File: Convicted Felons, NGP.

11. Craig Shirley, *Citizen Newt: The Making of a Reagan Conservative* (Nashville: Nelson Books, 2017), 42–43.

12. Sean M. Theriault, *The Gingrich Senators: The Roots of Partisan Warfare in Congress* (New York: Oxford University Press, 2013).

13. "Republicans Move to Expel Diggs, Convicted of Fraud, from House," *Los Angeles Times*, March 1, 1979.

14. Gingrich to Staff, March 7, 1979, box 147, File: Task Force Stuff, NGP.

15. "Gingrich Agrees with Decision on Diggs," *Atlanta Daily World*, July 8, 1979.

16. Frank Gregorsky, Personal Diary, December 13, 1980, in *The First Two Years: Oral Histories*, 45.

17. "Gingrich Unveils Proposals to Clean Up U.S. Congress," *Atlanta Daily World*, February 28, 1980.

18. Richard J. Cattani, "Reagan, Congressional Republicans Display Unified Front," *Christian Science Monitor,* September 16, 1980.

19. O.D. Resources, *Project Majority: Building a Republican Team*, November 5, 1979; Gingrich to Michel, May 5, 1981, box 40, File: Project Majority, NGP.

20. "Inaugural Day Notes: Being 15 Feet from Sinatra 'Neat' to Newt," *Atlanta Constitution*, January 21, 1981.

21. David Broder, "The Meaning of the Mandate," *Washington Post*, November 12, 1980.

22. Newt Gingrich, "Tip O'Neill Can Make Things Tough for Reagan," December 1980, box 288, File: Dump O'Neill Project, NGP.

23. Michael Burns, interview with Frank Gregorsky, December 16, 1980, in *The First Two Years*; Gingrich to Conservative Colleague, 1980, box 288, File: Dump O'Neill Project, NGP.

24. Craig R. Hume, "Mr. Gingrich Goes to Washington," *Atlanta Constitution*, January 14, 1979.

25. John M. Barry, *The Ambition and the Power: A True Story of Washington* (New York: Viking, 1989), 71.

26. Gingrich to Washington Team, June 8, 1981, box 291, File: Staff Memos 1982, NGP.

27. Dennis Farney, "Republicans Reflect on What They've Wrought," *Wall Street Journal*, August 6, 1981.

28. Michael Reese, "The Right-Wing Revolt," *Newsweek*, August 16, 1982, 24.

29. "Tax Vote Shows Politics Still Washington's Game," *Atlanta Constitution*, August 20, 1982.

30. Gingrich to Fellow Republican, March 18, 1982, box 456, COS Files 6–13, File: 12, NGP.

31. Ann Woolner, "Gingrich Tries to Shut Down Government to Prove Point," *Atlanta Constitution*, April 4, 1982; Peter Grier, "Washington Warms Up to Balanced-Budget Law," *Christian Science Monitor*, March 24, 1982.

32. Steven K. Beckner, "Rep. Newt Gingrich: A New Conservative Leader for the '80s," *Conservative Digest*, May 1982, 6–11.

33. "Newt Gingrich on the 1994 Republican Revolution."

34. Gingrich, *Lessons Learned the Hard Way*, 170; Zack Smith, "For Newt: 'Nixon's the One!,'" *Politico*, January 20, 2012.

35. Gail Sheehy, "The Inner Quest of Newt Gingrich," *Vanity Fair*, September 1995. For a study of the Conservative Opportunity Society (COS), see Zachary C. Smith, "From the Well of the House: Remaking the House Republican Party, 1978–1994" (Ph.D. diss., Boston University, 2012).

36. Newt to Friends, 1987, box 456, COS Files 6–13, File: 11, NGP.

37. Newt to Friends, 1987, box 456, COS Files 6–13, File: 11, NGP.

38. Gingrich to Whip Planning Group, June 14, 1983, box 456, COS Files 6–13, File: 12, NGP.

39. Gingrich to Colleague, February 8, 1983, box 460, COS, File: 30, NGP.

40. For a thoughtful collection of essays about Michel, see Frank H. Mackaman and Sean Q. Kelly, eds., *Robert Michel: Leading the Republican House Minority* (Lawrence: University Press of Kansas, 2019).

41. "The House: A Brash New Republican Style," *Newsweek*, February 27, 1984, 45.

42. Gingrich to Michel, June 8, 1983, box 458, COS, File: 22, NGP.

43. Bill Lee to Congressman Gingrich and Eddie Mahe Jr., January 31, 1984, box 1078, File: NA, NGP.

44. Lee to Gingrich and Mahe, January 31, 1984. See also Lee to Gingrich and Vin Weber, February 17, 1984, box 462, File: 55, NGP.

45. "Legislative Action," C-SPAN video archives, January 25, 1985.

46. Gingrich to Tom Coleman, Vin Weber, Mark Siljander, and Don Ritter, June 27, 1983, WHORM, Subject File, box F0008, File: 174424, RRPL.

47. Gingrich to Coleman, Weber, Siljander, and Ritter, June 27, 1983.

48. T. R. Reid, "Congress: The Best Little Soap Opera on Television," *Washington Post*, April 29, 1984.

49. Stephen E. Frantzich and John Sullivan, *The C-SPAN Revolution* (Norman: University of Oklahoma Press, 1996), 275.

50. Minutes, COS, December 17, 1983, box 44, File: Frank Gregorsky on Memos from Newt 1994, MSP.

51. "Symposium: Jack Kemp and the Reagan Revolutionaries in the House," March 6, 1982, Jack Kemp Oral History Archive, 20–21.

52. Richard Berke, "Trent Lott and His Fierce Freshmen," *New York Times*, February 2, 1997.

53. Newt Gingrich, interview with Morton Kondracke, December 13, 2012, Jack Kemp Oral History Archive, 25.

54. Zelizer, *On Capitol Hill*, 214.

55. Julian E. Zelizer, *Arsenal of Democracy: The Politics of National Security—from World War II to the War on Terrorism* (New York: Basic Books, 2010), 81–273.

56. Nancy J. Schwerzler, "Gingrich on Crusade Against Democrats," *Baltimore Sun*, May 21, 1984.

57. Gingrich to Reagan, July 1, 1983, WHORM Subject File, box F00303, File: 152945, RRPL.

58. Jim Wright, Personal Diary, April 24, 1984, JWA.

59. Frances E. Lee, *Insecure Majorities: Congress and the Perpetual Campaign* (Chicago: University of Chicago Press, 2016), 96.

60. Editorial, "'Dear Comandante,'" *Wall Street Journal*, April 17, 1984.

61. Jim Wright, Personal Diary, April 24, 1984, JWA.

62. "Televised Partisan Skirmishes Erupt in House," *Congressional Quarterly*, February 11, 1984, 246.

NOTES

63. Newt Gingrich, "House Floor Strategy for Republicans," 1984, box 692, File: June Files, NGP.

64. Bill Lee to Eddie Mahe and Newt Gingrich, July 15, 1983, box 458, File: 22, NGP.

65. Shirley, *Citizen Newt*, 100–101.

66. Marcus Stern, "Young Conservatives Make Waves at Every Chance on the House Floor," *Daily Breeze*, April 16, 1984.

67. Frantzich and Sullivan, *C-SPAN Revolution*, 51.

68. Michel to O'Neill, May 11, 1984, box 458, File: 26, NGP.

69. John Lawrence, *Class of '74: Congress After Watergate and the Roots of Partisanship* (Baltimore: Johns Hopkins University Press, 2018).

70. Chris Matthews, *Tip and the Gipper: When Politics Worked* (New York: Simon & Schuster, 2013), 295.

71. "Newt Gingrich on the 1994 Republican Revolution."

72. "A Conversation with Newt Gingrich," C-SPAN video archives, December 10, 1986.

73. Eileen McNamara, "Shouting Match," *Boston Globe*, May 16, 1984.

74. Shirley, *Citizen Newt*, 103–104.

75. Richard Cheney and Lynne Cheney, *Kings of the Hill: Power and Personality in the House of Representatives* (New York: Continuum, 1983).

76. Phil McCombs, "The Unsettling Calm of Dick Cheney," *Washington Post*, April 3, 1991.

77. "Republicans Assail O'Neill; Increasing Hostility Feared," *New York Times*, May 18, 1984.

78. Deborah Baldwin, "Pulling Punches," *Common Cause Magazine*, May/June 1985, 23.

79. T. R. Reid, "O'Neill, Colleagues Trade Static," *Washington Post,* May 15, 1984, www.washingtonpost.com/archive/politics/1984/05/15/oneill-colleagues-trade -static/72a6b45e-4e1a-4f36-8229-8f12d43f185e.

80. Katharine Q. Seelye, "Gingrich First Mastered the Media and Then Rose to Be King of the Hill," *New York Times*, December 14, 1994.

81. Matthews, *Tip and the Gipper,* 206.

82. David Osborne, "The Swinging Days of Newt Gingrich," *Mother Jones*, November 1, 1984; Myra MacPherson, "Newt Gingrich, Point Man in a House Divided," *Washington Post*, June 12, 1989; Peter Osterlund, "The Capitol Chameleon," *Los Angeles Times Magazine*, August 25, 1991.

83. Tom Shales, "As the Hill Turns," *Washington Post*, May 17, 1984.

84. Lungren to COS, May 29, 1984, box 458, File: 27, NGP.

85. David Crook, "House TV: Is It out of Control," *Los Angeles Times*, May 24, 1984.

86. Jim Wright, Personal Diary, May 16, 1984, JWA.

87. Greg McDonald, "Newt Gingrich Is Making His Mark on the GOP These Days," *Atlanta Constitution*, December 15, 1983.

88. Jonathan Alter et al., "Reagan's Roaring Start," *Newsweek*, September 3, 1984, 30.

89. "GOP Platform Panel Bars Tax Hikes, Defies Reagan," *Los Angeles Times*, August 14, 1984.

90. Greg McDonald, "Newt Gingrich Is Current Superman of GOP Convention," *Atlanta Constitution*, August 22, 1984.

91. Osborne, interview with author, April 17, 2017.

92. Osborne, "Swinging Days of Newt Gingrich."

93. David Boles, interview with Alan McConnell, 1985, box 24, File: Working Toward a Conservative Opportunity Society, 103, MSP.

94. Lois Romano, "Newt Gingrich, Maverick on the Hill," *Washington Post*, January 3, 1985.

95. Gingrich to Republican Colleagues, December 4, 1984, box 456, File: 10B, NGP.

96. Eleanor Randolph, "Odd Man Out in the House," *Washington Post*, January 1, 1985.

97. C-SPAN video archives, February 7, 1985.

98. The following account of Gingrich during the Indiana recount crisis comes from Nicholas Lemann, "Conservative Opportunity Society," *Atlantic*, May 1985, 22–36. Lemann followed Gingrich around for a profile as this crisis unfolded. See also Lois Romano, "Rep. Gingrich Still Thinks Big, but Without Being So Abrasive," *Boston Globe*, January 30, 1985.

99. Lemann, "Conservative Opportunity Society."

100. Lemann, "Conservative Opportunity Society."

101. Lemann, "Conservative Opportunity Society."

102. Lemann, "Conservative Opportunity Society."

103. Lemann, "Conservative Opportunity Society."

104. Lemann, "Conservative Opportunity Society."

105. Jim Wright, Personal Diary, March 5, 1985, JWA.

106. Guy Vander Jagt, press conference, April 16, 1985, transcript, box 471, File: Republican Leadership, NGP.

107. Zach Nauth, "House Task Force Vote Favors Democrat," *Los Angeles Times*, April 23, 1985.

108. Zach Nauth and Paul Houston, "GOP Protests Plan to Seat Democrat in 14 Hour Fight," *Los Angeles Times*, April 24, 1985.

109. "First Week of Democratic Dictatorship in the U.S. House," April 16, 1985, box 471, File: Republican Leadership, NGP.

110. Stephen Engelberg, "G.O.P. Plans a Showdown Today on Disputed Indiana Seat," *New York Times*, April 30, 1985.

111. Mark Starr, "Congress: A House Divided," *Newsweek*, April 22, 1985, 29.

112. Robert Michel et al. to Republican Colleagues, April 29, 1985, box 471, File: Republican Leadership, NGP.

113. C-SPAN video archives, April 30, 1985.

114. Newt Gingrich, "Notes on Self Government," *Atlanta Daily World*, May 5, 1985.

115. Steven V. Roberts, "A House Divided," *New York Times*, May 3, 1985.

116. Margaret Shapiro and Dan Balz, "House Seats McCloskey," *Washington Post*, May 2, 1985.

117. Shapiro and Balz, "House Seats McCloskey."

118. Gloria Borger, "Paralysis in the House," *Newsweek*, May 13, 1985, 36.

119. Newt Gingrich, "Notes on Self Government," *Atlanta Daily World*, May 12, 1985.

120. Jim Wright, Personal Diary, May 2, 1985, JWA.

Chapter 3: The Perfect Foil

1. Steven Roberts, "Democrats Also Select Foley as Majority Leader—Coelho Defeats Rangel for Whip Position; Wright Is Chosen as Next Speaker of House," *New York Times*, December 8, 1986.

2. "James C. Wright Jr.," *New York Times*, December 9, 1986.

3. "A Conversation with Newt Gingrich," C-SPAN video archives, December 10, 1986.

4. J. Brooks Flippen, *Speaker Jim Wright: Power, Scandal, and the Birth of Modern Politics* (Austin: University of Texas Press, 2018), 20–21.

5. Flippen, *Speaker Jim Wright*, 23; Ben Procter, "Jim Wright," in *Profiles in Power: Twentieth-Century Texans in Washington* (Arlington Heights, Ill.: Harlan Davidson, 1993).

6. John M. Barry, *The Ambition and the Power: A True Story of Washington* (New York: Viking, 1989), 44–45.

7. Nathan Koppel and Kristina Peterson, "Jim Wright, Former House Speaker, Dies at 92," *Wall Street Journal*, May 6, 2015.

8. Flippen, *Speaker Jim Wright*, 25.

9. Flippen, *Speaker Jim Wright*, 32–35.

10. Flippen, *Speaker Jim Wright*, 39.

11. Flippen, *Speaker Jim Wright*, 47–48.

12. Rowland Stiteler, "The Most Powerful Texan in Washington," *D Magazine*, March 1980.

13. Stiteler, "The Most Powerful Texan in Washington."

14. Paul West, "The Wright Stuff," *New Republic*, October 14, 1985.

15. Jack Z. Smith, "Growing Up Wright," *Fort Worth Star-Telegram*, February 17, 1985.

16. Jeff Prince, "The Speaker in Winter," *Fort Worth Weekly*, July 4, 2007.

17. Flippen, *Speaker Jim Wright*, 98.

18. Smith, "Growing Up Wright."

19. Brian Cervantez, *Amon Carter: A Lone Star Life* (Norman: University of Oklahoma Press, 2019), 202–3.

20. David R. Mayhew, *Congress: The Electoral Connection* (New Haven, Conn.: Yale University Press, 1974).

21. Fawn Vrazo, "How Texans See Wright's Predicament," *Philadelphia Inquirer*, July 5, 1988.

22. *The Changing Congress: The Rules of the Game*, National Educational Television Network, 1965, Texas Archive of the Moving Picture (Austin).

23. John Barry, "The Man of the House," *New York Times*, November 23, 1986.

24. Flippen, *Speaker Jim Wright*, 159.

25. Paul Burka, "Wright and Wrong," *Texas Monthly*, August 1988, 153.

26. Flippen, *Speaker Jim Wright*, 208.

27. Jim Wright, Personal Diary, December 30, 1971, JWA.

28. Jack Anderson, "Shooting at Fish in the Pork Barrel," *Washington Post*, March 17, 1972.

29. Jim Wright, Personal Diary, March 18, 1972, JWA.

30. Jim Wright, Personal Diary, June 22, 1972, JWA.

31. Julian E. Zelizer, *On Capitol Hill: The Struggle to Reform Congress and Its Consequences, 1948–2000* (New York: Cambridge University Press, 2004), 167.

32. Frances E. Lee, *Insecure Majorities: Congress and the Perpetual Campaign* (Chicago: University of Chicago Press, 2016), 32.

33. Bruce I. Oppenheimer and Robert L. Peabody, "How the Race for House Majority Leader Was Won—by One Vote," *Washington Monthly*, November 1977, 47; John Lawrence, *The Class of '74: Congress After Watergate and the Roots of Partisanship* (Baltimore: Johns Hopkins University Press, 2018); Jim Wright, interview with Richard Peabody, March 18, 1977, box 695, File: Interview of Jim Wright with Richard Peabody, 9, JWA.

34. Tom Matthews, "A Surprise in the House," *Newsweek*, December 20, 1976, 26.
35. Larry King, "A Single Card Held the Key to the House," *Washington Star*, December 8, 1976.
36. Stephen Nordlinger, "O'Neill, Wright Are Elected," *Baltimore Sun*, December 7, 1976.
37. Mary Russell, "Rep. Wright Is Elected House Majority Leader," *Washington Post*, December 7, 1976.
38. Richard Boeth, "Rebels on the Hill," *Newsweek*, August 8, 1977, 22–23.
39. Jacob S. Hacker and Paul Pierson, *Winner-Take-All Politics: How Washington Made the Rich Richer—and Turned Its Back on the Middle Class* (New York: Simon & Schuster, 2010), 186–222.
40. Greg Easterbrook, "The Business of Politics," *Atlantic*, October 1986; Hacker and Pierson, *Winner-Take-All Politics*, 177–82.
41. Easterbrook, "Business of Politics."
42. Hacker and Pierson, *Winner-Take-All Politics*, 116–36.
43. Easterbrook, "Business of Politics."
44. "Wright Blasts Reagan's Policies," *Atlanta Constitution*, January 25, 1984.
45. "Wright Accused of Threatening House Colleague," *Los Angeles Times*, July 2, 1985.
46. Bob Secter, "Lungren Says House Leader Threatened to Punch Him," *Los Angeles Times*, July 2, 1985.
47. Thomas E. Mann and Norman J. Ornstein, *The Broken Branch: How Congress Is Failing America and How to Get It Back on Track* (New York: Oxford University Press, 2006), 71–72.
48. Flippen, *Speaker Jim Wright*, 266.
49. West, "Wright Stuff."
50. Ernest Furgurson, "Dole, Others Glum as Democrats Win 100th Congress," *Baltimore Sun*, November 6, 1986.
51. Jim Wright, Personal Diary, November 5, 1986, JWA.
52. E. J. Dionne Jr., "Big Political Shift," *New York Times*, November 6, 1986.
53. Malcolm Byrne, *Iran-Contra: Reagan's Scandal and the Unchecked Abuse of Presidential Power* (Lawrence: University Press of Kansas, 2014), 276.
54. Ronald Reagan, Personal Diary, November 24, 1986, in *The Reagan Diaries*, ed. Douglas Brinkley (New York: Harper, 2007), 660–61.
55. Steven V. Roberts, "Top Legislators Promise Inquiry," *New York Times*, November 26, 1986.
56. Jim Wright, *Balance of Power: Presidents and Congress from the Era of McCarthy to the Age of Gingrich* (Atlanta: Turner, 1996), 439–40.
57. Minutes, COS Wednesday Morning Meeting, July 1, 1987, box 1019, File: Weekly COS 1987, NGP.
58. Editorial, "The Speaker and the Thrift Scandal," *New York Times*, June 24, 1987.
59. Thomas Rich and David Pauly, "The Wright Man to See: A Powerful Politician and His Efforts to Help Texas Thrift Operators," *Newsweek*, June 29, 1987, 44–45.
60. Gingrich to George Schultz, June 30, 1987, box 673, File: Newt Gingrich—Ethics, NGP.
61. Barry, *The Ambition and the Power*, 214.
62. Thomas Rosentiel, "How an Unheralded Reporter Wrote the Quiet Beginnings to Wright Case," *Los Angeles Times*, May 13, 1989.

63. Flippen, *Speaker Jim Wright*, 286–88.
64. Roberto Suro, "Wright's Partner Was a Quiet Friend," *New York Times*, April 24, 1989.
65. Barry, *The Ambition and the Power*, 692–93.
66. "Statement of House Speaker Jim Wright," June 10, 1988, box 672, File: Wright's Response to Our Complaint, NGP.
67. Michael Wines, "Wright's Path to Power: Debts, Deals, and a Book," *New York Times*, May 7, 1989.
68. Myra MacPherson, "The Speaker's Wife, Speaking Out," *Washington Post*, April 21, 1989.
69. Jackson, interview with author, December 17, 2014.
70. Brooks Jackson, "House Speaker Wright's Dealings with Developer Revive Questions About His Ethics and Judgment," *Wall Street Journal*, August 5, 1987.
71. Jim Wright, *Reflections of a Public Man* (Fort Worth, Tex.: Madison, 1984).
72. Editorial, "Wright-Gate," *Detroit News*, October 9, 1987.
73. Minutes, COS Wednesday Morning Meeting, September 9, 1987, box 1019, File: COS 1987, NGP.
74. Minutes, COS Executive Committee Meeting, September 15, 1987, box 1019, File: Weekly COS 1987, NGP.
75. Minutes, COS Wednesday Morning Meeting, September 16, 1987, box 1019, File: Weekly COS 1987, NGP.
76. Minutes, Wednesday Lunch Group, September 16, 1987, box 1019, File: Weekly COS 1987, NGP.
77. Newt Gingrich, GOPAC Masterfile letter, October 6, 1987, box 446, NGP.
78. "Bedlam on Wall St.," *Los Angeles Times*, October 19, 1987.
79. Flippen, *Speaker Jim Wright*, 359.
80. Barry, *The Ambition and the Power*, 469–72.
81. Trent Lott, *Herding Cats: A Life in Politics* (New York: ReganBooks, 2005), 98.
82. Jeffrey H. Birnbaum and Monica Langley, "House Passes Bill to Increase Taxes by $12.3 Billion," *Wall Street Journal*, October 30, 1987.
83. Charles Green, "House Passes Deficit-Cutting Bill as Republican Members Protest," *Hartford Courant*, October 30, 1987.
84. Newt Gingrich, "The House Republican Choice," 1987, box 664, File: Reconciliation Bill, NGP.
85. Zelizer, *On Capitol Hill*, 239; Jonathan Feurbringer, "Tax Rise Is Passed by House," *New York Times*, October 30, 1987.
86. Eli Rosenberg, "'Olliemania': The Stage-Worthy Scandal That Starred Oliver North as a Congressional Witness," *Washington Post*, May 8, 2018, www.washingtonpost.com/news/retropolis/wp/2018/05/08/the-nras-new-president-oliver-north-is-notorious-for-his-role-in-an-illicit-arms-deal.
87. Newt Gingrich, "Speech to Virginia Republican Party in Williamsburg," July 11, 1987, WHORM Alpha File, box 27, File: Gingrich, Newt (6), RRPL.
88. Barry, *The Ambition and the Power*, 362, 368–69.
89. Dale Russakoff and Tom Kenworthy, "House Speaker's Balancing Act," *Washington Post*, November 22, 1987.
90. "Nicaragua Ortega Program," *NBC Evening News*, November 13, 1987.
91. John Barry argues that Shultz directly contradicted what he told Wright. Barry, *The Ambition and the Power*, 493–515.

92. Jim Wright, *Worth It All: My War for Peace* (Washington, D.C.: Brassey's, 1993), 150–51.

93. Reagan, Personal Diary, November 16, 1987, in *Reagan Diaries*, 800.

94. Steven V. Roberts, "Reagan and Wright Caught Up in Feud," *New York Times*, November 15, 1987.

95. Kathryn McGarr, *The Whole Damn Deal: Robert Strauss and the Art of Politics* (New York: PublicAffairs, 2011), 307–8.

96. Joel Brinkley, "Wright, His Latin Role Contested, Signs a 'Peace Pact' with Shultz," *New York Times*, November 18, 1987.

97. "Gingrich Criticizes Wright Meeting with Daniel Ortega," *Atlanta Daily World*, November 24, 1987.

98. "Wright," *Fort Worth Star-Telegram*, November 17, 1987; Tom Fiedler, "Gingrich Calls Wright 'Corrupt,'" *Miami Herald*, November 17, 1987.

99. *Larry King Live*, November 17, 1987, transcript, box 678, File: Wright Stockyard, NGP.

100. Ernest Angelo to Roderic Bell, December 7, 1987, box 692, File: Republican Mailings, JWA.

101. Flippen, *Speaker Jim Wright*, 371.

102. Barry, *The Ambition and the Power,* 369.

103. Gingrich to Nader, December 1, 1987, box 673, File: Newt Gingrich—Ethics, NGP.

104. Barry, *The Ambition and the Power*, 530–36.

105. Brooks Jackson and Jeffrey Birnbaum, "Wright's First Year as Speaker Yields Success, but His Integrity Continues to Be Questioned," *Wall Street Journal*, December 4, 1987; Fox Butterfield, "Trump Urged to Head Gala of Democrats," *New York Times*, November 18, 1987; Michael Ryan, "Too Darn Rich," *People*, December 7, 1987.

106. Cort Kirkwood, "Jim Wright Makes It the Old-Fashioned Way," *National Review*, October 23, 1987.

107. "Role of House Speaker, Agenda for 1988," C-SPAN video archives, January 6, 1988.

108. Jost to Wright, November 16, 1987, box 745, File: DCCC, JWA.

109. Eric Pianin, "House GOP's Frustrations Intensify," *Washington Post*, December 21, 1987.

110. Barry, *The Ambition and the Power*, 369.

111. Susan Rasky, "The Speaker of the House: Everyone Has Something to Say About Wright," *New York Times*, December 18, 1987.

Chapter 4: Legitimating Gingrich

1. Mel Steely, *The Gentleman from Georgia: The Biography of Newt Gingrich* (Macon, Ga.: Mercer University Press, 2000), 190.

2. John M. Barry, *The Ambition and the Power: A True Story of Washington* (New York: Viking, 1989), 603–4.

3. Mair to Smith, December 15, 1987; Mair to Zuckerman, December 16, 1987; Mair to Bartley, December 15, 1987. These and other letters to the press are in box 676, Series II, File: Letters from Media, JWA.

4. "Reporters Given Wright Apology for Aide's Letters," *Los Angeles Times*, January 22, 1988.

5. William M. Adler and Michael Binstein, "The Speaker and the Sleazy Banker," *Bankers Monthly*, March 1988.

6. John Barry, "The Man of the House," *New York Times*, November 23, 1986.

7. Barry, *The Ambition and the Power*, 219–22.

8. Barry to Strauss, March 24, 1988, box 675, File: Bankers Monthly, JWA.

9. Lynam to Cross, April 1988, box 675, File: Bankers Monthly, JWA.

10. Gingrich to Michael Barone, March 21, 1988, box 673, File: Newt Gingrich—Ethics, NGP.

11. Gingrich to Gergen, February 16, 1988, box 673, File: Newt Gingrich—Ethics, NGP.

12. Gingrich to Rosenthal, February 25, 1988, box 673, File: Newt Gingrich—Ethics, NGP.

13. Gingrich to Colleagues, February 17, 1988, box 674, File: Staff Briefing on Wright, NGP.

14. Gingrich to Wertheimer, May 13, 1987, box 663, File: St. Germain Case, NGP; Gingrich to Wertheimer, December 1, 1987, box 673, File: Newt Gingrich—Ethics, NGP.

15. Gingrich to Wertheimer, February 16, 1988, box 673, File: Newt Gingrich—Ethics, NGP.

16. Wertheimer, interview with author, July 21, 2015.

17. Wertheimer to Gingrich, February 18, 1988, box 673, File: Newt Gingrich—Ethics, NGP.

18. Editorial, "Where's the Investigation?," *Wall Street Journal*, May 10, 1988.

19. Wertheimer, interview with author, July 21, 2015.

20. Common Cause, press release, May 18, 1988; and Wertheimer to Dixon, May 18, 1988, both in box 268, CCP.

21. Tom Kensworthy, "In Response to Group's Call for Ethics Probe, Wright Defends His Record," *Washington Post*, May 20, 1988.

22. Wertheimer to Julian Dixon, May 25, 1988, box 268, CCP.

23. Gingrich to Colleague, May 24, 1988, box 673, File: Dear Colleague—Complaint, NGP.

24. Maureen Dowd, "Bush Tries to Rough his Edges," *New York Times*, May 29, 1988.

25. Jeffrey A. Engel, *When the World Seemed New: George H. W. Bush and the End of the Cold War* (Boston: Houghton Mifflin, 2017), 27.

26. Jeremi Suri, "Ronald Reagan, 1981–1989," in *Presidential Misconduct: From George Washington to Today,* ed. James M. Banner Jr. (New York: New Press, 2019), 405–20.

27. Gerald Seib and Monica Langley, "Bush Wins a Clear Victory in TV Interview Spat but Doesn't Dispel His Iran Contra Problems," *Wall Street Journal,* January 27, 1988.

28. Susan Page, *The Matriarch: Barbara Bush and the Making of an American Dynasty* (New York: Twelve, 2019), 164.

29. Jean Edward Smith, *Bush* (New York: Simon & Schuster, 2016), 52; Antonino D'Ambrosio, "Lee Atwater's Legacy," *Nation*, October 8, 2008.

30. Atwater to Elizabeth Dole, May 31, 1981, box 2, File: Dole Memo, Lee Atwater Papers, RRPL.

31. Maureen Dowd, "Bush, in Jersey, Gets Tough on Drugs," *New York Times*, May 27, 1988, www.nytimes.com/1988/05/27/us/bush-in-jersey-gets-tough-on-drugs.html.

32. Sara Fritz, "Wright Inquiry May Undermine 'Sleaze Factor,'" *Los Angeles Times*, June 9, 1988.

33. Fritz, "Wright Inquiry May Undermine 'Sleaze Factor.'"

34. Scott Shepard, "Only Evidence in Wright Case: Press Clippings," *Atlanta Constitution*, May 28, 1988.

35. Jeff Gerth, "Meeting Follows Weeks of Partisan Debate—Outcome Due Today," *New York Times*, June 10, 1988.

36. Editorial, "Investigating the Speaker, Credibly," *New York Times*, May 27, 1988.

37. Citizens for Reagan, "Your Help Needed to Expose Most Corrupt House Speaker in History," press release, June 3, 1988, box 673, File: Newt Letters—Ethics, NGP.

38. Barry, *The Ambition and the Power*, 622–23.

39. Barry, *The Ambition and the Power*, 622–23.

40. Jim Wright, *Worth It All: My War for Peace* (Washington, D.C.: Brassey's, 1993), 161.

41. Frost, interview with author, March 2, 2018.

42. Oldaker, interview with author, July 9, 2015.

43. "St. Germain Defends Finances," *New York Times*, September 12, 1985.

44. Brooks Jackson and John E. Yang, "House Ethics Committee Suddenly Gets Tough to Quell Criticism of Leniency with Violators," *Wall Street Journal*, December 2, 1987.

45. Bill Minutaglio, "Power Failure," *Dallas Morning News*, June 16, 1989.

46. "House Panel to Investigate Jim Wright," *Hartford Courant*, June 11, 1988.

47. *Face the Nation*, CBS, June 12, 1988, transcript, box 672, File: Wright's Response to Our Complaint, NGP.

48. *This Week with David Brinkley*, ABC, June 12, 1988, transcript, box 672, File: Wright's Response to Our Complaint, NGP.

49. Karen Hosler, "Reagan Joins Chorus Calling for Independent Wright Review," *Baltimore Sun*, June 16, 1988.

50. "Speakergate Contd.," *Boston Herald*, July 7, 1988; "Let the Inquiry Begin," *Albuquerque Tribune*, June 14, 1988.

51. "The Speaker on the Spot," *Time*, June 20, 1988, 31.

52. "Albatross," *New Republic*, June 20, 1988, 5–7.

53. Peter Osterlund, "House Ethics: The Wright Stuff," *Christian Science Monitor*, May 31, 1988.

54. "Current Ethics Investigation of Jim Wright," C-SPAN video archives, June 9, 1988.

55. Eloise Salholz, "Wright's Alleged Wrongs," with Mark Miller, Eleanor Clift, and Timothy Noah, *Newsweek*, June 20, 1988, 14–15.

56. Robert Merry, "A New GOP Congressman Tries to Resolve His Dilemma over the President's Tax Bill," *Wall Street Journal*, August 19, 1982; "A Nice Day's Work," *Baltimore Sun*, June 8, 1984.

57. Brown, interview with author, August 4, 2016.

58. Arthur Foulkes, "Back Home, Myers Was the Face of D.C.," *Indiana Tribune Star*, January 28, 2015.

59. Martin Nolan, "O'Neill Lends Celebrity Status to Congressional Candidates," *Boston Globe*, October 21, 1978.

60. A. A. Mitchelson, "Atkins' Pros and Cons," *Boston Globe*, December 12, 1987; Eileen McNamara, "Strange Twists in Congressional Allegiances," *Boston Globe*, April 14, 1985; "Democrats Say Atkins on GOP Hit List," *Boston Globe*, March 19, 1985; David Espo, "Liberal Atkins Learns to Say No," Associated Press, May 1, 1985; Nancy J. Schwerzler, "Wright Votes Turn 2 Democrats into Lonesome Pair," *Baltimore Sun*, May 30, 1989; Harry Stoffer, "Eyes Focus on Panel of Wright 'Jurors,'" *Pittsburgh Post Gazette*, December 18, 1988.

61. Amy Roberts, "Richard Phelan's Uncompromising Positions," *American Lawyer*, January–February 1988, 19.

62. Michael Oreskes, "Aggressive and Exhaustive Lawyer," *New York Times*, May 12, 1989.

63. Flaherty to Gingrich, August 1, 1988, box 673, File: Newt Letter Ethics, NGP.

64. Elaine Povich, "Democratic Activist to Probe Wright," *Chicago Tribune*, July 27, 1988.

65. Weyrich to Gingrich, November 27, 1988, box 672, File: Wright, NGP.

66. Newt Gingrich, "A Proposed September–October Agenda of the House Republican Party," August 1988, box 434, File: Republican Info, NGP.

67. "House Republican Leaders Assail the Broken Branch of Government," press release, May 1988, box 18, File: Special Order, "Broken Branch of Government," RMP.

68. Robert Michel, "Special Order," May 24, 1988, Richard Cheney, "Special Order," and Trent Lott, "Special Order," May 24, 1988, all in box 676, File: Ethics Articles, NGP; Frances E. Lee, *Insecure Majorities: Congress and the Perpetual Campaign* (Chicago: University of Chicago Press, 2016), 108.

69. Newt Gingrich, "The House Republican Obligation to Focus on Ethics and Election Reform," September 6, 1988, box 434, File: Republican Info, NGP.

70. Gingrich to Colleague, September 2, 1988, box 664, File: Dear Colleague, NGP.

71. Newt Gingrich, "Conservative Movement and the 1988 Campaign: The Proposed October–November Perspective," August 31, 1988, box 434, File: Republican Info, NGP.

72. "Gingrich Urges Final Ethics Push for 100th Congress," press release, September 2, 1988, box 664, File: Dear Colleague, NGP.

73. House Committee on Ethics, *Executive Hearings*, September 14, 1988, transcript, 78.

74. Irvin Molotsky, "Wright Inquiry Examining Events Occurring Long Ago," *New York Times*, November 13, 1988.

75. "Wright's CIA Disclosure Sparks Call for Probe," *Chicago Tribune*, September 22, 1988; "House Panel Seeks Information on Wright Remark," *Washington Post*, October 1, 1988; "Wright vs. CIA," *Wall Street Journal*, September 29, 1988.

76. Peter Osterlund, "Controversial House Speaker Wright: Is He a Daring Leader or Ruthless Operator?," *Christian Science Monitor*, October 21, 1988.

77. Tom Kenworthy, "The Speaker's Cloudy Future," *Washington Post*, October 19, 1988.

78. Steven V. Roberts, "Wright's Style: Both a Strength and a Weakness," *New York Times*, October 25, 1988.

79. "Bush Meets with Wright," *Philadelphia Inquirer*, November 19, 1988.

80. Elaine Povich and George E. Curry, "Bush Spends a Busy Day Fence-Mending," *Chicago Tribune*, November 19, 1988.

81. Robert Shogan, "Sharp Partisan Split Threatens Bush Program," *Los Angeles Times*, January 22, 1989.

82. Lee, *Insecure Majorities*, 96–110.

83. Schlafly to George Eagle, October 31, 1988, box 1019, File: Campaign Political 1988, NGP.

84. William Eaton, "Wright, Renamed as House Speaker, Lists Party Goals," *Los Angeles Times*, December 6, 1988.

Chapter 5: Missing the Tempest

1. Charles Mohr, "Congress, Forget the Deficit, a Real Crisis Is Looming: Raises," *New York Times*, December 9, 1988.

2. Walter Shapiro, "Talking Wright," *Washington Post*, January 23, 1983.

3. "The Perks of Congress Pensions, Tax Breaks, Etc. Would Fill a Trunk," *Akron Beacon Journal*, January 29, 1989.

4. Sara Fritz, "Panel to Urge Big Pay Hike for Top Officials," *Los Angeles Times*, December 13, 1988.

5. Tyson Foods compensated Representative Tommy Robinson of Arkansas with $1,000 to take a cursory tour of its poultry plant. The Chicago Board of Trade, under federal investigation for fraud, contributed $130,000 in 1987 to members of the House and the Senate. The top earner of the time was Ways and Means Committee chairman, Dan Rostenkowski, whose jurisdiction included the tax code, Medicare and Medicaid, trade, and Social Security. These stories come from W. J. Michael Cody and Richardson Lynn, *Honest Government: Ethics Guide for Public Service* (Westport, Conn.: Greenwood, 1992), 54.

6. Fritz, "Panel to Urge Big Pay Hike for Top Officials."

7. Gregory Jaynes, "About New York: A Radio Nomad Enjoys a Pause in Life on the Air," *New York Times*, April 6, 1988.

8. Jeffrey Yorke, "Calling for a Confrontation," *Washington Post*, December 20, 1988; Richard Viguerie and David Franke, *America's Right Turn: How Conservatives Used New and Alternative Media to Take Power* (Chicago: Bonus Books, 2004), 182.

9. Bill McAllister, "Taxpayer Discontent Coming to a Boil," *Washington Post*, December 30, 1988.

10. Don Phillips, "For Long-Allied Activists, Raise Issue Fosters a Fight," *Washington Post*, January 30, 1989.

11. Michael Oreskes, "Congress Will Bar Honorariums as Soon as Pay Rises, Wright Says," *New York Times*, December 15, 1988.

12. Brian Rosenwald, *Talk Radio's America: How an Industry Took Over a Political Party That Took Over the United States* (Cambridge, Mass.: Harvard University Press, 2019).

13. "Now, Populist Radio," *New York*, February 27, 1989, 28.

14. Nichole Hemmer, *Messengers of the Right: Conservative Media and the Transformation of American Politics* (Philadelphia: University of Pennsylvania Press, 2016).

15. Sean Theriault, *The Power of the People: Congressional Competition, Public Attention, and Voter Retribution* (Columbus: Ohio State University Press, 2005), 61.

16. S. Robert Lichter and Richard Noyes, *Good Intentions Make Bad News: Why Americans Hate Campaign Journalism* (Lanham, Md.: Rowman & Littlefield, 1995), 238.

17. Mark Rozell, *In Contempt of Congress: Postwar Press Coverage on Capitol Hill* (Westport, Conn.: Praeger, 1996), 74–75.
18. Rozell, *In Contempt of Congress*, 75.
19. Nancy J. Schwerzler, "Raising Pay Also Raises Public Wrath, Call for Reforms, Congress Finds," *Baltimore Sun*, January 29, 1989.
20. Mary McGrory, "Reagan's Revenge," *Washington Post*, February 9, 1989.
21. Schroeder to Wright, January 23, 1989, box 734, File: Patricia Schroeder, JWA.
22. Michael Oreskes, "Wright Takes a Pounding from All Sides on Pay Raise," *South Florida Sun Sentinel*, February 6, 1989.
23. Michael Oreskes, "Senate Votes Against 50% Raise but the House Plans to Let It Stand," *New York Times*, February 3, 1989.
24. Susan F. Rasky, "Fury over Lawmakers' Raise Finds an Outlet on the Radio," *New York Times*, February 6, 1989.
25. "Congress/Pay Raise," *NBC Evening News*, February 1, 1989, VTA.
26. William Eaton, "Pay Issue Seen as Slowing Congress," *Los Angeles Times*, February 4, 1989.
27. Don Phillips and Tom Kenworthy, "Democrats Singing the Pay Blues," *Washington Post*, February 4, 1989.
28. Karen Hosler, "House Democrats Retreat from Heat over Pay at Spa," *Baltimore Sun*, February 5, 1989.
29. Robin Toner, "Democrats, Under Fire, Play It Cool," *New York Times*, February 6, 1989.
30. Steve Daley, "Democrats Can't Escape Pay Furor," *Chicago Tribune*, February 6, 1989.
31. Nancy J. Schwerzler, "House Vote on Pay Raise Set for Today," *Baltimore Sun*, February 7, 1989.
32. Robin Toner, "This Was No Day for a House Party," *New York Times*, February 8, 1989.
33. McGrory, "Reagan's Revenge."
34. Barbara Vobejda, "Citizens Celebrate as Raise Collapses," *Washington Post*, February 8, 1989.
35. Robert Shogan, "'90 Vote Offers GOP Big Chance to Score Gains," *Los Angeles Times*, February 21, 1989.
36. John Brady, *Bad Boy: The Life and Politics of Lee Atwater* (New York: Addison-Wesley, 1997), 222.
37. John Newhouse, "The Navigator," *New Yorker*, April 10, 1989, 81.
38. J. Brooks Flippen, *Speaker Jim Wright: Power, Scandal, and the Birth of Modern Politics* (Austin: University of Texas Press, 2018), 382.
39. Ed Rollins, *Bare Knuckles and Back Rooms, with Tom Defrank* (New York: Broadway, 1996), 201.
40. David Broder, "Wright Will Pay for Being Weak-Kneed," *Chicago Tribune*, February 12, 1989.
41. Robin Toner, "Wright Is Termed 'Target No. 1' By G.O.P. Aide Planning for '90," *New York Times*, February 23, 1989.
42. Thomas B. Edsall, "GOP Honing Wedges for Next Campaign," *Washington Post*, February 26, 1989.
43. Robin Toner, "Wright Is Termed 'Target No. 1' by G.O.P. Aide Planning for '90," *New York Times*, February 23, 1989.

44. Tom Kenworthy, "House Democrats Worry Fallout from Tower Fight Will Hurt Wright," *Washington Post*, March 5, 1989.
45. Helen Dewar, "Senate Kills Tower's Nomination as Defense Chief, 53–47," *Washington Post*, March 10, 1989.
46. Dewar, "Senate Kills Tower's Nomination as Defense Chief"; Michael Oreskes, "Air of Conciliation," *New York Times*, March 10, 1989.
47. "Senators and Sobriety," *New York Times*, February 25, 1989.
48. Kenworthy, "House Democrats Worry Fallout from Tower Fight Will Hurt Wright."
49. Kenworthy, "House Democrats Worry Fallout from Tower Fight Will Hurt Wright."
50. Andrew Rosenthal, "Bush's Safer Choice," *New York Times*, March 11, 1989.
51. "Newt Gingrich on the 1994 Republican Revolution and His Career in Politics," interview with William Kristol, November 21, 2014, conversationswithbillkristol.org/video/newt-gingrich.
52. Major Garrett, *The Enduring Revolution: How the Contract with America Continues to Shape the Nation* (New York: Crown, 2005), 47.
53. Garrett, *The Enduring Revolution*, 47.
54. "Newt Gingrich on the 1994 Republican Revolution and His Career in Politics."
55. Mel Steely, *The Gentleman from Georgia: The Biography of Newt Gingrich* (Macon, Ga.: Mercer Press, 2000), 202–3.
56. Don Phillips, "Reps. Madigan, Gingrich Vie for GOP Post," *Washington Post*, March 16, 1989.
57. "Newt Gingrich for Whip," *National Review*, April 7, 1989, 12–13.
58. Don Phillips, "Piggyback Entry into House GOP Race," *Washington Post*, March 17, 1989.
59. "Newt Gingrich on the 1994 Republican Revolution and His Career in Politics."
60. Rowland Evans and Robert Novak, "Revolt Against the GOP's Old Bulls," *Washington Post*, March 22, 1989.
61. Jeffrey H. Birnbaum, "Bitter Fight for Republican House Whip Places Divisions in Party Thinking in Stark Contrast," *Wall Street Journal*, March 21, 1989.
62. Paul A. Gigot, "Neutron Newt Could Become GOP's Coelho," *Wall Street Journal*, March 17, 1989.
63. Gigot, "Neutron Newt Could Become GOP's Coelho."
64. Douglas L. Koopman, *Hostile Takeover: The House Republican Party, 1980–1995* (Lanham, Md.: Rowman & Littlefield, 1996), 12.
65. Phillips, "Reps. Madigan, Gingrich Vie for GOP Post."
66. Robin Toner, "Race for Whip: Hyperspeed vs. Slow Motion," *New York Times*, March 22, 1989.
67. Charles Babcock, "Gingrich's Book Venture," *Washington Post*, March 20, 1989.
68. Newt Gingrich, *Window of Opportunity: A Blue Print for the Future,* with David Drake and Marianne Gingrich (New York: Tor, 1984).
69. See, for examples, "Rep. Gingrich Discloses Own Unusual Book Marketing Deal," *Los Angeles Times*, March 20, 1989; "Gingrich Said to Use Partnership on Book," *Baltimore Sun,* March 20, 1989.
70. "Unusual Arrangement on Gingrich Book Disclosed," *New York Times*, March 20, 1989.
71. "Gingrich, Too, Has Odd Book Deal," *Philadelphia Inquirer*, March 20, 1989; "Wright's Accuser Has 'Weird' Deal of His Own," *St. Louis Post-Dispatch,* March 20, 1989.

72. Babcock, "Gingrich's Book Venture."

73. Toner, "Race for Whip."

74. Steve Daley, "2 Illinoisans in House GOP Race," *Chicago Tribune*, March 17, 1989.

75. Steve Daley, "For House GOP Post, Sides Chosen—Sort Of," *Chicago Tribune*, March 22, 1989.

76. Don Phillips and Tom Kenworthy, "Gingrich Elected House GOP Whip," *Washington Post*, March 23, 1989.

77. Denny Hastert, *Speaker: Lessons from Forty Years in Coaching and Politics* (Washington, D.C.: Regnery, 2004), 94; Steve Daley, "GOP Elects Maverick House Whip," *Chicago Tribune*, March 23, 1989.

78. Robin Toner, "House Republicans Elect Gingrich of Georgia as Whip," *New York Times*, March 23, 1989.

79. Dan Balz and Serge Kovaleski, "Gingrich Divided GOP, Conquered the Agenda," *Washington Post*, December 21, 1994. See also John A. McDonald, "GOP Picks Conservative, Aggressive Gingrich for Key Post," *Hartford Courant*, March 23, 1989. For an interesting analysis of the final vote, see Matthew N. Green and Douglas B. Harris, *Choosing the Leader: Elections in the U.S. House of Representatives* (New Haven: Yale University Press, 2019), 78–85.

80. "House Republican Leadership Contest," C-SPAN video archives, March 22, 1989.

81. "House Republican Leadership Contest."

82. Daley, "GOP Elects Maverick House Whip"; McDonald, "GOP Picks Conservative, Aggressive Gingrich for Key Post."

83. Cartoon, *Clayton News Daily*, March 28, 1989.

84. "Newt Goes to the Whip," *Wall Street Journal*, March 23, 1989.

85. Stephen E. Frantzich and John Sullivan, *The C-SPAN Revolution* (Norman: University of Oklahoma Press, 1996), 275.

86. John Meacham, *Destiny and Power: The American Odyssey of George Herbert Walker Bush* (New York: Random House, 2015), 364–65.

87. Phillips and Kenworthy, "Gingrich Elected House GOP Whip."

88. John Crawley, "Gingrich Predicts Doom for Wright," *Atlanta Daily World*, March 31, 1989.

Chapter 6: Scandal Frenzy

1. U.S. Congress, House of Representatives, Committee on Standards of Official Conduct, *Report of the Special Outside Counsel in the Matter of Speaker James C. Wright*, February 21, 1989 (Washington, D.C.: U.S. Government Printing Office, 1989).

2. John Barry, *The Ambition and the Power: A True Story of Washington* (New York: Viking, 1989), 689–90, 701–2.

3. House Committee on Ethics, *Executive Sessions*, March 14, 1989, transcript, 18.

4. House Committee on Ethics, *Executive Sessions*, March 7, 1989, transcript, 45.

5. For a fantastic blow-by-blow analysis of the charges that fell apart, see Barry, *The Ambition and the Power*, 680–724.

6. Jim Wright, *Balance of Power: Presidents and Congress from the Era of McCarthy to the Age of Gingrich* (Atlanta: Turner, 1996), 482–84.

7. House Committee on Ethics, *Executive Hearings*, February 27, 1989, transcript, 27.

8. House Committee on Ethics, *Executive Hearings*, March 14, 1989, transcript, 157.

9. House Committee on Ethics, *Executive Hearings*, February 27, 1989, transcript, 30–32.

10. House Committee on Ethics, *Executive Hearings*, February 28, 1989, transcript, 32–63.

11. Barry, *The Ambition and the Power*, 710–11.

12. Van Brocklin to Gingrich, March 30, 1989, box 673, File: Newt Gingrich—Ethics, NGP.

13. Brooks Jackson, "Speaker Wright, Facing Ethics Battle, Mounts Strong 'It's All Politics' Defense," *Wall Street Journal*, March 14, 1989.

14. Brooks Jackson, "House Ethics Report on Wright Finished; Big Size Seen Suggesting Damaging Data," *Wall Street Journal*, February 23, 1989.

15. Tracy Updegraff to Speaker's Bureau, April 20, 1989, box 664, File: Pre-disciplinary Hearings, NGP.

16. Steve Daley, "Panel Narrows Probe of Wright," *Chicago Tribune*, April 6, 1989.

17. David Rogers, "Wright Seeking to Build His Defense Against Likely Adverse Ethics Report," *Wall Street Journal*, April 11, 1989.

18. Editorial, "The Old Accuse-the-Accuser Game," *Chicago Tribune*, May 7, 1989.

19. William J. Eaton and Sara Fritz, "Republicans Call Democratic Briefing by Wright Lawyer Possible Secrecy Violation," *Los Angeles Times*, April 12, 1989.

20. Susan Rasky, Nathaniel Nash, and Michael Oreskes, "Ethics Committee Expected to Find Violations by Wright on Finances," *New York Times*, April 5, 1989.

21. Eaton and Fritz, "Republicans Call Democratic Briefing by Wright Lawyer Possible Secrecy Violation."

22. "Critic Accuses Wright Counsel of Collusion," *Akron Beacon Journal*, April 12, 1989.

23. U.S. Congress, House of Representatives, Committee on Ethics, *Statement of Alleged Violation in the Matter of Representative James C. Wright Jr.*, April 13, 1999.

24. Barry, *The Ambition and the Power*, 680–724.

25. Brown, interview with author, August 4, 2016.

26. William Eaton, "2 Democrats Who Voted Against Wright Face Pressure," *Los Angeles Times*, April 15, 1989.

27. Wertheimer, interview with author, July 21, 2015.

28. David Cloud, "Of Party Fealty—and Revenge," *Congressional Quarterly*, April 15, 1989, 793.

29. Nancy J. Schwerzler, "Wright Votes Turn 2 Democrats into Lonesome Pair," *Baltimore Sun*, May 30, 1989.

30. Robin Toner, "Loyalists Are Enlisted for Wright's Defense," *New York Times*, April 14, 1989.

31. William Clayton, "The Wright Report—Votes Give Potent Signal—Ethics Panel Democrats Might Have Set Anti-Wright Tone," *Houston Chronicle*, April 18, 1989.

32. Bill Alexander, "My Fellow Democrats: Answer Gingrich or Lose," *New York Times*, April 25, 1989.

33. "Formal Ethics Complaint Filed Against Gingrich by Democrat," *Los Angeles Times*, April 12, 1989.

34. Tom Kenworthy, "Wright Begins Counterattack," *Washington Post*, April 14, 1989.

35. Margaret Carlson, "Wright Fights Back," *Time*, April 24, 1989, 16.

36. Sheila Dresser, "The Wright Charges and Other Scandals Become a Washington Growth Industry," *Baltimore Sun*, April 23, 1989.

37. Johanna Schneider to Republican Press Secretary, April 17, 1979, box 664, File: Pre-disciplinary Hearings, Karen Van Brocklin Files, NGP.

38. William J. Eaton, "Wright Violated Rules 69 Times, Ethics Panel Says," *Los Angeles Times*, April 18, 1989.

39. James M. Perry, "Report Reflects a Shift in Attitude on Ethics," *Wall Street Journal*, April 18, 1989.

40. Editorial, "Fair, Not Fearful, in the Wright Case," *New York Times*, April 14, 1989.

41. Tom Kenworthy, "House Committee Charges Wright with 69 Ethics-Rules Violations," *Washington Post*, April 18, 1989.

42. Elaine Povich and Steve Daley, "Ethics Panel Charges Wright," *Chicago Tribune*, April 18, 1989.

43. William Eaton, "Democrats Tell Concern as Wright Vows to Fight," *Los Angeles Times*, April 19, 1989. See also Tom Kenworthy, "Wright Courts Caucus, but Pessimism Thickens," *Washington Post*, April 19, 1989; "Wright Lays Out Defense for Colleagues," *Miami Herald*, April 19, 1989; Robin Toner, "Wright, Stepping Up His Defense, Releases Data on Work by Wife," *New York Times*, April 19, 1989.

44. David Hess, "Wright Stages Pep Rally with Democrats," *Akron Beacon Journal*, April 19, 1989.

45. Laura Mecoy, "Fazio Takes Heat on Wright, but Can't Talk About It," *Sacramento Bee*, April 18, 1989.

46. McClure, interview with author, September 9, 2016.

47. Alan Murray and Jeffrey Birnbaum, "Opposition Stirs to Possible Boost in Gasoline Tax," *Wall Street Journal*, May 2, 1989.

48. Richard E. Cohen, "Gingrich: Don't Expect 'Kinder, Gentler' Politics," *Los Angeles Times*, April 2, 1989.

49. David Broder, "Malarkey from Newt Gingrich," *Washington Post*, April 23, 1989.

50. Newt Gingrich, "The Gingrich Manifesto," *Washington Post*, April 9, 1989.

51. Ernest Furgurson, "No Celebration for Newt," *Baltimore Sun*, April 19, 1989.

52. Dan Balz, "Wright Decries Panel's 'Foot-Dragging,'" *Washington Post*, April 21, 1989; Karen Hosler, "Wright Accuses Ethics Panel of Foot-Dragging," *Baltimore Sun*, April 21, 1989.

53. Gingrich to Dixon, April 24, 1989, box 674, File: Dixon v. Gingrich, NGP.

54. "Gingrich Insists His Ethics Are Fine," *Mercury News*, April 26, 1989.

55. Steve Daley, "Questions About Ethics Rattle Gingrich's Wife," *Chicago Tribune*, April 26, 1989. See also Mike Christensen, "'What We Did Was Honest,' Gingrich Says of Book Promotion Deal," *Atlanta Journal-Constitution*, April 26, 1989.

56. Nancy J. Schwerzler, "Gingrich Defends Book Arrangement Involving Wife," *Baltimore Sun*, April 26, 1989.

57. Myron Waldman, "Wright, Gingriches Defend Book Deal," *Newsday*, April 26, 1989.

58. Horace Busby, "Gone How? Gone When? Gone Where?," April 26, 1989, box 1093, File: Wright Investigation, NGP.

59. David Rogers, "Wright's Attorneys Prepare Challenges to House Ethics Panel's Legal Analysis," *Wall Street Journal*, May 9, 1989.

60. Torricelli, interview with author, May 15, 2017.
61. Ringle, interview with author, November 24, 2015.
62. Small, interview with author, July 8, 2019.
63. Ringle, interview with author, November 24, 2015.
64. Barry, *The Ambition and the Power,* 72.
65. "Dear Friend of Law and Order," 1987, box 678, File: John Mack, NGP. The letter included news clippings: "Woman Assaulted," *Northern Virginia Sun,* August 30, 1973; "Woman Left for Dead; Man Held," *Washington Star News,* August 30, 1973.
66. Dave Montgomery, "Shadow of Violence Haunts Wright's Top Aide," *Fort Worth Star-Telegram,* August 2, 1987.
67. Barry, *The Ambition and the Power,* 72.
68. Edward Walsh, "The House Speaker's Team," *Washington Post,* March 17, 1987.
69. Mary Hadar, interview with author, December 8, 2015.
70. *Face the Nation,* June 12, 1988, transcript, box 672, File: Wright, NGP.
71. Ringle, interview with author, June 30, 2019.
72. Michael Oreskes, "Wright Aide's Past Shocks Capitol," *New York Times,* May 5, 1989; Ken Ringle, "Memory and Anger: A Victim's Story," *Washington Post,* May 4, 1989.
73. Eleanor Clift, "The Protégé and the Victim," *Newsweek,* May 15, 1989, 38.
74. Rehm recounts this story in Diane Rehm, *Finding My Voice* (Herndon, Va.: Capital Books, 1999), 183–86.
75. Clift, "The Protégé and the Victim."
76. Suzanne Garment, *Scandal: The Culture of Mistrust in American Politics* (New York: Random House, 1991), 237.
77. Van Brocklin to Gingrich, May 10, 1989, box 678, File: Mack, John, NGP.
78. Schroeder, interview with author, August 17, 2018.
79. Don Phillips, "Top Wright Aide Quits over Criminal Record," *Washington Post,* May 12, 1989.
80. Karen Hosler, "Wright Aide Quits Post After Uproar over Assault," *Baltimore Sun,* May 12, 1989.
81. Hosler, "Wright Aide Quits Post after Uproar over Assault."
82. Kim Mattingly, "Hill Women Help Push Mack Out," *Roll Call,* May 15, 1989.
83. Editorial, "The Departure of John Mack," *Washington Post,* May 13, 1989.
84. Richard Cohen, "Is Congress Deaf?" *Washington Post,* May 16, 1989, www.washingtonpost.com/archive/opinions/1989/05/16/is-congress-deaf/f6129e7f-a22f-4421-8182-506d0d747171.
85. Phillips, "Top Wright Aide Quits over Criminal Record."
86. Oldaker, interview with author, July 9, 2015.
87. Bill Minutaglio, "Power Failure," *Dallas Morning News,* June 16, 1989.
88. David Hess, "'73 Attack Catches Up with Aide—Mack Resigns; Wright OKs It," *Daily Press,* May 12, 1989.
89. Mona Charen, "John Mack Never Offered Compensation to Victim," *Moscow-Pullman Daily News,* May 15, 1989.
90. "Wright/Mack Resignation," *NBC News,* May 11, 1989.
91. "Capitol Offense," *Time,* May 15, 1989, 38.
92. Hess, "'73 Attack Catches Up with Aide."

93. Roger Simon, "The Deafening Silence on Capitol Hill," *Los Angeles Times*, May 14, 1989.

94. Steve Daley, "'73 Crime Forces Wright Aide to Quit," *Chicago Tribune*, May 12, 1989.

95. Andrea Dworkin, "Political Callousness on Violence Toward Women," *Los Angeles Times*, May 14, 1989.

96. Phillips, "Top Wright Aide Quits over Criminal Record."

97. National Republican Congressional Committee, "Why Does Coelho Defend Men Who Assault Women?," May 4, 1989, box 678, File: John Mack, NGP.

98. Robin Toner, "In Fighting Democrats, Almost Anything Goes on the Republican Campaign Committees," *New York Times*, May 15, 1989.

99. Dan Balz and Tom Kenworthy, "Wright Probe Puts House Leaders in Awkward Spot," *Washington Post*, May 9, 1989.

100. Karen Hosler and Nancy J. Schwerzler, "Legal Team of Embattled House Speaker Seeks Dismissal of Ethics Charges," *Baltimore Sun*, May 9, 1989.

101. "Statement of John P. Mack," May 11, 1989, box 678, File: Mack, John, NGP.

102. "Wright Aide Resigns 1 Week After Beaten Woman Tells Story," *Los Angeles Times*, May 11, 1989; Phillips, "Top Wright Aide Quits over Criminal Record."

103. Daley, "'73 Crime Forces Wright Aide to Quit"; David Hess, "Aide Quits Wright Staff After Publicized Attack," *Detroit Free Press*, May 12, 1989. See also "A Washington Morality Tale," *U.S. News & World Report*, May 22, 1989.

104. Robin Toner, "Wright Aide Quits Amid Furor on '73 Crime," *New York Times*, May 12, 1989.

105. Lloyd Grove, "Wright Wing Rally," *Washington Post*, May 11, 1989.

106. Tom Kenworthy, "Ethics Probe and Loss of Top Aide Put Speaker's Resilience to the Test," *Washington Post*, May 13, 1989.

107. E. J. Dionne Jr., "Coelho Says Bonds Were Bought for Him," *New York Times*, May 15, 1989.

108. Charles R. Babcock, "Coelho Changes Account of Investment," *Washington Post*, May 14, 1989.

109. Sara Fritz and Richard Meyer, "Coelho Targeted by GOP for House Ethics Inquiry," *Los Angeles Times*, May 20, 1989.

110. Rollins, interview with author, May 29, 2018.

111. Michael Oreskes, "The No. 3 Democrat: In Surprising Decision, He Speaks of Sparing His Party Turmoil," *New York Times*, May 27, 1989.

112. "Stop GOP Attacks, Coelho Tells Bush," *Newsday*, May 29, 1989.

113. Tom Kenworthy and Dan Balz, "Stunned Democrats Try to Regroup," *Washington Post*, May 28, 1989.

114. Sara Fritz and William J. Eaton, "Coelho to Resign in Face of Probe; Party in 'Disarray,'" *Los Angeles Times*, May 27, 1989.

Chapter 7: Gingrich on Top

1. "House Committee Stakeout," C-SPAN video archives, May 18, 1989.

2. Josh Getlin, "Wright Probe Is Gridlocking House, Michel Complains," *Los Angeles Times*, May 18, 1989.

3. Conservative Campaign Fund, "Help Put Jim Wright on Trial!," May 1989, box 675, File: Right Wing, JWA.

4. William Eaton, "No Outcry for House Members to Punish Speaker," *Los Angeles Times*, April 23, 1989; Mike Sante and David Hess, "Democrats Considering What to Do About Speaker's Growing Problems," *Austin American*, May 18, 1989.

5. Michael Oreskes, "Gloom on Wright Shakes Gathering of Key Democrats," *New York Times,* May 18, 1989, www.nytimes.com/1989/05/18/us/gloom-on-wright-shakes-gathering-of-key-democrats.html.

6. David Lauter, "Public Not Interested in Wright Case, Poll Finds," *Los Angeles Times*, May 18, 1989.

7. Paul West, "Wright Grows More Isolated as Crisis Deepens," *Baltimore Sun*, May 21, 1989.

8. R. Douglas Arnold, *The Logic of Congressional Action* (New Haven, Conn.: Yale University Press, 1990).

9. Sharp, interview with author, November 2, 2016; "IRS Probe Report Surprises Wright," *St. Louis Post-Dispatch*, May 19, 1989.

10. Sharp, interview with author; David Rogers, "Wright's Financial Footing Is Stronger on Eve of Battle Against Major Charges," *Wall Street Journal*, May 23, 1989.

11. Editorial, "It's Time for Wright to Step Down," *Chicago Tribune*, May 21, 1989.

12. Editorial, "Sufficient Reason to Go," *Los Angeles Times,* May 23, 1989.

13. William Oldaker to Julian Dixon and John Myers, May 10, 1989. Documents in possession of the author.

14. "House Committee Stakeout," May 18, 1989, C-SPAN video archives.

15. Gingrich and Van Brocklin to Steve Gunderson, May 23, 1989, box 664, File: Predisciplinary Hearings, NGP.

16. William J. Eaton, "Wright Defense Scheduled Tuesday," *Los Angeles Times*, May 19, 1989.

17. The hearings are available in the C-SPAN video archives.

18. Robert L. Jackson, "Wright Case Lawyers: Study in Contrasts," *Los Angeles Times*, May 24, 1989.

19. "Ethics Charges Against House Speaker Wright," May 23, 1989, C-SPAN video archives.

20. "Excerpts of Hearing on Wright," *Chicago Tribune*, May 24, 1989.

21. Michael Oreskes, "Wright Lawyer Asks Ethics Panel to Throw Out Main Accusation," *New York Times*, May 24, 1989.

22. Susan Feeney, "Panel Asked to Drop 2 Wright Charges—Opposing Lawyers Display Styles as Disparate as Their Arguments," *Dallas Morning News*, May 24, 1989.

23. Robin Toner, "Performers Show Style in a Theater of Careers," *New York Times*, May 24, 1989.

24. William J. Eaton, "'Stand in the Way of Lynch Mob' and Drop Charges, Wright Lawyer Asked," *Los Angeles Times*, May 24, 1989.

25. Mary McGrory, "Brilliance, All in Vain," *Washington Post*, May 25, 1989.

26. Walter Goodman, "Wright's Bad Fortune Is Turning into Good Viewing," *New York Times*, May 25, 1989.

27. Don Phillips, "Broadcast Confined to Background," *Washington Post*, May 24, 1989.

28. Toner, "Performers Show Style in a Theater of Careers."

29. Tom Kenworthy, "Wright Lawyer Urges Panel to Shun 'Lynch Mob' Mentality," *Washington Post*, May 24, 1989.

30. Paul West, "Panel Gives No Hint of Dropping Wright Charges," *Baltimore Sun*, May 24, 1989.

31. Peter Osterlund and Nancy J. Schwerzler, "All of Capitol Hill Glued to TV Hearings on Wright," *Baltimore Sun*, May 24, 1989.

32. "Speaker Wright & Atty. Stephen Susman," May 23, 1989, C-SPAN Video Archive.

33. Elaine Kamarck, "Will the Jim Wright Affair Rub Off on All Incumbents?," *Newsday*, May 22, 1989.

34. Robert Shogan, "Rush to Judge Politicians Held Damaging to Nation," *Los Angeles Times*, June 2, 1989.

35. John M. Barry, *The Ambition and the Power: A True Story of Washington* (New York: Viking, 1989), 748.

36. Barry, *The Ambition and the Power*, 748–49.

37. "Foley Could Be Speaker by Next Week," *Seattle Times*, May 25, 1989; Jackie Koszczuk, "Behind the Scenes at the Wright Negotiations—the Chain of Events That Led to the Collapse of Deal for His Exit," *Seattle Times*, May 28, 1989.

38. Steven Komarow, "Wright Is Offering to Quit Post as Speaker," *St. Paul Pioneer Press*, May 25, 1989.

39. Steve Daley, "Wright's Core of Support Melts," *Chicago Tribune*, May 25, 1989.

40. McGuire, interview with author, July 13, 2019.

41. Barry, *The Ambition and the Power*, 751–52.

42. Jim Wright, *Worth It All: My War for Peace* (Washington, D.C.: Brassey's, 1993), 234–35.

43. Myron S. Waldman, "Wright 'Liberated' By His Decision to Quit Congress," *Newsday,* June 2, 1989.

44. Ronald Ostrow, "Justice Department Ponders Action Against Wright," *Los Angeles Times*, April 7, 1989.

45. "Justice Department Plans Its Own Review of Wright," *St. Louis Post-Dispatch*, May 11, 1989.

46. Petri, interview with author, August 1, 2016.

47. Nancy J. Schwerzler, "Wright Decision Was Influenced by Vote Count," *Baltimore Sun*, June 1, 1989.

48. Jim Wright, *Balance of Power: Presidents and Congress from the Era of McCarthy to the Age of Gingrich* (Atlanta: Turner, 1996), 489.

49. E. J. Dionne Jr., "G.O.P. Keeping Up Ethics Pressure on the Democrats," *New York Times*, May 29, 1989.

50. Michael Oreskes, "War Drums in the House," *New York Times*, May 28, 1989.

51. Paul Houston, "Partisan Push Threatened in Ethics Problems," *Los Angeles Times*, May 29, 1989.

52. Jim Drinkard, "'I Know What I Should Do,' Wright Says," *Charlotte Observer*, May 31, 1989.

53. Basil Talbott, "Wright Might Get 'Reprieve'—Rep. Pepper Death Clouds Action," *Chicago Sun Times*, May 31, 1989; Michael Oreskes, "Wright Wrestles with Decision on Quitting House," *Daily News of Los Angeles*, May 31, 1989.

54. Don Phillips and Dan Balz, "A House Divided by Partisan Hostilities," *Washington Post*, June 1, 1989.

55. Robin Toner, "Climax to a Storm," *New York Times*, June 1, 1989.

56. Seth Kantor, "'Let Me Give You Back This Job You Gave to Me': Besieged Wright to Quit Congress," *Austin American-Statesman*, June 1, 1989.

57. Phillips and Balz, "A House Divided by Partisan Hostilities."

58. Phillips and Balz, "A House Divided by Partisan Hostilities."

59. Phillips and Balz, "A House Divided by Partisan Hostilities."

60. Phillips and Balz, "A House Divided By Partisan Hostilities."

61. Tom Shales, "Jim Wright's Final Hour in the Spotlight," *Washington Post*, June 1, 1989.

62. Paul West, "Texas Democrat, Under Fire, Also Leaving Congress," *Baltimore Sun*, June 1, 1989.

63. William Clayton Jr., "The Speaker Steps Down—a Speaker Makes His Last Speech," *Houston Chronicle*, June 1, 1989.

64. Brown, interview with author, August 4, 2016.

65. "Gingrich Should Cool It, GOP Minority Leader Says," *Los Angeles Times*, June 1, 1989.

66. Steve Daley and Elaine Povich, "House Speaker Wright Resigns," *Chicago Tribune*, June 1, 1989.

67. "Reactions to Wright's Resignation," C-SPAN video archives, May 31, 1989.

68. Newt Gingrich, Handwritten Notes, June 1, 1989, box 1093, File: Wright Investigation, NGP.

69. Newt Gingrich, Handwritten Notes, 1 June 1989, box 1093, File: Wright Investigation, NGP.

70. "Speaker Wright's Resignation," May 31, 1989, C-SPAN video archives.

71. Shales, "Jim Wright's Final Hour in the Spotlight."

72. William J. Eaton, "Wright Resigns, Urges End to This 'Mindless Cannibalism,'" *Los Angeles Times*, June 1, 1989; Michael Oreskes, "Turmoil in Congress; An 'Evil Wind' of Fear is Felt in House," *New York Times,* June 1, 1989, www.ny times.com /1989/06/01/us/turmoil-in-congress-an-evil-wind-of-fear-is-felt-in-house.html.

73. Susan Feeney, "Leader's Fall Leaves His Colleagues Somber—'What Is It You Can Say?' Supporter Asks," *Dallas Morning News*, June 1, 1989.

Chapter 8: Mindless Cannibalism

1. Steve Daley and Elaine Povich, "House Speaker Wright Resigns," *Chicago Tribune*, June 1, 1989.

2. "Reactions to Wright's Resignation," C-SPAN video archives, May 31, 1989.

3. "Reactions to Wright's Resignation," C-SPAN video archives, May 31, 1989.

4. "Reactions to Wright's Resignation," C-SPAN video archives, May 31, 1989.

5. Peter Osterlund, "Wright Resigns as House Speaker," *Baltimore Sun*, June 1, 1989.

6. Editorial, "Speaker Wright and the Cannibals," *New York Times*, June 1, 1989.

7. "Wright Resignation," *NBC Evening News*, May 31, 1989, VTA.

8. Editorial, "Jim Wright Resigns," *Washington Post*, June 1, 1989.

9. Don Phillips, "Gingrich Defends Part in Wright's Fall," *Washington Post*, June 3, 1989.

10. Don Phillips, "Republicans Bridle at Wright Speech," *Washington Post*, June 2, 1989.

11. Phillips, "Gingrich Defends Part in Wright's Fall."
12. "Gingrich Should Cool It, GOP Minority Leader Says," *Los Angeles Times*, June 1, 1989.
13. David Beers, "Newt Gingrich: Master of Disaster," *Mother Jones*, September 1, 1989, 43.
14. "Stop Mudslinging, Gephardt Urges," *Desert News*, June 15, 1989; Steve Daley, "House Democrats Rebuild at Top," *Chicago Tribune*, June 15, 1989.
15. George F. Will, "Character Assassination Is No Substitute for Political Purpose," *Hartford Courant*, June 1, 1989.
16. Mark Goodwin to Republican Leaders, May 31, 1989, box 674, File: Wright Resign, NGP.
17. James Pierobon, "Foley Tries to Quell Partisan Rancor," *Houston Chronicle*, June 7, 1989.
18. Nancy Traver, "The Republicans' Pit Bull," *Time*, June 12, 1989, 22.
19. Myra MacPherson, "Newt Gingrich, Point Man in a House Divided," *Washington Post*, June 12, 1989.
20. Tom Morganthau, Howard Fineman, and Eleanor Clift, "Ethics Wars: Frenzy on the Hill," *Newsweek*, June 12, 1989, 14–18.
21. Sara Fritz, "As Speaker, Foley Plans to Quell Partisan Fights," *Los Angeles Times*, June 4, 1989.
22. "Tom Foley: Out of the Liberal Closet," June 1989, box 674, File: Wright Resigns, NGP.
23. Ashley to Bush, June 7, 1987, GHWBP.
24. Amy Bayer, "GOP National Panel Gives Atwater Vote of Confidence," *Worchester Telegram & Gazette*, June 17, 1989.
25. Beers, "Newt Gingrich: Master of Disaster."
26. Interview Paul Weyrich, "The Long March of Newt Gingrich," *Frontline*, PBS, January 16, 1996, www.pbs.org/wgbh/pages/frontline/newt/newtintwshtml/weyrich.html.
27. Clarence Page, "Talk Like a Newt with the Gingrich Diatribe Dictionary," *Chicago Tribune*, September 19, 1990; GOPAC, "Language: A Key Mechanism of Control," 1990. There is a link to this document in the online publication of David Corn and Tim Murphey, "Gingrich in His Own Words," *Mother Jones*, April 7, 2011, www.motherjones.com/politics/2011/04/newt-gingrich-greatest-rhetorical-hits/2.
28. Richard L. Berke, "Gingrich, in Duel with White House, Stays True to his Role as an Outsider," *New York Times*, October 5, 1990, www.nytimes.com/1990/10/05/us/budget-agreement-gingrich-duel-with-white-house-stays-true-his-role-outsider.html.
29. Ronald Brownstein, *The Second Civil War: How Extreme Partisanship Has Paralyzed Washington and Polarized America* (New York: Penguin, 2007), 148.
30. Morton Kondracke and Fred Barnes, *Kemp: The Bleeding-Heart Conservative Who Changed America* (New York: Sentinel, 2015), 141.
31. Steve Gillon, *The Pact: Bill Clinton, Newt Gingrich, and the Rivalry That Defined a Generation* (New York: Oxford University Press, 2008), 99.
32. Stephen Mihm, "Echoes of 1990s Scandal Roll Across Capitol Hill," *Bloomberg*, December 27, 2017.
33. Clifford Krauss, "The House Bank: Gingrich Takes No Prisoners in the House's Seat of Gentility," *New York Times*, March 17, 1992.

34. Adam Clymer, "Michel, G.O.P. House Leader, to Retire," *New York Times*, October 5, 1993.

35. Jim Wright, "Worth It All," C-SPAN video archives, October 28, 1993.

36. Katharine Seelye, "With Fiery Words, Gingrich Builds His Kingdom," *New York Times*, October 27, 1994.

37. Robert Griffith, *The Politics of Fear: Joseph McCarthy and the Senate* (Amherst: University of Massachusetts Press, 1970).

38. Jim Wright to Newt Gingrich, February 15, 1995; Wright, note to files, February 23, 1995; and Gingrich to Wright, December 3, 1995, JWA, box 22, File: 10. Thanks to Garrison Nelson and James Riddlesperger for alerting me to this telling exchange.

39. Jason Zengerle, "These Democrats Will Soon Have the Power to Investigate the White House. How Far Will They Go?," *New York Times*, December 17, 2018.

40. Edward Walsh, "'Pit Bull' in the Chair," *Washington Post*, March 19, 1997.

41. Adam Clymer, "House, in a 395–28 Vote, Reprimands Gingrich," *New York Times*, January 22, 1997.

42. Sam Howe Verhovek, "To Jim Wright, What Goes Around," *New York Times*, January 5, 1997.

43. McKay Coppins, "The Man Who Broke Politics," *Atlantic*, November 2018.

44. Thomas E. Mann and Norman Ornstein, *It's Even Worse Than It Looks: How the American Constitutional System Collided with the New Politics of Extremism* (New York: Basic Books, 2012); Brownstein, *Second Civil War;* Benjamin Ginsberg and Martin Shefter, *Politics by Other Means: Politicians, Prosecutors, and the Press from Watergate to Whitewater*, 3rd ed. (New York: Norton, 2002).

45. Mann and Ornstein, *It's Even Worse Than It Looks*, xxiv.

46. Mann and Ornstein, *It's Even Worse Than It Looks*, 8–10.

47. Matthew Green, *Legislative Hardball* (New York: Cambridge University Press, 2019).

48. Todd Gillman, "Former House Speaker Jim Wright Recalls Gingrich as 'Sociopathic,'" *Dallas Morning News*, March 2012.

49. "Gingrich Advisor: He's Got Inside Knowledge, But He's an Outsider," *MSNBC*, January 22, 2016.

50. Nia-Malika Henderson, "Gingrich Says Birther Claims Not Racist, Are Caused by Obama's Radical Views," *Washington Post*, May 29, 2012.

51. Tim Alberta, *American Carnage: On the Front Lines of the Republican Civil War and the Rise of President Trump* (New York: Harper, 2019), 113.

52. Julia Ioffe, "The Millennial's Guide to Newt Gingrich," *Politico*, July 14, 2016.

53. John Helton and Alyssa McLendon, "Gingrich's 2012 Campaign Leaves Him with Mixed Legacy," CNN.com, May 2, 2012.

54. "Newt Gingrich on the 1994 Republican Revolution and His Career in Politics," interview with William Kristol, November 21, 2014, conversationswithbillkristol.org/video/newt-gingrich.

55. David Remnick, "It Happened Here," *New Yorker*, November 28, 2016. See also Alberta, *American Carnage*.

ILLUSTRATION CREDITS

ILLUSTRATION CREDITS

Insert pages 10, bottom; 11, top; and 16, middle: AP Photo/John Duricka

Insert page 11, bottom: Terry Ashe/The LIFE Images Collection via Getty Images/ Getty Images

Insert page 12, top: Getty Images

Insert page 12, bottom: Laura Patterson/CQ Roll Call via Getty Images

Insert page 13, top: AP Photo/*Fort Worth Star-Telegram*/Mark Gail

Insert page 13, bottom: Courtesy of Ken Ringle, personal collection

Insert page 14, top: AP Photo/File/Charles Krupa

Insert page 14, middle: CQ Roll Call via Getty Images

Insert pages 14, bottom; and 15, top: AP Photo/J. Scott Applewhite

Insert page 16, top: Cynthia Johnson/The LIFE Images Collection via Getty Images/ Getty Images

Insert page 16, bottom: Scott J. Ferrell/*Congressional Quarterly*/Getty Images

INDEX

INDEX

INDEX

INDEX

INDEX

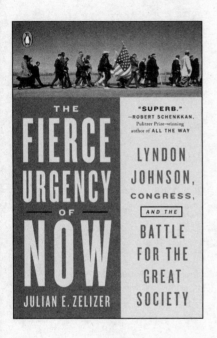